The Edinburgh History of Reading: Common Readers

THE EDINBURGH HISTORY OF READING

General Editors: Mary Hammond and Jonathan Rose

Bringing together the latest scholarship from all over the world on topics ranging from reading practices in ancient China to the workings of the twenty-first-century reading brain, the four volumes of *The Edinburgh History of Reading* demonstrate that reading is a deeply imbricated, socio-political practice, at once personal and public, defiant and obedient. It is often materially ephemeral, but it can also be emotionally and intellectually enduring.

Early Readers, edited by Mary Hammond
Modern Readers, edited by Mary Hammond
Common Readers, edited by Jonathan Rose
Subversive Readers, edited by Jonathan Rose

The Edinburgh History of Reading: Common Readers

Edited by Jonathan Rose

EDINBURGH
University Press

Edinburgh University Press is one of the leading university presses in the UK. We publish academic books and journals in our selected subject areas across the humanities and social sciences, combining cutting-edge scholarship with high editorial and production values to produce academic works of lasting importance. For more information visit our website: edinburghuniversitypress.com

© editorial matter and organisation Jonathan Rose, 2020, 2022
© the chapters their several authors, 2020, 2022

Edinburgh University Press Ltd
The Tun – Holyrood Road, 12(2f) Jackson's Entry, Edinburgh EH8 8PJ

First published in hardback by Edinburgh University Press 2020

Typeset in Sabon and Futura
by R. J. Footring Ltd, Derby, UK

A CIP record for this book is available from the British Library

ISBN 978 1 4744 6188 7 (hardback)
ISBN 978 1 4744 9487 8 (paperback)
ISBN 978 1 4744 6189 4 (webready PDF)
ISBN 978 1 4744 6190 0 (epub)

The right of Jonathan Rose to be identified as the editor of this work has been asserted in accordance with the Copyright, Designs and Patents Act 1988, and the Copyright and Related Rights Regulations 2003 (SI No. 2498).

Published with the support of the University of Edinburgh Scholarly Publishing Initiatives Fund.

Contents

List of Figures, Plates and Tables	vii
List of Contributors	ix
Introduction *Jonathan Rose*	1
1 British Commonplace Readers, 1706–1879 *Jillian M. Hess*	9
2 Reading in God's Treasure-House: The Societies for Purchasing Books in Leadhills and Wanlockhead, 1741–1820 *Margaret J. Joachim*	30
3 The School Library and Childhood Reading in Lowland Scotland, 1750–1850 *Maxine Branagh-Miscampbell*	55
4 'Although ambitious we did not aspire to such dizzy heights': Manuscript Magazines and Communal Reading Practices of London Literary Societies in the Long Nineteenth Century *Lauren Weiss*	75
5 Space and Place in Nineteenth-Century Images of Women Readers *Amelia Yeates*	96
6 Asian Classic Literature and the English General Reader, 1845–1915 *Alexander Bubb*	116
7 Readers and Reading During Russia's Literacy Transition, 1850–1950: How Readers Shaped a Great Literature *Jeffrey Brooks*	137
8 F. F. Pavlenkov's Literacy Project: Popular Serials and Reading Rooms for the Russian Masses *Carol Ueland and Ludmilla A. Trigos*	157

9 Formal and Informal Networks of Book Provision for Rural
   Children in Australia and New Zealand, 1900–60   180
   Bronwyn Lowe

10 Putting Your Best Books Forward: A Historical and
   Psychological Look at the Presentation of Book Collections   198
   Nicole Gonzalez and Nick Weir-Williams

11 In Search of the Chinese Common Reader: Vernacular
   Knowledge in an Age of New Media   218
   Joan Judge

12 From 'Bookworms' to 'Scholar-Farmers': Tao Xingzhi and
   Changing Understandings of Literacy in the Chinese Rural
   Reconstruction Movement, 1923–34   238
   Zach Smith

13 The Voice of the Reader: The Landscape of Online Book
   Discussion in the Netherlands, 1997–2016   258
   Peter Boot

14 Novel Ideas: The Promotion of North American Book Club
   Books and the Creation of Their Readers   280
   Samantha Rideout and DeNel Rehberg Sedo

15 Making the Story Real: Readers, Fans and the Novels of
   John Green   299
   Jennifer Burek Pierce

Select Bibliography   319
Index of Methods and Sources   342
General Index   343

Figures, Plates and Tables

Figures

1.1	Locke's index in the first English edition of *A New Method of a Common-Place-Book*	15
5.1	Charles W. Cope, *Life Well Spent*, 1862	99
8.1	The Pavlenkov 1865 Russian-language edition of A. Ganot's *Complete Course of Physics with a Brief Review of Meteorological Phenomena*, translated from the French (12th edition) by F. F. Pavlenkov and V. Cherkasov (1866), part I of IV	159
8.2	F. F. Pavlenkov's *Illustrated Alphabet Primer for Learning and Self-Taught Literacy*, with 600 illustrations (1873). Price 10 kopeks. Typography of A. M. Kotomin, p. 3	165
10.1	The IKEA 'Billy' bookcase	213
11.1	A bookstall in Shanghai in the 1930s	230
13.1	Number of posts to Dutch book discussion sites per year, by platform	272
13.2	Post length by platform (all posts on Ezzulia, blog posts on weblogs, reviews on all other sites)	274
14.1	Proportional use of seven different bestseller lists in promotional material	290

Plates

1. William Nicol, *Quiet*, 1860
2. John Callcott Horsley, *A Pleasant Corner*, 1865
3. Alexander Rossi, *Forbidden Books*, 1897
4. William Powell Frith, *Ramsgate Sands*, 1854
5. Nolinsk Library, memorial exhibition dedicated to F. F. Pavlenkov
6. The Penguin Books edition of *Lady Chatterley's Lover*, at its affordable cover price

7   The Tianjin Binhai Library of China
8   Simon and Schuster book clubs newsletter web page, 11 December 2013
9   Random House 'Reader's Circle' newsletter, 12 February 2009
10 Video Spotlight from HarperCollins CA, 'The Savvy Reader', 24 September 2012
11 Random House CA, BookClubs.ca, 'Books Buzz', 15 June 2011
12 Harper Collins Canada, 'The Savvy Reader', 28 April 2011

Tables

2.1	Numbers and proportions of books by category in the libraries of the Societies for Purchasing Books at Leadhills and at Wanlockhead	38
2.2	Number of Wanlockhead titles also in Leadhills library, 1800	39
2.3	Numbers and proportions of books by category, Wanlockhead library, 1820	40
2.4	Booksellers used by the Wanlockhead Society, 1784–1820	41
2.5	Books donated to Wanlockhead library, 1784–1820	43
2.6	Donated and purchased books at Westerkirk, 1793	45
2.7	Wanlockhead books rebound between 1785 and 1820	46
2.8	Sample extracts from the Wanlockhead annual book valuation, 1785–1820	50
14.1	Novel Ideas dataset	283
14.2	Identified themes of promoted books	285
14.3	Examples of the uses of the *New York Times* bestseller list in promotional copy	290
14.4	Ways in which authors are identified in publishers' newsletters	292

Contributors

Peter Boot is a senior researcher at the Huygens Institute for the History of the Netherlands. He wrote a PhD about annotation in digital scholarly editions ('Mesotext: Digitised Emblems, Modelled Annotations and Humanities Scholarship'). His current research centres on online reading and writing cultures, focusing on what they can say about reading and readers in general as well as the changes that the online world is bringing to reading and writing.

Maxine Branagh-Miscampbell is a PhD candidate at the University of Stirling. Her research focuses on young Scottish readers in educational institutions between 1750 and 1850 and is supervised by Dr Katie Halsey and Dr Bethan Benwell. Her work is funded by the Arts and Humanities Research Council's Doctoral Training Partnership, the Scottish Graduate School for the Arts and Humanities.

Jeffrey Brooks is the author of *When Russia Learned to Read: Literacy and Popular Literature, 1861–1917* (1985, winner of the Wayne S. Vucinich Book Prize), *Thank You, Comrade Stalin: Soviet Public Culture from Revolution to Cold War* (2000), *Lenin and the Making of the Soviet State: A Brief History with Documents* (2006, with Georgiy Chernyavskiy) and *The Firebird and the Fox: Russian Culture Under Tsars and Bolsheviks* (2019). He is a professor of history at the Johns Hopkins University, and in the past has taught at the universities of Chicago, Minnesota and Dar es Salaam.

Alexander Bubb is a senior lecturer in English at Roehampton University in London. He works on nineteenth-century poetry and reading culture, and has also written on aspects of Indian colonial history. His first book, *Meeting Without Knowing It: Kipling and Yeats at the Fin de Siècle* (2016), won the University English Book Prize 2017. Currently he is writing on popular accessible translations of classic literature from Asian languages targeted at the general reading public in the late nineteenth century.

Jennifer Burek Pierce is an associate professor in the School of Library and Information Science at the University of Iowa. Her books include *What Adolescents Ought to Know: Sexual Health Texts in Early Twentieth-Century America* (2011), *Sex, Brains, and Video Games: Information and Inspiration for Youth Services Librarians* (2nd edition 2017) and *Mapping the Imaginary: Supporting Creative Writers Through Programming, Prompts, and Research* (2019, with Riley Hanick and Micah Bateman).

Nicole Gonzalez is a professor in the Psychology Department at Middlesex County College in New Jersey, where she teaches social psychology and the psychology of death and dying.

Jillian M. Hess is an associate professor of English at Bronx Community College, City University of New York (CUNY) and a former visiting scholar at the American Academy of Arts and Sciences. Her work has appeared in the journals *Book History*, *European Romantic Review* and the *Journal of the History of Ideas*. Her current book project, *The Commonplace Method*, explores the influence of commonplace books on Romantic and Victorian literature.

Margaret J. Joachim is a late convert to book history, having abandoned early academic study as a geologist for a thirty-five-year career in information technology management and ordination as an Anglican priest. Finally retired, she took an MA in the history of the book at the University of London and is now undertaking PhD research on the significance of heraldry in medieval psalters. She accidentally discovered the miners' libraries while looking for disused lead mines and traces of gold on holiday in Scotland.

Joan Judge is a fellow of the Royal Society of Canada and professor in the Department of History at York University, Toronto. A cultural historian of print and knowledge in modern China, she is the author of *Republican Lens: Gender, Visuality, and Experience in the Early Chinese Periodical Press* (2015), *The Precious Raft of History: The Past, the West, and the Woman Question in China* (2008) and *Print and Politics: 'Shibao' and the Culture of Reform in Late Qing China* (1996), as well as co-editor of *Women and the Periodical Press in China's Global Twentieth Century: A Space of Their Own?* (2018), *Beyond Exemplar Tales: Women's Biography in Chinese History* (2011) and *Women Warriors and National Heroes: Global Histories* (forthcoming).

Bronwyn Lowe published her first book, *'The Right Thing to Read': A History of Australian Girl-Readers, 1910–1960*, with Routledge in 2018 and has published articles in *Book History* and *History Compass*. She works as the Academic and Student Wellbeing Coordinator at St Hilda's College, University of Melbourne.

DeNel Rehberg Sedo is a professor in the Department of Communication Studies at Mount Saint Vincent University in Halifax, Nova Scotia. She published *Reading Beyond the Book: The Social Practices of Contemporary Literary Culture* (2013) with her research partner, Danielle Fuller. The two recently edited a special themed edition of *Participations: Journal of Audience and Reception Studies* (2019) titled 'Readers, Reading and Digital Media'.

Samantha Rideout has a graduate degree in public relations from Mount Saint Vincent University, where she has lectured in research methods. She published an article about book cover design in PR News's *Visual Storytelling Guidebook* (2016) and has published two works of fiction, *The People Who Stay* (2016) and *Pieces* (2013). At the annual Atlantic Schools of Business conference (2014) she presented a conference paper on how email marketing shapes reader identity. With a Bachelor of Commerce (co-op) and Bachelor of Arts degrees from Memorial University of Newfoundland, she currently works as a marketing manager in New York.

Jonathan Rose is William R. Kenan Professor of History at Drew University. He was the founding President of the Society for the History of Authorship, Reading and Publishing, and a founding editor of the journal *Book History*. He currently edits (with Shafquat Towheed) the monograph series 'New Directions in Book History' (Palgrave Macmillan). His books include *The Intellectual Life of the British Working Classes* (2nd edition, 2010), *The Holocaust and the Book: Destruction and Preservation* (2001), *The Literary Churchill: Author, Reader, Actor* (2014); *Readers' Liberation* (2018) and (with Simon Eliot) *A Companion to the History of the Book* (2nd edition, 2019).

Zach Smith is Assistant Professor of History and Director of the Asian Studies Program at the University of Central Arkansas. He specialises in the intellectual and cultural history of modern China, and his current research focuses on the relationship between popular education, citizenship and colonial forms of power in the early twentieth century. His article 'Reading Pingmin: Popular Education and the

Democratic Ideal in Republican Beijing, 1917–1924' was published in the January 2018 issue of *Twentieth-Century China*.

Ludmilla A. Trigos, an independent scholar, received her PhD in Russian literature from Columbia University. She has taught at Columbia, Barnard College, Drew University and New York University. Her books include *The Decembrist Myth in Russian Culture* (2009) and *Under the Sky of My Africa: Alexander Pushkin and Blackness* (co-edited with Catharine Theimer Nepomnyashchy and Nicole Svobodny, 2006). She and Carol Ueland have recently contributed articles on Russian print culture to *Writing Russian Lives: The Poetics and Politics of Biography in Modern Russian Culture* (edited by Polly Jones, 2018) and the *Slavic and East European Journal*.

Carol Ueland is Professor Emerita of Russian at Drew University. Recent papers and chapters include 'Women's Poetry in the Soviet Union', 'The Eastern Path of Exile: Russian Women's Writing in China' (co-authored with Olga Bakich), 'Joseph Brodsky and Aleksandr Kushner: The Relationship in Verse' and 'Pseudonyms and Personae of Marianna Kolosova: Creating a New Feminine Voice in Emigration'. Book translations include Aleksandr Kushner's *Apollo in the Grass: Selected Poems* (with Robert Carnevale, 2015). She and Ludmilla A. Trigos are the editors of *Biography for the Masses: The Lives of Remarkable People in Russia, 1890 to the Present* (forthcoming).

Nick Weir-Williams is Director of Strategic Partnerships at Ingenta, and has worked in publishing for forty years in the United States, the United Kingdom and Australia. Books published under his directorship at Northwestern University Press won the Nobel Prize and National Book Award. As Stephen Weir he authored *Encyclopedia Idiotica: History's Worst Decisions and the People Who Made Them* (2005), published in eight countries.

Lauren Weiss is a research associate at the University of Strathclyde for 'Piston, Pen & Press', a project funded by the Arts and Humanities Research Council. Her publications include 'The Manuscript Magazines of the Wellpark Free Church Young Men's Literary Society, Glasgow: A Case Study', in *Media and Print Culture Consumption in Nineteenth-Century Britain: The Victorian Reading Experience* (edited by Paul Raphael Rooney and Anna Gasperini, 2016) and '"All are instructive if read in a right spirit": Reading, Religion and

Instruction in a Victorian Reading Diary', in the journal *Library and Information History* (2016).

Amelia Yeates is Senior Lecturer in Art History at Liverpool Hope University. She has published on Pygmalionism, women's reading practices, and artistic masculinities in the nineteenth century. She was co-editor (with Serena Trowbridge) of *Pre-Raphaelite Masculinities: Constructions of Masculinity in Art and Literature* (2014) and editor of a special issue of *Visual Culture in Britain* (2015): 'The Male Artist in Nineteenth-Century Britain'. She is co-editor, with Beth Palmer, of the forthcoming *Picturing the Reader: Reading and Representation in the Long Nineteenth-Century* (Peter Lang).

Introduction

Jonathan Rose

It really all began with Richard Altick. In *The English Common Reader: A Social History of the Mass Reading Public, 1800–1900* (1957), he sketched in the agenda of what would later be known as 'the history of the book'.[1] This grand project would bring together research on literacy, basic education, libraries, the book business, newspapers and periodicals, and situate it all in the social and cultural milieu of the times. (Altick was actually one step ahead of the volume that is often credited with launching book history, *L' apparition du livre*, which Lucien Febvre and Henri Jean Martin published in 1958.)

Although Samuel Johnson invented the term and the concept, it was Altick who wonderfully focused the minds of historians on the 'common reader'. Tracking the literary tastes of authors, intellectuals, divines and statesmen was relatively easy, but as for the untold millions of ordinary readers – those who read not for professional reasons, but for pleasure and edification – what paper trails did they leave behind? Could we ever hope to enter into their minds and recapture reading as they experienced it? Scarcity of sources was an obstacle to Altick, who in fact devoted only one chapter of his book to 'The Self-Made Reader'. But since 1957 scholars have discovered ingenious ways to approach the subject and to recover what once seemed to be hopelessly lost to history. The case studies in the present volume make clear that we have advanced very far and in many directions since *The English Common Reader*. Much of that research has focused on Britain, if only because England and especially Scotland were early achievers of mass literacy, and both left behind rich documentary evidence of everyday reading. But this volume also offers pioneering research on Russia, China and isolated Australasian and New Zealand farmsteads.

Commonplace books have long been used by scholars to reveal which texts readers read and which specific passages they thought important enough to copy. Most of these notebooks have survived only in manuscript, but some were published, as Jillian M. Hess explains in Chapter 1, 'British Commonplace Readers, 1706–1879'. The compilers were often apologetic for presuming to make public their work, which might appear to be a farrago of random, unoriginal jottings. Frederick Locker-Lampson tellingly titled his printed commonplace book *Patchwork* (1879), and wondered whether a 'Commonplace-book is a book kept by a commonplace sort of person'. David Allan concluded that these apologias reflect the 'terminal decline' of this genre in the nineteenth century, but Hess sees here an attempt to adapt an ancient literary form to a modern culture of reading, in three specific ways. First, commonplace books were increasingly presented as creative acts that reflected the personality of the compiler. Second, by the eighteenth century, commonplace books had become something to be read at home rather than at school, designed to 'delight' their readers rather than merely 'instruct'. Finally, the strict organisation of some early modern commonplace books was abandoned, leaving the reader-editors free to structure their compilations as they wished.

In Chapter 2, 'Reading in God's Treasure-House: The Societies for Purchasing Books in Leadhills and Wanlockhead, 1741–1820', Margaret J. Joachim explores two reading societies established by and for Scottish miners, the earliest working-class subscription libraries in Britain and, indeed, (as far as we can tell) in the world. Borrowing records appear to be lost, but we have some carefully kept minute books of the miners' monthly meetings, lists of book purchases, and catalogues. The miners governed these libraries and established strict rules that barred any interference by their bosses. Joachim focuses on the years 1741 to 1820, and the minute books and catalogues show that, to an impressive extent, the workers were reading the Scottish Enlightenment, which was not necessarily what their employers wanted them to read. But that independence came at a price: ledger books show that the finances of such libraries were inevitably precarious, given that they depended on dues from the miners themselves.

Where Joachim concentrates on two working-class Scottish libraries, Maxine Branagh-Miscampbell ranges more broadly in 'The School Library and Childhood Reading in Lowland Scotland, 1750–1850'. She mines institutional records and anecdotal evidence for a wide variety of schools to show how they furnished reading materials for children. She explores public grammar schools for upper-middle-class boys, hospital schools for the sons and daughters of merchants, pauper schools for the poor, and parish and burgh schools in rural and urban areas. This approach reveals how reading habits, library provision, library usage and attitudes towards reading differed for children of different social strata. It also illuminates important cultural changes over time: school libraries assumed an increasingly important role in the curriculum; there was greater emphasis on enjoyment and leisure reading; children's literature and periodicals were introduced; and novels were made more available.

In the nineteenth century and well into the twentieth, manuscript magazines were a common form of grassroots popular literary expression, yet scholars have almost entirely ignored them. A search of the MLA International Bibliography turns up just two hits, one of them by Lauren Weiss, and here, in Chapter 4, '"Although ambitious we did not aspire to such dizzy heights": Manuscript Magazines and Communal Reading Practices of London Literary Societies in the Long Nineteenth Century', she shows how much these amateur periodicals can reveal. These magazines included poetry, prose, art and even music, all created by groups of common readers, which, at the time, were called 'mutual improvement societies'. As such, they illuminate communal reading, individual reading, interactive reading, silent reading, reading aloud, intensive and extensive reading, guided reading and, of course, self-education. Reader responses were often scribbled on the back pages of these magazines. Weiss has found about ninety mutual improvement magazines based throughout the United Kingdom. They show (if any more evidence is needed) that manuscript publication did not end with Gutenberg, but continued into modern times, even in highly literate and industrialised societies.

The historiography of reading is rarely art history, but Amelia Yeates brings that perspective to bear in 'Space and Place in Nineteenth-Century Images of Women Readers'. Artists commonly depicted women reading in diverse sites: public and home libraries, parlours, attics, window seats, gardens, beaches or railway carriages; reading alone, among strangers or with friends or family; and perusing a wide variety of materials. Of course, Victorian fiction is replete with reading scenes, where authors used physical space to illuminate the imaginative spaces of their characters (Jane Eyre, for instance). Taken together, these images reveal much about sexuality, education, class, religion and domesticity, especially when they are studied in the context of Victorian literary guidebooks that warned young women away from romantic and sensation novels.

The Victorian canon was not entirely Western. In 1845 Louisa Costello published the first successful oriental anthology, *The Rose Garden of Persia*, and Edward FitzGerald's classic translation of *The Rubáiyát of Omar Khayyám* achieved phenomenal sales and renown. A pocket edition of the latter was owned by Thomas Ambrose Palmer, an Australian farmer who served on the Western Front in 1916, and he annotated it with quotations from Tennyson's 'Akbar's Dream', something by Kipling in the style of the medieval Indian poet Kabir and a ninth-century Japanese poem by Yasuhide. Taken together, these oriental classics communicated a kind of multicultural ecumenicism to Western common readers, who were perhaps not so ethnocentric as they are sometimes portrayed. In Chapter 6, 'Asian Classic Literature and the English General Reader, 1845–1915', Alexander Bubb discusses the proliferation of cheap and accessible editions of Persian, Arabic, Sanskrit, Chinese and Japanese works. Most were not direct translations but were, rather, rewritings by profit-maximising self-described 'popularisers'. They were not respected by academic experts, but the publishers employed shrewd marketing, illustration and pricing strategies. Some of the works were briefly popular and are now forgotten; others failed completely. But they were all part of a grand Victorian effort to bring the best that was known and thought in the world to the masses – and here the world included the East. Bubb shows how these popular translations were interpreted (and misinterpreted) and recast as musical and theatrical performances. For evidence of reader response he relies especially on marginalia and commonplace books, culled from wide-ranging research in British, American and Australian libraries. Their personal comments show how ordinary Victorians strove to read across cultural boundaries and achieve a universal literary perspective.

The Russians have long prided themselves on being a 'reading nation' (*samyi chitaiushchii narod*), not without some justification. In 'Readers and Reading During Russia's Literacy Transition, 1850–1950: How Readers Shaped a Great Literature', Jeffrey Brooks surveys the creation and cultivation of that mass reading public, from the emancipation of the serfs to the death of Stalin. It was an era when Russians endured hideous repression, some of the bloodiest wars and civil wars in human history, famines (largely manmade) and mindless censorship. Nevertheless, under both the tsars and the communists, education, literacy and popular reading expanded continuously and at an explosive pace. And those common readers were serious readers, devouring Tolstoy and Chekhov, though they also enjoyed 'Pinkertons' (the Russian counterpart of dime novels). After the Revolution, belles-lettres were largely swept aside by propaganda, and a market-driven literary economy gave way to top-down planning. But Russians learned to read between the lines, for example when newspapers tried to obscure reports of Red Army defeats in the opening phase of the Great Patriotic War.

Edwardian Britain is renowned for its great popular education projects, such as Everyman's Library and the Workers' Educational Association. But there were very similar ventures in late tsarist Russia, as Carol Ueland and Ludmilla A. Trigos chronicle in Chapter 8, 'F. F. Pavlenkov's Literacy Project: Popular Serials and Reading Rooms for the Russian Masses'. An enterprising capitalist of conviction, Pavlenkov developed innovative publishing and marketing methods to sell progressive literature to newly literate Russian readers. He made them repeat customers for his various series, such as the biographical 'Lives of Remarkable People' (200 titles), the illustrated 'People's Popular Science Library' (forty titles), the 'Cultural History Library' (thirteen titles) and 'The Popular Law Library' (eleven titles), all of which were highly lucrative. He also aimed to establish free reading rooms throughout the Russian Empire. Following his death in 1900, his will dedicated 100,000 roubles to that mission, and by 1911 his executors had opened a total of 2,018 reading rooms. Some of them outlived the Soviet regime and are still functioning in Putin's Russia.

In the first half of the twentieth century, many rural regions of Australia and New Zealand were too sparsely populated to support schools and public libraries (let alone bookshops), so children in these remote areas had to develop other ways of accessing reading material. In 'Formal and Informal Networks of Book Provision for Rural Children in Australia and New Zealand, 1900–60', Bronwyn Lowe draws on memoirs, autobiographies and oral history to reconstruct reading experiences in isolated farms and sheep stations. Starting in the 1920s, state libraries and bush book clubs despatched book parcels to country families, but the supply was limited, and librarians made sure that no 'unsuitable' literature was included. Nevertheless, children found ways around these limits and cultivated their own independent literary tastes, corresponding and exchanging books with like-minded readers.

Books are not only read: they also furnish rooms. Eighteenth-century aristocrats and twenty-first-century twenty-somethings have this in common: they both use their personal libraries to communicate something about themselves. They want to impress visitors with their literary and intellectual breadth, and they do it by displaying shelves of books that they may or may not have read. On the other hand, there are other books that we do not display in our public rooms, because they are either utilitarian and uninteresting (cookbooks, repair manuals) or downright embarrassing (pornography, *The Hunger Games*): these we hide away in the kitchen, the tool shed or the bedroom. In Chapter 10, 'Putting Your Best Books Forward: A

Historical and Psychological Look at the Presentation of Book Collections', Nicole Gonzalez and Nick Weir-Williams investigate and explain this sociological dynamic, starting with Samuel Pepys and carrying forward to the present day.

Having studied the Western common reader, we naturally want to know more about common readers in the rest of the world. When I raise this question with historians of non-Western nations, they often point to the special difficulties they face: specifically, low literacy rates and a lack of source material. These obstacles are real, but they do not deter Joan Judge, who deploys ingenious research strategies in her chapter, 'In Search of the Chinese Common Reader: Vernacular Knowledge in an Age of New Media'. Republican China witnessed the emergence of what the Anglophone countries called 'middlebrow' literature. The Chinese called it *wanbao quanshu*: 'comprehensive compendia of myriad treasures'. These were cheap, popular manuals of useful information about such mundane matters as home remedies, gardening, recognising counterfeit coins (an important skill in the chaotic Warlord Era of Republican China) and how to win friends and influence people. The target audience was neither the mostly illiterate peasantry nor the educated elites, but a middling class of urban manual, clerical, service and sex workers. These books helped the Chinese common reader to understand and adjust to a society that was modernising rapidly, unevenly and with great turmoil.

One salient aspect of that modernisation was a huge expansion of popular literacy, which provided the audience for popular books. In 'From "Bookworms" to "Scholar-Farmers": Tao Xingzhi and Changing Understandings of Literacy in the Chinese Rural Reconstruction Movement, 1923–1934', Zach Smith explains that, in the 1920s, reformers who had worked to promote literacy among urban workers redirected their energies towards the far larger population of peasants. The Rural Reconstruction Movement (*Xiangcun jianshe yundong*) drew its pedagogical theory and teaching practice from its leader, Tao Xingzhi, who also rethought the objectives of Chinese literacy education. Initially, reformers promoted mass literacy as intrinsically good, essential for general popular enlightenment, but Tao came to the conclusion that this was a Western liberal ideal, not appropriate to an economically underdeveloped country like China, and he turned towards a more utilitarian approach. His Xiaozhuang Experimental Normal School valued literacy as a 'tool' that would make workers more productive contributors to the national economy. And that in turn implied a concept of Chinese citizenship very different from the Western liberal model.

In the twenty-first century, the World Wide Web has proven to be a revolutionary empowering tool for the common reader. Professional literary critics from Thomas Carlyle to Lionel Trilling were once respected and influential arbiters of taste: now they are a rare and endangered species, as newspapers either drop their book review sections or go out of business entirely. Enrolment in college-level literature courses has plummeted, but readers have not stopped reading: to a remarkable extent, this literary vacuum has been filled by DIY criticism, where readers offer their own opinions and recommendations online. In a sense, we have circled back to the 'mutual improvement societies' of the nineteenth century, except that these autodidact groups are now virtual communities on the web. Peter Boot offers a case study in Chapter 13, 'The Voice of the Reader: The Landscape of Online Book Discussion in the Netherlands, 1997–2016'. He concentrates on Holland, but students of such sites in other countries may find many of his conclusions generalisable and universal. Boot sees the web as home to a highly diverse public sphere, open to reasonably free discussion, where individual sites vary greatly in focus and sophistication. Many of these sites are ephemeral, appearing and disappearing like supernovas, and that presents obstacles to scholars who are trying to write their histories. But they do have one common denominator: though their members are often educated and well read, no professional critics need apply. In literature as in politics, populism is ascendant.

However, an important caution is in order here: big corporate publishers use the web too, as Samantha Rideout and DeNel Rehberg Sedo illustrate in 'Novel Ideas: The Promotion of North American Book Club Books and the Creation of Their Readers'. 'Novel Ideas' was the title of an electronic newsletter link that was carried in the January 2008 edition of the Random House 'Reader's Circle'. There were literally hundreds of similar newsletters that big American and Canadian publishers electronically transmitted to book club members from 2008 to 2013. They were all part of a shrewdly planned marketing strategy by huge conglomerates, and they succeeded because they effectively used social media to engage book club readers as individuals, making them feel part of an intimate literary community. For instance, one newsletter asked its mostly female audience 'Has your book club ever had a "bring your husband to your meeting" night?' The published responses, from women all over North America, gave club members the sense that they all belonged to a grassroots circle of real housewives with common domestic lives and common literary interests. In actuality, however, such circles were largely created and run by the boys in the PR department, who had manufactured an idealised reader as a means of selling backlist books to niche audiences. So yes, readers are eschewing professional literary critics and setting up their own web communities, but those communities can be manipulated by marketers. The trick is to address those readers over the web in an intimate and conversational voice. But there is no real conversation, just a postmodern salesperson making a pitch. Intimacy can be faked.

Precisely because they fear corporate control, younger readers are striving to create their own anarchic sites for reading, as Jennifer Burek Pierce explains in the final chapter, 'Making the Story Real: Readers, Fans and the Novels of John Green'. The brothers in question were Hank Green (an enterprising populariser, much like F. F. Pavlenkov, except that Green used the Internet to promote *Pride and Prejudice*) and John Green (a bestselling novelist). On 1 January 2007 they posted their first Vlogbrothers YouTube video, and it quickly blossomed into a channel where readers and authors could interact every which way. Here the boundary between reader and author virtually disappeared, given that readers posted their own videos, fan art and critical analyses. You could call it a species of fandom, but who is the fan and who is the celebrity? The distinction between reading and doing likewise broke down, for this community was deeply engaged in raising money for non-profits and granting microloans for projects in the developing world. This literary culture is radically different from what we observe in the eighteenth century: scholars of that era could focus sharply on the well defined memberships of subscription libraries, or the 'close-knit system called the Republic of Letters' (to quote Gérard Genette).[2] But now all the boundaries have dissolved, and the very nature of reading is morphing. And that makes the historiography of the common readers as exciting as it is disorienting.

Notes

1. A second edition was still in print as of 2019: Richard D. Altick, *The English Common Reader: A Social History of the Mass Reading Public, 1800–1900*, 2nd edition (1957; Columbus: Ohio State University Press, 1998).
2. Gérard Genette, *Paratexts: Thresholds of Interpretation*, trans. Jane E. Lewin (Cambridge: Cambridge University Press, 1997), p. 361.

Chapter 1

British Commonplace Readers, 1706–1879

Jillian M. Hess

'What say you, Mary? for you are a young lady of deep reflection I know, and read great books, and make extracts.' Mary wished to say something very sensible, but knew not how. (Jane Austen, *Pride and Prejudice*[1])

Poor Mary Bennet! For all the reading she has done, and the careful 'extracts' of choice quotations she inscribes in her commonplace book, she often remains silent, finding her reading does not offer an entry into conversation. Centuries earlier, the commonplace book had been the cornerstone of humanist pedagogy: students were taught to collect quotations that they might then weave into their own arguments. By the nineteenth century, reading – no longer reserved for the male elite – had become part of the lives of women and the masses. Commonplacing, despite its illustrious history as an aid to the likes of Erasmus, Bacon and Milton, had become a source of social concern. As historians of reading have taught us, at the end of the eighteenth century England saw a 'rapid expansion in reading . . . across all strata', which, as William St Clair explains, cultivated an anxiety about the effects of common reading practices – particularly as more women and middle-class men joined the ranks of the literate.[2] Mary, like many in the nineteenth century's expanding literate class, could read and make extracts, but struggled to turn her reading into usable knowledge. And so Mr Bennet passes over his daughter: 'While Mary is adjusting her ideas . . . let us return to Mr. Bingley.'[3] Of course, the conversation never returns to Mary.[4] All of her reading and commonplacing fail her.

Mary represents a particular kind of reader that novelists parodied and pedagogues worried over: the new Georgian reader who could amass quotations from books but could not figure out how to use them. I call this variety of reader the commonplace reader because they were both widespread and reliant on the commonplace tradition, often in its printed form as collections of anecdotes, verse or witty sayings. Mary's knowledge comes from a passive form of reading – of making extracts without thinking them over and making them her own. As readers gravitated towards 'extensive' rather than 'intensive' reading practices,[5] they consumed more books, but often in a desultory fashion. Such reading led to a passive kind of learning that we find in Mary as she recycles commonplaces. Consider how she glosses the most important word of the novel as though she were reading a page from her commonplace book:

> 'Pride,' observed Mary, who piqued herself upon the solidity of her reflections, 'is a very common failing I believe. By all that I have ever read, I am convinced that it is very common indeed, that human nature is particularly prone to it, and that there are very few of us who do not cherish a feeling of self-complacency on the score of some quality or other, real or imaginary. Vanity and pride are different things, though the words are often used synonymously. A person may be proud without being vain. Pride relates more to our opinion of ourselves, vanity to what we would have others think of us.'[6]

Mary organises her thoughts under the headings 'pride' and 'vanity', and because traditional commonplace book form (assembling reading notes and quotations under general topics) serves the purposes of private study, it is only a state of undigested learning. Mary is hardly to blame. The growing industry of printed commonplace books – sometimes called books of scraps – became a staple of literacy and embodied the kind of indiscriminate reading that seemed to plague the nation. Although keeping a commonplace book of one's own was preferable to buying one 'ready made',[7] compiling one's own collection did not guarantee skilful use of one's extracts. A common criticism levelled at authors' works was comparing them to a commonplace book. For example, one notoriously nasty periodical likened Keats's verse to 'the refuse of a school-boy's common-place book'.[8] In *Spirit of the Age*, William Hazlitt criticised the poet laureate, Robert Southey, by claiming his manner of speaking 'has a little resemblance to a common-place book';[9] as we shall see, Southey was a committed compiler, and his printed commonplace books proved extremely popular. These critiques suggest that readerly skill lay not in accumulating quotations and anecdotes, but in digesting extracts (to use Seneca's metaphor of commonplacing as akin to the way a stomach digests food[10]) into a unique whole.

With the expanding readership of the eighteenth and the nineteenth century came a massive market for printed texts that catered to general tastes. Printed commonplace books were part of the growing trend for reading short texts curated by someone else: literary annuals like *The Keepsake* or *Fisher's Drawing Room Scrapbook* assembled the most popular contemporary authors, while the anthology, as Leah Price has explained, arranged canonical texts.[11] Such assemblages usefully controlled for acceptable material by wiping out indecent or provocative sections. As Richard Altick describes, throughout the nineteenth century, middle-class libraries consisted of 'nosegays from . . . authors whose works it was deemed imprudent to read in their original form', especially Shakespeare's plays.[12]

The key difference between the printed commonplace book and these associated traditions of literary annuals and anthologies is that the former were arranged according to a single person's reading habits and taste. The majority of printed commonplace books discussed in this chapter started as private manuscripts that might be shared with a select group of friends and family. My objective in this chapter is twofold: to uncover how editors represented their collections in prefatory material, and, using the evidence of printed commonplace books, to analyse the kinds of reading practices they modelled. These concerns unfold over three sections: 'Reading commonplace books', 'Marketing commonplace books' and 'Learning to be a good reader'. The dominant eighteenth- and nineteenth-century perception of printed commonplace books was that they fostered a lazy kind of reading; however, even as authors derided the printed commonplace book tradition, they tried to use their collections to teach more engaged reading practices. As I argue, those who printed their commonplace books anxiously negotiated their market success with the desultory reading practices the tradition seemed to encourage. In what follows, I explore printed commonplace books from the eighteenth to the nineteenth centuries that modelled active reading habits.

Reading commonplace books

> I have avoided confusion in my thoughts: the scheme I had made serving like a regular chest of drawers, to lodge those things orderly, and in the proper places, which came to hand confusedly, and without any method at all. . . . Reading, methinks, is but collecting the rough materials, amongst which a great deal must be laid aside as useless. (John Locke, 'Study'[13])

Histories of reading in the West have long been influenced by Roger Chartier's call to analyse ways of reading that have disappeared, as he encouraged scholars to engage 'the task of retracing forgotten gestures and habits'.[14] Since then, researchers have uncovered practices of reading that range from unfamiliar to bizarre.[15] Among the historical reading practices that Chartier outlined are the book wheel, which allowed readers to keep several texts open and easily accessible, and the commonplace book, which allowed readers to transcribe extracts from various books, stored and indexed according to general topics. The latter tradition continued to influence reading practices through the nineteenth century, even as its name lost its original ancient rhetorical meaning. Aristotle and Cicero theorised commonplaces not as hackneyed truisms but as the essential building blocks of debate. Ancient rhetoricians imagined commonplaces as mental locations that store argumentative templates fit for a variety of cases. Aristotle's *koinos topos* – a general topic – influenced Cicero, who translated the term into *locus communis* – from which we get our word 'commonplace' – which featured in his discussion of legal forms of argument. Cicero also added content to some of these 'places' and suggested that orators should use quotations from great thinkers to build authority (*auctoritates*). As the two words (common and place) merged into one (commonplace), the term shed its rhetorical meaning. Perhaps the minor poet Frederick Locker-Lampson put it best when he opened his printed commonplace book, *Patchwork* (1879), by playing on the dual meanings of the term:

> I do not know whether a reference to Dr. Johnson's Dictionary would show that a Commonplace-book is a book kept by a commonplace sort of person, but I should not be surprised if the Doctor had thought so, and, certainly, there is a very general opinion that collections of such scraps are mighty poor reading: in sustained and coherent interest not a whit better than the Doctor's own lexicon.[16]

Of course, this sentence takes a defensive turn at the end, as Locker-Lampson suggests that those who would criticise printed commonplace books for their fragmentation ought to consider that Johnson's great dictionary was similarly formed. Scholars such as David Allan[17] have seen the apologetic tenor of printed commonplace books as a symptom of the tradition's 'terminal decline' in the nineteenth century; however, in this chapter I interpret anxious prefatory material as attempts to fit the ancient tradition of keeping commonplaces to a new culture of reading in Georgian and Victorian England.[18]

Indeed, the commonplace book tradition had long been a comedic source for writers who used its formal qualities to illustrate an embarrassing form of learning. While Shakespeare created Polonius,[19]

Sir Walter Scott crafted his own commonplace character, a crusty antiquarian, the reverend Dr Jonas Dryasdust. This recurring character's name evokes both the boring pedantry of an antiquarian and the dustiness associated with old, mostly forgotten volumes. He lards his speech with Latin quotations – in his prefatory letter for *Peveril of the Peak* (1822), Dryasdust writes, 'To your last letter I might have answered, with the classic, "*Haud equidem invideo, miror magis*"'.[20] It is not surprising that in 1825 Walter Scott published a commonplace book under Dryasdust's name: *The Common-Place Book of Literary Curiosities, Remarkable Customs, Historical and Domestic Anecdotes, and Etymological Scraps*, attributed to 'the Rev. Dr. Dryasdust of York, somewhile Preface-Writer to the Great Unknown'. Scott himself kept commonplace books, and his own antiquarian interest aligns him with Dryasdust.[21] A friend recalls walking into Scott's study and finding him 'occupied in transcribing from an old manuscript volume into his common-place book'.[22] In the introduction to his printed commonplace book, Scott (writing as Dryasdust) announces that the collection aims to instruct and amuse its readers. It does so with a blend of quotations and anecdotes.

A popular form in the eighteenth century, the anecdote straddled the line between fiction and history, between instruction and entertainment. The Georgian writer Isaac Disraeli traces the root of the word back to Cicero, who 'gave the name of Anecdote to a work which he had not yet published'.[23] Disraeli explains that anecdotes, rarely read with attention, are easily forgotten:

> Yet, when anecdotes are not merely transcribed, but animated by judicious reflections, they recal [sic] others of a kindred nature: and the whole series is made to illustrate some topic that gratifies curiosity, or impresses on the mind some interesting conclusion in the affairs of human life.[24]

Disraeli admits that the anecdote had a great potential to educate, but only if the reader actively engaged it. Rather than merely making extracts, he suggests that those who wish to learn from anecdotes must approach them not for 'frivolous' interest, but to 'consult the annals of history, as a son and a brother would turn over his domestic memoirs'.[25] Such engaged reading, in which the reader imagines himself part of a larger family, becomes a form of patriotism. Being a good reader of historical anecdotes, according to Disraeli, involves yoking one's self-interest to that of the larger society – in so doing, the reader develops a passionate relationship to a text. For Disraeli, commonplace books were the height of passive reading:

> The common-place book is crouded [sic] with facts, while the mind makes not the acquisition of one solitary idea. This Erudition is a gross lust of the mind; it seizes on every thing indiscriminately, yet produces nothing; it is passion without fruition.[26]

Georgians often saw commonplacing as a means of reading without learning – a physical exercise in transcription that had little effect on knowledge. Nevertheless, many were not ready to abandon the commonplace tradition. Instead, they printed their commonplace books to model better reading habits.

Another critic of the commonplace book tradition was none other than the Enlightenment philosopher John Locke (1632–1704), even though he would become the most significant figure in the history of commonplacing after the tradition's Renaissance revival. Locke was an inveterate commonplace book compiler and went so far as to publish his technique in *A New Method of a Common-Place-Book*.[27] Locke mistrusted the commonplace book tradition because he believed that we should not accept information simply because it comes from authorities, but should evaluate it with our faculty of reason. This is a significant departure from older traditions of the commonplace book, which explicitly collected wise sayings from respected thinkers as sources of *auctoritas*. Furthermore, Locke maintained that a well stocked commonplace book was not the same thing as knowledge. He criticised men who filled their minds with a 'great stock of borrowed and collected arguments'[28] and thereby risked contradicting themselves. Instead, Locke suggested that students ought to supplement their reading with 'meditation and discourse' because, as he explained, good readers know what to keep and what to discard. Locke argued that readers must find the method that suits their particular needs, but that strict organisation made his own reading useable. He honed his method for organising reading notes throughout his lifetime and compiled upwards of forty commonplace books.[29]

Ultimately, Nicolas Toinard, a friend from Paris with whom Locke carried on an extensive correspondence, convinced the great philosopher to share his method. Despite its personal usefulness, Locke, like other people in his position, found publishing his commonplace book embarrassing and wrote that it was 'so mean a thing, as not to deserve publishing'.[30] Whatever Locke's reservations, his method dominated printed commonplace book culture in the eighteenth and nineteenth centuries. Dozens of posthumous collections of Locke's works would include his 'New Method'. For Georgian readers, Locke's method for organizing his notes was part and parcel with his legacy of empiricism.

Originally written in French, in 1706 Locke's *A New Method of a Common-Place-Book* was translated into English, inspiring a market for blank commonplace books, fitted with Locke's unique index, which he describes as follows:

> ADVERSARIORUM METHODUS.] I take a paper book of what size I please. I divide the two first pages that face one another by parallel lines into five and twenty equal parts, every fifth line black, the other red. I then cut them perpendicularly by other lines that I draw from the top to the bottom of the page, as you may see in the table prefixed. I put about the middle of each five spaces one of the twenty letters I design to make use of,[31] and a little forward in each space, the five vowels, one below another, in the natural order. This is the index to the whole volume, how big soever it may be.[32]

Locke divides his explanation into general topics such as *Epistola* and *Adversariorum Methodus*. He then notes the page number for each topic in his index: *Epistola* under 'Ei' and *Adversariorum Methodus* under 'Ae' (see Figure 1.1). In this way, Locke models the very method

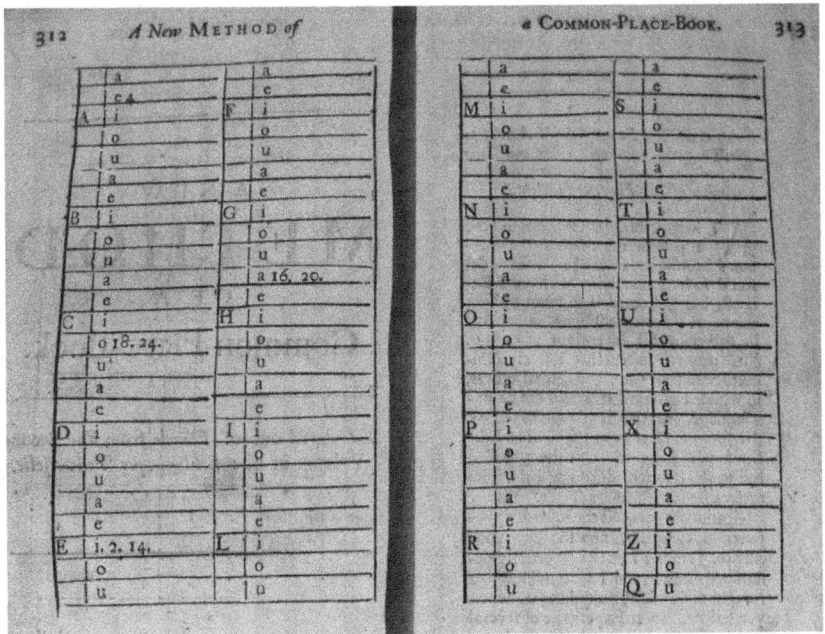

Figure 1.1 Locke's index in the first English edition of *A New Method of a Common-Place-Book*. From John Locke, *The Posthumous Works of Mr. John Locke* . . . (London: Printed by W. B. for A. and J. Churchill at the Black Swan, 1706), pp. 312–13

he describes. Locke suggests that headings ought to be written in Latin, preferably in the nominative case, though he observes that the particular language is less important than the reader's consistency. But Locke thought it most important that readers choose their own general topics, thereby facilitating critical engagement.

Marketing printed commonplace books

> To couple information with anecdote – to blend wit with instruction – to present novelty to his readers where abundance already reigns – is the aim of the editor. (Dryasdust [Walter Scott][33])

Introductory materials in printed commonplace books consciously addressed the twin issues of an ostensibly lazy readership and a cultural desire for more active consumption of texts. To address both concerns, editors announced that their compilations would instruct *and* delight the readership. Through entertainment, they hoped to hook the reader so that they might also supply some instruction, including effective strategies for reading. This dual purpose also provided cover for eighteenth- and nineteenth-century editors who, like Locke, worried over reproducing something so 'supremely egotistical and subjective'[34] as a commonplace book. Yet, eighteenth- and nineteenth-century compilers were especially attuned to the market value of such assemblages. As Dr Jeremiah Newman admits, he hoped *The Lounger's Common-Place Book* (1792) would make money for him:

> to select what struck me in the course of my reading as either curious, entertaining, or applicable to the purposes of human life; in short, to *make* a book which people would like to read, and the bookseller give me money for, are motives which enticed me to the press.[35]

Newman's collection was successful enough to survive through multiple editions well into the Victorian period, presumably because he correctly observed that the audience of desultory readers is 'more numerous than is generally imagined'.[36]

Jeremiah Newman fills *The Lounger's Common-Place Book* with anecdotes that readers might remember when they 'wish not to appear wholly ignorant of what has been said or sung'.[37] Newman presents his work as an abridgement for the lazy reader who wishes to know enough to sound educated when in company:

> I offer the Common-place Book as an easy tooth-pick companion, for idle, dissipated, forgetful men (and such, my friendly critic, there ever will be,

in spite of wisdom and gray hairs) who pass their mornings in Hyde-park, or the fruit-shop, *****'s, or St. James's-street; and yet, at the club, or after dinner, wish not to appear wholly ignorant of what has been said or sung on any careful subject of private converse, or public discussion.[38]

This book, Newman claims, is for the lazy and dissolute, for those who care more for pleasure than learning. With this collection, even they can pretend to be at least somewhat learned. Towards the end of his preface, Newman folds in his own concession to morality, and hopes that 'under the guise of literary bagatelle' he might instruct, enlighten or inspire his debauched readers, given that they would 'start at a serious volume, yawn at a moral essay, and slumber over a sermon'.[39]

To accomplish his goal, Newman compiled a series of brief biographies and encyclopaedic entries on topics listed in alphabetic order. The reader might learn about the scandalous story of Polly Baker, a Connecticut woman who, having had a child out of wedlock, was put on trial, where she persuaded the audience that her so-called crime was actually a patriotic act. 'Can it be a crime, in the nature of things, to add to the number of His Majesty's subjects, in a new country, that really wants peopling?'[40] Alternatively, readers might learn the history and advantages of the guillotine, 'an instrument of death, introduced and improved in the year 1791, by a French physician, from whom it takes its name, and who was said himself to have suffered beneath its stroke'.[41] Newman praises this 'expeditious' tool, which was 'calculated and designed to diminish pain, and shorten as much as possible the agonies of death'.[42] Newman's readers would not only learn short historical stories, but they might draw on Newman's collection for illustrations in their own works, as Leigh Hunt did when he quoted multiple stories from *The Lounger's Common-Place Book* in his collection *The Town: Its Memorable Characters and Events* (1848).[43]

As Newman writes:

in the present day, a book wholly and solely useful and instructive, incurs the risque [sic] of never being perused: and a publication merely entertaining without any view towards improving the understanding or amending the heart, I think no one ought to write.[44]

In a similar vein, the anonymously published *The Scrap Book; or, A Selection of Interesting and Authentic Anecdotes* (1825) differentiates itself from similar 'compilations' that 'have too often been made with the sole view of furnishing amusement for an idle hour; and often has this object been pursued without regard to the moral or immoral tendency of the anecdotes selected'.[45] Readers might therefore build their moral character while browsing the collection.

In addition to advertising the educational and entertaining aspects of their collections, many editors used Locke's name to promote their product. Indeed, almost as soon as British publishers discovered Locke's method, they updated it to fit a broad population of readers. Worried that the rigour of Locke's method might dissuade consumers, however, most editions offered amendments to make commonplacing easier. For example, *Bell's Common-Place Book for the Pocket; Form'd Generally upon the Principles Recommended and Practised by Mr. Locke* (1770) suggests that the common reader use the vernacular. 'Mr. Locke recommends the use of the Latin for the Index; which, though it may possibly answer the purpose of the learned, is by no means adapted to general use'.[46] Some printed commonplace books on specific topics also drew on Locke; for instance, *Stenography Compendized; or, An Improvement of Mr. Weston's Art of Short-Hand* (1780) began with a 'A Specimen of Mr. Locke's Index to a Commonplace book'. Publishers continued to use Locke's name to market their books, even as they quickly dismissed his method in their prefaces because, as *A New Commonplace Book* (1799) declared, 'The inconveniences of Mr. Locke's method are palpable'.[47] In the 1820s Taylor and Hessey promoted their *Improved Commonplace Book or Literary Diary* by including Locke's index with the suggestion (announced in the title) that the reader might choose not to use it at all and instead record entries chronologically, as though it were a diary.

Parts of Locke's commonplace book appeared in print in 1830 when Peter King published a collection of the philosopher's manuscripts. This particular sample focuses on religion and incorporates a mix of others' ideas and Locke's own commentary, organised under general headings. Under ECCLESIA he summarises 'Hooker's description of the Church', along with its volume and page number for later reference.[48] And, under ELECTIO he writes a paragraph that describes his problems with 'the Doctrine of Election' and references Calvin.[49]

Like Locke's, other celebrated authors' commonplace books often appeared posthumously. As the Victorian editor of Robert Burns's commonplace book explained, this collection provides a privileged glimpse into the reading and writing practices of a successful poet: 'there is something awe striking in thus, as it were, looking over the shoulder of the greatest lyrical Poet our country has produced, wrestling with his genius in its very birth-pangs'.[50] The poet's commonplace book begins with the title 'Observations, Hints, Songs, Scraps of Poetry, &c.'[51] and includes Burns's original creations as well as Scottish verse and a selection of epitaphs – including one for his 'Ever honored father'.[52] In 1876 the Camden Society published John Milton's commonplace book along with 'a Latin Essay and Latin Verses Presumed to be by Milton'.[53] Once again, both of these texts purport to give the reader a special view into the workings of a brilliant writer's mind. In his introduction to Milton's commonplace book, the editor explains that the manuscript's owner, 'Sir Frederick Graham, thinking it unwise to leave such a record of some of the studies of a great man to the charge of a single manuscript, very kindly approved my suggestion to have the contents printed, and mostly liberally entrusted the volume to my hands for that purpose'.[54] The immeasurable value printed commonplace books hold for histories of reading have been most visible when it comes to the collections of important figures.[55]

After Locke's, some of the most famous printed commonplace books of the nineteenth century belonged to Robert Southey. After the poet laureate's death, his commonplace books would recirculate in four printed volumes edited by his son-in-law, John Warter Wood. Southey planned on publishing his collection and most entries are strikingly impersonal. As Pamela Woof writes, 'The compilation is encyclopaedic rather than personal and the reader feels relief when tiny individual recollections occasionally appear'.[56] Though Wood attempted to check Southey's quotations and citations, if the reader were to find an error, he explains, it is only a testament to 'the wonderful stores, the accumulated learning, and the unlimited research, of the excellently single-hearted, the devout, and gifted Collector'[57] The preface introduces this collection as a rare glimpse into the practices of a great reader. Southey, we are told, read quickly and extensively. In the fourth volume of the first edition, Wood quotes from a letter his father-in-law had written in 1822, comparing his extensive reading and collection of quotations to the behaviour of an antique collector:

> Like those persons who frequent sales, and fill their houses with useless purchases, because they may want them some time or other; so am I for ever making collections and storing up materials which may not come into use till the Greek Calends. And this I have been doing for five and twenty years! It is true that I draw daily upon my hoards, and should be poor without them; but in prudence I ought now to be working up those materials rather than adding to so much dead stock.[58]

Southey transformed his 'stock' into 'a saleable commodity' with the publication of his poems.[59]

Southey's son-in-law would go one step further and package the poet laureate's raw materials into an expensive collection – each volume sold from between eighteen shillings to one guinea.[60] A full collection of Southey's volumes would have been extravagantly expensive to own. Another popular example, Anna Jameson's *A Commonplace Book of Thoughts, Memories, and Fancies: Original and Selected* (1854), cost twenty-one shillings in 1855.[61] Thankfully, most lending libraries had Jameson's printed commonplace books in addition to extracts from Locke's commonplace book, attached to King's *The Life of John Locke*. From Leeds[62] to Derbyshire[63] to Edinburgh,[64] subscription and free public libraries offered middle- and working-class readers the opportunity to peruse these collections. Mudie's Select Library, one of the nineteenth century's most popular lending libraries, carried all the volumes of Southey's and Jameson's printed commonplace books.[65]

Learning to be a good reader

> We are often told that an era is opening in which we are to see multitudes of a common sort of readers, and masses of a common sort of literature; that such readers do not want and could not relish anything better than such literature, and that to provide it is becoming a vast and profitable industry. (Matthew Arnold[66])

Though literacy and access to books were steps towards mass education, they were by no means sufficient. Many printed commonplace books specifically aimed to teach the 'common sort of readers' (to use Arnold's words) good taste and active reading. They were produced against a backdrop of Cardinal John Henry Newman's warning about the effects of industrialisation on the mind: 'What the steam engine does with matter, the printing press is to do with mind; it is to act mechanically, and the population is to be passively, almost unconsciously enlightened, by the mere multiplication and dissemination of volumes'.[67] Knowledge learned passively was not really knowledge at all. We have seen that editors often expected an undisciplined readership and they consequently arranged their collection with small selections on a variety of topics. Once the editor gained readers' attention, he or she might teach them more active modes of reading. *The Lounger* assembles a variety of stories for readers to recirculate in either conversation or their own writing. Similarly, *The Scrap Book* arranges 'true' stories that might provide the reader with 'useful information' and moral instruction; it portrays 'some virtue to be imitated' and 'some vice which is to be avoided'.[68] While *The Scrap Book* presented prose, others offered verse meant to teach good taste.[69] All of these collections assumed the reader would apply their lessons to his or her own life.

In addition to demonstrating morality and good taste, other editors modelled what we would now call critical reading. They taught the reader to converse with texts. Anna Jameson hoped her popular collection, *A Commonplace Book of Thoughts, Memories and Fancies*, might spark new ideas and interests in her audience. She explained that printing one's commonplace book

> can do good only in one way. It may, like conversation with a friend, open up sources of sympathy and reflection; excite to argument, agreement, or disagreement; and, like every spontaneous utterance of thought out of an earnest mind, suggest far higher and better thoughts than any to be found here to higher and more productive minds. If I had not the humble hope of such a possible result, instead of sending these memoranda to the printer, I should have thrown them into the fire.[70]

Rather than incinerating her memoranda, Jameson hoped that publishing them might encourage new, better ideas among her readers. In other words, the utility of this commonplace book rested entirely in the reader's hands. It was a modest work, in her opinion: 'truly what its name sets forth – a book of common-places and nothing more'.[71] In the Victorian period, Jameson was known for her histories of art and literature. Her prolific writing career, we learn, was supported by her devotion to commonplacing:

> For many years I have been accustomed to make a memorandum of any thought which might come across me – (if pen and paper were at hand), and to mark (and *remark*) any passage in a book which excited either a sympathetic or an antagonistic feeling. This collection of notes accumulated insensibly from day to day. The volumes on Shakespeare's Women, on Sacred and Legendary Art, and various other productions, sprung from seed thus lightly and casually sown. . . . But what was to be done with the fragments which remained – without beginning or end – links of a hidden or broken chain?[72]

Jameson offered a challenge for the common reader. There might have been another study hidden in these leftover unpublished bits of her commonplace practice; she wondered if her readers might discover the 'links of a . . . chain' in the extracts. Yet, to accomplish such a task required a particular kind of reader: one who was attuned to omission, skilled at argumentation and able to find connections among extracts.

Anna Jameson's *Commonplace Book* resembles Locke's and Southey's in the way she interweaves quotations with her own reflections, modelling a form of responsive reading. Yet one of the problems with engaged note-taking is that it can become difficult to sort the original from the borrowed:

> all those passages which are marked by inverted commas must be regarded as borrowed, though I have not always been able to give my authority. All passages not so marked are, I dare not say, original or new, but at least the unstudied expression of a free discursive mind.[73]

Jameson modelled an active form of reading with her 'free discursive mind', which often interwove itself into quotations. For the most part, she reflected on others' ideas, for instance the question of historical difference as it related to gender:

> I READ in the life of Garrick that, 'about 1741, a taste for Shakespeare had lately been revived by the encouragement of some distinguished persons of taste of both sexes; but more especially by the ladies who formed themselves into a society, called the "Shakespeare Club"'. There exists a Shakespeare Society at this present time, but I do not know that any ladies are members of it, or allowed to be so.[74]

Jameson never simply offered quotations for her readers, but wrapped them in her own essayistic prose, demonstrating a way of reflecting on, and engaging with, her reading. Hers was a questioning mind that did not readily accept what she read as truth. The most obvious example of her proclivity to enter into a text came in the form of her revision of Wordsworth's 'Character of the Happy Warrior'. Jameson used this poem to illustrate the fallacy in 'the belief that there are essential masculine and feminine virtues and vices'.[75] She first illustrated this point 'by quoting the axiom of the Greek philosopher Antisthenes . . . "The virtue of the man and the woman is the same"'.[76] This, she pointed out, was 'a sort of anticipation of the Christian doctrine'.[77] Following this ancient reference, Jameson turned to 'an illustration which is at once practical and poetical, and plain to the most prejudiced among men or women'[78] – an adaptation of Wordsworth's 'The Happy Warrior'. While this poem originally referred to a man, Jameson demonstrated how it might equally refer to a woman by changing 'warrior' to 'woman' and revising gendered pronouns. Doing so reveals that, 'almost from beginning to end it is literally as applicable to the one sex as to the other':[79]

CHARACTER OF THE HAPPY WOMAN.

Who is the happy *woman*? Who is *she*
That every *woman* born should wish to be?
It is the generous spirit, who, when brought
Among the tasks of real life, had wrought
Upon the plan that pleased *her* childish thought;
Whose high endeavours are an inward light,
That make the path before *her* always bright. . . .

With her revisions, Jameson exhibited a kind of readerly engagement that brought a text's hidden assumptions or prejudices to the surface in order to interrogate them. While Wordsworth meant his poem to portray ideals of masculinity, Jameson used it to make a different point. These lines, in her view, did not refer just to men, but to humanity in general.

The catalogues of lending libraries attest to the popularity of Jameson's collection, but Leigh Hunt's assemblages of his favourite verse were even more popular.[80] Hunt, the man who first published Shelley and Keats, loved collecting extracts and he published them in multiple collections with engaging titles such as *A Book for the Corner* (1849) – which Hunt describes as 'a book . . . of favourite passages, not out of the authors we most admired, but those whom we most loved'[81] – or *A Jar of Honey* (1848) – which references Seneca's famous metaphor for commonplacing, the honey bee.[82] The first of this series, *Imagination and Fancy* (1844), successfully appeared in three editions in as many years. The third edition's release coincided with the second work in the series, *Wit and Humour* (1846), which was reprinted in 1848. With Hunt's signature jovial style, he not only reproduced his extracts for readers' perusal, he mimicked the act of reading with his audience by italicising key parts of a text he would comment on. Readers were supposed to feel as though Hunt were looking over their shoulders, analysing the text with them through a '*principle of co-perusal*'.[83] Hunt not only modelled close reading practices, but guided his audience line by line through what he considered to be great poetry – including the verse of his friend John Keats. Hunt reproduced Keats's 'The Eve of St Agnes' interspersed with his own comments. For instance, he italicised the poem's second line, alerting his readers to a note at the end of the poem:

St. Agnes' Eve – Ah, bitter chill it was!
 The owl, for all his feathers, was a-cold;
 The hare limp'd trembling through the frozen grass,

The corresponding note burst forth with praise:

> Could he have selected an image more warm and comfortable in itself, and, therefore, better, contradicted by the season? We feel the plump, feathery bird in his nook, shivering in spite of his natural household warmth, and staring out at the silent strange weather.[84]

In this way, Hunt simultaneously taught the reader to notice juxtaposition in Keats's imagery and to *feel* the cold night pressed against the owl's feathers. Nicholas Roe encourages us to think of these collections as extensions of Hunt's criticism of authors in his periodical essays, filled as they were with extensive quotations.[85] We might also view these 'Jewel Cases' as precursors to Victorian literary criticism built around extensive quotation – Matthew Arnold would do something similar with his collection of choice literary extractions, which he called 'touchstones', in *The Study of Poetry* (1880). Both of these texts aimed to model good taste and active practices of reading for the public. Hunt's friend Francis Jeffrey wrote to congratulate him on *Imagination and Fancy*; he hoped for a

> succession of such Jewel Cases . . . for the sake of the *reading public*, as much as for yours, being persuaded that the best way of breaking in careless readers to a true taste in poetry, is by thus parsing and expounding, as it were, to them a few exquisite passages, and so enabling them, by their light and the master's magnifying commentary, to distinguish the elements in which all poetical beauty consists.[86]

It would seem that the reading public needed guidance, that 'careless readers' needed breaking in.

The ambivalent and sometimes contradictory narrative of printed commonplace books in the eighteenth and nineteenth centuries has long been overshadowed by the more recognisable anthology tradition. Moreover, the commonplace book's (now) unfamiliar name makes it all the easier to overlook. Yet, as a literary technology that assisted readers for hundreds of years, printed commonplace books preserve debates around reading practices. We have seen commonplace book compilers model different forms of engaged reading: Locke described his method of organising reading notes, Newman presented a range of short anecdotes for his readers' various uses, and Jameson demonstrated critical engagement with texts. For his part, Hunt taught his audience to become what we would now call close readers, attuned to the figurative language, imagery, diction and rhythm of verse. Additionally, befitting his own characteristically cheery disposition, he hoped to instil a love of poetry in his readers.

By way of conclusion, if we return to Longbourn, along with Jane and Elizabeth Bennet (who have finally met Mr Bingley) we find their sister Mary 'deep in the study of thorough bass and human nature' with 'some new extracts to admire, and some new observations of thread-bare morality to listen to'.[87] Austen humorously juxtaposes two divergent topics: a very specific form of musical notation (thorough bass) and the most general of all topics (human nature). It is unclear how exactly these two subjects relate to one another, but this is, after all, the point: Mary's desultory reading habits draw her in different directions so that her learning remains superficial because she does not know how to read actively. Instead, she accumulates information without critically engaging it, making her susceptible to shallow morality. After all, 'Mary had neither genius nor taste',[88] and though she was industrious, her learning was not of her own making. What, we might wonder, would Mary's character have been if she had used Locke's index or written engaged summaries of her reading in the model of Southey and Jameson? Then, rather than being just another commonplace reader, perhaps Mary would have been more memorable.

Notes

1. Jane Austen, *Pride and Prejudice* (1813; London: Penguin, 2002), p. 9.
2. William St Clair, *The Reading Nation in the Romantic Period* (Cambridge: Cambridge University Press, 2004), p. 11.
3. Austen, *Pride and Prejudice*, p. 9.
4. As Alex Woloch points out, Mary all but disappears from the second half of the novel. See Alex Woloch, *The One vs. the Many: Minor Characters and the Space of the Protagonist in the Novel* (Princeton: Princeton University Press, 2009), especially ch. 1.
5. Rolf Engelsing invented this now famous distinction. See Rolf Engelsing, *Zur Sozialgeschichte deutscher Mittel- und Unterschichten* (Göttingen: Vandenhoeck and Ruprecht, 1978).
6. Austen, *Pride and Prejudice*, p. 21.
7. 'Commonplace Books', *Chambers's Journal*, 3 January 1880, p. 217.
8. *Literary Chronicle and Weekly Review*, 31 March 1821, p. 206.
9. William Hazlitt, *The Spirit of the Age* (London: H. Colburn, 1825), p. 182.
10. Lucius Annaeus Seneca, *Seneca: Works* (Cambridge, MA: Harvard University Press, 1971), vol. v, letter 84.
11. Leah Price, *The Anthology and the Rise of the Novel: From Richardson to George Eliot* (Cambridge: Cambridge University Press, 2003).

12. Richard D. Altick, *The English Common Reader: A Social History of the Mass Reading Public, 1800–1900*, 2nd edition (Chicago: University of Chicago Press, 1998), p. 127.
13. Peter King, *The Life of John Locke: With Extracts from His Correspondence, Journals, and Common-Place Books* (London: Henry G. Bohn, 1858), p. 108.
14. Roger Chartier, *The Order of Books: Readers, Authors, and Libraries in Europe Between the Fourteenth and Eighteenth Centuries* (Palo Alto: Stanford University Press, 1994), p. 9.
15. For example, Ellen Gruber Garvey describes how African-Americans used scrapbooks to create 'alternative histories' that were both 'weapons' and 'communal knowledge'. See Ellen Gruber Garvey, *Writing with Scissors: American Scrapbooks from the Civil War to the Harlem Renaissance* (New York: Oxford University Press, 2012), p. 23. Additionally, Leah Price theorises an entire category of 'non-reading' and describes Byron's shock at seeing a butcher use a page from *Pamela* to wrap meat. See Leah Price, *How to Do Things with Books in Victorian Britain* (Princeton: Princeton University Press, 2012), p. 233.
16. Frederick Locker-Lampson, *Patchwork* (London: Smith, Elder, 1879), p. vii.
17. David Allan, *Commonplace Books and Reading in Georgian England* (Cambridge: Cambridge University Press, 2010), p. 265.
18. Doing so, I continue the work Ann Moss did to elaborate the differences between Latin and vernacular commonplace books printed in the Renaissance. See Ann Moss, *Printed Commonplace-Books and the Structuring of Renaissance Thought* (Oxford: Clarendon Press, 1996), p. 211.
19. Marjorie Garber calls Shakespeare's Polonius 'a walking commonplace book'. See Marjorie Garber, *Profiling Shakespeare* (New York: Routledge, 2008), p. 291.
20. Walter Scott, *Peveril of the Peak* (Edinburgh: Adam and Charles Black, 1871), p. 7.
21. Scott's commonplace books are held at Abbotsford and in the National Library of Scotland, MS 1568.
22. Robert Pearse Gillies, *Recollections of Sir Walter Scott, Bart* (London: J. Fraser, 1837), p. 96.
23. Isaac Disraeli, *Literary Miscellanies* (London: Murray and Highley, 1801), p. ii.
24. Ibid., p. 6.
25. Ibid., p. 7.
26. Ibid., p. 145.
27. This text was originally published in 1685 in French, under the title *Méthode nouvelle de dresser des recueils*.
28. King, *The Life of John Locke*, p. 105.
29. For more on Locke's commonplace books see Richard Yeo, *Notebooks,*

English Virtuosi, and Early Modern Science (Chicago: University of Chicago Press, 2014), especially ch. 7.
30. Ibid., p. 444.
31. Locke explains that he omits several letters from this index because he finds he never uses them.
32. Ibid., p. 444.
33. Dryasdust (Walter Scott), *The Common-Place Book of Literary Curiosities, Remarkable Customs, Historical and Domestic Anecdotes, and Etymological Scraps* . . . (London: John Bumpus, 1825), p. i.
34. Anna Jameson, *A Commonplace Book of Thoughts, Memories, and Fancies: Original and Selected* (London: Longman, 1854), p. vii.
35. Jeremiah Whitaker Newman, *The Lounger's Common-Place Book; or, Alphabetical Arrangement of Miscellaneous Anecdotes* (London: printed for the author: and sold by Kerby and Co., 1792), p. ii.
36. Jeremiah Whitaker Newman, *The Lounger's Common-Place Book; or, Alphabetical Arrangement of Miscellaneous Anecdotes* (London: printed for the author: and sold by Kerby and Co., 1796), p. ii. Newman's various editions contained different introductions and new material.
37. Ibid., p. ii.
38. Ibid., p. ii.
39. Ibid., p. ii.
40. Newman, *The Lounger's Common-Place Book* (1792), p. 21.
41. Newman, *The Lounger's Common-Place Book* (1796), p. 217.
42. Ibid.
43. Leigh Hunt, *The Town* (1848; London: Smith, Elder and Company, 1859), p. 252.
44. Newman, *The Lounger's Common-Place Book* (1796), p. ii.
45. *The Scrap Book; or, A Selection of Interesting and Authentic Anecdotes* (London: Chambers & Halligan, 1825).
46. John Bell, *Bell's Common-Place Book for the Pocket; Form'd Generally upon the Principles Recommended and Practised by Mr. Locke* (London: printed for John Bell, 1770), p. v.
47. *A New Commonplace Book; Being an Improvement on That Recommended by Mr. Locke* (London: printed for J. Walker, 1799), p. 1.
48. King, *The Life of John Locke*, p. 295.
49. Ibid.
50. Robert Burns, *Robert Burns' Common Place Book* (Edinburgh: privately printed, 1872), p. vi.
51. Ibid., p. 1.
52. Ibid., p. 19.
53. John Milton, *A Common-Place Book of John Milton*, ed. Alfred J. Horwood (Westminster: printed for the Camden Society, 1876).
54. Ibid., p. xx.
55. This trend continued well into the twentieth century, with scholarly editions of celebrated authors' commonplace books. See Wystan Hugh

Auden, *A Certain World: A Commonplace Book* (London: Faber & Faber, 1982); E. M. Forster, *Commonplace Book* (Palo Alto: Stanford University Press, 1987); D. L. Wilson, *Jefferson's Literary Commonplace Book* (Princeton: Princeton University Press, 2014).
56. Pamela Woof, 'The Uses of Notebooks', *Coleridge Bulletin*, New Series 31 (summer 2008), 15.
57. Robert Southey, *Southey's Common-Place Book*, ed. John Warter Wood (London: Longman, Brown, Green and Longmans, 1850–1), p. iii.
58. Ibid., p. v.
59. Dahlia Porter, 'Poetics of the Commonplace: Composing Robert Southey', *Wordsworth Circle*, 42:1 (2011), pp. 27–33.
60. As a point of comparison, in 1815 a ham and potato dinner for two would have cost around seven shillings.
61. Mrs Anna Jameson, *Sisters of Charity: Catholic and Protestant, Abroad and at Home* (London: Longman, Brown, Green and Longmans, 1855), p. 12.
62. *Catalogue of the . . . Central Lending Library.* (Leeds: Goodall and Suddick, 1884).
63. Free Public Library and Museum, *Catalogue of the Lending Library* (Derbyshire: Wilkins and Ellis, 1879).
64. Edinburgh (Scotland) Public Library, *Catalogue of Books in the Lending Library* (Edinburgh: Edinburgh Public Library Committee at the Darien Press, 1890).
65. *Catalogue of the Principal Books in Circulation at Mudie's Select Library, January, 1865* (London: Mudie's Select Library, 1865).
66. Matthew Arnold, 'The English Poets', *Library Magazine*, 4 (1880), p. 125.
67. John Henry Newman, *The Idea of a University* (1852; New Haven: Yale University Press, 1996), p. 203.
68. *The Scrap Book*, p. 7.
69. Examples include *The Poetical Common-Place Book* (London: John Anderson, 1822) and *The Common-Place Book of Ancient and Modern Ballad* (Edinburgh: J. Anderson, 1824).
70. Jameson, *A Commonplace Book*, p. vi.
71. Ibid., p. v.
72. Ibid., pp. v–vi; original emphasis.
73. Ibid., p. vii.
74. Ibid., p. 305.
75. Ibid., p. 85.
76. Ibid., p. 86.
77. Ibid.
78. Ibid.
79. Ibid., p. 87.
80. Like most other lending libraries at the time, Mudie's also carried Leigh Hunt's collections of extracts.

81. *Selected Writings of Leigh Hunt*, ed. Michael Eberle-Sinatra and Robert Morrison (London: Pickering and Chatto, 2002), vol. V, p. 7.
82. Seneca, Letter 84.
83. Hunt, *Selected Writings*, vol. V, p. 3.
84. Ibid., vol. IV, p. 111.
85. Nicholas Roe, *Fiery Heart: The First Life of Leigh Hunt* (New York: Random House, 2010).
86. Leigh Hunt, *The Correspondence of Leigh Hunt* (London: Smith, Elder and Company, 1862), vol. II, p. 37.
87. Austen, *Pride and Prejudice*, p. 59.
88. Ibid., p. 25.

Chapter 2

Reading in God's Treasure-House: The Societies for Purchasing Books in Leadhills and Wanlockhead, 1741–1820

Margaret J. Joachim

In 1876 James Moir Porteous, minister of the kirk in Wanlockhead, a small village in the Lowther Hills in south-west Scotland, published a book. The hills were – and still are – remote and bleak, but their mineral resources were so rich that they provided more than four-fifths of Scotland's lead production until the 1920s. This, combined with the wild natural beauty of the area, prompted him to call his book *God's Treasure-House in Scotland*.[1] Over 100 years earlier, the lead miners in Wanlockhead and Leadhills, two isolated villages 1,000 feet up in the hills, had set up two reading societies, the earliest working-class subscription libraries in Britain. Both survived as lending libraries until the mines closed 200 years later, and the library buildings and most of the books have been preserved.[2] The miners kept meticulous records of their monthly meetings and book purchases and produced library catalogues. Many of these have also survived.

This study draws on the minute books, catalogues and related documents for the period 1741–1820. Records confirm that each society's membership was drawn almost entirely from the mining community. The catalogues reveal the miners' choice of books, the topics covered and the extent to which their reading was influenced by works characteristic of the Scottish Enlightenment. Wanlockhead's minute book details purchase and binding costs, the extent to which books were bought new or second-hand, the booksellers used and the contrasting subject matter of purchased and donated books. Although no borrowing records have survived, we can guess which works were most heavily read from evidence of rebinding and replacement. The increasing value of the Society's assets can be traced, as can the financial difficulties it experienced when its members decided to subscribe for a multipart encyclopaedia. Early records from a third library, established thirty miles away at the end of the eighteenth century by a gift of books from the mine managers, show the continuing disparity between what the managers thought the miners ought to read and what the miners bought with their own money.

The Society for Purchasing Books at Leadhills was founded in 1741. Its membership list begins on 15 April 1743 with twenty-three founder members and concludes with member number 840 in 1902.[3] Manuscript and printed copies of the articles and laws survive from 1760,[4] a handwritten library catalogue dates from 1767[5] and a printed one from 1800.[6] An undated register lists volumes in accession order from 1 to 4,820.[7] The first 1,000 entries appear to be in the same hand, suggesting that one or more earlier registers were copied into a new book. Minute books record monthly, quarterly and annual meetings and committee meetings from 1821 to 1991; one is missing (covering October 1851 to September 1870).[8] 'Bargain books', which identify miners and record their agreements for work, span 1739–1854, and three of the earliest of these come within the period under discussion.[9] A comprehensive catalogue of books remaining in the library is in draft, to which Mr Robin Harbour has kindly given me access.

In 1756 the Society for Purchasing Books at Wanlockhead was established a mile to the south. The Society's journals record members' and committee meetings, 'Deaths, Demissions and Entreys', and details of book purchases, repairs and replacements from 1784 to 1946.[10] The articles and laws of the Society are listed at the start of the first volume of the journal, and an incomplete printed copy survives from 1820.[11] A printed library catalogue dates from 1819[12] and a detailed catalogue of the surviving books was produced when the library was restored in 1979.[13] One bargain book for Wanlockhead has been found, covering the period 1747–51.[14] Wanlockhead mining journals, dating from 1755–69 and 1773–81, recorded daily or weekly progress at the mines owned by the Duke of Queensberry and Buccleuch.[15] Excerpts from these documents are reproduced here as they were written.

The articles and laws of the two societies were almost identical and both open with statements of purpose, revealing a strong ethos of mutual improvement and the need for rigorous organisation and self-discipline:

> We, Subscribers, having agreed to form Ourselves into a SOCIETY, in order to purchase a Collection of Books, for our Mutual Improvement, did, upon the twenty-third Day of *November*, One thousand seven hundred and forty-one, condescend upon certain ARTICLES, to be observed by us, for the Establishment and Regulation of this our SOCIETY.[16]

The rules which follow cover eligibility for membership, the entry money and annual subscription to be paid by members, the frequency of meetings, the election and responsibilities of officers, the procedure for weekly exchange of books, the requirement to make borrowed books available for inspection, the fines for missing meetings, declining elected office and damaging books, the conditions for inheriting or transferring a membership right, and the ability of a member to 'demit' (place membership and subscription payment on hold for a period). The rules of both societies emphasised that members had to live in Leadhills or Wanlockhead unless any new mines were opened within a six-mile radius, in which case the new miners could also become members.

From the perspective of book choice, four rules were particularly important. Both versions of Article 7 stipulated that 'neither the Society in general, nor any Member thereof shall contract for Books or any effects whatever in the name of the Society beyond the amount of the annual payments of the then current year'. Rule 37 (Wanlockhead only) prescribed exclusion for any member who recommended or introduced 'such Books as are known to hold forth, or maintain erroneous tenets or doctrines, & which may have a manifest tendency to corrupt the principles of the Society'.[17] Rule 8, for both societies, placed decision-making firmly in the hands of the miner members: 'no such person as Overseer or Grieve in this place or elsewhere who by his office may have an influence over the Members shall be capable of holding public office in this Society lest he should use his influence to the prejudice of the same'. And rule 20 provided that 'Members reading a book of more volumes than one shall not be deprived of the next succeeding volume by Members chusing before them'.[18]

Mark Towsey argued that 'the evidence suggests that not only were the miners not the founders of the original [Leadhills] library, they were not even its original membership', and a similar claim was made by John Crawford.[19] Others have proposed that the libraries were paternalistic enterprises by mine company owners, designed to foster a tractable workforce.[20] Examination of the source documents supports neither hypothesis. While the inspiration for a subscription library at Leadhills probably came from James Stirling, the renowned mathematician and enlightened manager of the Scots Mine Company who introduced numerous social and environmental improvements for his workforce, the majority of founder members were miners. This can be demonstrated by comparing names on the membership list with names in the company's bargain books, in which groups of miners signed agreements (bargains) to undertake specified work for defined periods at agreed rates.[21] Among the first 100 members at Leadhills were thirty men who can be positively identified as signatories to bargains. Eight of these were among the founder members, together with three mine overseers, a senior clerk and the village schoolmaster and surgeon. Many mine workers (e.g. lead-washers, smiths, general labourers) did not take bargains and thus did not appear in the bargain books. In fact, there was nothing in the area except lead mining, so nearly everyone there (except for a tiny middle class) worked for the mines.

The reasons for the establishment of a second library, at Wanlockhead, are not clear, but again miners led the way. Of the thirty-four men who joined the Society before 1780, seventeen were included on bargains. Of the first 100 members, forty-five names appear on bargains and there is one mine overseer.[22] Library members who cannot be identified with bargains mostly have connections to other family members who can. James and Robert Ramage were Wanlockhead Society members but do not appear in the bargain books, but bargains are recorded for Charles, John and William Ramage in the same period.[23] As this example demonstrates, there were strong elements of kinship among members. The same surnames occur repeatedly, and records of the transfer of membership rights reveal additional relationships where the direct name link was obscured by marriage.[24] Probably the longest-sustained family connection was that of the Dalziels, which began with John and Andrew, founder members of the Leadhills Society. Samuel was an early Wanlockhead member, another Andrew inherited Samuel's right in 1790 and William inherited Andrew's right in 1798.[25] Dalziel names continued to feature regularly in the membership list until 1932, when Elizabeth Dalziel was the last reader to be registered at Wanlockhead before the library closed.[26]

Wanlockhead's membership was unique in one respect. A woman, Isobel Rutherford, was admitted on 1 July 1783, having inherited her right from her brother. On 1 January 1785 she assigned her right to her nephew George McCall. No other women were admitted until in 1813 two decisions were made: workmen's widows could have reading rights until their sons were old enough to inherit, and females could become members with heritable rights but no vote.[27] Women were not admitted to the Leadhills Society until the 1880s.

Miners were not employees, but nor were they entrepreneurs or employers of labour. A group who signed up for one bargain might then take another, or subsequently split up and collaborate with different miners. They were paid at the conclusion of each three- or six-month bargain. Their earnings averaged about 5s per week in 1750,[28] rising to 9s in 1791 and even more at the height of the Napoleonic War, but fell back after 1815, when the demand for lead slackened, cheap imports arrived from Spain and the mine companies started to cut back.[29] The entry money and annual subscription (5s and 2s.6d respectively for Leadhills membership) were major outlays, and the fines (from 1d for failing to return a book to 6d for missing a quarterly meeting and 1s for declining elected office) encouraged responsible behaviour.

Geographical isolation meant that it was a long distance to a source of reading material for anyone who could not afford to maintain their own collection (which may have been one reason why both libraries survived into the 1930s, long after many similar enterprises had closed). There is some evidence that Leadhills had an active reading community before 1741. Bibles, catechisms and other devotional books were encouraged by the Kirk, and chapbooks, school books, almanacs and newspapers would be brought in by carriers (or with the returning carts which took 4,000 loads of lead to Leith each year). Eight Leadhills names occur on the subscription list for the 1737 reprint of *Prima, Media and Ultima* (a religious work by Isaac Ambrose, originally published in 1657), four of whom (John and Andrew Dalziel, Edward Douglas and John Weir) were library founders.[30] Twenty-three men were listed as founder members in 1743, but in the following two years only four more joined, suggesting the library had been launched by a core group which had already coalesced around reading as a mutual activity.

One contemporary diary excerpt survives, attributed to Matthew Wilson, a senior clerk for the Scots Mine Company.[31] He appears on the Leadhills membership list as member number 33 on 1 October 1745,[32] but in the diary he reports attending a quarterly meeting on 1 July that year and a book-choosing meeting on 10 July. Between June and November 1745 he read *Leonidas* by Richard Glover, the *London Magazine*, Paul de Rapin Thoyras's *History of England*, *The Christian Hero* by Richard Steele, a book the diary titles *Dilections*, by Sir Edward Coke, René d'Aubert de Vertot's *Revolutions of Portugal*, *The History of the Late Rebellion* by Peter Rae, Alexander Pope's *An Essay on Man*, *Don Quixote* by Miguel de Cervantes, a book by Samuel von Pufendorf and John Cramer's *Elements of the Art of Assaying Metals*. Of these, Rapin, Vertot and Cramer can be traced in the 1767 library catalogue. All have very early accession numbers in the catalogue of existing books. *Don Quixote* and Pufendorf's *Introduction to the History of the Principal Kingdoms and States of Europe* are listed in the current catalogue but both are editions published in 1748, so cannot have been the actual books Wilson read. He does not comment on his reading, other than that he could read Pufendorf and Rapin at sixteen pages per hour and *Don Quixote* at twenty-eight pages. He later improved his Rapin reading rate to thirty pages per hour.[33]

Honorary members were important to both societies. The Earls of Hopetoun were honorary members and patrons of Leadhills from the outset, and Wanlockhead received cash and book donations from the local aristocracy and gentry, who were given honorary membership in return. They were entitled to use the library, but there is no indication that they ever did so. Other honorary members were mine managers, lessees and concession-holders, some of whom gave active support and may have borrowed books.[34] They certainly formed part of the reading communities, possibly recommending purchases and lending their own books to other members.

Members were keen to restrict the privileges of their libraries to those who had paid for them. Both societies had rules which prohibited lending books to anyone who was not a member. But a member's family would certainly have had access to the books, so the actual reading community was much wider. One volume, on a month-long loan, would probably have been available to three or four people, or more if it had also been lent to another member. Most children could read well. At Leadhills, James Stirling mandated full-time schooling for all children until the age of nine and part-time until boys started work underground at fourteen or fifteen.[35] Crauford's, the company which operated the principal Wanlockhead mines, followed suit. Books and reading would have been subjects of discussion not just at the weekly meetings for book exchange, but also in the home and at the workplace. Notices about library business were posted in public places.[36] Dorothy Wordsworth, visiting both villages on her 1803 Scottish tour, encountered boys who had learned Latin and Greek, heard from a villager that what looked like a school in Leadhills was in fact a library, and stayed overnight in Mrs Otto's cottage, in which she noticed several books.[37] Some may have been from the library, as Otto men had been library members since 1741.

As two of the earliest subscription libraries to be founded in Scotland, Leadhills and Wanlockhead could not adopt the strategy followed by some later institutions which scrutinised the catalogues of earlier libraries to assemble a corpus of suitable literature.[38] Nor, it appears, did they have regular subscriptions to periodicals which reviewed new publications. Surviving copies of the *Edinburgh Review* at Leadhills date from 1813 and at Wanlockhead from 1822, though some members may have subscribed individually and circulated the magazines or passed on suggestions. The mine managers, minister, doctor and schoolmaster would have had professional and social contacts outside the village. Monthly book-exchange meetings would provide opportunities to discuss book choices, as would informal conversations at work. There would also have been many contacts between miners in the two villages.

Books were chosen by the standing committee, which was elected at the annual anniversary meeting and which held a book-choosing meeting shortly afterwards, with another later in the year if funds permitted. Any member could recommend a book and attend the committee meeting to argue for his choice, but only committee members had a vote. Wanlockhead minutes usually recorded only purchased titles, so there is no way of knowing which books were turned down. However, in 1804 the committee proposed twenty-three titles:

> Booths reign of Grace, Browns Christian Journal, McEwens Essays, Bradburys Sermons, Pike & Haywards cases of Conscience, Edwards on religious Affection, Owen on Communion with God, Owen on the 130th Psalm, Bennets Christian Oratory, Witherspoons leading truths, Halliburtons Communion Sermons, Browns Scripture metaphors, Robertsons History of Scotland, Youngs History of the French Revolution, Imisons School of arts, The Rambler, the Lounger, Orphan of the Castle, Emily, Cecilia, Beggar Girle, Citizen of the World and Fergusons Astronomy.

The meeting decided to reject 'Young's History of the French Revolution' and purchase the 'Continuation of Smolletts History from the end of the American War'. There is no trace in the catalogues of Witherspoon, Halliburton, Brown, *Emily* or *Orphan of the Castle*, and no gaps in the sequence of accession numbers, so these books were presumably never ordered.[39] Two years later the committee proposed:

> John Erskine of Edinburgh Sermons 2 volumes, Sir Harry Moncrieffs Sermons, Sherlock on Judgement, & on a Future State, Evangelical Preacher 2 volumes, Youngs Night Thoughts 2 volumes, McNeights Harmony, Reids Inquiry, Hunters Biography, Charnocks Life of Lord Nelson, Alphonso or Wanderer of the Alps, Children of the Abbey, Orphan of the Castle, Cecilia 5 volumes, Monk 3 volumes, Orphan Marion 2 volumes, History of Joseph, Bostons Body of Divinity 3 volumes. The Clerk to write to Mr Hill to establish prices.

But they were short of funds and restricted their purchases that year to Erskine, Moncrieff, Young, Charnock, Boston, the *Evangelical Preacher*, *Cecilia*, *Children of the Abbey* and *Orphan Marion* at an initial cost of £5.15s.6d, which included 7s.8d for binding *Children of the Abbey* and *Orphan Marion* in calfskin.[40]

There is no evidence that rule 37 was invoked at Wanlockhead before the mid-nineteenth century, so members must have had a clear (if unwritten) understanding of what would be impermissible. Contrary to the practice in some other subscription libraries of the time, there were no religious or political tracts in either library. This exclusion persisted until the Reverend Henderson donated his library to Wanlockhead in 1814 (when the miners were desperate for new reading matter). Given the daily flow of transport to Edinburgh and Leith, it is unlikely that such material never reached the villages; presumably it circulated informally.

The Leadhills Society was older than the Wanlockhead one; it had higher fees, greater patronage and more members, so its stock of books was larger at any point in time. These factors, combined with the absence of detailed minutes for Leadhills until 1821 and differences and duplications in the way the societies recorded book titles in their printed catalogues, make it difficult to compare the contents of the two libraries. However, two useful comparative benchmarks can be established for both libraries: the book stock approximately twenty-six years after foundation and the stock in 1800. The problems which beset Wanlockhead between 1803 and 1820 (described below) make subsequent comparison unrealistic. To facilitate this study, titles have been allocated to one of nine subject categories: biography, geography, history, miscellaneous, novels, poetry, religion, science and natural history, and travel. The 'miscellaneous' category includes belles-lettres, law, periodicals, commercial arithmetic, translations of classical literature and other subjects for which there are few titles.[41] Table 2.1 shows the number and proportion of books in each category in each library at these dates.

A manuscript catalogue from Leadhills has survived from 1767, when the Society had been in existence for twenty-six years, and the Wanlockhead minutes list books in the library in 1783, twenty-seven years after its foundation.[42] Leadhills had 191 titles (496 volumes), while Wanlockhead had accumulated forty-three titles (116 volumes). Wanlockhead got off to a much slower start, and its stock was proportionately richer in novels and miscellaneous titles, while Leadhills held more history. Both libraries acquired A. M. Ramsay's *The Travels of Cyrus*, *The Adventures of Roderick Random* by Tobias Smollett

Table 2.1 Numbers and proportions of books by category in the libraries of the Societies for Purchasing Books at Leadhills and at Wanlockhead

Category	First twenty-six years				Books to 1800			
	Leadhills		Wanlockhead		Leadhills		Wanlockhead	
	No. of titles	% of titles	No. of titles	% of titles	No. of titles	% of titles	No. of titles	% of titles
Biography	14	7	2	5	19	5	6	3
Geography	6	3			8	2	6	3
History	34	18	3	7	48	13	20	11
Miscellaneous	34	18	12	28	88	23	28	15
Novels	8	4	7	16	27	7	22	12
Poetry	5	3	2	5	10	3	11	6
Religious	74	39	16	37	151	39	82	44
Science	9	5			17	4	7	4
Travel	7	4	1	2	16	4	8	4
Total	191		43		384		190	

and *The Adventures of Telemachus* by François de Salignac Fenelon, but otherwise their stock of novels was different. Leadhills had *Memoirs of an Unfortunate Young Nobleman* by Richard Annesley, *Don Quixote*, Henry Fielding's *Tom Jones*, *Gil Blas* and *The Devil on Crutches* (both by A. R. Le Sage), while the early Wanlockhead members could read *The Vicar of Wakefield* by Oliver Goldsmith, *Mogul Tales* by Thomas-Simon Gueulette, *Pamela* by Samuel Richardson and Smollett's *The Adventures of Peregrine Pickle*.

Almost 40 per cent of the stock of each library was made up of religious publications. The tone was Protestant, with numerous books of sermons, but initially neither strongly evangelical nor anti-Catholic. One reason for the establishment of a separate Wanlockhead library may have been that local kirk dignitaries felt that the Leadhills content was insufficiently devotional. John Laurie, described as 'preacher', and Robert Wilson, 'elder', are among the first half-dozen members. But if this was their intention, they were unsuccessful. Both libraries maintained an almost constant proportion of religious books throughout the period under discussion, and Wanlockhead always had proportionately more novels.

Table 2.2 Number of Wanlockhead titles also in Leadhills library, 1800

	Titles in both libraries	% of category at Wanlockhead
Biography	3	50
Geography	1	17
History	13	65
Miscellaneous	15	54
Novels	18	82
Poetry	5	45
Religious	37	45
Science	4	57
Travel	4	50
Total	100	

The Leadhills Society printed a catalogue in 1800 which included 384 titles while the Wanlockhead minute book recorded the library's 190th purchase in October 1800.[43] Leadhills had a slightly larger proportion of history and miscellaneous books but otherwise it broadly maintained its earlier pattern of purchases. Wanlockhead now had books in all categories, and consequently the proportion of novels had fallen; nevertheless the proportion of novels and poetry was almost double that of Leadhills. Although only half the size, Wanlockhead library had eleven poetry titles to ten at Leadhills, and twenty-two novels compared with twenty-seven at Leadhills. Moreover, as Table 2.2 shows, 100 of the Wanlockhead books were also available at Leadhills, but almost half the Wanlockhead content was unique to that library, including all but one of its geography titles. Despite being so physically close, the two reading communities had noticeably different preferences.

It is not possible to determine accurately which books had entered the Leadhills library by 1820, but a detailed list for Wanlockhead can be constructed from the minutes. Two versions of the content are given in Table 2.3, one of which includes the 118 titles donated in 1814 by the Reverend Henderson, the local minister, whose library was composed almost entirely of religious works. Only seven of his books were on secular topics: Daniel Defoe's *Tour Through the Whole Island of Great Britain*, Daniel Fenning's *The Use of the Globes*, Charles Hall's *The Effects of Civilisation on the People in European States*, two further titles on the political state of Europe for which it has not been possible to identify authors, *A New Musical Grammar* by William Tansur and John Williamson's *The British Angler*. It is

Table 2.3 Numbers and proportions of books by category, Wanlockhead library, 1820

	Without the Henderson donation		With the Henderson donation	
	No. of titles	% of titles	No. of titles	% of titles
Biography	10	3	10	2
Geography	6	2	7	2
History	30	10	37	8
Miscellaneous	64	21	66	16
Novels	34	11	34	8
Poetry	12	4	12	3
Religion	125	41	236	56
Science	16	5	16	4
Travel	11	4	12	3
Total	308		430	

reassuring to think that this intensely serious man might occasionally have entertained himself with a song or a fishing expedition.

When Henderson's donation is excluded and the titles bought by the miners are categorised, it can be seen that the pattern of purchases from 1801 to 1820 was very similar to that which obtained in earlier years, with one significant exception. In 1803, acting on advice from their Edinburgh bookseller, Peter Hill, the members contracted to purchase the new edition of the *Cyclopaedia* compiled by Abraham Rees and to be published by Longmans in thirty-six volumes. They carefully calculated that, if they purchased the volumes as they were published, their annual outlay would not be more than £4.10s, which would leave them at least £2 a year to buy other books.[44] But they experienced problems almost immediately and over the following seventeen years this commitment brought the Society to the brink of extinction. By 1819 the publisher had managed to stretch the *Cyclopaedia* over thirty-nine volumes and was issuing supplements. The price started to increase from 1804. From 1807 Wanlockhead was unable to buy any other books, any cash remaining to the Society being spent on rebinding existing volumes, binding the occasional donated book and making urgent repairs to the library roof.[45] By 1819 the Society was paying £1.9s per bound *Cyclopaedia* part, far more than originally planned for.[46] This coincided with wildly fluctuating inflation and the falling price of lead after the end of the Napoleonic wars, resulting in decreasing activity at the mines and a consequent reduction in the number of subscribing members. The Society consistently owed money to Peter Hill from 1808. It increased the subscription, then imposed a 1s levy on all members, and finally heroically raised £11.6s.1½d in a week (a minimum 2s.6d from each member and £3.11s.6d in other donations). Still, it was unable to clear the debt until November 1819.[47] In January 1817 the clerk of the Society had been instructed to write to Hill that 'when the work is through the Alphabet, if there are any supplements as is the case of most publications of such extant [sic] the Society are unanimously resolved that they will have no concern with it'.[48] This episode demonstrates clearly that, for a working-class library with very limited resources, a commitment to a major long-term purchase could be extremely risky.[49]

When the Society had finally met its obligations, it returned to the serious business of choosing books, though at first these had to be purchased second-hand. The library rarely acquired used books: just five times between 1792 and 1797,[50] and again in 1820, when Mr John Gracie, an honorary member then living in Edinburgh, was sent £4 and a list of books and asked to see how many he could buy in good condition on the second-hand market. The Society had just emerged from its troubles with the *Cyclopaedia* and wanted to build its stock as quickly as possible. Gracie duly obliged, reporting that he had obtained the library's first works by Walter Scott: *Rob Roy* at half price and his series of novels 'Tales of My Landlord' for £1, when the price new was £1.12s. Two weeks later he sent another set of 'Tales of My Landlord' as well as Mary Brunton's *Discipline*, and volunteered to look for the rest of Scott. The clerk had to tell him to wait, as the Society could not afford more.[51]

Between 1784 and 1820 the Society used a series of booksellers, listed in Table 2.4. The relationship with Boyd ended because he did not fulfil commissions quickly enough. He ordered books from London and this took too long; they could be supplied more quickly from an Edinburgh outlet.[52] In 1789 eight guineas and a list were given to Mr John Stevenson in Edinburgh, probably a private individual, to

Table 2.4 Booksellers used by the Wanlockhead Society, 1784–1820

Bookseller	Location	Dates
Mr Boyd	Dumfries	1784–July 1785
Charles Elliot	Edinburgh	July 1785–June 1788
Peter Hill	Edinburgh	August 1790–1795
Mr Jarna (stationer)	Glasgow	July 1792
Mr Creech	Edinburgh	April 1795–mid-1797
William Dickinson	Edinburgh	December 1797–December 1799
Peter Hill	Edinburgh	February 1801–1819

buy 'at as low prices as he could whether at auctions or in shops'. The minutes record that he delivered:

[Comte de] Buffon Natural History 8 vol	£3	0	0
[William] Robertson History of America 3 vol		15	0
[Samuel Richardson] Adventures of Grandison 7 vol		14	6
Limestreet Sermons 2 vol		5	6
[Jonathan] Edwards on Redemption		3	0
[Isaac] Watts Sermons		6	0
[Allan] Ramsays Poems 2 vol		3	0
[Matthew] Henry on the Sacrament 'to the bargain'		Free	
2 Quires of Paper		1	2
1 Quire common (?)			9
¼ Hundred Quills and stick of sealing wax		2	0
	£6	5	5

Shortly afterwards he fulfilled a further order:

[James] Cooks Voyages 4 vol 12mo		10	6
[Axel] Cronstedt Mineralogy 2 vol		14	0
[Tobias Smollett] Sir Launcelot Gr.		1	6
[Tobias Smollett] Count Fathom 2 vol		3	0
[George] Muir on Parable of Sower		1	6
	£1	10	6

He returned the unspent 12s.1d the following July.[53] No reasons are given for other changes of suppliers, but in 1797 the Reverend John Henderson went to Edinburgh and bought books for the Society from William Dickinson, presumably the bookseller he used himself.[54] The Society stayed with Dickinson until 1800, when Dr Milligan bought books from an unnamed Glasgow bookseller, but in 1801 its custom again went to Peter Hill. The *Cyclopaedia* purchase locked the Society into that relationship until 1819.[55]

Between 1784 and 1820 Wanlockhead received eighty-three donated titles (excluding the 118 from Reverend Henderson discussed above), summarised in Table 2.5. The Countess of Dumfries gave fourteen titles in 1787–90, as did Miss Katherine Crawford in 1790 and the Countess of Loudon contributed three in 1803.[56] These donations covered a wide range of topics, giving the impression that the ladies had gone through their shelves to see what would be suitable. All three women also made early financial contributions, but after 1803 the Society had no further patronage from the aristocracy or gentry until 1820. Gilbert Meason, an honorary member and a partner in Crauford's, was another substantial donor, coming to the members'

Table 2.5 Books donated to Wanlockhead library, 1784–1820

Donor	Biography	Geography	History	Miscel-laneous	Novels	Poetry	Religion	Science	Travel
Mr Boyd (bookseller)							1		
Countess of Dumfries		1	1	2		3	5	1	1
Katherine Crawford		2	3	2		2	5		
Gilbert Meason	1		7	7		1	6	5	1
Gilbert Laing				3			6	2	
Countess of Loudon				1			1		1
Samuel Laing					2				
William Nelson							1	1	
Anonymous	1								
Dr Milligan							2		
John Gracie							2		
James Moffatt							1		
Rev. Swan							1		
Mr Richardson				1					
Total titles	2	3	11	16	2	6	31	9	3
% by category	2.5%	4%	13%	19%	2.5%	7%	37%	11%	4%
% of category in 1820 stock	20%	50%	37%	25%	6%	50%	25%	56%	27%

assistance with a gift of twenty-seven titles in 1810 (after he had given an initial one in 1809), when they had bought no books for four years.[57] He was the most prolific donor of books on science and engineering, providing five of the sixteen books in this category. He probably bought these books for his own professional purposes and passed them on to the library in the expectation that the miners would also be interested. Two features stand out from Table 2.5: almost every donor gave books on religion and nobody, apart from Samuel Laing in 1809, gave novels. Half the geography, half the poetry and more than half the science titles in the 1820 stock had been donated. Donors clearly thought that the miners should be reading for self-improvement rather than entertainment.

The records of a third miners' library, at Jamestown, thirty miles south-east of Leadhills, established in 1793, provide a further perspective.[58] Unlike Leadhills, the initiative for this library came from the mine company. The first entry in the minute book records:

> The miners in this place received from the Westerkirk Mining Co^y the following Books for our mutual improv^{mt}
> [John] Tillotsons Sermons
> [William] Guthries Grammar
> [Robert] Dodsleys Preceptor
> [Comte de] Fourcroys Chemistry
> [Elisha] Coles Lectures
> [John] Ray on the Wisdom of God Spectator
> [Robert Dossie] Handmaid to the Arts
> [William] Robertsons History of Scotland
> [Antoine] Lavoisiers Chemistry
> [Johann Friedrich] Henkel on the Pyrites
> [Lucius Annaeus] Senecas Morals
> [William] Derham on the Being

> The following gentlemen hearing of the Companys good intentions thought fit to present the miners with the following Books. Mr Martin Minister Langholm [Matthew] Hales Contemplations, Mr Otto [Claude-François-Xavier] Millots History of England, Wm Little Minister Westerkirk [George] Horn[e] on the Psalms, Lewis Grant Bustler at Westerhall [Thomas] Bostons Four fold State. Likewise by Mr Otto [William] Wisharts Discourses Constitution of America & [James] Herveys Meditations, Mr Henderson [John] Williams Mineral Kingdom.[59]

The next entry reads:

> We the miners in this place finding the Books sent us by the Company & others will lend greatly to our Improvement have thought proper to advance five shillings each man for purchasing more Books & ordered the following to be sent for directly by Mr Henderson to Peter Hill Bookseller Edinburgh.

It is followed by a list of twenty-nine books costing in total £12.1s after Hill's discount. At five shillings per man, there must have been at least forty-nine subscribers.[60]

By October 1793 the miners had organised a society, elected officers and were exchanging books and imposing fines, in true Leadhills fashion.[61] This is unsurprising. The *History of England*, originally given by one of the gentlemen, is still on the shelves, inscribed: 'Presented to the Library at Jamestown by Mr William Otto, 1793'. Otto is an unusual name but occurs three times in the Leadhills membership list before 1793. William Otto was a founder member, number 23, Henry Otto became member number 93 and Henry Otto junior was member number 170 in 1782.[62] William, another family member, must have become a manager at Jamestown. He knew the benefits of a library and doubtless suggested to his employers that they establish one. He was the manager most in tune with the miners' interests, as can be seen in Table 2.6, which demonstrates the contrast between the titles donated to begin the library and those the miners bought.

No borrowing registers have survived for this period from any of the societies. Nor are there any blot books, which recorded damage. As members were fined for damaging books, it was in their interest to ensure that they did not pay for damage caused by an earlier reader. There are several entries in the Wanlockhead minutes describing the purchase of blank foolscap books for this purpose, and between 1794 and 1819 there are notes of the election of a blot clerk at the anniversary meeting.[63] Blots frequently resulted when members copied passages from books for their own reference. Some idea of the frequency of copying (and thus reader use) might be obtained from inspection of damage to surviving books, but this would be prohibitively time-consuming. A better, albeit partial indication of the intensity with which books were read can be derived from records of rebinding and replacement (which assumes that all books were equally

Table 2.6 Donated and purchased books at Westerkirk, 1793

	Religious	History	Miscellaneous	Novels	Science/mining
Company proportion	7 41%	1 6%	4 24%		5 29%
Individual donors proportion	5 63%	2 25%			1 12%
(of which Otto)	(2)	(2)			
Miners' proportion	8 27%	6 21%	9 31%	6 21%	

robust when initially acquired). Table 2.7 summarises this information for Wanlockhead. There are no biography, geography or science titles in this list, indicating that they were less popular. Books were borrowed by volume, not by title, so the number of volumes rebound is also shown, revealing that the *Ancient Universal History* and *World Displayed* were well read. The former was the first book listed in the minutes, and the record of rebinding shows that it was consistently popular for over fifty years. Joseph Alleine's *Works* was perhaps the most-used title; he was a seventeenth-century Puritan divine and influential preacher. These two volumes were replaced twice (in 1785 and

Table 2.7 Wanlockhead books rebound between 1785 and 1820

Author	Title	Date first acquired	Date rebound	No. of vols	Cost s	Cost d
	Ancient Universal History (20 vol)	Pre-1784	18/7/1785	7	7	0
			5/11/1812	1	2	3
			2/12/1813	1	2	3
			7/9/1815	1		
			7/4/1818	4		
Joseph Alleine	Works (2 vols)	Pre-1784	7/1/1807	2		
Flavius Josephus	History of the Jews (3 vols)	Pre-1784	18/7/1785	2	1	6
	Spectator (8 vols)	Pre-1784	7/9/1815	8		
Humphrey Ditton	On the Resurrection	Pre-1784	18/7/1785	1	1	2
Thomas Dyches	Dictionary	Pre-1784	18/7/1785	1	1	2
John Ray	On the Creation	Pre-1784	7/1/1807	1		
George Buchanan	History of Scotland (2 vols)	Pre-1784	18/7/1785	1		10
			7/4/1818	1		
Tobias Smollett	Roderick Random (2 vols)	Pre-1784	7/9/1815	2		
	Arabian Nights Entertainment (4 vols)	Pre-1784	7/1/1807	1		
James Hervey	Works (6 vols)	Pre-1784	7/9/1815	3		
Samuel Richardson	Pamela (4 vols)	Pre-1784	7/1/1807	2		
			7/9/1815	3		
John Hawkesworth	Adventures of Telemachus (2 vols)	Pre-1784	7/1/1807	1		
	The World Displayed (20 vols)	7/7/1785	7/1/1807	2		
			24/3/1809	1		
			5/11/1812	3	4	0
			7/9/1815	5		
Tobias Smollett	History of England (13 vols)	1/12/1785	7/1/1807	2		
Samuel Ancell	Siege of Gibraltar	6/7/1786	24/3/1809	1		
Jonathan Edwards	On Redemption	3/1/1790	7/4/1818	1		

1790) and rebound in 1807. The eight-volume *Spectator* was replaced in 1790 and rebound in 1815. *The Vicar of Wakefield* was replaced in 1790, and at least one volume of *Pamela* was rebound twice. The only religious work to be rebound twice was Johnston's *Commentary on the Revelation of St John*. Fifteen volumes were rebound before 1807, but seventy-eight thereafter. While this would be expected, as the books were getting older, it also demonstrates the much heavier use of the existing book stock during the period when the Wanlockhead Society was unable to expand its collection.

Where the minute book gives the rebinding cost of a volume this is also shown in Table 2.7. Comparing the 7s cost of rebinding seven volumes of the *Ancient Universal History* or 10d for a volume of

James Cook	Voyages (4 vols)	4/3/1790	7/9/1815	2		
Tobias Smollett	Adventures of Count Fathom (2 vols)	4/3/1790	7/9/1815	1		
Maximilian de Bethune, duc de Sully	Memoirs (6 vols)	1/7/1790	7/9/1815	1		
William Whiston	New Theory of the Earth	1/7/1790	7/9/1815	1		
Richard Watson	Body of Divinity	1791	7/1/1807	1		
Alexander McEwen	Essay on the Types	1791	7/9/1815	1		
Robert Burns	Poems (2 vols)	2/4/1794	7/9/1815	2		
John Swanston	Sermons	2/4/1794	2/121813	1	2	3
Hugh Blair	Sermons (vol. 4)	2/4/1794	4/2/1796	1		
Bryce Johnston	Commentary on the Revelation of St John (2 vols)	6/11/1794	4/2/1796	1		
			7/9/1815	2		
Ralph Erskine	Works (10 vols)	6/11/1794	5/11/1812	1	2	3
			7/9/1815	3		
Frances Burney	Evelina (2 vols)	6/11/1794	7/1/1807	2		
Algernon Sydney	On Government	6/11/1794	4/2/1796	1		
Jacob Bryant	On the Authenticity of the Scriptures	7/12/1797	7/1/1807	1		
	Scots Worthies (4 vols)	7/12/1797	7/4/1818	1		
John Flavel	Works (6 vols)	6/3/1800	5/11/1812	3	7	6
	Protestants Defence on a Popish Catechism	5/3/1801	7/4/1818	1		
John Young of Hawick	Sermons (3 vols)	3/4/1801	24/3/1809	3		
Jonathan Edwards	On Religious Affection	1804	7/9/1815	1		
Benjamin Bennet	Christian Oratory (2 vols)	1804	7/9/1815	1		
	Evangelical Preacher (2 vols)	6/6/1806	24/3/1809	2		
Regina Maria Roche	Children of the Abbey (4 vols)	6/6/1806	7/4/1818	1	5	8
Total titles	40		Total volumes	93		

Buchanan's *History of Scotland* in 1785, with the cost for single volumes in 1812 and 1813 reveals inflationary pressures the Society faced. In 1807 a bookbinder in Thornhill charged them 19s.9d plus 1s carriage to rebind fourteen volumes, but five years later he was charging 2s.3d per volume and carriage had increased to 2s for eight. By 1818, a Sanquhar bookbinder was offering slightly lower prices, but the Society still could not afford to rebind all the most worn books.[64]

Many of the books in both the Leadhills and Wanlockhead libraries were from what William St Clair calls the 'old canon'. These included novels (*Don Quixote, Gil Blas, The Vicar of Wakefield, Sir Charles Grandison* and works by Smollett and Sterne), reprinted periodicals (*Spectator, Lounger, Mirror, Tatler, Rambler*) and books promoting good conduct and pious living by authors including Philip Doddridge, Elizabeth Singer Rowe, James Hervey, Archibald Mason, William Sherlock, John Young and Isaac Watts.[65] St Clair classifies these authors as promoting a 'counter-Enlightenment' worldview, because they predated the Enlightenment, although their books continued to be reprinted for many years. They were popular with the miners to the extent that many at Wanlockhead had to be rebound or replaced before 1820, but they were not the only influence.

The progress of the Scottish Enlightenment was reflected in the content of many libraries during the eighteenth century. Mark Towsey lists twenty-four authors whom he considers representative of this period, including David Hume, William Robertson, Adam Ferguson, Francis Hutcheson, John Millar and Adam Smith, and he regards Joseph Black, William Cullen, Hugh Blair, James Hutton, John Home, Henry Mackenzie, James 'Ossian' Macpherson, Scott, Robert Watson and Henry Home, Lord Kames as being of significant influence.[66] In 1800 Leadhills held books by eleven of these authors and Wanlockhead nine. Towsey also examined the catalogues and sales prospectuses of 440 gentlemen's private libraries between 1720 and 1830, and ranked fifty-one Scottish Enlightenment books which featured in at least a fifth of them.[67] Leadhills and Wanlockhead each had twenty-one of these titles. Leadhills had thirteen of Towsey's top twenty and Wanlockhead ten. The gentlemen's libraries frequently included works by Fielding and Voltaire, Buffon's *Natural History*, Cook's *Voyages*, Charles-Louis de Secondat, Baron de Montesquieu's *Esprit*, the *Monthly Review* and the *Encyclopaedia Britannica*.[68] The miners' libraries had the first four of these, and Wanlockhead also purchased an encyclopaedia, though not the *Britannica*. Checking the libraries' content against Towsey's review of the books most frequently found in Scottish middle-class subscription libraries reveals that the miners' libraries differed in having no books on local Scottish history. Nor did they hold many books which would have improved their readers' working practices, in contrast to the works on agricultural improvement found in some provincial libraries at this period, which is an indication of the predominantly working-class readership and leadership of the miners' libraries.[69]

The Wanlockhead minutes record the cost of almost every book purchased between 1785 and 1820. They also include the valuation which was presented to the anniversary meeting in January each year. The value of the library building once acquired, the bookshelves and other minor possessions remained relatively constant. Table 2.8 summarises the increasing value of the Society's overall assets, the variation in the number of reading members, the cost of books purchased each year, and financial donations received. The decline in membership between 1811 and 1817 is obvious, as is the resurgence once the Society's financial difficulties had been resolved.

The Society for Purchasing Books at Leadhills is the oldest working-class subscription library anywhere in the British Isles, predating Mechanics' Institutes by some fifty years, and differing from them in that members, rather than employers or local philanthropists, chose and paid for the books. Southern Scotland was the most literate area of the British Isles in the eighteenth century, and there is evidence that some members of the two mining communities read serious books before the establishment of the two libraries. Once the Leadhills miners had set up their reading society, it was not long before Wanlockhead followed suit.

Members of both societies were motivated by mutual improvement and were proud of the organisations they had created. They valued formality and discipline in their conduct of meetings, library organisation and book-borrowing procedures. They were keen to preserve their assets, willingly shared the responsibilities involved and made considerable financial sacrifices when circumstances demanded. They maintained an atmosphere of mutual respect, welcomed local professionals as members and accepted donations from them and from honorary members of higher social classes, but refused to be influenced in their choice of books by their employers.

Neither society was notably conservative in its choice of books. Although Wanlockhead had a rule prohibiting erroneous doctrine, it was not invoked during this period. Members read books ranging from long-established standard works to those stimulating intellectual discussion in the clubs and universities of the major cities, but without the formal education and opportunity for academic debate which

Table 2.8 Sample extracts from the Wanlockhead annual book valuation, 1785–1820

Year	Valuation			Reading members	Titles purchased	Cost of purchases[a]			Notes
	£	s	d			£	s	d	
1785	21	4	10		5	8	0	0	2 guineas from Countess of Dumfries, 1 guinea from Lady Elizabeth Crichton
1790	42	14	9		13	4	1	0	Society acquired its house in 1788 – initial valuation £12
1795	62	4	2		13	5	5	6	Value of house now £32 following repairs
1800	71	19	6	49	5	6	6	0	
1805	107	16	9	63	3 (3C)[b]	6	15	2	
1810	156	5	7	76	6 (6C)	5	5	0	Annual subscription raised to 2s.6d. Substantial binding/rebinding excluded
1811	164	8	3	75	7 (7C)	6	13	0	
1812	171	7	6	73		6	11	2	Substantial rebinding excluded
1813	192	19	3	69	16 (16C)		12	9	'Advance shilling' collected Binding only
1814	210	7	9	65	3 (3C)	20	1	0	Entry money raised to 6s Binding/rebinding included
1815	223	19	0	67	3 (3C)	7	1	5	1 guinea from Rev. Robert Swan Binding/rebinding excluded
1816	243	1	9	62	13 (13C)	17	17	6	
1817	255	4	6	57	3 (3C)	4	2	9	Levy of 2s.6d on all members. Entry money raised to 8s.6d. 2 guineas from Gilbert Laing. 1 guinea from Mr Bramwell
1818	261	16	0	62	4 (4C)	6	17	6	Rebinding excluded
1819	269	9	10	65	4 (4C)	9	12	6	
1820	273	2	5	75	9 (2C)	5	18	0	Entry money reduced to 5s. All members donate 'advance shilling' and 2s.6d levy to Society

[a] Cost of purchase figures are not rigorously comparable, as binding/rebinding and/or carriage is included in some years and not in others.
[b] Each part of the Cyclopaedia (C) is treated as one book. Cyclopaedia parts were not always paid for (and recorded as cost) in the year in which they were received.

prevailed in those circles. They read about revolutions in Europe and America, travel to distant parts of the world, and different legal, political and economic systems, but stayed in their villages and continued to work in the mines. They maintained respectful relations with their church ministers and followed the progress of evangelicalism, but at the same time they enjoyed the diversions afforded by novels and were as keen as Edinburgh high society to read Walter Scott as soon as he was published. They were serious readers but had no intention of spending their money and leisure time to read about work or what others thought would be good for them. They wanted to widen their horizons, understand more about the world they lived in and be entertained.

The Wanlockhead Society's experience when subscribing to the *Cyclopaedia* reveals many of the economic and practical difficulties facing printers, publishers, bookbinders and booksellers in the early nineteenth century. It also exhibits the determination of the miners to avoid debt, keep their reading society in existence, complete the purchase to which they had committed and avoid the more predatory tactics of the publisher.

These early documents furnish a unique insight into the first working-class subscription libraries and the social history of the people who organised and supported them. The record of the first eighty years of the two reading societies is testimony that while the natural resources of the Lowther Hills formed one element of God's treasure-house, the carefully husbanded resources of the libraries were another.

Notes

1. James Moir Porteous, *God's Treasure-House in Scotland* (London: Simpkin, Marshall and Co., 1876).
2. Leadhills library is now in the care of the Leadhills Reading Society, a direct descendant of the original society. The books are presently undergoing conservation. Wanlockhead library is preserved by the Wanlockhead Museum Trust.
3. National Library of Scotland, Edinburgh, MS 20497: A List of the Members of the Reading Society in Leadhills and the Time of Their Admission.
4. Hopetoun House, Edinburgh, NRA(S) 888/bundle 610 (Leadhills Mining Papers): Leadhills Reading Society Articles and Laws, 1761; Hornel Library Kirkcudbright, M 31-6 10956: *Articles and Laws of the Leadhills Reading Society, 1760* (printed 1761).

5. Hopetoun House, NRA(S) 888/Vol.661 Class IV, 100 (Leadhills Papers): Library Catalogue and List of Honorary Members.
6. Leadhills Miners' Library, Leadhills: *A Catalogue of Books Contained in the Miners' Library at Leadhills, 1800* (photocopy).
7. Leadhills Miners' Library, LML054: Accessions Register.
8. Leadhills Miners' Library, LML050: Leadhills Reading Society Minute Book, 1821–51.
9. Leadhills Miners' Library LML024: Bargain Book 1742–46; LML025: Bargain Book 1746–48; LML026: Bargain Book 1749–50.
10. Wanlockhead Museum Trust, Wanlockhead, CAB 13: Journal of the Society for Purchasing Books in Wanlockhead, 1756–1833 (henceforth WSJ). This is unpaginated; early page numbers are in square brackets; later references are cited by date.
11. Hornel Library, M31-S 10955: *Articles and Laws of the Society for Purchasing Books in Wanlockhead, 1783* (printed 1820).
12. Hornel Library M31-S 10954: *A Catalogue of Books Belonging to the Miners' Library of Wanlockhead* (Dumfries: Joseph Swan, 1819).
13. *Catalogue of the Miners' Library* (Paisley: Paisley College of Technology, 1979).
14. Buccleuch Archives, Drumlanrig Castle, Thornhill, NRA(S) 1634: Wanlockhead Lead Trials Bargain Book.
15. Hornel Library, K37-1: Wanlockhead Mines Journal, 1755–69; K36-1: Wanlockhead Mines Journal, 1773–7; Buccleuch Archives, vol. 1a (136): Wanlockhead Mining Company Day Book, 1778–81.
16. Hornel Library, M 31-6 10956, *Articles and Laws of the Leadhills Reading Society 1760* (printed 1761).
17. Rule 37 of the Leadhills Society provided for an anniversary dinner. This is the most significant difference between the two sets of rules.
18. WSJ, [10].
19. Mark R. M. Towsey, *Reading the Scottish Enlightenment: Books and Their Readers in Provincial Scotland, 1750–1820* (Leiden: Brill, 2010), p. 61; John C. Crawford, 'Leadhills Library and a Wider World', *Library Review*, 46 (1997), pp. 539–53.
20. See, for example, Peter Jackaman, 'The Company, the Common Man and the Library: Leadhills and Wanlockhead', *Library Review*, 29 (1980), pp. 27–32; and Keith A. Manley, *Books, Borrowers and Shareholders: Scottish Subscription and Circulating Libraries Before 1825* (Edinburgh: Edinburgh Bibliographical Society, 2012).
21. National Library of Scotland, Edinburgh, MS 20497; Leadhills Miners' Library, LML024: Bargain Book 1742–6; LML025: Bargain Book 1746–8; LML026: Bargain Book 1749–50.
22. Margaret J. Joachim, 'Reading in God's Treasure House: The Societies for Purchasing Books at Leadhills and Wanlockhead, 1741–1820', unpublished MA dissertation (Institute of English Studies, School of Advanced Study, University of London, 2016), pp. 9–10.

23. Ibid., pp. 67–9.
24. Ibid., pp. 78–88.
25. National Library of Scotland, MS 20497.
26. John C. Crawford, 'Reading and Book Use in Eighteenth-Century Scotland', *Bibliotheck*, 19 (1994), pp. 24–5.
27. WSJ, 6/1/1813.
28. Old British currency, denoted as £.s.d. There were twelve pence (d) in a shilling (s) and twenty shillings in a pound (one shilling therefore equals five pence in current decimal currency). A guinea was £1.1s.
29. T. C. Smout, 'Lead Mining in Scotland', in Peter L. Payne (ed.), *Studies in Scottish Business History* (London: Frank Cass, 1967), p. 129.
30. Crawford, 'Reading and Book Use', pp. 24–5.
31. The diary was in the private possession of its transcriber but its current whereabouts is untraced.
32. National Library of Scotland, MS 20497.
33. James Williams, 'A Leadhills Diary for 1745, Transcribed by Miss E. M. Brown', *Transactions of the Dumfries and Galloway Natural History and Antiquarian Society*, 3rd series, 54 (1979), pp. 105–31.
34. This could be very practical, such as the gift of a house to Wanlockhead in 1787, and subsequently wood to repair the roof. WSJ, 3 May 1787, 7 October 1789.
35. Smout, 'Lead Mining in Scotland', p. 125.
36. As, for example, when an emergency meeting of members was called by posting a notice on the company smithy door. WSJ, 9 November 1816.
37. Dorothy Wordsworth, *Recollections of a Tour Made in Scotland A.D. 1803* (Edinburgh: Edmonston and Douglas, 1874), pp. 15–19.
38. Towsey, *Reading the Scottish Enlightenment*, p. 81.
39. WSJ, 4 March 1804.
40. Ibid., 11 February 1806, 6 June 1806, 13 June 1806.
41. The early catalogues do not categorise titles. The 1800 Leadhills catalogue has been informally annotated by a much later hand to designate ten categories: literature, politics and periodicals are separated, poetry is included with literature, and geography with 'Voyages'.
42. Hopetoun House, NRA(S) 888/Vol.661 Class IV, 100 (Leadhills Papers), WSJ, [15,16].
43. Photocopy held in Leadhills Library; WSJ, 3 October 1800.
44. WSJ, 3 February 1803. The original cost per bound volume was £1.2s.6d.
45. Ibid., 4 January 1809, 7 August 1811.
46. Ibid., 2 May 1805.
47. Ibid., 5 October 1814, 1 January 1817, 13 November 1819.
48. Ibid., 10 January 1817.
49. Margaret J. Joachim, 'The Cyclopaedia Saga: Pitfalls of a Serial Publication Purchase in the Early Nineteenth Century', *Journal of the Edinburgh Bibliographical Society*, 13 (2018), pp. 81–103.
50. WSJ, 4 March 1792, 5 April 1792, 9 July 1795, 3 January 1797.

51. Ibid., 14 January 1820, 4 February 1820, 11 February 1820.
52. Ibid., 18 July 1785.
53. Ibid., 3 January 1790, 5 February 1790, 7 July 1790.
54. Ibid., 7 December 1797.
55. Ibid., 6 March 1800.
56. Ibid., 3 May 1787, 1 July 1790, 6 October 1790, 5 January 1803.
57. Ibid., 1 January 1810.
58. The library moved from Westerkirk to Bentpath in 1800 but is still known as the Westerkirk Library.
59. Westerkirk Library, Bentpath, Dumfries and Galloway: Jamestown (later Westerkirk) Reading Society Minute Book January 1793–December 1894, 26 January 1793.
60. Ibid., 1 August 1793. The books would have cost £13.2s.9d without the discount.
61. Ibid., 1 October 1793.
62. National Library of Scotland, MS 20497, 15 April 1743, 3 January 1764, 2 January 1782.
63. For example WSJ, 6 January 1794, 3 July 1805.
64. WSJ, 7 January 1807, 5 November 1812, 27 June 1818.
65. William St Clair, *The Reading Nation in the Romantic Period* (Cambridge: Cambridge University Press, 2004), pp. 130–1.
66. Towsey, *Reading the Scottish Enlightenment*, pp. 3–5.
67. Ibid., pp. 27, 35–6.
68. Ibid., pp. 34–6.
69. Ibid., pp. 66–7.

Chapter 3

The School Library and Childhood Reading in Lowland Scotland, 1750–1850

Maxine Branagh-Miscampbell

This chapter traces the establishment of school libraries across Lowland Scotland between 1750 and 1850. Although the majority of this chapter discusses Lowland Scotland, where records of Sabbath school, parish school and juvenile libraries exist in communities in the Scottish Highlands, Islands and Aberdeenshire these have also been included in order to give a fuller picture of library provision across Scotland, and a flavour of the wide geographical spread of these facilities. What is not discussed is the provision of reading materials in the Gaelic-speaking Highlands and Islands.

During this period, there was a key shift in the perceived importance of the library within a variety of different schools educating children from a wide range of social backgrounds. In the first half of the nineteenth century, particularly between the 1830s and 1850s, there was an increased awareness of the importance of access to a variety of reading materials for children, albeit in a supervised and moderated environment. There was also an increased recognition of the importance of school library space, and funds were channelled to ensure that institutions were able to provide this. Alongside this, there was an increase in the number and types of texts available to school pupils of all social classes. Using institutional records, it is possible to see what the perceived importance of the school library was, including its collections and the types of childhood reading practices which took place in schools. In so doing, we can reveal a little more about the books that children had access to and therefore give a new dimension to the study of childhood reading practices. There are, of course, limitations to this type of evidence in terms of what it can tell us about historical reading practices. Where the institutional records are augmented by borrowers' records, however, as in the case of the Royal High School, we can glean a little more insight into what the reading habits of children at these schools might have been. Such records are rare though, and often we have to rely on short reports in governors' minutes or in the *Statistical Accounts of Scotland* to ascertain the types of materials children were engaging with. What these records can reveal is how the child reader was perceived within these institutions and the various purposes that childhood reading was deemed to have in this context.

Using a combination of archival sources and the *New Statistical Account of Scotland* (1845), I trace the development of school libraries from 1750 to 1850, but focusing on the early nineteenth century, when there was a particular increase in the number of schools with libraries, particularly Sabbath schools.[1] Robin Alston's directory of libraries in Scotland has offered a useful starting point for tracing the establishment of school libraries in this period and from this some quantitative evidence of the number of school libraries has been taken.[2] The *Statistical Accounts of Scotland* were collated by Sir John Sinclair, Member of Parliament for Caithness at Westminster, based on the responses of parish ministers to a range of queries designed to get a sense of the 'quantum of happiness' in Scottish communities and to provide a means for planning 'future improvement'.[3] The first of these records was completed in 1799 and the second in 1845, with the later *Account* much richer and more detailed and, crucially, containing records of the library provision in each parish. These records ought to be used with some degree of caution, in that they are subjective accounts. However, they are useful in offering a full picture of educational and library provision, alongside a detailed picture of the demographics of communities and the services and resources available to them. These records are particularly useful in placing school libraries in the wider context of the whole community, as records of these often also contain an account of how they were used and the value they were perceived to have in the local community.

It is vital here to address the limitations of this evidence, as well as the opportunities for what it can tell us about historical child readers. School library catalogues and records of acquisitions can only ever tell us the books that children had access to, and specifically only the books they had access to at school, not necessarily what was read. As David Allan points out in *A Nation of Readers: The Lending Library in Georgian England*, what is needed is:

> a more systematic analysis of the kinds of texts that actually found their way into different people's hands, as well as the practices that they might have employed when reading them, rather than simply a study of the books that crowded the shelves of the libraries that they happened to frequent.[4]

Where more substantial institutional records exist, at the Royal High School and George Heriot's Hospital in Edinburgh for example, these can give a small insight into how these libraries were used by children and offer an addition to the work on historical readers which focuses on anecdotal, personal and empirical evidence of childhood reading.[5] The use of library records does avoid some of the potential problems with anecdotal evidence of reading experiences in that childhood reading can be misremembered or misrepresented by the adult recounting their own experiences and can, therefore, offer a more impartial view of historical childhood reading practices.

Before a discussion of the evidence of school libraries in Scotland, it is important to address some of the key ways in which Scottish education was different to that in England in this period, particularly in relation to literacy. Due to the distinct ways in which mass education and literacy developed in Scotland and England, it is necessary to take a more regional and localised approach to the child reader in order to ascertain whether location and cultural expectations had an impact on the types of texts read by children, as well as attitudes towards teaching literacy espoused by the education systems of the two societies. In Scotland, for those who were educated publicly, children of all ranks of society were often sent to parish or burgh schools between the ages of seven and nine, with boys and girls educated together in many cases from the 1750s.[6]

Critics have often marked out Scotland's early and relatively well developed national school system as unique in Europe in this period. Donald J. Withrington, for example, argues that, by the early seventeenth century, 'there is good evidence that in the majority of Lowland parishes there was schooling of some kind', and stresses the impact that this had on Scotland's higher-than-average literacy rates.[7] However, R. A. Houston and others have challenged the assumption that 'Scotland had enjoyed a substantially superior progress in education and literacy when compared to England',[8] arguing that '[e]ven the most basic statistics on Scottish literacy attainments for any period before the nineteenth century are lacking'.[9] In terms of national educational provision, though, R. D. Anderson argues that, although the church was responsible for much of the public education in the eighteenth century, there was 'statutory backing' from the state, which resulted in 'an unusually uniform and effective national system of parish schools'.[10] This parochial system of education operated between 1696 and the introduction of compulsory education under the Education Act of 1872. The Act for Settling of Schools (1696) had made it a legal requirement for every parish in Scotland to have a school 'under the supervision of the kirk session and partly supported by a tax on local landowners'.[11] Tom Devine has argued that 'the Act anent (concerning) the Settling of Schools in 1696 was the climax of a process of school foundation which had been going on apace in earlier decades', and that 'by the 1660s it was already a "normal thing" for a Lowland parish to have a school under supervision of the kirk session and partly supported by a tax on local landowners'.[12] As discussed later in the chapter, between the 1810s and 1840s some of these parish schools would also give pupils access to a school library, though the library itself was often founded by independent bequest.

In terms of urban educational records, James Grant's *History of the Burgh Schools of Scotland* (1876) provides a well researched and referenced overview of educational provision in eighteenth-century Scottish towns but more recent criticism is limited. Lindy Moore offers a brief overview of urban educational provision in her chapter in *The Edinburgh History of Education in Scotland* (2015). Here she argues that the towns 'supported a higher concentration of gentry and families from the expanding middle ranks . . . which led to a greater availability and higher standard of schooling'.[13]

There was a variety of schools available to children in the towns of Scotland. As well as the grammar schools, which provided a public education to the sons of the upper classes and gentry, there were also a number of hospital schools in Edinburgh, which were aimed at burgesses, merchants and guildsmen. These schools were 'designed to ensure that people of the middling ranks retained their status within the burgh even if they fell into poverty', and they provided both an education and room and board for children of the middling ranks of society, either orphans or whose parents had fallen on hard times.[14] Examples of these include George Heriot's Hospital, Donaldson's Hospital and the Merchant Company Schools discussed below. Other urban educational provision was through the town councils. In Edinburgh, for example, four 'English' schools (so called to emphasise the fact that teaching was in English rather than Latin or Scots) were established in 1759 to provide a public education to the middling ranks of society away from the traditional Latin grammar or Scots systems.[15] Provision for the poor at that time took the form of workhouses, but also orphan, pauper and charity schools, which were supported by 'private individuals from the urban middling ranks who established a variety of educational institutions in increasing numbers in the Scottish towns in the second half of the eighteenth century'.[16] At the same time, public education for both boys and girls of the upper ranks of society was becoming more common through the grammar schools of Scottish cities, and by the end of the eighteenth century private boarding schools for young ladies were increasingly popular.[17] The number of public schools available to children of this rank of society grew exponentially in the first half of the nineteenth century. This growth in public educational provision at the beginning of the nineteenth century, alongside increasing provision for children of the lower ranks of society, points to a democratisation of schooling for all children, particularly in the urban context of post-Enlightenment Edinburgh. This change is also reflected in the greater provision of school libraries at the beginning of the nineteenth century.

Using *Pigot's Directory of Scotland* (1827) and *Crockford's Scholastic Directory for 1861*, Alston lists eleven grammar schools and twenty-three academies with school libraries by the mid-nineteenth century. The *New Statistical Account* sometimes provides a little detail about the size and usage of these school libraries. For example, the Academy of Kirkcudbright in Dumfries and Galloway in the south-west of Scotland is noted to have had, in 1837 '[a]ttached to the grammar school [. . .] a library consisting of between 300 and 400 volumes of useful literature'.[18] We therefore get a sense both of the size of the library and when it began, with many of the school libraries formed in the 1830s and 1840s. Where more detailed records of what these libraries contained and how they were used by pupils exists, these offer a valuable insight into the use of school libraries in both the eighteenth and nineteenth centuries. The Royal High School in Edinburgh's archives are particularly useful, with records of acquisitions, catalogues and borrowers' records dating back to 1739.

The Royal High School in Edinburgh began as a seminary school attached to the Abbey of Holyrood in 1128 before moving to its first school-house site, in Blackfriars' Garden, in 1578, where it remained until 1777. The school library was established upon order of the town council in 1658. The council minutes of 6 January that year state:

> The Provost, Bailies and Council taking to their serious consideration the good and commendable motion of Master John Muir, Master of the Grammar School of this Burgh, representing to the Council how convenient and expedient it will be for the good of the Grammar School both masters and scholars that shall be hereafter, to erect a Library in the said school for all sort of books that may concern humanity and the knowledge of languages and desiring the Council's authority as Patrons and Superiors to be granted for the foundation of the same.[19]

This shows that the school library was for the benefit of 'both masters and scholars'. What is also evident is that this library had a specific academic purpose, rather than a moral or improving one, which many school libraries established in the nineteenth century were explicitly set up to have. *The Statistical Account of Scotland* in 1791 describes the building of a new school-house in 1777, the first of the iterations of the Royal High School to have a purpose-built library:

> In 1777 – a new, elegant and commodious edifice for a Grammar-school was built by voluntary subscriptions. This school house cost L. 4000. It consists of one great hall, five teaching rooms, and a library with smaller appartments [sic].[20]

This reveals the perceived importance of the school library at the Royal High School by the 1770s: it was a purpose-built library space to house collections. This move coincides with an increase in the number of books purchased for the school library, presumably thanks to the sudden increase in space to house these titles.

Where pupils did not have access to a school library, they often used public libraries. For example, there is no specific record of a school library at Stirling High School, a burgh grammar school in Central Scotland, during this period. However, school-aged borrowers can be traced in the borrowing records of the Leighton Library in Dunblane, approximately seven miles from the school. This suggests that scholars either had no access to a school library or that they were augmenting their reading with the books available at the Leighton Library. One such borrower, D. Munro, a student at Stirling High School, borrowed a selection of both Greek and Latin texts between 1821 and 1825. At this time, only Latin and English were taught at the high school and so his selection suggests that his borrowing augmented his school studies rather than being a means of accessing books necessary for his school subjects.[21]

A small number of specifically juvenile libraries can also be traced in Alston's databases, all founded in between 1817 and c. 1850: in Wick in Caithness, in the far north of Scotland; in Banff in Aberdeenshire and Elgin in Moray, in the Scottish Highlands; in Paisley, near Glasgow; in Doune, in Stirlingshire and Benholme in Kinrosshire, in the central belt; and in Rothesay, on the Isle of Bute. These provided young people with access to books either in addition to a school library or, in some cases, as the only means of borrowing texts. The geographical spread of these suggests that, although there was no distinct, named movement behind the establishment of juvenile libraries, in the first half of the nineteenth century various communities across Scotland saw a need for a specific library space for their young people.

Some records surrounding hospital and charity schools either refer to petitions for school libraries or present specific accounts of the foundation of these spaces and collections, suggesting that, even with rather limited funds, the school library was seen as a priority. In some cases, brief mention of the types of works the libraries ought to contain exist. In the absence of the extensive library catalogues available for the likes of the Royal High School in Edinburgh, these provide a valuable insight into the purposes of the school library. Drawing on records from some of the charity and hospital schools in Edinburgh it is possible to see a snapshot of the reading materials valued by educators during the period, and, what is particularly telling, the variety of reading materials these libraries contained.

One such example of the materials available in the school library occurs in a history of George Heriot's Hospital in Edinburgh, published in 1872. William Steven writes that:

> Not the least of the privileges enjoyed by the pupils of this Institution is a large and well-assorted library, containing, in addition to most of the standard works of literature, a large number of such books as are most likely to form a gradual taste for reading. On the tables of the Reading Rooms are spread several of the current publications of the day, such as 'The Illustrated London News', 'Illustrated Times', 'Punch', 'Chambers' Journal', 'Dickens' Household Words', 'Leisure Hour', 'Christian Treasury'. During the Sabbath, these publications are exchanged for religious periodicals, tracts and Christian tales.[22]

It is unclear from this particular record when the practice of laying out specific publications for the students to access began. However, the publication dates of these periodicals suggest that this particular example of the practice occurred in the 1850s. The school chose to vary these publications from those which may have been seen as useful or entertaining, to those which had a religious and moral purpose, with the latter to be read on a Sunday, suggesting that the school saw distinct reasons for having a school library. It was a space for reading for entertainment, scholarly and general knowledge, and a morally improving Christian purpose. The specific periodicals mentioned hint at the wide range of reading material available to pupils and the various purposes that reading in the school environment could have. These publications cover news and general knowledge in the *Illustrated London News* and the *Illustrated Times*, comedy and satire in *Punch* and fiction in Dickens's *Household Words*, wherein appeared Charles Dickens's *A Child's History of England* between 1851 and 1853 and *Hard Times* in 1854, and works by Elizabeth Gaskell and

Wilkie Collins. Christian religious periodicals are also included in *Leisure Hour*, produced by the Religious Tract Society, and *Christian Treasury*, showing that reading for religious and moral purposes was not limited to Sundays. What is also notable is the predominance of London-based periodicals, with *Chambers's Journal* the only Edinburgh-based publication. This suggests that the reading materials accessed by children at George Heriot's Hospital were drawn from across Britain, rather than having a distinctly Scottish focus. This eclectic range of texts is similar to the variety of works available at the Royal High School of Edinburgh, albeit on a much smaller scale, and the mixture of entertaining and improving works also matches with the provision at parish school libraries, discussed below. The swap to works of a wholly religious nature on a Sunday matches much more closely the collections available at the Sabbath school libraries.

Another mention of the school library appears in *Regulations for the Internal Management and for the Offices of Treasurer and Superintendent of Works of George Heriot's Hospital* (1851). This encourages the house governor to promote the use of the school library among the pupils:

> To form and foster a habit of private study, to train to reflection, and store the mind with general information, the House-Governor shall take care that every facility be afforded to the Boys to avail themselves of the Hospital Library, under such restrictions, however, as shall be contained in the Library Regulations.[23]

Here we can see another purpose to the use of the school library: that is, for the pupils to be able to practise the habits of private study and reflection. They are also encouraged to broaden their general knowledge through access to a wider range of books and the use of the library space in and of itself. By the 1850s, the library space therefore became an important one for Heriot's Hospital, with the role of the library moving beyond a means for students to borrow and read books to a use of the space itself as a means of improvement. The laying out of papers and periodicals in the room, as noted previously, shows that students were encouraged to use the space itself for reading, rather than to borrow books for reading elsewhere, suggesting a supervised reading environment. However, the wide range of these texts, which included works of fiction and satire, suggest that the library space had a purpose beyond 'private study' and 'reflection', as a space for entertainment and relaxation as well.

Donaldson's Hospital in Edinburgh was founded in 1830 when James Donaldson of Broughton Hall left his 'property, heritable and personal, to build and found an hospital for boys and girls, to be called Donaldson's Hospital, preferring those of the name Donaldson and Marshall – to be after the plan of the Orphan Hospital in Edinburgh and John Watson's Hospital'.[24] The school admitted both hearing and deaf children, making Donaldson's Hospital unique in Britain at the time. Children with hearing impairments were to be 'taught the usual branches of education – the English Language, Writing, Arithmetic, Geography, the Doctrines of the Christian Religion, and Drawing'.[25] On 29 November 1850, the minutes of a meeting of the education committee at Donaldson's Hospital state:

> The House Governor having suggested that it would be of great importance to have a small library of suitable works to be used by the Children in their leisure hours, he was requested to prepare a List, on a moderate scale, of such Books as he would recommend for this purpose, to be laid before the committees.[26]

By 1850, therefore, it was seen as 'of great importance' for the children of Donaldson's Hospital to have access to 'suitable works . . . in their leisure hours'. With the list being 'laid before the committees' it is evident that the selection of texts came under careful consideration, though records of these particular meetings are lost. This suggests that, even when no library space was available, leisure reading practices in schools could take place outside a recognised library space.

The Merchant Company Schools included George Watson's Hospital, which was founded by bequest in 1723 by George Watson, who left £144,000 Scots 'to raise a Hospital for entertaining and educating of the male children and grandchildren of decayed merchants in Edinburgh, which Hospital is to be called in all succeeding generations George Watson's Hospital'.[27] At the beginning of the twentieth century, there is a record which states that boys of the school 'are now furnished with a proper library of books',[28] with the library founded by the school's literary society and school governors in 1884.[29]

The library at the Merchant Maiden Hospital, also managed by the Merchant Company, in Edinburgh had a different purpose to the educational and improving one of some of the other schools in the city, namely as a means for a new governess to bond with her pupils. The Merchant Maiden Hospital was founded in 1694 by the bequest of Mary Erskine and with the support of the Merchant Company, which raised subscriptions to fund the school. It was intended 'for maintenance of Burges [sic] children of the female sex'.[30] In a history of the school, Margaret K. B. Somerville remarks that, in 1831:

> To induce happy relations between the new governess and her charges, it was agreed that she should have under her care a small library from which she would distribute books 'according to her best direction', and that she should have a few of the girls to tea with her occasionally in the evening, when she would converse with them on the subject of their reading and on the progress of their studies generally. £20 was allowed to form the library; some years later £10 more was spent on recent publications.[31]

The school library at the Merchant Maiden School had a specifically pastoral purpose, designed to provide a means for a new governess to become closer to her pupils. Therefore, the school library could have a number of different functions and its presence within a school often came about for different reasons.

As well as the perceived importance of the school library space in the hospital schools of the period, there was also a call for charity schools to have their own libraries. Indeed, provision for a school library was occasionally written into the establishment of charity or pauper schools. In his history of George Heriot's Hospital, William Steven states that, in 1838, the Hospital's school committee set out a series of regulations for the establishment of charity 'out-door schools', which were to extend the free education offered by the trust to many 'destitute children of all classes and both sexes' throughout Edinburgh.[32] One of these regulations was '[t]hat a library should be provided for the use of scholars, to be kept under the charge of the teachers'.[33] The presence of a school library was not, then, to be a privilege only for the sons of burgesses, but also for the 'destitute children' of the foundation schools. Other charity schools also had provision for a small school library and this may be linked to the idea of the moral and improving benefits of these spaces, as well as the recognition that these children would have had limited or no access to books at home. For example, the abstract of rules for Archibald Millar's Charity School for Girls in Glasgow states that, in 1811, 'FIVE Pounds may be expended in establishing a Library for the Girls – in which 20s. yearly may afterwards be expended'.[34] A specific library space was then to be attached to the school in March 1823.[35] Although these libraries would be small and somewhat limited in their collections, they were deemed important enough to be included in the plans for charity schools.

Outside of the big towns of Lowland Scotland, parishes often had limited access to libraries. However, as Mark Towsey has demonstrated, access to books in rural areas was not as difficult as previously thought.[36] School libraries were no different. Parish school libraries also served an important role, particularly in rural communities. These were often founded by individuals, emphasising the fact that there was very little uniformity in the founding of school libraries across Scotland. For example, in Old Deer, Aberdeenshire, it was noted in 1845 that 'there are fully 200 volumes belonging to the original parish school, purchased from the interest of money left for the purpose by a Mr Shirras, a native of this parish, who died in America'.[37] In St Mungo, Dumfries, 'Mrs Hart of Castlemilk, has this year [1834] established a school library. It contains upwards of 200 volumes, which appear to be judiciously selected',[38] and in Kenmore, Perth, in c. 1830, 'a small library of well selected, simple publications has been attached to the parochial school, by Lady Breadalbane, for the use of the pupils of that seminary; – a measure likely to stimulate the rising generations to the habit of reading, and so to generate and widen the desire of useful knowledge'.[39] The parish school library at Colinton, Edinburgh, was in 1833 noted also to be 'the gift of a friend', with the books 'lent to the advanced children as a reward for diligence in their studies'.[40] These examples give a sense of the standard size of a parish school library as well as the importance of having carefully chosen, or 'judiciously selected', books within them.

The types of books within the parish school library appear to have varied a great deal more in their nature than those at the Sabbath schools, perhaps due to the patchwork way in which they were often formed. For example, at the parish school in New Kilpatrick, Dumbartonshire (Central Scotland) in c. 1830, '[t]he books are chiefly religious, biographical, historical, and agricultural' and were 'much read'.[41] They also give us a sense of the perceived benefits of the library in terms of supplying pupils with 'useful knowledge', alongside the 'taste for reading' and moral benefit of the Sabbath school libraries.

Robin Alston lists a total of fifty-six Sabbath school libraries in his database and the large number of these, as well as their importance in the parish communities, is reflected in their mention in the *New Statistical Account* of 1845. The accounts of these libraries show a wide variation in their usage and size, with some free to use and others requiring a small payment. It is often mentioned that the parents of Sabbath school pupils could have access to these. For example, in Salton, Haddington (in the Scottish Borders) in 1834 it is remarked that the Sabbath school library 'now consists of 130 volumes, chiefly of works of a religious character. They are eagerly read by the young people, in many instances by their parents also.'[42] In New Machar, Aberdeen, in 1841 it is noted that '[t]he books were selected with care, and, through the children, not unfrequently [sic] find their way into the hands of the parents'.[43] Often the Sabbath school library was the only library in the parish, and so it is no surprise that the parents of pupils who had access to these books, often free of charge, would make use of them too. In Deskford, Banff (Aberdeenshire), for example, it is specifically remarked in c. 1830 that: 'There is no other public library than the Sabbath school one; but it is of great use to parents, and the other friends and connexions of the young who attend school'.[44] These libraries are generally well regarded in the *Statistical Accounts* and there is often mention of their specific benefits to the pupils and wider public who could make use of these. At Salton, it was remarked that through the Sabbath school library 'may be found a means of advancing the moral and religious welfare of the young, who appear in general, from the commencement of this little institution, to have imbibed a greater desire for serious and profitable reading'.[45] These reports talk about the development of a 'taste for reading'[46] among the children and note that the works 'are read with the greatest avidity'.[47] At Coldstream in Berwickshire (Scottish Borders) in c. 1830, it is also evident that the benefits of these libraries move beyond a religious and moral one to a recognition of the broader benefits of reading for children, not just of religious texts but of other works as well: 'The recent establishment of a small library connected with the church Sabbath school has created a fondness in the young for reading works on religion, history, and travels, from which very beneficial results may be anticipated'.[48] This particular selection of books is unusual for a Sabbath school library, though it does reveal a wider purpose to the use of these libraries. Nonetheless, where the types of books are specified, they are generally works of religion, such as this example referring to the Sabbath school library in Kinross (Dumfries and Galloway in the south-west of Scotland) in c. 1830:

> There are besides, three juvenile libraries, or rather small selections of books, chiefly of such as are suited to the years and capacities of the scholars of the Sabbath classes, and almost all of a strictly religious character. These are purchased by public collections at the church doors, or by individual bounty.[49]

Although the collections of the Sabbath school libraries were, unsurprisingly, largely religious in their nature, there is the occasional reference to other works, such as travels and history at Coldstream. These wider collections more closely reflect the materials at the Royal High School, for instance, where the most extensive records of what an eighteenth-century grammar school library contained exist and offer an insight into the types of works which were deemed appropriate for children in the period.

Where such records exist, library acquisitions can tell us a great deal about the books that were available to the students and, moreover, what was valued enough to be purchased in any given year. However, it is impossible to see why a particular book was purchased at any given time and so it is important to augment these records with other evidence of how the library was used, such as borrowers' records and school records relating to the use of the library. When texts were purchased as just single copies we must be careful not to assume that these were specifically for borrowing by pupils – as the schoolmasters had ultimate say over the works purchased for the school library, they have may have used this as a means to acquire texts that they themselves were interested in reading. This is perhaps most clearly evident in the purchasing of texts about education, such as Vicesimus Knox's *Liberal Education: Or, A Practical Treatise on the Methods of Acquiring Useful and Polite Learning* (1781) and Lord Kames's *Loose Hints Upon Education* (1781) in 1781.[50]

Records as extensive as those for the Royal High School are rare, but a small mention of acquisitions of books for pupil use was discovered among materials relating to Donaldson's Hospital in Edinburgh. As seen above in the justifications for the establishment and founding of certain school libraries, particularly those in the charity and Sabbath schools, there was also a moral and religious purpose to inculcating particular reading practices in schools. The acquisitions for Donaldson's Hospital reflect this moral purpose of reading. The only record of texts at Donaldson's Hospital is a mention of books and stationery purchased by the governors in the minutes of a meeting in 1850. These do not necessarily reflect the contents of the school library, as there is no record of why these works were purchased. They certainly do tell us, though, something about the nature of the books read in the school, with a heavy emphasis on reading for a religious purpose reflected in the purchase of Bibles and Catechisms, alongside the schoolbooks of English grammars, dictionaries and geographies:

  80 Bibles strongly bound in calf
  50 New Testaments bound in calf
  80 School Associations no. 3
  80 School Associations no. 4
  120 School Associations 1st geography
  30 MacCulloch's Series
  50 Douglas English Grammar
  50 English Dictionaries
  4 Reid's English Dictionaries
  30 Hittas' Palestine

94 Shorter Catechism w. Meanings
46 Mothers' Catechism
70 slates clamped with tin at the edges
Besides various Sheets of Alphabets, Reading lessons, and illustrated prints to be mounted on board.
96 ruled copy books
400 Quills

The committee also authorised Mr. M. McDiarmid to procure the following articles for the use of the Deaf Dumb Children

12 Bibles
40 copies geography
12 dictionaries
3 Reid's Dictionaries
50 Shorter Catechisms
50 Mother's Catechisms
50 slates
48 copy books for writing
200 Quills[51]

The reading practices taking place in the school library were, by their very nature, supervised reading experiences. Even in the absence of records of a named librarian, it is clear from records that the works placed in the library stacks, and thereby in children's hands, were carefully selected and curated by schoolmasters and governors.

The changing nature of the school library across this period can be seen in the acquisitions and catalogues of the library at the Royal High School. Towards the end of the eighteenth century, the Royal High School began to purchase a variety of periodicals, with regular issues of *The Scots Magazine* from 1787, *The Monthly Review* from 1792/3, *Edinburgh Gazetteer* and *The Classical Journal* from 1817/18, and *The Edinburgh Philosophical Journal* from 1819/20, which could suggest an increased focus on leisure reading.[52] Prior to this, the school library at the Royal High School was largely populated by Latin and Greek texts. By the early nineteenth century, the acquisitions at the School tended to include a great deal more fiction. Frances Burney's *Evelina* (1778) and *Cecilia* (1782), Sir Walter Scott's early works, and Maria Edgeworth's *Tales of Fashionable Life* (1809), *Popular Tales* (1804) and *Moral Tales* (1801) were purchased in the school year 1812/13. Edgeworth's *Comic Dramas* (1817), *Harrington* (1817) and *Ormond* (1817) were all purchased in 1817/18. In 1821, the library also contained a much larger number of Scott's works, including *Ivanhoe* (1820), *The Abbot* (1820) and *The Monastery* (1820) and Horace Walpole's *Castle of Otranto* (1764).[53] However, such novels do represent a small proportion of the titles available to the pupils; even into the nineteenth century, high proportions of the library purchases were devoted to classical Latin and Greek texts, philosophical and religious works, and history.

There is, however, a noticeable turning point in the works purchased in the 1820s and 1830s, with the introduction of juvenile works. This foreshadowed the introduction of a specific juvenile library for the youngest schoolboys (aged nine to ten) in 1848, which contained: works relating to history, physical geography, encyclopaedic works such as the SPCK's *Instructor*, biographies, a little poetry, voyages and travels such as *Anson's Voyages* (1748), *Cook's Voyages Around the World* (1771) and *Gulliver's Travels* (1726); some fiction, such as Elizabeth Hamilton's *The Cottagers of Glenburnie* (1808), religious works such as John Bunyan's *Pilgrim's Progress* (1678); and works specifically written for children, such as *The Boy's Own Book* (1828), Edgeworth's *Moral Tales*, *Early Lessons* (1801) and *Parents' Assistant* (1796), and *The Children's Friend*, a periodical specifically written for children, first published in 1824. What is notable here is the complete absence of works in Latin and Greek for this age group, which reflects a move away from a purely classical education for boys of the upper middle classes.

Though it is impossible to ascertain what exactly was read, we can draw some conclusions about how the students were using the library from the texts that they were borrowing. Patterns of borrowing at the Royal High School of Edinburgh seem to suggest that, after the 1780s, possibly coinciding with the increased space allocated to the library discussed above, and with the subsequent growth in the collections, students were borrowing more and more varied titles. This reflected a change in the usage of the library from one that was focused on an academic purpose to reading for a broader purpose, including entertainment. What can also be traced is an increased borrowing of titles from a wider variety of genres. Historical works were widely borrowed in the 1770s but by the 1780s voyages and travels were increasingly borrowed.[54] In 1810, the most popular works remained travels and voyages. Particularly popular were *Cook's Voyages*, William Mavor's *General Collection of Voyages and Travels* (1810) and John Campbell's *Lives of the British Admirals* (eight volumes, 1812–17).[55] By the 1820s, voyages and travels remained popular among the boys but a much wider range of books were also engaged with, with works of fiction such as Edgeworth's *Popular Tales*, Burney's *Evelina* and *Cecilia*, and Sir Walter Scott's novels all frequently borrowed.[56] Eventually, by the time of the establishment of a specific juvenile catalogue in 1848, it is possible to see students borrowing those books specifically written or marketed for children, such as Bunyan's *Pilgrim's Progress*, Hamilton's *Cottagers of Glenburnie* and Edgeworth's *Early Lesson*.[57] The changing nature of the works borrowed by pupils at the Royal High School gives an insight into how the school library changed over the period, both in its purpose and in its use by the students themselves. The shift from pupils borrowing histories to voyages and travels and eventually to fiction and works for children shows how the children at the Royal High School were increasingly perceived as child readers by the mid-nineteenth century, with a distinct need for works written for and to entertain them.

Records of acquisitions and catalogues ought certainly to be used with caution. However, what these can reveal is a little more about the nature of the library in question and specifically, here, what texts were available to young readers. The inclusion of voyages and travels, fiction and poetry may not in itself be enough evidence to support a sudden recognition of the importance of reading for enjoyment or pleasure for children in the school environment. However, it does suggest a movement away from reading purely for academic purposes. These works were often seen as a way for children to develop a taste for reading, and travels and voyages were seen as a safe and appropriate genre for children to read.[58] From the evidence available, it is possible to see a variety of purposes and uses of the school library space in Lowland Scotland in this period, particularly in the first half of the nineteenth century, when a number of school libraries across Scotland were founded. Records relating to school libraries in the eighteenth century are limited; however, it is clear from the records surrounding the Royal High School what usage of a grammar school library could look like. The changing role of the school library at the Royal High School reveals a shift towards the recognition of children as a distinct group of readers with a need and desire for a literature of their own. It is also evident from a number of the records that schools were keen to encourage a taste for reading among their pupils, and the inclusion of more entertaining works may well be speaking to this desire.

There was, nonetheless, a clear academic purpose to the use of the school library, particularly at the Royal High School and George Heriot's Hospital. There was also evidently a moral and religious impetus to the establishment of school libraries in the charity and Sabbath schools in this period, not just for the pupils but in many cases for their parents too. The establishment of school libraries in Scotland was, though, inconsistent; in particular, the parish school libraries came about mostly through the generosity of one or two individuals. However, towards the end of the period there was an increased recognition of the importance of the school library. In 1840, a petition was sent to the Lord Provost in Perth, requesting that the money used for school prizes across the schools in the town be spent on the establishment of school libraries instead. This letter argued that 'the formation of a small Library at each of the Schools' is 'a thing which, in the opinion of your Petitioners will, in the end tend more to promote the religious, moral, and intellectual improvement of those under their care'.[59] This petition highlights some of the benefits of the school library perceived at this time. These encompassed both the intellectual improvement of the pupils – as is clear in the establishment of school libraries at the grammar schools in the seventeenth and eighteenth centuries – as well as their moral and religious improvement, which was especially the impetus behind the provision of libraries in many of the charity and Sabbath schools at the beginning of the nineteenth century. Although records relating to school libraries are somewhat limited in their scope, what they can tell us is a little more about how children were perceived as a group of readers and what the perceived benefits of reading for this group looked like. Supplemented with other evidence of childhood reading practices (letters and memoirs, for example) these provide a useful insight into both how young readers were perceived and how and what they might have read.

Notes

1. *The Statistical Accounts of Scotland 1791–1845* can be found online at <https://stataccscot.edina.ac.uk/static/statacc/dist/home> (last accessed October 2019).
2. Robin Alston's database of libraries in Scotland can be found online at <https://www.scribd.com/document/63097322/Robin-Alston-Library-History-Scotland> (last accessed October 2019).
3. 'An Introduction to the *Statistical Accounts of Scotland*', at <https://stataccscot.edina.ac.uk/static/statacc/dist/support/introduction> (last accessed October 2019).
4. David Allan, *A Nation of Readers: The Lending Library in Georgian England* (London: British Library, 2008), p. 227.
5. See Matthew Grenby, *The Child Reader, 1700–1840* (Cambridge: Cambridge University Press, 2012).
6. See James Grant, *History of the Burgh and Parish Schools* (Glasgow: William Collins, Sons and Co., 1876), pp. 535–7.

7. Donald J. Withrington, *Going to School* (Edinburgh: National Museums Scotland, 1997), p. 11.
8. R. A. Houston, *Scottish Literacy and the Scottish Identity* (Cambridge: Cambridge University Press, 1985), p. 4.
9. Ibid., p. 11.
10. R. D. Anderson, *Scottish Education Since the Reformation* (Dundee: Economic and Social History Society of Scotland, 1997), p. 4.
11. T. M. Devine, *The Scottish Nation 1700–2007* (London: Penguin, 2006), p. 68.
12. Ibid.
13. Lindy Moore, 'Urban Schooling in 17th- and 18th-Century Scotland', in Robert Anderson, Mark Freeman and Lindsay Paterson (eds), *The Edinburgh History of Education in Scotland* (Edinburgh: Edinburgh University Press, 2015), p. 80.
14. Ibid., p. 87.
15. Ibid., p. 89.
16. Ibid.
17. Ibid., p. 90.
18. *The New Statistical Account of Scotland*, 1845, vol. IV, p. 33.
19. See J. B. Barclay, *The Tounis Scule* (Edinburgh: Royal High School Club, 1974), p. 40.
20. *The Statistical Account of Scotland*, 1791–9, vol. VI, p. 591.
21. For more on the Leighton Library and its borrowers see Jill Dye, 'Books and Their Borrowers from the Library of Innerpeffray 1680–1850', PhD thesis (University of Stirling: 2018), available at <https://dspace.stir.ac.uk/handle/1893/28881#.XcVzTFX7SHs> (accessed November 2019).
22. William D. D. Steven, *History of George Heriot's Hospital with a Memoir of the Founder and an Account of the Heriot Foundation Schools*, 3rd edition revised and enlarged by Frederick W. Bedford, LL.D., D.C.L., House Governor and Head-Master of Heriot's Hospital and Inspector of Heriot Foundation Schools (Edinburgh: Bell and Bradfute, 1872), p. 221.
23. Mitchell Library, Glasgow, TBK157/3, *Regulations for the Internal Management and for the Offices of Treasurer and Superintendent of Works of George Heriot's Hospital* (Edinburgh: Neill and Company, 1851), p. 16.
24. National Library of Scotland, Edinburgh, ACC11896/197, *History of the School from 1st October, 1924*.
25. National Library of Scotland, ACC11896/66, *Answers to Queries, and a Few Remarks on the Proposal to Devote Part of Donaldson's Hospital to the Deaf and Dumb*.
26. National Library of Scotland, ACC1896/33, Donaldson's Hospital, *Minute of Meeting of the Education Committee of the Governance of Donaldson Hospital, 29th November 1850*.

27. John Harrison, *The Merchant Company and Its Schools* (Edinburgh: Merchants' Hall, 1920), p. 17.
28. Ibid., p. 19.
29. Les Howie, *George Watson's College: An Illustrated History* (Edinburgh: Butler and Tanner, 2006), p. 60.
30. Harrison, *The Merchant Company*, p. 14.
31. Margaret K. B. Somerville, *The Merchant Maiden Hospital of the City of Edinburgh* (Edinburgh: Former Pupils Guild of the Mary Erskine School, 1970), p. 82.
32. Steven, *History of George Heriot's Hospital*, p. 253.
33. Ibid., p. 257.
34. Mitchell Library, THH3/7/3, *The Rules of Archibald Millar's Charity: To which are annexed The Deed of Mortification and Royal Charter of Incorporation* (Glasgow: John Graham, 1852).
35. Mitchell Library, TBK157/7, Millar's Charity School Abstract of the Rules of Archibald Millar's Charity School for Girls, 1842.
36. See Mark R. M. Towsey, *Reading the Scottish Enlightenment: Books and Their Readers in Provincial Scotland, 1750–1820* (Leiden: Brill, 2010).
37. *The New Statistical Account of Scotland, 1834–1845*, vol. XII, p. 163.
38. Ibid., vol. IV, p. 215.
39. Ibid., vol. X, p. 482.
40. Ibid., vol. I, p. 131.
41. Ibid., vol. VIII, p. 62.
42. Ibid., vol. II, p. 127.
43. Ibid., vol. XII, p. 1034.
44. Ibid., vol. XIII, p. 76.
45. Ibid., vol. II, p. 127.
46. Ibid., vol. IV, p. 347
47. Ibid., vol. X, p. 824.
48. Ibid., vol. II, p. 212.
49. Ibid., vol. IX, p. 25.
50. Edinburgh City Council Archives, SL137/12/1, Royal High School, 'Accounts of books purchased for the school library 1784–1868'.
51. National Library of Scotland, ACC11896/33, 'Minutes of Joint Meeting of the Education Committees of the Governors of Donaldson's Hospital 20th August, 1850'.
52. Edinburgh City Council Archives, SL137/12/1, Royal High School, 'Accounts of books purchased for the school library 1784–1868'.
53. Ibid.
54. Edinburgh City Council Archives, SL137/14/3, Royal High School, 'Books borrowed from the school library by masters and boys sessions 1777/78–May 1788'.
55. Edinburgh City Council Archives, SL137/14/5, Royal High School, 'Books borrowed from the school library by masters and boys sessions 1809/10–1811/12'.

56. Edinburgh City Council Archives SL137/14/6, Royal High School, 'Books borrowed from the school library by masters and boys sessions 1823/24–1825/26'.
57. Edinburgh City Council Archives, SL137/14/10, Royal High School, 'Books borrowed from the school library by masters and boys sessions 1848/49'.
58. See, for example, Maria Edgeworth and Richard Lovell Edgeworth, *Practical Education* (1798).
59. Letter in Perth Council Archives, B5924/6/156.

Chapter 4

'Although ambitious we did not aspire to such dizzy heights': Manuscript Magazines and Communal Reading Practices of London Literary Societies in the Long Nineteenth Century

Lauren Weiss

This chapter discusses communal reading practices and the interactive, individual *and* collective responses of small voluntary groups in the long nineteenth century, particularly those formed for the purpose of 'mutual improvement'. Some of these groups produced their own manuscript magazines – a newly discovered genre in nineteenth-century periodical studies. Their miscellanies were created by and for group members, and consist of original poetry, prose, artwork and even music. These groups provide examples of individual and group reading, silent reading and reading aloud, intensive and extensive, guided as well as self-directed purposeful reading for self-education. Their magazines offer not only new materials for historians of reading and of the book, but also for researchers in nineteenth-century history, the history of education, cultural studies and literature.

These materials are generally unknown to other book historians and historians of reading, and with the exception of my own research, there are currently no other published studies on the magazines of British mutual improvement societies.[1] Richard Altick and Jonathan Rose thought these societies left behind minimal evidence.[2] While Altick mentioned the production of essays by society members for internal critical review, David Vincent and recently Martyn Walker overlook the societies' periodicals.[3] Andrew King, Alexis Easley and John Morton, in their edited collection on British newspapers and periodicals, should have said more about the culture of producing magazines in manuscript by working-class 'improving' societies, as evidence of what they call 'the intensity of the social permeation of print'.[4]

Research on handwritten nineteenth- and early twentieth-century 'improvement' newspapers and magazines appears to be still in its nascent stages. Heather Murray notes the production of literary society manuscript magazines in Ontario but does not explore them in detail.[5] Elizabeth Webby's work on Australian literary societies offers important insights but does not treat their production of manuscript magazines per se.[6] Kirsti Salmi-Niklander is one exception, and her research on the handwritten newspapers created by young Finnish working people, and on Finnish-Canadian groups in the early twentieth century, reveals many parallels with Scottish and English groups, and demonstrates the continued vigour of manuscript culture internationally well into modern times.[7]

Scholars have known for about forty years (at least) that small voluntary groups of (mostly) non-professionals produced their own manuscript periodicals during this period, and evidence from around the world has been steadily accumulating. In 1980 Roy Alden Atwood began work on 'The Handwritten Newspaper Project', a valuable open-access research tool that includes community, school and shipboard papers in addition to 'Organization Newspapers'.[8] However, there are listings for only seven English newspapers, six of which are shipboard periodicals and one of which is a children's paper.[9] There are no listings of any genre for Scotland.

This chapter intervenes in the current scholarship by presenting a range of new evidence. To date, my research has uncovered ninety groups across Scotland and England that produced magazines, predominantly in manuscript; 322 extant issues were created by English groups and 330 by groups in Scotland.[10] Although produced by a range of different associations, their stated objects, with few exceptions, included 'improvement'. These periodicals demonstrate that there was a national – indeed, international – trend for producing 'improving' periodicals that was part of a larger mutual improvement movement during the long nineteenth century (here defined as 1800 to 1915).

I argue that these magazines are important: first, they offer new evidence for group reading, an area currently under-represented in the scholarship of the history of reading; second, they demonstrate groups' different responses to print culture; and third, they demonstrate that communal reading practices centring on a manuscript culture continued to flourish as a *result* of the ubiquity of print culture by the end of the nineteenth century. I focus on the manuscript magazines produced by 'literary societies' – one type of mutual improvement society – in London between 1848 and 1915, principally the Park Church Literary Society (1859–1937?), Islington Presbyterian

Church Young Men's Association (1862–93?), St Martin's Literary Society (1901?–4?) and Friends' Hall Literary Society/Bethnal Green Literary Society (1906–15). Most of these magazines were produced by aspirational young men, though it was not unusual for the network of contributors and readers, men *and* women, to extend well beyond London. Through a brief overview of their format and content, I consider how these magazines could be viewed as a response to the mass-market periodicals that had become ubiquitous by the end of the nineteenth century. Finally, I consider readers' written critical responses, added at the back of these magazines, to fellow members' contributions. This dynamic interactive feature was considered important by some societies and provides evidence of critical communities of readers.

From the evidence I have uncovered to date in England, magazine-producing societies were concentrated in the north-west of the country and in and around London, with a couple of outliers.[11] As was the case in Scotland, in the long nineteenth century, groups that produced magazines were mainly based in larger urban areas, with London having the greatest number (ten), followed by Manchester (five) and Sheffield and Hertford (at least two each); Newcastle upon Tyne, Halifax, Oldham, Warrington/St Helens, Liverpool, Shrewsbury and Bristol all had at least one. In Scotland, I located evidence for thirty-one groups that produced magazines in Glasgow, twelve in Edinburgh, eight in Dundee, and others in Kirkwall, Wick, Elgin, Aberdeen, Helensburgh, Airdrie, Paisley, Melrose and Dumfries.[12] This represents only those magazines that I discovered through a search that was not fully comprehensive due to time constraints. It is highly likely that targeted searches in the local and regional archives across England and Scotland will uncover more. The largest number of groups that produced magazines in England were church mutual improvement/literary/young men's societies (thirteen), followed by secular groups of the same type (four) and mixed-gender groups all associated with various churches or religious groups (three). Here I will focus on three churches and one adult school and their magazines.

Park Church Literary Society

Park Church was located on Grosvenor Lane, Highbury, London. Completed in 1863, it was built for a congregation of Scottish Presbyterians who had outgrown their former premises in Myddleton Hall, Upper Street, Islington.[13] According to J. Ewing Ritchie, author of *The*

Religious Life of London (1870), Highbury was a firmly middle-class residential area that had 'no poor people'.[14] At the time of his writing, the congregation was 'active and flourishing' and numbered between 400 and 500 people.[15] He noted that '[t]o the stranger the principal novelty is the vast preponderance of young men in the congregation'.[16] Ritchie gave a glowing description of the church's architecture and amenities, which included rooms below the chapel that were 'fitted up with every convenience' for lectures and meetings. He listed the organisations then running through the church, which included a 'Missionary Association, a Psalmody Association, [and] a Ladies' Working Association'; in addition, there was a Young Men's Literary Institute and the Young Men's Christian Fellowship Association.[17]

The Park Church Literary Society was established in 1859. The evidence from this group comes from the minutes from 1859 to 1861, two minute books dating from 1882 to 1890, and some printed reports and syllabi. Members had to be 'Adherents of the Presbyterian church of England and other Evangelical Churches'.[18] Women could attend open meetings, but membership was restricted to men until 1895.[19] Like the Islington Presbyterian Church Young Men's Association discussed below, this reading community was connected to a larger network of similar societies through the London Presbyterian Literary Societies Union.[20] The Society was initially made up of young Scottish men living in London, but after 1895 both married and unmarried women were allowed to join.[21] It had an average of sixty-three members between 1881 and 1897, and seventy-seven between 1901 and 1914.[22] The meetings regularly featured talks on Scotland and Scottish literature and culture. Its social meetings occasionally even included traditional Scottish songs and instrumental music. It appears that while Scottish nationalism played a defining role in this society's identity and activities, its magazines did not share the same agenda. This is a notable contrast to the magazines produced by the Glasgow Orkney and Shetland Literary and Scientific Association (1862–present), a society whose members (or their parents) hailed from the islands and then moved to Glasgow. While the Glasgow Orkney and Shetland Association's syllabi also regularly included Scottish literature and culture, its magazines in particular were used to channel their expressions of love of their former northern homes, and feelings of nostalgia and homesickness.[23]

There are fifteen extant magazines (all issued as annuals, with a single copy produced and distributed to members) from the Park Church Literary Society, eight of which date before 1915 and form the basis for this overview. These contain roughly an equal mixture of fiction and non-fiction. As was not unusual for these magazines, original poetry was included more than short prose pieces. Some writers displayed their cultural literacy by citing literary influences directly, as in the case of 'Sonnet. After the French of Joachim du Bellay',[24] or when the author of 'Fra Ugo Bassi' states his indebtedness to Mrs Hamilton King's collection of poems supporting Italian unification, *The Disciples*.[25] Alternatively, reference might be made to contemporary literary trends, for example when the author of 'A Ballad of Sorrow and Song' complained of the then current 'fashion' for morbid verse, and sardonically encouraged 'Brother-singers': 'Let us all be unhappy in rhyme!'[26]

Among the non-fiction contributions are essays on current affairs, accounts of visits to various locales/events, science (e.g. psychology), didactic pieces and journalism ('An Old Magazine. 1814. La Belle Assemblée', with clippings of its fashion plates, and 'Journalism Behind the Scenes').[27] There are several biographical essays with critical reviews of an author's work: Hans Christian Andersen, Charles Kingsley, Thomas Hood, Charles Lamb and John Locke. One essay commented on current word usage ('The Fortune of Words'),[28] another on the decline in the 'correct' use of language ('Prenez garde; il y a des pièges').[29] Purposeful educative reading was the subject of a long essay entitled 'The Chief End of Reading', which suggested that reading 'should be towards the Growth of Character. The Character of the Heart, the Soul, the Mind'.[30] The author stressed that on that 'Great Day', readers would be answerable to having wasted time on materials that did not provide nourishment and sustenance like the Bible.

Distribution of the single copy of each magazine was most likely organised through a list of readers, as was common in other societies. The April 1911 issue has a list of readers/members and their addresses at the front, and readers were enjoined to hand the issue over 'with as little delay as possible'.[31] The Park Church magazine had a 'Correspondence Column' and an 'Editor's Waste Paper Basket',[32] which included fictional letters to the editor and humorous responses, as well as satirical advertisements.

Unlike most other literary society magazines produced during the early twentieth century, Park Church's manuscript magazines were elaborate handmade productions influenced by the Arts and Crafts movement. While many other societies' magazines also had members' decorative artwork adorning their covers, issues of the Park Church magazine were carefully bound, using wide colourful ribbons, with its pages hand-stitched together with similarly colourful cord, or embroidered in the case of a 1908 cover.[33] This level of care in their production suggests that these magazines were meant to be shared, but also cared for and preserved, and not meant to be ephemeral items.

Another distinguishing element is that at least six of the eight magazines produced in the early twentieth century were edited by women.[34] The group was founded by and for young men, but after 1895, when women were allowed to join, their numbers grew quickly: by 1914 they made up 60 per cent of the membership.[35] I estimate that a sizeable proportion of the contributions were written by women.[36] The only other society that had a similarly large percentage of female contributors was St Martin's Literary Society (discussed below), which almost solely comprised women. While the 'ordinary meetings' of the Park Church Literary Society between 1911 and 1914 predominantly consisted of lectures and essays read by men, ten years earlier its magazine had already become largely the preserve of women.

Islington Presbyterian Church Young Men's Association

The precursor to the Islington Presbyterian Church Young Men's Association was founded in 1854. Two of the Association's minute books and four manuscript magazines survive.[37] The group was 'chiefly composed of young Scotchmen', and their object was the 'moral, intellectual and religious improvement of the Young men connected with the church'.[38] Women were allowed to become full members in January 1891.[39] Four years after its formation, the Association founded its own manuscript magazine. Two articles in the first bound issue offer unique insights into one group's establishment of a periodical for its members' 'improvement' and the difficulties involved in such a venture. In this case, it is illustrated through a series of heated exchanges between individual members, the editor and possibly a church official.

The first issue of the *Aemulus* appeared in 1866, and its articles offer insights into the group dynamics around the time of the magazine's founding, revealing the tensions that were involved in the process. The magazine consists of nine parts, being a collection of contributions read aloud by the editor at the Association's 'magazine nights'. These evenings were a regular part of the syllabus, and between 1869 and 1894 they occurred variously between two and five times a year with their popularity cooling slightly during the later years. With the addition of visual and musical materials, the first volume amounted to thirty-five prose pieces, fourteen poems (of which two were acrostics), a musical score for piano and one voice, three illustrations, and six photographs of office bearers. In the article 'Our Magazine' by 'Justitia', the author sets out the magazine's role as 'the *receptacle* [my emphasis], in which is gathered, not only Articles, that are very creditable; Poems which are really good, and papers exhibiting signs of great ability, on all kinds of subjects, including Religion, Science, Politics, and social subjects'.[40]

The author, or perhaps authoress,[41] then goes on to say that some 'articles . . . have no right to be inserted and . . . ought to be expunged from the Aemulus for ever', in fact 'would have been better had they never seen the light'.[42] According to Justitia, among the materials which had been 'no credit to its pages' were one or two poems (which she does not identify) and an equal number of articles, but 'we speak more particularly of the Reviews'.[43] The author was wholly in favour of readers writing reviews of other contributors' work:

> Review by all means. Review severely, be just & hit hard, when it is deserved, but in a Society like this politeness and Refinement ought to be one of our standards, and gentlemanly and courteous criticism ought to be another.[44]

Justitia gives the *Saturday Review* as a model, 'but even in that paper we do not remember ever seeing an article that would compete with the coarse language contained in the two reviews above referred to', and while not explicitly named, for certain 'every member has by this time either heard or read them for himself and felt as harmed, that any member of this society could be guilty of such coarseness, bitterness and scurrility'.[45] One of the reviews in question could be 'The Poetry of the Colebrook Magazine', by 'R. B.', which appears earlier in the same volume. The author uses six of his ten pages to take to task a poem by 'Mac', which R. B. states is 'neither English nor Poetry'.[46] If Mac had chosen to write a 'Scottish Poem, or verse in the Northern dialect', he would not have objected, but, in his opinion, it was 'neither a poem nor a fair grammatical production', his final verdict being that the poem was 'worthless and insipid'.[47]

Justitia wrote of the difficulties, indeed *battles* waged by the editor over the inclusion of various pieces in the magazine:

> our Faithful Editor with his peculiar, unruly, and we may say dangerous charge (for there have been several explosions) has had to buffet with and fight hard with his assailents [sic] amid tremendous and harassing showers of bullets; not only this, but he has also been called out to do battle singly with some mighty man, strongly and securely cased in mail, while his

assailents [sic] in a body have ceased their firing to look on with pleasure at the interesting duel. Who among us can envy him his position?[48]

Thus, these disagreements might not have been solely between the editor and the Association's members, but might have involved a church official. The editor, Thomas Thacker, himself sets out the difficulties in managing the enterprise in his article 'The Editor versus The Editor', yet proclaims the success of the magazine despite 'every kind of opposition':

> Some have openly cried it down, some have insidiously endeavoured to undermine it, some have promised support month after month and up to this very day have backed out, some have given excuses as 'want of time,' – 'would rather write an essay and read it myself,' – while others have candidly admitted that they tried, but were ashamed of their production and therefore would not send it.[49]

Thacker comes to the defence of the 25 per cent of the Association's members who *did* contribute, being young, inexperienced men, some of them 'not always cognisant with the rules of literary etiquette',[50] who as a whole had been 'fiercely assailed and uncharitably if not shamefully treated'.[51] His policy of 'kindness, forbearance, and liberality', and reluctance to edit out objectionable views, and the need to respect the anonymity of the contributors, placed him in a difficult position. And it is interesting to reflect that the magazine was nonetheless started with the unanimous support of the Association.

The *Aemulus* was a contested medium of reading *and* writing for this literary society. It allowed young inexperienced writers a forum for practising their compositional skills that would elicit criticism, either orally when pieces were read aloud at magazine nights, or through reviews written by members that were included in the material magazine. Some of these reviews fell outside the explicit and implicit norms set externally (by established journals like the *Saturday Review*) or internally through the highly contested, more ambiguous set of standards set somewhere between the editor, the officers of the Association, and possibly by a more senior official of the church. What constituted 'acceptable' reading materials in the magazine applied to what was written for inclusion in the first place, and included the subject matter, style and tone. The magazine's official gatekeeper, the editor, or its unofficial one, the Association's administrative committee, or the church itself – as well as the Association's members themselves – were perhaps anxious to define and thus to control what could be seen as a public reflection of the church and its members.

St Martin's Literary Society

The church of St Martin-in-the-Fields, Trafalgar Square, opened in 1724, but the St Martin's Literary Society dates only from the early twentieth century, or possibly the late nineteenth. The only extant records from this group are four issues of its manuscript magazine, for what was called a 'Newspaper Evening'.[52] The chairman was Reverend J. O. Murray, the minister of the church, and the editor was also a man, but a letter to the editor in the first issue suggests that the majority of the members were women[53] and most likely part of the church congregation. Society meetings were held biweekly on Thursdays at 8.00 p.m. in the vestry room.[54]

The first number of their magazine, *St Martin's Review*, dates from May 1901. The 'Preface' gives the journal's origins and the basic rules for contributing:

> The following Papers are the result of a general invitation issued to the members of St. Martin's Literary Society to contribute towards a 'Newspaper Evening'. Members were free to choose a subject; failing that to adopt one suggested by the Editor. It is significant that few availed themselves of the latter privilege. The only conditions imposed, were the length of the contributions and the strict observance of secrecy as regards the names of the writers.[55]

The issues of the magazine were created between 1901 and 1904 (at least), but issue 2 is missing. The Society produced at least two copies of each issue, each having a different cover design. In the cases of issues 3 (June 1902) and 4 (1903), both copies have survived. There was not a reading order for the limited number of copies – no designated list of recipients in a sequenced circulation – as there was for other literary society magazines, but members signed their names and recorded the 'Date[s] Lent' and 'Date[s] Retd' in the spaces provided on the front flyleaves in some issues. Members had two weeks to read the issue, whereupon they had to return it to either of the secretaries. A 'Notice' in the third issue strictly forbids members from passing the magazine between themselves.[56] The magazines would be read aloud at the meetings and 'Discussion was invited at the close'.[57] Members voted for the best paper, and each member could vote for two papers. From the results of the votes as recorded in the front of the issues, I estimate there were approximately twelve members at this time, a decrease from a reported forty members in previous years.[58]

With the exception of a handwritten poem inserted at the front of one issue, all of the issues are in typescript – red, blue or green, or purple from the copying process – but the publication is nonetheless called a manuscript magazine.[59] The contents are mostly prose fiction and non-fiction, with only a small percentage of poetry. Unlike other literary society magazines, the *St Martin's Review* appears to have been solely for the group's entertainment rather than for any notions of providing a means for 'improvement'.

Friends' Hall Literary Society/Bethnal Green Literary Society

The origins of the *Friends' Hall Literary Society MSS Magazine* lie in the colourful history of a literary society formed by a group of London East End working men who were members of an adult school class. The Friends' Hall Literary Society is particularly interesting because it clearly demonstrates the influence that one literary society had on its individual members. While the group began as a local weekly discussion class, its impact could be felt nationally, and arguably internationally: the Society could count among its former members prominent novelists, politicians, scholars and community leaders.

The records for the Society are fairly complete and include minute books, manuscript magazines, various loose manuscripts of papers read at its meetings as well as records of its library. Also in the collection are two manuscripts written by a former president of the group, Arthur Hadley. One is his autobiography, while the other is a history of the Society, both of which were written in his later life. Hadley's autobiography offers a good opportunity to contextualise this Society through the history of one of its members. In its pages, we also learn of the fates of the various members after they left the Society.

Hadley's memoir is of interest as he recounts his early life in poverty, his being sent to work at a very young age, and the influence of literature and its transformative effect on him.[60] He discusses the range of materials that he and his brother read, which included 'anything from Marcus Aurelius to Marie Corelli'.[61] The brothers had founded 'The Excelsior M.S.S. Magazine',[62] which Hadley described as being 'very much like other schoolboy magazines . . . [whose] circulation was the lowest on record', being confined to immediate family members.[63] They even formed their own mutual improvement society, Hadley recalled: 'This serious effort at self-education played a considerable part in my development. Todd's "Students manual" and Smiles's "Self Help" were among our text books.'[64]

Hadley discussed the origins of the Friends' Hall Literary Society in more detail in another manuscript, 'A Little Athens in the Slums'.[65] The original members all attended the adult school classes that were run by the Quakers at Friends' Hall, located on Barnet Grove in Bethnal Green, London. Hadley distinguished himself as attending evening classes in 'Shorthand, Typewriting, Book-keeping[,] Political Economy, English Literature and technical subjects'.[66] A small group of men at the school – which included Hadley – were given permission to form a discussion class, and this developed into a Shakespearian reading circle. The circle became so popular that the group decided to transform it into a literary and debating society, and this was duly launched on 9 February 1906.[67] Hadley describes the 'vogue' for such organisations at the time, but modestly places his own small society within the framework of a mutual improvement society:

> Such societies when [sic] were then the vogue in nonconformist chapels, some of which, like the City Temple, secured the leading publicists of the period – Bernard Shaw, Sir Oliver Lodge, Jerome K. Jerome, Madam Sarah Grand[,] G. K. Chesterton &c. to lecture to their large membership. Although ambitious we did not aspire to such dizzy heights. Our purpose was mutual improvement and we relied upon our own members to provide the programme.[68]

The group met on Friday evenings in the Red Room at Friends' Hall 'to discuss literature, to acquire literary taste and judgment, to engage in literary activities and public speaking'.[69]

Hadley later had a falling out with the superintendent of the adult school, the result of a 'somewhat bohemian lecture on "Shelley"' and Hadley's unconventional religious views.[70] The group then moved temporarily to a coffeehouse, the Traveller's Rest, on Bethnal Green Road and changed its name to the Bethnal Green Literary Society.[71] Shortly thereafter, the Society moved to a room rented at the Town Hall on Cambridge Road. Among its activities, the Society had a study group, a summer reading programme and a manuscript library of its members' literary works. In addition, the members produced plays, one of which, *The Celestial Pierrot*, was published.[72] It was while the group was based at Friends' Hall that they began a manuscript magazine.

There are eight extant issues of the *Friends' Hall Literary Society MSS Magazine*, which date from 1907 to 1911, along with some loose contributions, not attributed to any issue, that date from December 1911 to June 1912. Contributions to the magazine were sent to the editor, who selected those to be included in the current issue. The magazines were read at Society meetings devoted to the purpose. At a meeting held on 13 November 1909, the Society voted to form a library for the purpose of preserving the magazines and papers delivered to the Society.[73] In some of the issues can be found a handwritten list of dates when the issues were borrowed. A line has been scored through these, presumably to show that the issue was returned.

The magazines consist of original poetry and prose fiction, along with puzzles, humorous advertisements, letters to the editor and 'Answers to Correspondents'. The authors use pen-names or, less frequently, their own names or identifiable initials. Compared with other literary society periodicals, the issues contain on average a considerably higher proportion of original prose fiction. And while the magazine included a 'Critics' Chat' section, there was only a single response, and it appears not to have come from one of the Society's members.

In the May 1908 issue a new feature appeared called 'Critic's Chat', which offered criticism on the *previous* issue. While intended to be a continuing feature, this is the only issue in which it appears. 'Critic's Chat' differs from other literary societies' 'criticisms', in that the comments were provided by an unnamed critic who (the magazine explained) 'is well qualified both from a literary & a general standpoint to pass an opinion on the merits or demerits of the various articles comprised in our last issue'.[74] The comments do have the flavour and tone of a professional critic, and great attention is given to each piece, including punctuation, grammar, style, originality and overall conformity to genre. Specifically in reference to poetry, the critic assessed metre and general 'poetic merit'. Some comments were very positive, as on the poem 'Our Lady of Gain': the critic wrote that it 'shows very considerable poetic merit & skill. A good imitation of Swinburne's style. The last verse "L'Envoi" is perfect Swinburneian.'[75] But more often the critic found faults, even calling the essay 'The Age of Sentiment' 'hopelessly wrong [sic]'.[76] In light of its members' future accomplishments (see below), it is tempting to see the Society's decision to have a critic from outside the circle provide feedback on their work as a sign of members' larger ambitions – aspirations that could be traced back to the early years of their associational activities.

The physical properties of this magazine vary between issues, and do not show the same level of care in production. The contributions are in both manuscript and typescript, typical for a magazine produced during this period, but there is an assortment of paper sizes that varies more than that in any other literary society magazine I have examined. There was even a poem that was sent to the editor on a postcard, and he included it *in totum* in the next issue.[77] These contributions are held together in a variety of ways: hand-stitched with string or twine, metal clips, hole-punched for a ring notebook, staples, or a combination thereof.

But the amateurish appearance of this magazine belies its contributors' later, more mature productions, literary and otherwise. In Hadley's history of the Society, he proudly outlines their future careers:[78]

- Edmund Dutton, the Society's first president: 'a cork manufacturer of Hackney Road ... afterward became a councillor of the City of London Corporation and finally an alderman'.
- Mrs H. Wynne, the Society's first female member, who was elected vice-president: 'This distinguished lady had conducted a Literary and Debating Class at the old Bethnal Green Free Library. ... She was the widow of a General, a blue-blooded aristocrat with titled relatives, and added lustre to our gatherings. She was a member of the Royal Society'.
- Samuel Cottage: 'joined the Lit at its inception and at that time lived in a squalid slum in Virginia Row. He worked in the Cabinet making industry'. Under the pen-name George Acorn he published *One of the Multitude* (1911) and *The Driving Force* (1915).
- William Kean Seymour (1887–1975) began his career as a bank clerk. He 'dabbled in verse in his boyhood, and started his literary career by contributing poems to local papers and chapel magazines. Subsequently poems from his pen were accepted by The Pall Mall Gazette, The Westminster Gazette, Country Life, The New Age, John o' London's Weekly, The New Witness, G.K.'s Weekly, Eve, Everybody's Weekly etc. His first volume of poems was published in 1914 under the title of "The Street of Dreams" [1914]'. Seymour became a Fellow of the Royal Society of Literature.
- Beatrice Kean Seymour, née Beatrice Mary Stapleton (1886–1955). Hadley recounts: 'I well remember how thrilled we were when her first short story "The long [sic] Arm" appeared in a popular magazine. Little did we dream that she was destined to become a famous novelist and best seller, with two dozen novels to her credit'.
- Horace Shipp (1891–1961): 'His output has been scattered over the Parnassian fields of Poetry, Drama, Fiction, Art and Belles-lettres'. Hadley gives details of his published collections of poetry, essays, plays, literary criticism and school books.

And the list goes on. Interestingly, Hadley himself worked as a bank clerk, but if he had any literary aspirations, he did not mention them.

The Society's last meeting was in December 1915, and it never reformed: 'the dispersal of our members owing to the war necessitated closing down'.[79] Hadley's short manuscript very aptly details the history of a society which was indeed 'A Little Athens in the Slums'.

Conclusion

The literary society magazines discussed here should be seen in the larger context of a tradition of producing magazines in manuscript by various groups in London that had been established at the beginning of the nineteenth century (at least). Staff and students at the Worship Street Sunday School produced *The Monthly Instucter* (sic) between 1823 and at least 1830,[80] and a group of young Freethinking Christians founded a magazine in 1844.[81] An adult education group formed at the College for Working Women (later the Francis Martin College for Women) had its own manuscript periodical.[82] The Hackney Literary and Scientific Institution founded one, perhaps as early as 1856.[83] Company staff had their own handwritten magazines: employees working for James Budgett and Son Limited founded *Budgett's Budget*, in which they shared news, gossip, cartoons and humorous biographies of company staff.[84] As I have shown with the four groups discussed in this chapter, literary societies adopted the form to suit their members' various perceived needs, especially improving their writing and critical reading skills. The circumstances of the founding and running of these magazines, and the material objects themselves – their style, format, contents and distribution patterns – are as individual as their members.

By the end of the nineteenth century, like newspapers and periodicals, literary societies were ubiquitous across England and Scotland, and as King, Easley and Morton highlight, '[j]ournalism and daily life were increasingly entwined'.[85] I would add that these societies – which collectively had thousands of members across the country (and beyond) – also benefited from 'improvements in printing technology; advances in methods of information gathering and dissemination; increases in literacy rates; and the elimination of the taxes on knowledge'.[86] In the second half of the century, while some literary groups responded to the 'surging sea of print'[87] by adopting this medium and technology to produce their own magazines in print, other groups chose to create handwritten periodicals, a tradition that has been overlooked in the scholarship.

Contrary to theories of technological determinism, which underlines the 'causal force of print technology' in bringing about social change, many voluntary 'improving' societies in the long nineteenth century clearly *resisted* change.[88] Indeed, technology itself was a causal force for what can be seen as an entrenchment of social practices that included a long tradition of manuscript production. In reviewing the work of scholars who 'have all demonstrated the continuing vitality of a manuscript tradition for the circulation of text of all kinds in seventeenth-century England and, indeed, the new ways in which it was valued and employed', David McKitterick rightly stated that 'the boundary between manuscript and print is as untidy chronologically as it is commercially, materially or socially'.[89] This is equally true for the long nineteenth century.

Michael Bristol and Arthur Marotti argue that 'manuscript transmission belonged to a culture that valued personal intimacy, sociality and participation, if not also intellectual and social exclusivity – all features that generally distinguished it from print transmission'.[90] Citing Harold Love, they continue: 'Closer to the world of orality and its sociological assumption, the manuscript medium could be used to foster familial and kinship ties, group solidarity, local identity, and factional or partisan interests'.[91] Orality is associated with physical experience (including sight, sound and smell) as well as an immediate direct experience, or what is referred to in literary theory as 'presence'. Walter J. Ong asserts that presence is based in orality, and is thus dispelled in a written work and further still in print: chirographical transmission 'represents an intermediate stage between oral and typographical transmission in which the values of orality – and the fact of presence – are still strongly felt'.[92] Following Love's Ong-inspired spectrum of diminishing levels of presence the further away from orality the experience is,[93] I argue here that the continued use of manuscript texts by literary societies in the nineteenth and early twentieth centuries was due to its commingling of both the oral recitation of essays in 'ordinary meetings' and on 'magazine nights', and the material magazine itself, when the experience or presence of the auditor/editor was interfused. The manuscript medium, in this case society magazines, did indeed 'foster familial and kinship ties, group solidarity, local identity, and factional or partisan interests', as Love rightly states. Presence helps explain not only the popularity of these groups, and in some cases the long-standing nature of the groups as well as of a few of their members, but also the longevity of their creative handwritten productions.

Notes

This research would not have been possible without the assistance of the Santander Award, and I extend my sincere thanks for that support. Also, I thank the archivists at the London Metropolitan Archives, Tower Hamlets Archive and Westminster City Archives for all their advice and kind assistance.

1. See Lauren Weiss, 'The Manuscript Magazines of the Wellpark Free Church Young Men's Literary Society', in Paul Raphael Rooney and Anna Gasperini (eds), *Media and Print Culture Consumption in Nineteenth-Century Britain: The Victorian Reading Experience* (Basingstoke: Palgrave Macmillan, 2016), pp. 53–73. For a review of previous work on eighteenth- and nineteenth-century literary societies and mutual improvement groups more generally, along with an overview of research on nineteenth-century working-class writings, see Lauren Weiss, 'The Literary Clubs and Societies of Glasgow During the Long Nineteenth Century: A City's History of Reading Through Its Communal Reading Practices and Productions', PhD dissertation (University of Stirling, 2017), pp. 19–29.
2. Richard Altick, *The English Common Reader* (Chicago: University of Chicago Press, 1957), p. 205; Jonathan Rose, *The Intellectual Life of the British Working Classes* (New Haven: Yale University, 2001), p. 58.
3. Altick, *The English Common Reader*, p. 205. It is unclear whether Altick was aware of the production of society magazines. See David Vincent's discussion of artisan groups and working-men's education clubs in *Bread, Knowledge and Freedom: A Study of Nineteenth-Century Working Class Autobiography* (London: Europa, 1981), pp. 134–7. See also David Vincent, *The Rise of Mass Literacy: Reading and Writing in Modern Europe* (Cambridge: Polity Press, 2000), pp. 117–18; Martyn Walker, *The Development of the Mechanics' Institute Movement in Britain and Beyond* (Abingdon: Routledge, 2017).
4. Andrew King, Alexis Easley and John Morton, 'Introduction', in Andrew King, Alexis Easley and John Morton (eds), *The Routledge Handbook to Nineteenth-Century British Periodicals and Newspapers* (London: Routledge, 2016), pp. 1–13 (p. 2).
5. See Heather Murray, *Come, Bright Improvement! The Literary Societies of Nineteenth-Century Ontario* (Toronto: University of Toronto Press, 2002), p. 15, note 34.
6. See Elizabeth Webby, 'The Beginnings of Literature in Colonial Australia', in Peter Pierce (ed.), *The Cambridge History of Australian Literature* (Cambridge: Cambridge University Press, 2009), pp. 34–51; Elizabeth Webby, 'Not Reading the Nation: Australian Readers of the 1890s', *Australian Literary Studies*, 22 (May 2006), pp. 308–18.
7. See Kirsti Salmi-Niklander, 'Manuscripts and Broadsheets: Narrative

Genres and the Communication Circuit Among Working-Class Youth in Early 20th-Century Finland', *Folklore*, 33 (2006), pp. 109–26; Kirsti Salmi-Niklander, 'Crooks and Heroes, Priests and Preachers: Religion and Socialism in the Oral-Literary Tradition of a Finnish-Canadian Mining Community', in Tiiu Jaago (ed.), *Lives, Histories and Identities* (Tartu: University of Tartu, 2002), vol. I, pp. 131–58. Other work on specifically socialist handwritten newspapers has covered Sweden (Ronny Ambjörnsson, *Den skötsamme arbetaren: Idéer och ideal i ett norrländskt sågverkssamhälle 1880–1930* [Stockholm: Carlsson, 1988]), Norway (Christian Berrenberg, *'Es ist deine Pflicht zu benutzen, was du weisst!' Literatur und literarische Praktiken in der norwegischen Arbeiterbewegung 1900–1931* [Würzburg: Ergon Verlag, 2014]), Finland (Risto Turunen, 'From the Object of History to the Subject of History: The Writing Factory Workers in Finland in the Early 20th Century', in Heiko Droste and Kirsti Salmi-Niklander [eds], *Handwritten Newspapers as an Alternative Medium During the Early Modern and Modern Periods* [forthcoming]) and Finnish immigrants in Australia (Anne Heimo, 'Socialist Endeavors, Fist Presses and Pen Wars: Literary Practices of Early Finnish Migrants in Australia', in Ann-Caterine Edlund, T. G. Ashplant and Anne Kuismin [eds], *Reading and Writing from Below: Exploring the Margins of Modernity* [Umeå: Umeå University, 2016], pp. 97–114). For these last references, I thank Risto Turunen.
8. Roy Alden Atwood, 'The Handwritten Newspapers Project: An Annotated Bibliography and Historical Research Guide to Handwritten Newspapers from Around the World', at <https://handwrittennews.com> (accessed 17 November 2017). This site continues to collect and publish evidence of handwritten newspapers and magazines, though it is by no means exhaustive or representative.
9. Atwood, 'Handwritten Newspapers Project', at <https://handwrittennews.com/category/england/> (accessed 14 November 2017).
10. See appendices III–V in Weiss, 'The Literary Clubs and Societies of Glasgow', pp. 261–7.
11. Ibid., pp. 173–5.
12. Ibid., figure 6.3, p. 172.
13. A. P. Baggs, Diane K. Bolton and Patricia E. C. Croot, 'Islington: Protestant Nonconformity', in T. F. T. Baker and C. R. Elrington (eds), *A History of the County of Middlesex, Vol. VIII: Islington and Stoke Newington Parishes* (London: Victoria County History, 1985), pp. 101–15, available at 'British History Online' <https://www.british-history.ac.uk/vch/middx/vol8/pp101-115> (accessed 29 September 2016).
14. J. Ewing Ritchie, *The Religious Life of London* (London: Tinsley Brothers, 1870), pp. 139–40.
15. Ibid., p. 140.
16. Ibid., p. 141.
17. Ibid., p. 140.

18. London Metropolitan Archives, LMA/4303/E/02/039, 'Park Church, Highbury. The Literary Society. Rules', Minute book, 1882–90 (front endpaper). Hereafter, all materials from this archive are simply listed with the LMA reference number.
19. LMA/4303/E/02/040, Programme appended to minute entry, 23 January 1882; 'Thirty-Seventh Annual Report', Park Church Literary Society, Minute book, 1890–98 (report appended to minute entry, [?] November 1895).
20. LMA/4303/E/01/003, 'Origin of the Literary Societies' Union', London Presbyterian Literary Society Union minutes, 1874–1935, p. i.
21. LMA/4303/E/02/041, Roll of membership for the Literary Society in connection with Park Church, Highbury, 1901–1915.
22. The average number of members between 1881 and 1897 was calculated from the total membership numbers given in the annual reports, but are non-inclusive as reports for 1886–88 are no longer extant. Membership between 1901 and 1914 was calculated from official membership lists for these years. Ibid.
23. Weiss, 'The Literary Clubs and Societies of Glasgow', p. 161.
24. W. G. H., 'Sonnet. After the French of Joachim du Bellay', *Highbury Magazine*, 3 (24 March 1902), p. 14 (LMA/4366/B/009).
25. J. C. Y. [James C. Young], 'Fra Ugo Bassi', *Highbury Magazine*, 3 (24 March 1902), pp. 30–48 (p. 48).
26. W. G. H., 'A Ballade of Sorrow and Song', *Highbury Magazine*, 3 (24 March 1902), pp. 28–9.
27. A. M., 'An Old Magazine. 1814. La Belle Assemblée', *Highbury Magazine*, 6 (April 1905), pp. 1–12 (LMA/4366/B/011); S.U.B., 'Journalism Behind the Scenes', *Highbury Magazine*, 9 (1908), pp. 33–9 (LMA/4366/B/013).
28. A. C. H., 'The Fortune of Words', *Highbury Magazine*, 2 (22 April 1901), pp. 22–9 (LMA/4366/B/008).
29. J. M. W. [Rev. J. Macartney Wilson], 'Prenez garde; il y a des pièges', *Highbury Magazine*, 6 (April 1905), pp. 61–72.
30. D. A. A. [David Alexander Adams], 'The Chief End of Reading', *Highbury Magazine*, 9 (1908), pp. 3–12 (p. 6).
31. Editor's note and reading list, *Highbury Magazine*, 12 (April 1911), pp. 1–2 (LMA/4366/B/015).
32. 'Jack and Jill', 'The Editor's Waste Paper Basket', *Highbury Magazine*, 10 (April 1909), pp. 70–5 (LMA/4366/B/014).
33. The most elaborate cover is this one made for the 1908 issue, which is a needlepoint that, the editor informs us, was 'sewn by a member of the Society and is an enlarged copy of a bookcover in the British Museum said to have been worked by "that bright occidentel [sic] star", Queen Elizabeth'. See 'Editorial Remarks', *Highbury Magazine*, 9 (1908), p. 1.
34. The 1902 issue did not have an editor listed, while the 1911 issue was edited by W. Blake, a male society member.

35. See note 22.
36. It was not possible to identify all the authors in these magazines as some used pen-names, while others used initials that were not always identifiable from the rolls. Identification is complicated further by the fact that 'friends' of the society were also allowed to contribute to the magazine.
37. At the time of writing, the 1886 issue is missing from the LMA collection.
38. Minute entry, 20 November 1871, [Ninth Annual Report], Islington Presbyterian Church Young Men's Association, Minute book, 1869–78 (LMA/4303/E/04/012); Minute entry, 23 November 1874, 'Twelvth [sic] Annual Report', Minute book, 1869–78.
39. Minute entry, 19 January 1891, Islington Presbyterian Church Young Men's Association, Minute book, 1878–94 (LMA/4303/E/04/013).
40. 'Justitia', 'Our Magazine', *Aemulus*, 1 (1866), pp. 339–47 (p. 339) (LMA/4303/E/04/015).
41. Although initially barred from membership and 'debarred from expressing their opinions at the meetings', women were permitted to contribute to the magazine 'if they c[ould] obtain the good offices of any of the members to place their contributions in the hands of the Editor'. Minute entry, 20 November 1871, [Ninth Annual Report].
42. *Aemulus*, 1 (1866), pp. 339, 343.
43. Ibid., p. 343.
44. Ibid., p. 344.
45. Ibid., p. 344.
46. 'R.B.', 'The Poetry of the Colebrook Magazine', *Aemulus*, 1 (1866), pp. 273–82 (p. 274).
47. Ibid., pp. 274–8.
48. 'Justitia', 'Our Magazine', pp. 339–40.
49. Editor [Thomas William Thacker], 'The Editor versus The Editor', *Aemulus*, 1 (1866), pp. 349–58 (p. 350).
50. Ibid., p. 354.
51. Ibid., p. 350.
52. 'Preface', *St Martin's Review*, ed. Thomas Barnard, no. 1 (May 1901), p. i. The issues of the *St Martin's Review* are held at Westminster City Archives, London, STM/1851/1/5/6.
53. 'A Candid Friend' [letter to the editor], ibid.
54. Title page, ibid.
55. 'Preface', ibid.
56. 'Notice', *St Martin's Literary Society Manuscript Magazine*, no. 3 (June 1902), (front endpaper). Westminster City Archives, STM/1851/1/5/7.
57. 'Preface', ibid.
58. 'A Rank Outsider', 'The Lay of the Faithful Jew', *St Martin's Magazine*, 5 (June 1904) (loose supplement, front endpaper). Westminster City Archives, STM/1851/1/5/9.
59. Ibid. The pen-name suggests that the author was not a member, and

the poem appears to have been a late addition to the issue. The poem is about the 'faithful' Society members who have remained in the group over the years.
60. Another member of the Friends' Hall Literary Society, Samuel Cottage, also wrote a memoir. His 'autobiographical novel' was published under the pen-name of 'George Acorn' as *One of the Multitude* (1911).
61. Arthur Hadley, 'Penny Plain: Autobiography of a Bethnal Green Boy', unpublished manuscript (1947), p. 30 (Tower Hamlets Library, LC8386 (100 HAD)).
62. The title of the Hadley brothers' magazine is taken from Henry Wadsworth Longfellow's poem, 'Excelsior'. Published in 1842, it was used in working-class culture as a motto for about a century thereafter. I am grateful to Kirstie Blair for pointing out this association.
63. Hadley, 'Penny Plain', pp. 28–9.
64. Ibid., pp. 29–30.
65. Arthur Hadley, 'A Little Athens in the Slums: The Story of the Bethnal Green [formerly Friends Hall] Literary Society, 1906–1916' (unpublished manuscript, c. 1955 [or October 1958?]). The manuscript is held in the Tower Hamlets Local History Library and Archives (hereafter TH), P/MIS/376/2.
66. Ibid., p. 4.
67. Ibid., pp. 4–6.
68. Ibid., p. 5.
69. Ibid., p. 3.
70. Ibid., pp. 7–8.
71. Ibid., p. 10.
72. Ibid., pp. 11–12. According to Hadley's manuscript, '"The Celestial Pierrot" was published in "The Odd Volume" for 1913 edited by John G. Wilson, a bibliophile, who subsequently became manager of Bumpus', the famous bookshop in Oxford Street. I have not been able to locate a copy of this.
73. Tower Hamlets Local History Library and Archives (hereafter TH), S/BGL/1/1, Friends' Hall Literary Society, Minute Book, 1908–9, Minute entry, 13 November 1909.
74. Editorial, *Friends' Hall Literary Society M.S.S. Magazine*, 3 (May 1908), p. 1 (TH, S/BGL/2/2).
75. 'The Critic's Chat Concerning the Christmas Number of the MSS Magazine', ibid.
76. Ibid.
77. The poem, 'For the M.S.S. Magazine, Life (from the french. [sic])', is written on the back of a blue postcard. It was sent to 'T. A. Nichols Esq, Friends Hall Lity. Socy., Friends Hall, Barnet Grove, Bethnal Green Road E.', and was posted on 28 May 1909. 'XYZ', 'For the M.S.S. Magazine, Life (from the french.)', *Friends' Hall Literary Society M.S.S. Magazine*, 5 (May 1909) (TH, S/BGL/2/4).

78. Hadley, 'A Little Athens in the Slums', pp. 6–7, 14–22.
79. Ibid., p. 14.
80. Only volumes V–VII (1827–30) have survived (LMA, CLC/229/MS 07513A/001-003).
81. Freethinking Christians, *The Manuscript Magazine of the Church of God at the Meeting House, St John's Square, London*, August to December 1844, 5 vols (LMA, CLC/197/MS02199).
82. *The College Magazine*, ed. Miss [Francis] Martin, March and November 1886 (LMA, A/FMC/CM/001-004). See also: *A Reminiscence of the College for Working Women*, December 1911 (LMA, A/FMC/CM/005); *Our Journal*, January 1913 (LMA, A/FMC/CM/006a); *Chronicle of the Frances Martin College*, 1927–8 (LMA, A/FMC/CM/007a).
83. *Hackney Literary and Scientific Institution Manuscript Magazine*, January–June 1857, vol. 2, no. VIII (Hackney Archives, D/F/TYS/70/15). See also records for St Thomas' Institute, which produced a magazine in manuscript (Hackney Archives, *St. Thomas' Institute Magazine*, 22 vols, 1876–81, D/E/215/THO).
84. James Budgett and Son Limited, *Budgett's Budget*, April–September 1909, March–April 1910, April and June 1914, October 1919 (LMA, CLC/B/133/MS20372).
85. King et al., 'Introduction', p. 1.
86. Ibid.
87. From 'Repose', *Saturday Review*, 23 July 1864, pp. 110–11, as quoted in King et al., 'Introduction', p. 2.
88. See Bristol and Marotti's overview and discussion of the 'social meaning of print', particularly in its relation to the traditional manuscript culture of the early modern period: Michael D. Bristol and Arthur F. Marotti, 'Introduction', in *Print, Manuscript, and Performance: The Changing Relations of the Media in Early Modern England* (Columbus: Ohio State University Press), pp. 2–29.
89. David McKitterick, *Print, Manuscript and the Search for Order, 1450–1830* (Cambridge: Cambridge University Press, 2003), p. 11–12.
90. Bristol and Marotti, 'Introduction', p. 13.
91. Ibid., pp. 13–14.
92. See Harold Love's discussion of Ong's versus Derrida's concepts of 'Presence and the Scribal Text': Harold Love, *Scribal Publication in Seventeenth-Century England* (Oxford: Clarendon, 1993), pp. 141–4.
93. Ibid., p. 144.

Chapter 5

Space and Place in Nineteenth-Century Images of Women Readers

Amelia Yeates

Studies of women readers have considered the concept of space, both real and imagined, as integral to the reading process. Kate Flint, for example, proposes that the act of reading be seen as a means of claiming personal space.[1] Similarly, Janis Bergman-Carton argues that paintings of women readers comprise 'interior spaces, [both] domestic and psychological'.[2] The focus on space in recent studies of women's reading is prompted by the importance attached to space in nineteenth-century accounts, with didactic texts often focusing on the issue of reading spaces, articulating where women's reading should and should not take place. John Ruskin, in 'Of Queens' Gardens' (1865), for example, dealt with the role of fiction-reading for young unmarried women in relation to the household library.[3] Maintaining this focus on space, the chief argument of this chapter is that the depicted locations of women's reading were crucial in the construction of meaning around the 'woman reader'. I argue that spatial access determined women's reading practices and that the visual arts, in privileging the visual depiction of space, were crucial in the articulation and representation of those practices.

In the visual arts, the woman reader was a popular trope, with depicted reading locations including public and domestic libraries, parlours, marginal and interstitial places such as attics, corners and window seats, public spaces such as the beach or the train carriage and liminal spaces such as gardens. Readers were pictured alone, among strangers or with friends or family, reading a range of texts. This chapter examines some of these spaces and places and explores the ways in which these depictions helped to construct meaning surrounding reading spaces. As I demonstrate, readers could be confined by their spaces or, conversely, transgress potentially confining reading spaces and their boundaries.

Studies of nineteenth-century readers have proliferated over recent years, but have seen relatively little intervention from the discipline of art history, despite the popularity of women reading as a motif for artists and illustrators during that century. Visual representations are therefore often absent from, or neglected in, this scholarship. Leah Price is strangely silent on the illustrations she reproduces in her *How to Do Things with Books in Victorian Britain*,[4] while the important resource UK RED (UK Reading Experience Database)[5] limits itself to documented evidence of 'actual' reading experiences, and therefore excludes both fictional accounts of reading and visual representations of reading. Kate Flint's ground-breaking *The Woman Reader* reproduces important paintings, photographs and illustrations featuring women readers, some of which are discussed closely in her account, but her chief sources of evidence remain textual. However, an examination of the visual iconography of women reading can further our understanding of meanings surrounding the spaces and places in which women's reading might take place. Images of women reading do not tell us how women read any more or less than do fictional accounts but form part of a cultural history of reading, suggesting to us the available range of tropes of reading on which artists drew, as well as creating their own formal intrigues and imaginative constructions, themselves to be read.

This chapter focuses on the nineteenth century as a period which saw a proliferation of literature and literacy, as well as concomitant advice and didactic texts about how, where and with whom reading should take place, advice directed particularly at young female readers, who were seen as most in need of guidance, and who were viewed as the susceptible consumers of problematic genres, such as romance and sensation novels. The chapter examines a range of paintings depicting women readers in particular locations or types of space, and the ways in which such images are productive in the construction of meaning and values surrounding reading practices. It considers specifically middle- and upper-class female readers, for whom distinctions between public and private spaces took on very different meanings than they did for working-class women.

Books were a mainstay of respectable households across the class spectrum. Photographs of nineteenth-century living spaces show books casually lying on tables, ready to be perused at any point. But the seeming informality of such arrangements belies the complex expectations surrounding when, where and with whom reading should and should not take place, especially for women. The locations in which reading took place were crucial, for, as Patricia Okker notes, portraying women reading in a familial area such as the sitting room could 'domesticate women's pleasure in reading'.[6] The conscious decision by critics to identify both allocated and prohibited spaces for reading within the home can be seen not only as an attempt to create a separation between the domestic/feminine and the cultural/masculine but also to limit the physical space to which a female reader had access.

In images of interior spaces, a common mode of reading depicted was that between mother and child. The importance of the maternal figure to her children's reading habits can be traced to images of the Madonna with child, often shown in the act of reading. Examples are numerous, and include the fifteenth-century *Virgin and Child Reading* (sometimes known as the *Ince Hall Madonna*) after Van Eyck,[7] in the Netherlandish tradition of women reading in a domestic interior. In the nineteenth century, secularised versions of this iconography could be found in works such as William Nicol's *Quiet* (1860) (Plate 1), depicting a mother and her child reading, and which, as Susan Casteras notes, 'exalts motherhood and harmonious domesticity'.[8] The motif of the reading mother was familiar in other Victorian paintings, for example *Life Well Spent* by Charles W. Cope (1862) (Figure 5.1), featuring a mother knitting industriously while looking attentively at her son, who is guided by the book on his mother's lap. In a reinforcement of the importance of women to the moral development of their family members, the elder daughter reads close to her mother, while tending to the baby, mimicking the dynamics enacted by the mother, and foreshadowing the expectations of her own role as she grows older. The daughter, like a mother in training, emblematises sororal maternality. Likewise, in didactic literature, the importance of reading in maternal functions extended to elder female siblings. For example, in a chapter on 'The Elder Sister', *The Young Ladies' Treasure Book* advised girls that they had a duty to instruct their younger siblings.[9]

It was because of the huge importance placed on women's moral responsibilities as wives and mothers that in Augustus Egg's trilogy of paintings *Past and Present* (1858),[10] a woman's infidelity, prompted by her illicit reading of Balzac, leads to the dissolution of her family, as the woman has failed both her wifely and her motherly duties. Within the home it was the mother who was seen as having influence over the moral upbringing of the children, and therefore her own reading practices were of utmost importance. One critic wrote:

> On them, as mothers and sisters, rests a great responsibility, for, as is well known, they are childhood's first teachers . . . and thus it is imperative that a mother should read so that she might direct her family in their choice of books.[11]

Figure 5.1 Charles W. Cope, *Life Well Spent*, 1862

A mother's reading was important not only in order to prevent corruption entering the home, as in *Past and Present*, but also so that she could influence her family in what to read, acting as spiritual and moral guide and protector. As Susan Casteras notes in *Images of Victorian Womanhood*, it was a mother's role to preserve the home as a 'safe haven of domesticity, male recuperation, moral edification of children and others'.[12] Even when another family member read out loud, maternal approval was seen as crucial, as expressed by

Mrs Sarah Ellis, who wrote that there are few more satisfying scenes than 'that of a thoroughly united and intelligent family, the female members of which are busily at work, while a father or brother reads aloud to them some interesting book approved by the mother, and delighted in by her daughters'.[13] For Ellis, reading aloud within the family was to be highly prized, as it maintained family contact and diverted attention away from idleness. The scene she describes was an ideal way of passing an evening: family unity was achieved and, in being read to, the women were able to busy themselves (with tasks such as needlework) and not be idle, while still obtaining the benefits of the book's content.

The need for maternal approval of reading material was also expressed by other female writers. Matilda Pullan in *Maternal Counsels to a Daughter* (1855), for example, wrote: 'Nothing should enduce a daughter to read such as are not sanctioned by her mother'.[14] John Tosh suggests that whereas in the eighteenth century 'child-rearing advice literature . . . had commonly been addressed to the father . . . now it tended to be written for mothers'.[15] While Tosh argues that 'One should obviously be wary of accepting prescriptive literature as evidence of practice',[16] my interest here is not so much in didactic texts as reflective of lived practice, but in how, when considered alongside the copious imagery of mothers, or of female educators such as governesses reading with children, such texts indicate the significance of the maternal figure to reading and represent a key part of nineteenth-century cultural histories of women reading.

Had *Life Well Spent* originally been exhibited alone, it would perhaps merely have contributed to the many contemporary representations of virtuous maternal devotion. However, the painting was exhibited with a companion work entitled *Time Ill Spent*, now lost, featuring a very different kind of reader. The *Art Journal* described the scene in the latter painting as a woman 'addicted to French novels, and whose household is confusion'.[17] The review, which emphasises absorption, neglect and chaos, draws on the trope of the unmonitored addicted woman reader, identifying French novels as the source of these vices, in contrast to the ordered households in paintings such as Nicol's *Quiet* and Cope's *Life Well Spent*. John Tosh notes that 'The properly ordered household was widely taken by religious people of all persuasions to be a microcosm of the divinely ordered universe'.[18] Perhaps the most well known example of the disordered interior as an indicator of moral and sexual transgression is William Holman Hunt's *The Awakening Conscience* (1853),[19] where the carefully depicted chaotic interior signifies the moral laxity of the kept woman.

The chaotic interior was a particularly recognisable trope in descriptions of avid novel readers. In an article addressed in warning to young women, one critic described the following 'real life' scenario:

> A whole family, brought to destitution, has lately had all its misfortunes clearly traced by the authorities to an ungovernable passion for novel-reading entertained by the wife and mother. The husband was sober and industrious, but his wife was indolent, and addicted to reading everything procurable in the shape of a romance. This led her to utterly neglect her husband, herself, and her eight children. One daughter, in despair, fled the parental home and threw herself into the haunts of vice. Another was found by the police chained by the legs, to prevent her from following her sister's example. The house exhibited the most offensive appearance of filth and indigence. In the midst of this pollution, privation, and poverty, the cause of it sat reading the latest 'sensation work' of the season, and refused to allow herself to be disturbed in her entertainment.[20]

As is evident in this passage, the literary form which was of particular concern to moralists during the nineteenth century was the novel. Although some articles suggested to worried relatives that novel-reading in moderation was perfectly healthy and that novels could instruct young women well, novels were generally thought to be the most unwholesome and insidious form of reading, and were central to many debates over women's reading practices (French novels were of particular concern).[21] The title given to Cope's pair of works was *Two Mothers*,[22] emphasising the significance of the maternal figure in both paintings.

The contrast between ordered virtuous reading and disordered unwholesome reading was evident in the writings of John Ruskin. In his description of one of his favourite paintings, Carpaccio's *The Dream of St Ursula* (1497–8),[23] Ruskin repeatedly returns to the theme of order. St Ursula is still and peaceful, possessing a 'Royal power over herself and happiness in her flowers, her books, her sleeping, and waking, her prayers, her dreams, her earth, her heaven',[24] which Ruskin contrasts to the chaos of two young American female readers he apparently saw on a train journey in Italy:

> They pulled down the blinds the moment they entered the carriage, and then sprawled, and writhed, and tossed among the cushions of it . . . they had French novels, lemons, and lumps of sugar, to beguile their state with; the novels hanging together by the ends of string that had once stitched them, or adhering at the corners in densely bruised dog's ears, out of which the girls, wetting their fingers, occasionally extricated a gluey leaf.[25]

The imperative for order recurs throughout Ruskin's writings, and, as Hilary Fraser notes, is central to Ruskin's 'ideas about beauty'.[26] However, order is also central to his moral vision. Pitting the slovenliness of the American girls in their carriage against the order of Ursula in her chamber is both a moral and an aesthetic choice. However, even Ursula can lapse, Ruskin noting that in the corner of Ursula's room is her reading table, 'some two feet and a half square, covered by a red cloth with a white border and dainty fringe'. On the table sits a book, 'set up at a slope fittest for reading'. This is almost the perfect reading corner, functional and in order; however, the door of the shelf 'has been left open, and the books, I am grieved to say', writes Ruskin, 'are rather in disorder, having been pulled about before the princess went to bed, and one left standing on its side'.[27] Ruskin was right to be concerned, as discarded books feature as a negative symbol in a range of artworks. In Victor Orsel's *Le Bien et le Mal* (1832),[28] the sexually fallen woman ('le mal') tramples on her discarded book; in Emily Osborn's *The Governess* (1860),[29] depicting an indignant mother indulging her disobedient children while the governess is reprimanded for failing to discipline them, the discarded book at the bottom right of the painting is a signifier of the children's unruliness; while Albert Morrow's poster for Sydney Grundy's 1894 play *The New Woman* features a pile of books and papers in disarray on the floor. The moral polarising of order and disorder within a quasi-religious context was so pervasive that arguably the relative lack of disorder in *Past and Present* indicates the complexity of the moralising at work in the painting and the degree of its potential sympathy with the woman. While the narrative of the work is familiar to many viewers today, the painting prompted an array of readings at the time of its initial display. The *Athenaeum*, for example, supposed that the viewer's sympathies were intended to lie with the woman, rather than the man, who had struck his wife to the floor.[30] In fact, it was due to the existence of various readings that Ruskin felt the need to offer his authoritative reading of the painting: the woman 'can't ready [sic] French well enough to understand the least bit of de Balzac's subtlety'.[31]

Most of the paintings so far discussed have involved reading within a familial group. As important as communal family reading in the home was, women were often depicted reading alone in a temporarily seized space. In R. B. Martineau's *The Last Chapter* (1862),[32] for example, the reader kneels by the fireside one evening, taking advantage of the firelight, and some spare moments, to read a book. While solitary female reading was seen as always potentially dangerous, some texts addressed to young women did sanction, and indeed encourage, the creation of a private space for reading. An article entitled 'What Shall We Read?', published in *Young Woman* in 1892, for example, stated:

> every grown-up girl should have a little place in her father's house that is altogether her own. Let it be only a glorified attic, let it be only a bedroom, – but let it be exclusively hers where . . . anything that requires special attention can be read.[33]

While the patriarchal aspect of the home ('her father's house') is clearly apparent in this advice, such sources must have offered to their readers a welcome legitimisation of private female reading spaces. Furthermore, when exclusion from the household library was upheld, a 'glorified attic' or bedroom was, in fact, often the only space a young middle-class woman did have in which to read. In situations where exclusion from the household library was upheld, or where the family was not wealthy enough to possess a library, women of the house were forced to find alternative reading locations.

Numerous paintings of the period depict women reading in such private spaces, for example Alice Squire's *Young Girl Reading in an Attic Bedroom* (1861).[34] In this picture, while the woman's position is slightly less temporary than in *The Last Chapter*, and the comfort of her surroundings is indicated by the curled up cat on the bed, the scene is nevertheless claustrophobic, with the patterning of the floor and the walls closing up the space, and the tilt of the woman's head paralleled by the sloping of the attic wall on the left of the painting. As an attic space, the ceiling of the room is lower than that found in alternative reading spaces, such as parlours, and the room itself is clearly not spacious, leading some sources to suggest that the woman depicted is a governess.[35]

A more salubrious setting is that in John Callcott Horsley's *A Pleasant Corner* (1866) (Plate 2),[36] depicting a young woman reading a large leather-bound volume in an old-English-style house, with wooden panelling, an open fire and a seat near a window. Her space is indeed pleasant, but pictorially it is confined. She is flanked by the large fireplace and by the curtain on the viewer's right. Unlike the protective red curtain Charlotte Brontë's Jane Eyre draws around her during her window-seat reading (considered further below), which allows her to create mentally rewarding spaces conjured up by her reading, the curtain in *A Pleasant Corner* threatens to curtail the reader's experience and close in on her, potentially cutting her off from the rest of the house.[37]

While Squire's and Horsley's readers are depicted at a moment of reverie, or distraction from their reading, visual representations of absorbed women readers during this period were common, for example Edward Ward's *Girl Reclining on a Sofa* (1854).[38] In Ward's painting, the close proximity of the artist, and therefore the viewer, to the subject invests the scene with a sense of voyeurism, as the viewer enjoys uninhibited access to the reading figure. Departing from classic feminist accounts of the male gaze, Kathryn Brown has attempted to incorporate less binary approaches to the gaze in her interpretation of women reading in nineteenth-century French painting.[39] I would argue, however, that the presentation of female reading figures for an eroticised (male) gaze remains a key characteristic of visual representations of women readers, in part due to the appeal of female interiority, represented by scenes of reading. The critic W. R. Greg wrote in 1859 about the impressionability of women readers, 'in whom at all times the emotional element is more awake and more powerful than the critical, whose feelings are more easily aroused and whose estimates are more easily influenced than ours'.[40] Depictions of lone female readers offered viewers an opportunity to witness such intense emotional engagement with a text. Likewise, George J. Romanes claimed that, having difficulty in concentrating, women's minds are 'more prone to what is called "wandering"'.[41] Such views about the attention spans of women were evident in depictions of female readers, in many of which they have become distracted from their reading, or are enjoying daydreaming. Male readers, by contrast, were depicted as concentrating on their reading material, or taking a break for contemplation, or looking away for inspiration, rather than in reverie. Arguably, therefore, viewing images of women readers offered appealing opportunities to witness women at moments of reverie.

A particularly significant female lone reading experience, especially in terms of space, is that found in *Jane Eyre*, where Jane steals away from the drawing room into the breakfast room and hides herself away in a window seat, with a curtain drawn around her, to read Bewick's *History of British Birds*. Jane's reading position is marginal, in that it is on the outskirts of the patriarchal Reed drawing room (Jane is reminded that, as a 'dependant', she has no right to touch the Reed family books),[42] but what is most striking about this scene is that Jane makes her reading space into one of power and vision. The act of reading is instrumental in establishing Jane's capacity to imagine an alternative existence for herself and is a scarce source of relative happiness during her painful childhood. For Jane, reading was an activity through which she could engage in identification with the imagery presented in her reading material as she lingered over the passages recalling bleak landscapes.[43] As Rachel Rackham notes, Jane is drawn to the 'solitary rocks' and 'dreary space' of the birds.[44] Susan B. Taylor also examines in detail parallels between Bewick's book and the narrative of *Jane Eyre*.[45] In *Feminisms and the Self: The Web of Identity* (1995), Morwena Griffiths suggests that reading involves 'self-identification' and the process of 'being ourselves', which 'has far-reaching consequences affecting private feelings and public spaces'.[46] Similarly, Suzanne Leonard has explored the role of second-wave feminist fiction in encouraging self-awareness in readers.[47] The negotiation of the relationship between the reader's 'self' and the 'other' of the text, to use Lynne Pearce's metaphors about the interactions which take place during reading, was therefore crucial, hence the concern over how women read.[48] For Jane, as for many other readers, the interactions between text and self also involve space and place, as the possibilities offered by imaginative worlds replace, temporarily, the confines of everyday life.

The temporary nature of either the pose or the reading space in the paintings of lone female readers discussed here is testimony to the opportunist nature of women's reading, especially when compared with the many images of male readers seated comfortably in their libraries or studies, exercising a command over the space around them and enjoying more sustainable positions. For example, in James Lobley's *The Demurer* (1873), the books on the bookshelves sit squarely behind the country squire and are aligned to his side of the painting.[49] The comfort of the depicted male readers contrasts with the temporary nature of women's reading activities, resulting from either a self-produced retreat, as with Jane Eyre, or a rare escape from other duties. A striking feature of nineteenth-century texts for women which deal with reading are the numerous constraints placed on not only what a woman should read but at what time of day and under what circumstances. Certainly, reading was sanctioned and even encouraged as part of the daily life of middle-class women, and was structured into their daily schedule. But it is also clear that reading, while acceptable and valuable, should be undertaken only in certain circumstances, and not at the cost of more important duties, such as assisting with household tasks or domestic management. *The Young Ladies' Treasure Book* of 1884, for example, advised of appropriate activities to take place after lunch in the drawing room. These include 'light fancywork or other sociable pursuit which does not forbid conversation', or, if the girl's mother is enjoying a post-prandial sleep, 'the daughter can, with an easy conscience, read a favourite book'.[50] Here the contingent nature of female recreational activities is clear: reading, and even the archetypally female needlework, can be undertaken in a domestic setting, provided the activity does not isolate the young woman or interfere with inter-female familial relationships. Similarly, the same text suggested that if a girl chooses to undertake independent study beyond school age, this is permissible, 'but as it is a duty to herself, it must be subservient to her duty to her mother and those to whom she has to make home as pleasant a place as she can'.[51]

Arguably, the reason for the array of domestic settings in the depictions of readers so far discussed is women's exclusion from the household library. In an 1871 edition of *The Gentleman's House: or, How to Plan English Residences*, Robert Kerr advised that a library should be 'essentially a private retreat . . . for a man of learning', but reluctantly admitted: 'at the same time the ladies are not exactly excluded'.[52] Kerr's figuring of the library as a 'retreat' implies a withdrawal from the domestic space of the house, and the desire to exclude women from the library can be seen as an attempt to uphold gender distinctions between gendered space, whereby women's recreational reading and men's scholarly reading did not coexist in the same room. The household library could be a male sanctuary, a place of retreat from female company. In dealing with the issue of reading spaces, and women's access (or lack of) to those spaces, Kerr's text is representative of key concerns in discourses surrounding women's reading practices in the nineteenth century.

Patricia Okker claims that as the nineteenth century progressed, 'The family-centred sitting room gradually replaced the once masculine home library . . . as the primary site for reading'.[53] During this time, visual and textual sources demonstrate an ongoing dialogue about women's place in the household library. In Robert Edis's *Decoration and Furniture of Town Houses* of 1881 the author advised:

> The library of the house should also be as comfortable as possible, with broad easy chairs, low centre table for books and periodicals, a large pedestal desk with circular revolving top, to shut up all papers and keep them free from dust. This kind of desk I consider invaluable to any man who really uses his library as a work-room, whether it be for real literary work and study, or for the ordinary examination and arrangement of household accounts; . . . this circular-headed desk shuts down at once papers as they lie, which cannot be 'tidied' by the housemaid, who would seem to take a pleasure in putting away papers and notes in all kinds of out-of-the-way corners.[54]

In this account, where the library is naturalised as a masculine space, the only woman mentioned is the officious housemaid, insensitive to the masculine needs of the male library-dweller.

Other critics advised that women of the family should indeed be allowed in the library of the house.⁵⁵ A pictorial representation of women's lack of inclusion in the atmosphere of the library, even when physically permitted into it, can be seen in C. R. Leslie's *The Library at Holland House* of 1838.⁵⁶ This painting depicts Lord Holland and his wife, as well as their librarian and their secretary, in the library of the house.⁵⁷ Lady Holland is the only figure shown not reading or holding a book, document or newspaper, and seems somewhat bored as she stares out of the painting and fans herself. Physically she occupies the library but her presence, unlike that of her male companions, is not naturalised.

A representation of a solitary female reader in the library can be found in J. H. Henshall's *Thoughts* of 1883,⁵⁸ which depicts a young woman in the household library: perching in a temporary position on a stool, as she looks up from her reading to consider her thoughts. The woman's impromptu reading has provoked reverie, which, as already established, is a common trope in visual and literary depictions of the female reader. The woman's act of reading also affords the viewer opportunity to survey her face and body as she faces front but does not challenge our gaze. The makeshift reading position of Henshall's reader, who has found something that arrested her attention during a visit to the library, suggests women's lack of belonging in the household library, contrasting with depictions of men in libraries, who look rooted, comfortable and at ease, seated in heavy wooden furniture. See, for example, W. P. Frith's *Charles Dickens* (1859),⁵⁹ or Helen Allingham's *Alfred Lord Tennyson* (1880).⁶⁰ It is significant that the latter paintings are portraits – images of named, known, individual men, marking further the distinction between abstracted images of femininity, such as Henshall's, and particular men; images of anonymous female readers are common, while images of anonymous male readers are comparatively rare, indicating the visual appeal of scenes of nameless women readers.

Such male inhabitants of the household would have enjoyed unrestricted access to the contents of their libraries and could feel at home in the space. Women's access, on the other hand, was to be monitored and mediated via paternal authority. It is unsurprising, therefore, that a frequent trope in paintings of women in household libraries was illicit reading. In Alexander Rossi's *Forbidden Books* (1897) (Plate 3), six young women are secretly accessing the household library, with books discarded on the floor. One woman rests, indolently and erotically, with her arms raised behind her head, perhaps satiated by her reading. Likewise, in Auguste Toulmouche's *In the*

Library (1869),[61] young women avidly take books down from the bookcase in the household library, again discarding them on the floor when they are no longer of interest. In both paintings, threat of discovery is present: in Rossi's painting the girls are about to be discovered by the figure at the door, while in Toulmouche's scene one of the girls listens for a possible intruder. Both works, therefore, present women's access to certain texts as atypical, the women not knowing how to behave appropriately when accessing household libraries. At the same time, the works are frivolous rather than punitive in tone, the scenes creating an erotic frisson through the threat of discovery, and allowing the viewer a voyeuristic insight to the ways in which unmonitored groups of women might indulge themselves (this is a fantasy specifically about groups of girls; note that Toulmouche's 1872 work of the same title, *In the Library*, represents a much more pensive solo reader).[62] Kate Flint suggests that the sexualisation of the women in Toulmouche's *In the Library* occurs due to the 'inference that what they are reading about is sex',[63] but arguably the women are made the subject of an erotic gaze regardless of the content of their reading, by virtue of their collectivity and their absorption.

The significance in both *Forbidden Books* and *In the Library* of the door as the threshold between the properly masculine but temporarily violated space of the library, and the means by which the women's discovery will be made, serves to reinforce the significance of the gendered space of the library. As Kate Flint notes, both paintings 'employ the convention that there are some books which are habitually kept well out of the reach of young women readers, but that, given half a chance, these same young women will fall enthusiastically upon these very volumes and become engrossed in their contents'.[64] In the case of Toulmouche's painting, this convention is expressed through the use of a step-ladder – a common trope in images of women in the library – to reach otherwise inaccessible volumes. The ladder emblematises the idea of books being otherwise out of reach of women, and unintended for their use. For John Ruskin, the library was an acceptable place for women if its content was monitored:

> if she can have access to a good library of old and classical books, there need be no choosing at all. Keep the modern magazine and novel out of your girl's way: turn her loose into the old library every wet day, and let her alone.[65]

Some scholars, such as Joseph Bristow[66] and Elizabeth Helsinger,[67] have seen Ruskin's comment as representing a permissive attitude towards women's reading. However, arguably, Ruskin's household library is a paternalistic space, with 'modern' texts (magazines and novels) removed and therefore his advice involves a gendering of the library space.

So far, this chapter has considered domestic interior spaces. I wish now to turn our attention to the beach. While this shifts our focus to outdoor spaces, I argue that the beach represents a hybrid space – outside but sharing certain of the tropes of domestic spaces. As Pamela Horn notes,[68] reading at coastal resorts was a common activity, so much so that the chief resorts often featured a circulating library, as can be seen in Thomas Rowlandson's *Summer Amusement at Margate, Or a Peep at the Mermaids* (1815).[69] The extensive advice available to women on reading included conduct while travelling, a situation where women were thought to be particularly vulnerable.[70] Books were recommended as a safeguard for young travelling females, as they could 'shut out the attack of that intolerably sociable stranger'.[71] The idea of reading as a means of protection from strangers was not, however, confined to travelling but rather extended to any situation outside of the home where women did not enjoy the protections of private domestic space. A notable example was excursions to the beach, where the likelihood of encountering strangers, including those from other social classes (unlike in the class-segregated space of the train carriage), was high. C. W. Nicholls's *Courtship on the Beach* (1867)[72] depicts a respectable woman who has stopped reading (her book is Braddon's *Lady Audley's Secret* [1862]) to listen to the advances of a suave young man, but who firmly holds onto her book and remains guarded. The act of interrupting her reading exposes her to danger, emblematised by the exposed petticoat at the foot of her dress. Another painting by the same artist, *A Seaside Romance* (c. 1869),[73] continues the theme of seaside readers. Here, a woman, apparently in mourning, looks up from her reading at two men who look on, one adjusting his spectacles to take a particularly close look. Yet another example of coastal readers is Abraham Solomon's *By the Seaside* (1862), depicting two respectable women on a day out, one of them reading, the other staring into the distance. In this painting no stranger is present, but the reading of the book, together with the guarded pose of the woman, helps to protect her from any possible unwelcome advances.

As with depictions of indoor readers, women reading at the beach were a subject of the male gaze, a gaze pictured within the space of Alexander Rossi's *On the Shores of Bognor Regis* (1887),[74] where a seated woman reads a newspaper, which another woman behind her reads over her shoulder. A man stops behind them to look on, unheeded. It is no accident that it is the reading figures, rather than picnicking figures, he stops to look at. Absorbed in their reading and facing away from him, they are unable to challenge his gaze. Furthermore, as the range of nineteenth-century paintings of women readers discussed here suggests, the erotic and visual appeal of the female reader was strong. A poem by 'Cecil' entitled 'Experientia Doucet' (1862) describes 'flirting' being 'all the go / On sea-side beaches'.[75] An illustration accompanying the poem in *Once a Week* presents familiar themes in images of beach-goers.[76] The ankles of three women at the beach are exposed by the coastal gusts, and the bathing machine acts as a reminder of the promise of semi-clad women. A young lady reads alone, watched by two men behind her. The solitude of the reading figure is highlighted by the groupings of the non-reading female figures at the right of the picture, not watched by the two men.

A painting particularly significant for its depiction of readers in the public space of the beach is William Powell Frith's panoramic *Ramsgate Sands* (1854) (Plate 4). The painting contains an array of figures, both men and women, reading newspapers and books. In the painting, books themselves, as well as the activity of reading, can be seen to act as safeguards against strangers, in the way that contemporary sources recommended, for example in the case of the woman in yellow in the right-hand half of the painting who diligently reads her book. Furthermore, it is significant that where a figure is distracted by the attention of strangers, her reading is temporarily abandoned, as in the case of the lady near the centre of the painting, who had been reading under a green parasol but whose attention is momentarily arrested by the travelling salesman kneeling by the water, demonstrating his mice. Likewise, the woman in black to the right of the salesman has placed her book on the chair in front of her to instead pay attention to the young man next to her. As Caroline Arscott rightly argues, vision is a central theme in the painting.[77] Various motifs in the painting emblematise this theme of vision. For example, several characters use ocular devices, such as a monocle or telescope. Arguably the activity of reading is central to the ocular economy of the painting. The viewer is not able to see the faces of several of the reading characters. For example, the face of the figure reading the newspaper in the left half of the painting is obscured, while the figure next to him or her reads a book but her eyes are hidden from us by her bonnet. Similarly, the woman in yellow on the right side of the painting reads a book but we do not see her head or her face. In the case of the woman in black conversing with the man in the brown suit, the fringe of her parasol is placed exactly to cover her eyes. This obscuring and shrouding of figures within the painting is not explicable within the usual schema of Frith's narrative paintings. His comparable panoramas, for example *The Railway Station* (1862) or *Derby Day* (1856–8), feature clearly depicted faces and figures, intended to be highly readable denotations of character and emotion. *Ramsgate Sands*, with its obscured faces, shrouded heads and overlapping figures, thwarts this attempt at legibility, while the figures themselves engage in a range of ocular activities (reading, not reading, looking, not looking).

Caroline Arscott has persuasively read *Ramsgate Sands* as 'an elaborate commentary on bathing – on the demure aversion or lowering of women's eyes and the surreptitious male voyeurism permissible at the margins of the picture'.[78] She argues that the painting attempts to preserve 'private domestic space within the public crowd' and within 'a situation which offers threats to social boundaries'.[79] While Arscott does not explore the depiction of reading within the scene, the act of reading (or sometimes merely the physical possession of a book) is arguably crucial in these attempts to transport some of the protections of private space into the more fluid space of the beach, where, as Christiana Payne observes, 'social segregation' was not always possible,[80] and where Virginia Richter and Ursula Kluwick suggest that 'incongruent social elements meet and mix'.[81] Indeed, as Kathryn Brown has argued in her study of women reading in French nineteenth-century painting, reading could be a 'form of portable privacy' facilitated by the 'porous nature of boundaries between public spaces and private interiors'.[82] Feminist scholars have contributed to Victorian studies the important notion of 'separate spheres'. While the notion has been much disputed and qualified, the idea of gendered spheres does highlight the significance that the domestic sphere was believed to hold for women and can further our understanding of the 'portable privacy' emblematised by the act of women's reading, evident in *Ramsgate Sands*. Prompted by the *Art Journal*'s description of the central group in *Ramsgate Sands* as being 'remarkable in their exclusiveness', and the assertion that 'at Peckham their garden wall is higher than that of anybody else',[83] Arscott sees the work as transporting domestic space to public outdoor space. Arscott's reading of the relationships between public and private space in *Ramsgate Sands* is persuasive but, arguably, the depicted activity of reading is a crucial motif in the denotation of such spaces and their meanings.

In conclusion, the paintings examined here suggest that both location and space are productive in the construction of meaning and values surrounding women's reading practices in nineteenth-century art and wider culture. As many scholars have shown, spaces, both in and out of the home, were inherently sexualised during the Victorian period. The activity of reading could either contribute to or guard against the sexualisation of space, as in scenes of beach readers. While the activity of reading was seen to carry with it a permanent hazardous potential for women, who were perceived as highly susceptible to the influences of what they read, it could also offer means of both protection and escape.

Notes

I would like to thank Beth Palmer and Liz Mitchell for their reading and comments on this chapter.

1. Kate Flint, *The Woman Reader 1837–1914* (Oxford: Oxford University Press, 1994), p. 102.
2. Janis Bergman-Carton, *The Woman of Ideas in French Art, 1830–1848* (New Haven: Yale University Press, 1995), p. 107.
3. John Ruskin, 'Of Queens' Gardens', in *Sesame and Lilies, The Two Paths and The King of the Golden River* (1864; London: J. M. Dent and Sons, 1953), pp. 49–76.
4. Leah Price, *How to Do Things with Books in Victorian Britain* (Princeton: Princeton University Press, 2012).
5. UK RED (UK Reading Experience Database) is at <https://www.open.ac.uk/Arts/RED/index.html> (last accessed October 2019).
6. Patricia Okker, *Our Sister Editors: Sarah J. Hale and the Tradition of Nineteenth-Century American Women Editors* (Athens: University of Georgia Press, 1995), p. 126.
7. National Gallery of Victoria, Melbourne.
8. Susan Casteras, *Images of Victorian Womanhood in English Art* (Madison: Fairleigh Dickinson University Press, 1987), p. 56.
9. *The Young Ladies' Treasure Book: A Complete Cyclopædia of Practical Instruction and Direction for All Indoor and Outdoor Occupations and Amusements Suitable to Young Ladies* (London: Ward, Lock and Co., 1884), p. 227.
10. Tate Gallery, London.
11. 'Female Influence on Reading', *Library Journal*, 3 (1878), pp. 380–1, quoted in Flint, *The Woman Reader*, p. 41.
12. Casteras, *Images of Victorian Womanhood*, p. 50.
13. Sarah Ellis, *Mothers of England, Mothers of England* (London: Fisher, Son and Co., 1843), p. 39.
14. Matilda Pullan, *Maternal Counsels to a Daughter. Designed to Aid Her in the Care of Her Health, the Improvement of Her Mind, and the*

Cultivation of Her Heart (London: Darton and Co., 1855), p. 52, quoted in Flint, *The Woman Reader*, p. 93.
15. John Tosh, *Manliness and Masculinities in Nineteenth-Century Britain: Essays on Gender, Family, and Empire* (Harlow: Pearson Longman, 2005), p. 134.
16. Ibid., p. 134.
17. 'The Royal Academy', *Art Journal*, 24 (1862), p. 134, quoted in Casteras, *Images of Victorian Womahood*, p. 55.
18. John Tosh, 'Domesticity and Manliness in the Victorian Middle Class: The Family of Edward White Benson', in Michael Roper and John Tosh (eds), *Manful Assertions: Masculinities in Britain Since 1800* (London: Routledge, 1991), pp. 44–73 (p. 50).
19. Tate Gallery, London.
20. 'T. C.', 'Novel Reading: A Letter to a Young Lady', *Christian's Penny Magazine and Friend of the People*, 14 (1859), p. 155, quoted in Flint, *The Woman Reader*, p. 149.
21. For a defence of novels, see 'The Uses of Fiction', *Saturday Review*, 22 (1866), pp. 323–24.
22. Kendall Smaling Wood, 'George Elgar Hicks's Woman's Mission and the Apotheosis of the Domestic', *Tate Papers*, 22 (autumn 2014), available at <https://www.tate.org.uk/research/publications/tate-papers/22/george-elgar-hicks-womans-mission-and-the-apotheosis-of-the-domestic> (accessed 23 August 2018).
23. Gallerie dell'Accademia, Venice. This painting is discussed (and reproduced as Plate 7) by Mary Hammond, 'Reading While Travelling in the Long Nineteenth Century', in Mary Hammond (ed.), *The Edinburgh History of Reading: Modern Readers* (Edinburgh: Edinburgh University Press, 2020), pp. 104–23.
24. John Ruskin, *The Works of John Ruskin*, ed. E. T. Cook and Alexander Wedderburn (London: Longmans, Green and Co., 1903–12), vol. XXVII, pp. 344–5.
25. Ibid., p. 346.
26. Hilary Fraser, *Beauty and Belief: Aesthetics and Religion in Victorian Literature* (Cambridge: Cambridge University Press, 1986), p. 114.
27. Ruskin, *The Works of John Ruskin*, vol. XXVII, p. 343.
28. Musée des Beaux-arts de Lyon.
29. Yale Centre for British Art.
30. The *Athenaeum*, quoted in Lynda Nead, *Myths of Sexuality: Representations of Women in Victorian Britain* (Oxford: Basil Blackwell, 1988), p. 77.
31. Quoted in John Lewis Bradley, 'An Unpublished Ruskin Letter', *Burlington Magazine*, 100:658 (January 1958), pp. 25–6 (p. 25).
32. Birmingham Museum and Art Gallery.
33. 'What Shall We Read?', *Young Woman*, 1 (1892), p. 26, quoted in Flint, *The Woman Reader*, p. 105.

34. Geffrye Museum, London.
35. For example, Lee Christine O'Brien, *The Romance of the Lyric in Nineteenth-Century Women's Poetry: Experiments in Form* (Newark: University of Delaware Press, 2013), p. 28; and Joanna Banham, Sally MacDonald and Julia Porter, *Victorian Interior Style* (London: Studio Editions, 1995), p. 42.
36. Royal Academy of Arts, London.
37. On Jane Eyre's reading see Mark M. Hennelly, Jr, 'Jane Eyre's Reading Lesson', *ELH*, 51:4 (winter 1984), pp. 693–717.
38. Private collection.
39. Kathryn Brown, *Women Readers in French Painting 1870–1890: A Space of the Imagination* (Farnham: Ashgate, 2012).
40. W. R. Greg, 'False Morality of Lady Novelists', *National Review*, 8 (1859), pp. 144–67 (p. 145).
41. George J. Romanes, 'Mental Differences Between Men and Women', *Nineteenth Century*, 21 (1887), pp. 654–72 (p. 659).
42. Charlotte Brontë, *Jane Eyre* (1847; London: Penguin Books, 1994), p. 9.
43. Ibid., p. 10.
44. Rachel Rackham, 'Like a "Caged Bird": Jane Eyre's Flight to Freedom Through Imagery in *Jane Eyre*', *Criterion: A Journal of Literary Criticism*, 10:2 (2017), pp. 85–92 (p. 86).
45. Susan B. Taylor, 'Image and Text in *Jane Eyre*'s Avian Vignettes and Bewick's *History of British Birds*', *Victorian Newsletter*, 101 (spring 2002), pp. 5–12.
46. Morwena Griffiths, *Feminisms and the Self: The Web of Identity* (London: Routledge, 1995), p. 2.
47. Suzanne Leonard, '"I really must be an Emma Bovary": Female Literacy and Adultery in Feminist Fiction', *Genders*, 51 (2010). Also see Flint, *The Woman Reader*, on identification and reading.
48. Lynne Pearce, *Feminism and the Politics of Reading* (London: Arnold, 1997), p. 17.
49. Private collection.
50. *The Young Ladies' Treasure Book*, p. 151.
51. Ibid.
52. Robert Kerr, *The Gentleman's House: or, How to Plan English Residences from the Parsonage to the Palace*, 3rd edition (London: J. Murray, 1871), pp. 118, 116.
53. Okker, *Our Sister Editors*, p. 111.
54. Robert W. Edis, *Decoration and Furniture of Town Houses: A Series of Cantor Lectures Delivered Before the Society of Arts, 1880, Amplified and Enlarged* (London: C. Kegan Paul and Co., 1881), p. 188.
55. Jane Panton, *A Gentlewoman's Home: The Whole Art of Building, Furnishing, and Beautifying the Home* (London: Gentlewoman Offices, 1896), pp. 220–24, quoted in Flint, *Woman Reader*, p. 103.
56. Private collection.

57. Graham Reynolds, *Painters of the Victorian Scene* (London: B. T. Batsford, 1953), p. 50.
58. Private collection.
59. Victoria and Albert Museum, London.
60. Private collection.
61. Private collection.
62. Private collection.
63. Flint, *The Woman Reader*, p. 253.
64. Ibid., p. 253.
65. Ruskin, 'Of Queens' Gardens', p. 66.
66. Joseph Bristow, 'Coventry Patmore and the Womanly Mission of the Mid-Victorian Poet', in Andrew H. Miller and James Eli Adams (eds), *Sexualities in Victorian Britain* (Bloomington: Indiana University Press, 1996), pp. 118–39 (p. 126).
67. Elizabeth Helsinger, 'Authority, Desire, and the Pleasures of Reading', in Deborah Epstein Nord (ed.), *Sesame and Lilies* (New Haven: Yale University Press, 2002), pp. 113–41 (p. 124).
68. Pamela Horn, *Pleasures and Pastimes in Victorian Britain* (Stroud: Sutton Publishing, 1999), p. 125.
69. Royal Collection.
70. Hammond, 'Reading While Travelling in the Long Nineteenth Century'.
71. Charles Allston Collins, 'Our Audience', *Macmillan's Magazine*, 8 (May–October 1863), p. 164.
72. Scarborough Art Gallery.
73. Private collection.
74. Private collection.
75. Cecil, 'Experientia Doucet', *Once a Week*, 22 March 1862, p. 364.
76. The picture is by Hablot Knight Browne (Phiz), and can be seen at the Database of Mid-Victorian Illustration <https://www.dmvi.org.uk/details.php?type=creator&idcreator=263&offset=1&refOffset=0&refView=listview> (accessed June 2019).
77. Caroline Arscott, '*Ramsgate Sands*, Modern Life, and the Shoring-Up of Narrative', in Brian Allen (ed.), *Towards a Modern Art World* (New Haven: Yale University Press, 1995), pp. 157–68 (p. 162).
78. Ibid.
79. Ibid.
80. Christiana Payne, *Where the Sea Meets Land: Artists on the Coast in Nineteenth-Century Britain* (Bristol: Sansom, 2007), p. 93.
81. Virginia Richter and Ursula Kluwick, '"Twixt Land and Sea: Approaches to Littoral Studies', in Virginia Richter and Ursula Kluwick (eds), *The Beach in Anglophone Literatures and Cultures: Reading Littoral Space* (Farnham: Ashgate, 2015), pp. 1–20 (p. 9).
82. Brown, *Women Readers*, p. 32.
83. 'The Royal Academy', p. 161.

Chapter 6

Asian Classic Literature and the English General Reader, 1845–1915

Alexander Bubb

On 9 January 1886, the banker and Liberal MP Sir John Lubbock gave a lecture at the Working Men's College in Great Ormond Street, London. His objective was to advise the College's students on what reading to prioritise in their limited leisure hours. Lubbock had entered Parliament in the very same month that the Elementary Education Act was introduced – February 1870 – and it would hardly have escaped his attention that among his audience were members of the first generation to benefit from the Act's provisions. How the newly literate classes might be led away from the dangerous (Paine's *Rights of Man*) and the sensational (the *Illustrated Police News*), and guided towards the morally and politically uplifting, was a question that had troubled their social betters throughout the nineteenth century. Lubbock's view was that this socialising process would best be effected through exposure to all that was most excellent in culture and philosophy, in contrast to the evangelical-cum-utilitarian mind-set that had prevailed earlier in the century, and that had regarded imaginative literature as a pernicious distraction from the working man's proper occupation of studying pious tracts and acquiring 'useful knowledge'.[1] Lubbock was by no means the only proponent of sweetness and light, and the books he recommended would likely have passed without wider comment had it not been for the manner in which he laid them before his public, in the form of a list: not merely 100 good books, but the 100 *best* books – or, to use Lubbock's own phrase, those books 'most worth reading'.

Lubbock's list has chiefly been remembered for the mockery, criticism and controversy it provoked (a controversy fixed initially on his surprising omission of the Bible), and for the series of rival lists promulgated in subsequent years by Frederic Harrison, William Morris, Lord Acton, Clement King Shorter and others.[2] Reviewing it today, what is remarkable is Lubbock's diverse, even cosmopolitan selection, and the universal application of his didactic purpose – something the middle-class daily which publicised the list, the *Pall Mall Gazette*, picked up on when it titled its report on 11 January 'Sir John Lubbock's Liberal Education'. Lubbock intended his choices to be representative of human achievement across cultures, and by giving them the status of a canon, he was hazarding the implication that anyone who aspired to consider themselves an educated person – whether they be a self-improving mechanic of the Working Men's College or an Oxford undergraduate – should emulate the seriousness and catholicity of taste his list upheld.

Those with the means, but not the time or inclination, to have yet sampled every dish in Lubbock's banquet of knowledge were somewhat abashed. And that portion of the feast where they may have felt themselves quite as much, if not even more, at a loss than Lubbock's working-class audience was the oriental buffet. 'There are in your list about a dozen books which I humbly confess', wrote Lord Iddesleigh, 'to not having read myself, – Marcus Aurelius, Epictetus (barely glanced at once or twice), Confucius, Spinoza, Wake, Mahabharata, Ramayama [sic], Shahnameh; and I am afraid I must add Miss Martineau's two books'.[3] John Ruskin was more violent and openly satirical in his reaction, posting to the *Pall Mall Gazette* a vandalised copy of Lubbock's list in which he had brutally scored through the sections on 'Eastern Poetry', 'Non-Christian Moralists' and 'Philosophy' (sparing only Sir Francis Bacon) and erased every text of an Asian origin with the sole exception of the *Arabian Nights*.[4] Indeed, besides Lubbock's tactless omission of the Bible, the greatest source of reproach and debate were these items drawn from the scripture or classical literature of India, Persia, China and the Middle East. In the original list, they numbered seven: the Qur'an, the *Arabian Nights*, three epic poems (the *Shahnameh* from Persian, and the *Ramayana* and *Mahabharata* from Sanskrit), the *Analects* of Confucius and the *Shijing* or *Classic of Poetry*, a canonical Chinese anthology compiled between the eleventh and seventh centuries BC. When Lubbock revised his list in February 1886 for the *Contemporary Review*, he made space for the Bible but stood by his oriental selection, adding St-Hilaire's *Le Bouddha et sa Religion* (intended perhaps as a substitute for actual Buddhist scriptures, only a fraction of which had at that time been translated into English). A further addition, the ancient Sanskrit drama *Sakuntala*, appeared when the list was published in Lubbock's self-help manual *The Pleasures of Life* (1887) – or, to be exact, it features from the 1890 edition (remarkably, already the twentieth) onwards. Moreover, Lubbock explicitly defended his position in a new preface written for that landmark edition:

> The Ramayana and Mahabharata, and St. Hilaire's Buddha, are not only very interesting in themselves, but very important in reference to our great oriental Empire. Kalidasa's Sakoontala is generally regarded as the gem of the Hindoo Drama, and the Shahnameh is the great Persian Epic. Of the Koran, I suggest portions only. We must remember that 150,000,000 of men regard it not merely as the best of books, but as an actual inspiration. Surely, then, it could not have been excluded.[5]

Lubbock's list made two normative presumptions of its audience: as it neared full literacy, the British public would – or should – aspire to educate itself universally in a standard canon of worthy texts; and being an imperial public, it either was, or else *should become*, interested in the literature of Asia. Implicit in these two norms is a third expectation: that those books of Asia 'most worth reading' should be made available in English translation to all readers irrespective of prior knowledge or financial means. As already mentioned, Lubbock was obliged to nominate a history of Buddhism (and a French one, at that) in the absence of genuine Buddhist scriptures, while for the Hindu epics he recommended the synopses given in J. Talboys Wheeler's *History of India*. The *Mahabharata* in 1886 was available only in abridgement, while R. T. H. Griffith's five-volume *Rámáyan of Válmíki* retailed at 18s per volume.[6] Where exactly were his impecunious clerks and mechanics – let alone bankers and peers – to buy or borrow these poems? This problem touches directly on the task for historians of books and reading, and brings us to the questions for this chapter: what Asian texts were available in Lubbock's time, and were they usable by readers with no specialist training? What motivated them to read these books, what texts did they favour over others, and what benefit did they derive from them? And above all, how large really was the orientophile public that Lubbock seems to imagine?

Asian texts in the nineteenth-century marketplace

Of the overall volume of English translations made from Asian languages in the nineteenth century, Persian accounts for much the largest share. John D. Yohannan spent his career illuminating the influence of its poetry on writers from Byron to Basil Bunting, and his *Persian Poetry in England and America* (1977),[7] along with the work of Hasan Javadi (1987),[8] are the first points of reference for investigators in this area. Other languages have been treated less comprehensively, with research focusing instead on particular texts like the *Arabian Nights*[9] or specific instances of linguistic encounter such as Ezra Pound's engagement with Chinese.[10] Biographies have also appeared of several orientalists, including William Jones[11] and James Legge.[12] One finds these sometimes in danger of heroising their subjects, but they have highlighted how individual dispositions and motives govern translation activity as much as the larger colonial project, analysed first by Edward Said and more recently by Tejaswini Niranjana,[13] to study, categorise and – for a variety of reasons not necessarily malign – appropriate Asian culture.

Existing scholarship on orientalism has thus generally focused on the imperial forces and the developments in European thought (the Enlightenment, Romanticism) driving it, and its influence on a small number of writers and intellectuals. Less attention has been given to the dissemination and consumption of translations among the wider public, and the place they occupied in the Victorian literary economy. Today, a reader can enter any large bookstore and walk out with a copy of the *Ramayana* or *Mahabharata* in Penguin Classics. If he or she wishes to make deeper forays into Sanskrit literature, the same series will afford him or her the *Hitopadesha*, *Panchatantra* or *Baital Pachisi* at no great cost. The aspiring Buddhist will find the *Jatakas* and *Dhammapada*, while a Persian enthusiast may enjoy most of that language's classic poetry – though most of these texts will not be readily found on the shelves, and will have to be ordered in. In late nineteenth-century Britain and America, the book market could not adequately satisfy all these wants. But it could offer some things that even Amazon cannot. Firstly, it was considerably easier to obtain Asian texts in their original languages, by writing directly to specialist firms like the publisher Nicholas Trübner of Ludgate Hill, London. In its heyday that firm put out a bimonthly *American and Oriental Literary Record* advertising new items in stock: a customer who had consulted, for example, the issues for March and May 1889 could ask to have posted to him or her books printed in Arabic, Persian, Sanskrit, Urdu, Hindi, Bengali, Marathi, Gujarati, Kannada, Malayalam, Tamil, Telugu, Burmese, Japanese and Armenian. The clientele for these titles would principally have consisted of those who had some professional investment in those languages: orientalists, pioneers of comparative mythology, missionaries and colonial administrators. But the *Literary Record* was a hunting ground too for bibliophiles, Indians and other expatriates living in Britain, and that small but remarkable class of readers who, for various personal reasons, decided to teach themselves Asian languages (notably the dialect poet William Barnes, who studied Persian for decades in the privacy of his Dorset rectory).[14]

Turning to translations, while a greater range is available today than at any other point in history, the visibility of certain texts in the nineteenth century was dramatically enhanced. By 1900, the *Rubáiyát* attributed to the medieval Persian astronomer Omar Khayyám had circulated in millions of copies, bearing the names of over a dozen different translators into English (not to mention a babel of other languages, ranging from Afrikaans to Yiddish).[15] Conversely, many other texts were comparatively invisible. The systems that create demand for and availability of books were, for oriental translations at least, much more asymmetric than they are now, as well as less settled and static. Today, academics are more numerous and in firmer consensus about the worth of various texts. Degree courses in Asian languages are fully established, and reading lists guarantee that the must-reads stay in print. In contrast, what Victorians could obtain, or obtain affordably, in their marketplace was subject to inconstant factors and – to an appreciable extent – to public demand (whether real or anticipated). Government subsidy, a bulk order from a missionary society, an ambitious publisher snapping up an expiring copyright or the enthusiasm of a prominent literary figure were all circumstances that could lead to the proliferation of a text among one or two generations of readers, before an equally rapid eclipse. Thus, certain texts that loomed perceptibly on the horizon of many people's cultural knowledge in the nineteenth century are practically unheard of in general conversation today. The unhappy browser on amazon.co.uk searching for an up-to-date version of the episode of the lovers Salaman and Absal from Jami's *Haft Awrang* (*Seven Thrones*), or the fables in Kashefi's *Anvār-i Suhaylī* (*Lights of Canopus*), will find only print-to-order paperbacks of the translations made from Persian in the 1850s by Edward Fitzgerald and Edward Eastwick.[16] Though they may be obscure now, both are texts that could have been found on the shelves of educated Victorians.

The great bibliophile Lord Amherst kept a copy of the *Anvār-i Suhaylī* in his library at Didlington Hall,[17] while the doctor G. F. Rogers (whose books are now at Newnham College in Cambridge) preferred the eccentric paraphrase made by Lafcadio Hearn in *Stray Leaves from Strange Literatures* (1884).[18] I have in my own collection a copy of Fitzgerald's *Salámán and Ábsál* (bundled with the fourth, 1879 edition of his *Rubáiyát of Omar Khayyám*), which was formerly owned and annotated by the Radical statesman John Bright.

For both these reasons – the availability of source-language documents, and the turbulence and eccentricity of the translation market – the Western consumer of oriental literature would, in some ways, have been better served by the bookshops of Trübner's era than by their modern-day equivalent. And here one final contrast with the present is worth noting: genres which today would be stocked only by specialised retailers were then available generally. In London, a reader wanting the *Jataka* in Pali in 1889 may have gone to Bernard Quaritch, a bookseller in Piccadilly whose shop stocked a wide range of translated literature, and paid twenty-eight shillings for it. Or she could have had a used copy for five shillings from Jesse Salisbury in the Gray's Inn Road. As early as 1847, Henry G. Bohn in York Street, Covent Garden, had a good range of Arabic, Persian, Sanskrit and Hebrew books, running to some 200 titles. In the fashionable West End, F. Horncastle of the Burlington Arcade was offering more than 100 books printed in Arabic, Turkish, Hebrew, Syriac, Chinese, Armenian, Bengali and 'Laplandish', while at his bankruptcy in 1851 the nearby premises of Alexander Black were found to contain a German translation of *Sakuntala*, and an Arabic text of the sixth-century poet 'Antar' printed at Paris in 1841. Even in rural England, local booksellers sold off obsolete texts at discounted prices. In Saffron Walden in 1907, P. M. Barnard advertised a copy of Stanislas Julien's French translation of the Yuan Dynasty verse drama *The Chalk Circle* from 1832, at two shillings and sixpence, and an ancient copy of the 'Odes of Hafey' (read Hafez) at two shillings.[19]

Scholarly versus popular translations

The great historical tide that, when it ebbed, left *The Chalk Circle* washed up in an Essex bargain bin was of course European imperialism. For the English-speaking world, the chief locus for translation activity was colonial India. From Calcutta especially – where Sir William Jones founded the Asiatic Society in 1784 – officials of the East India Company turned out grammars and dictionaries for Persian, Sanskrit, Arabic and a variety of modern Indian vernaculars, along with a representative selection of literary translations to serve as aids in learning these tongues. Joseph Champion gave English readers a first, much abridged, version of Firdausi's *Shahnameh* (the Persian *Epic of Kings*) in the style of Pope's *Iliad*, while his contemporary Francis Gladwin authored a reliable version of Sadi's *Gulistan* (*Rose Garden*), a collection of didactic stories that later found favour with Emerson and the American Transcendentalists.[20] Jones himself first brought to English notice Kalidasa's *Sakuntala* (from the Sanskrit), the *Muʻallaqāt* (seven Arabic odes that were supposedly hung on the

Kaaba in pre-Islamic times) and the great Persian lyricist Hafez. The last was introduced in the form of his famous and much-imitated couplet on the Shirazi Turk, for a mole on whose cheek the poet offered to exchange all the riches of Samarkand and Bokhara. Unexpectedly, the earliest English translations of the Confucian classics were also made in Bengal, although the instrumental figure in Sinology would be the missionary James Legge, who laboured in Hong Kong through the middle decades of the nineteenth century on his versions of the *Analects*, *Classic of Poetry*, *Classic of History* and other texts. Japan, closed to prying Westerners for so long, had the last major literature to be interpreted, beginning with the *Japanese Odes* (1866) and *Chiushingura* (1876) of F. V. Dickins. It is crucial to appreciate, however, that European notions of East Asian literature were at this stage heavily skewed towards antiquity.[21] The eighth-century Tang Dynasty poets like Li Po and Du Fu, whose names are now common currency in the West, began to enter the general frame of reference only in the 1910s, while most of the classic 'novels' (such as the *Tale of Genji* from medieval Japan and the sixteenth-century *Journey to the West* from China) would not be properly appreciated until the advent of Arthur Waley's still-popular versions between 1925 and 1942.

The bulk of these pioneer translations were never intended seriously as commercial propositions, except as textbooks. Many were subsidised by the Oriental Translation Fund, set up in London in 1828. Nevertheless, they would become a ready quarry for the authors of popular translations and anthologies, intended for general readers – many of which were produced with no reference to the source text, but rather by paraphrasing existing versions in English, French or German. For the sales-minded men and women who projected these books, the guiding star was ultimately the *Arabian Nights*, which had entered English literature from the French of Antoine Galland in the early eighteenth century. Unauthorised 'Grub Street' translations of Galland ensured the *Nights* a special status in English reading culture long before the first Arabic-to-English version appeared in 1838,[22] by which point the tales already formed part of the furniture of every affluent (and many working-class) English child's imagination. They were enjoyed as fervently by Alfred Tennyson and Walter Bagehot as by the dyer's son and future Chartist Thomas Cooper, who borrowed the 'enchanting' collection in the late 1810s from the circulating library run by Mrs Trevor, a stationer at Gainsborough in Lincolnshire.[23]

The popularity of the *Nights* encouraged publishers to support a range of analogous ventures. The editor of *Tales of the East*, brought out by Ballantyne of Edinburgh in 1812, ransacked the work of out-of-copyright European orientalists to fill his three volumes. Anything answering to the description 'popular romance' was admissible, including Alexander Dow's version of a Persian textbook used by the Mughal nobility, the *Bahar-i-Danish* – one story from which gave Thomas Moore the scenario for his 1817 *Lalla Rookh*. In a period when taxation and paper costs kept the price of new works of literature relatively high, oriental *rechauffés* made economic sense, whether in book form or in sixpenny number publications like *The Library of Romance* and *The Story-Teller*, which carried both *Nights*-style tales and *caizi jiaren* (scholar and beauty) stories popular in Ming and Qing China.[24] Publications like these catered to, and in their turn bolstered, a fabular notion of Asia, and the general reception of more 'serious' genres was slower to develop. But if the taste for exotic fiction persisted through the nineteenth century and beyond, the reading public was also influenced by the priority given in Victorian translation discourse to poetry, as the form of writing that most candidly represents a foreign nation's culture and characteristics.[25] In the field of Asian languages, the poetry of Persia was the first to achieve general recognition in Britain and America. Byron, Shelley, Southey, Leigh Hunt and their Romantic peers all eagerly digested William Jones, though, as Yohannan was at pains to point out, only Moore made any serious effort at study, and the so-called Persian vogue of these years was more successful at introducing common tropes (such as the nightingale's love for the rose) into the British frame of cultural reference than any firm textual knowledge.[26] The various editions of Hafez, for example, published in this period were all intended more or less as cribs and were not targeted at the general public. Romantic 'oriental' fantasies like *Lalla Rookh*, however, did prepare readers for what was to follow, and it was a young friend and admirer of Moore who marked an unacknowledged epoch in 1845 by publishing a book titled *The Rose Garden of Persia*.

Louisa Stuart Costello (1799–1870) was the impecunious orphan of an Irish army officer who was obliged to support herself by her pen. Her knowledge of French and German opened to her the pages of continental scholars like Garcin de Tassy and Joseph von Hammer-Purgstall, and while completely untrained in Persian she tentatively asked the orientalist H. H. Wilson to check the spelling of the couplet of Hafez that appears on her title page. The book, she explained to him, 'gives biographies and specimens of Persian poets, merely for the English reader, but I think a great Oriental scholar like yourself will not disdain the attempt to do honour to his favourites, even though the unskilful should presume to do so'.[27] Selecting short excerpts that she judged most likely to appeal, Costello edited and rewrote her material (sometimes turning prose into verse), ordered her extracts by poet and subject (e.g. 'On True Worth', 'In Praise of Wine') and added light-touch historical context and explanatory notes. The resulting volume is, in three respects, exemplary of the Victorian popular translation: it is conceived wholly for the general public and was taken up by a mainstream press; it is appealingly ornamented, with arabesque designs created by Costello's brother Dudley; and it is consciously representative, offering its reader not the haphazard harvest of *Tales of the East*, but a cohort of sixteen major poets that gives a superficial but effective crash course in the Persian literary canon.

The Rose Garden was ahead of its time, at least in respect to the economics of book production in the 1840s. In its first year it sold 517 copies, at 12s.9d, but by 1848 it must have become apparent to Longman & Co. that at that price it could only ever have a limited public, and the remaining stock was disposed of cheaply to the bookseller Henry Bohn.[28] General readers, it must be remembered, were not necessarily poor ones, and indeed several of the noted popular translations of the period were conceived as art books for wealthy non-experts and bibliophiles. But if it is difficult to credit Costello with direct influence, her book set a number of precedents for succeeding decades. Productions like W. A. Clouston's *Arabian Poetry for English Readers* (1881) and Samuel Robinson's *Persian Poetry for English Readers* (1883) encapsulate in their titles the project to make accessible to educated people a representative sample of a foreign canon of writing. Illustration was used to great effect in Richard Burton's *Vikram and the Vampire* (1870), also published by Longman (and a very free adaptation of the exploits of the Indian hero Vikramaditya), and in A. B. Mitford's *Tales of Old Japan* (1871). And the oriental anthology format was taken up by a trio of American Unitarians – William Rounseville Alger, Moncure Conway and Charles D. B. Mills – to create ecumenical digests that juxtaposed texts from various languages to demonstrate the unity of religious traditions.[29]

By the time Lubbock's list of 100 books was publicised in 1886, the various strands making up the weave of Victorian oriental translation are much more plainly visible. In her *Epic of Kings* (1882), a redacted retelling of the *Shahnameh*, Helen Zimmern had candidly excused her ignorance of Persian by explaining that it had been her goal not to translate, but 'to popularize the tales told by the Persian poet Firdusi [sic] in his immortal epic'.[30] In 1886 her work went into a second edition, retitled *Heroic Tales* and adapted specially for children. Not only was the populariser now a defined role: professional scholars, too, were now more alive to the lay audience. The Cambridge don E. J. W. Gibb, who targeted his publications at what he called 'the non-orientalist reader',[31] brought out a rendition of the Turkish romance *The History of the Forty Vezirs* in the same year, while in 1887 the elderly Oxford Professor of Sanskrit, Monier Monier-Williams, succeeded in reissuing his old academic translations with the mainstream press of John Murray. His new edition of *Sakuntala* is likely to have prompted Lubbock's inclusion of the Indian play in his revised list.

From the 1880s onwards, consumers enjoyed increased choice as translators competed with one another, or reinterpreted major texts to serve alternative functions. Serious readers of the Qur'an, for example, could now benefit from the objectivity of E. H. Palmer instead of putting up with the supercilious J. M. Rodwell, a mid-century clergyman who seems to have translated the holy revelation mainly in order to discredit it. Another symptom of this diversification was Richard Burton, whose erotic, ribald retelling of the *Arabian Nights* (1885–8), loaded with anthropological observations and circulated only to subscribers, represents an attempt to reclaim the text for a privileged coterie.

Fittingly, 1887 also saw the reappearance of Costello's *Rose Garden of Persia*, from the press of George Bell and Sons, at seven shillings and sixpence. In 1899, another publisher would issue it in 18mo at five shillings, and by 1911 it would be available at one and six. Finally, the anthology was priced and sized for the pocket of the clerk or even workman, and not destined only for the library of the moneyed dilettante. By this point the *Rose Garden* was, admittedly, obsolete technology. Indeed, excepting the works of Edwin Arnold – by far the most commercially successful oriental populariser of the era – the cheapest bracket of translation in the 1880s and 1890s exclusively comprised reprints of the stodgy prose and heroic couplets characteristic of the early decades of the century. Perhaps for this reason, in 1905 the editors of John Murray's new 'Wisdom of the East' series determined whenever possible to take up unpublished translations or to commission new ones – and met with considerable success. The ledgers in the Murray archive prove the existence, at least by the Edwardian period, of a sizeable readership for such offerings as a two-shilling *Sayings of Confucius* (3,811 copies sold in its first ten years) or a one-shilling *Gulistan* of Sadi (2,817 sold in its first five).[32]

So far, then, we have our macro-data: we know what texts from the canonical literatures of Asia were available, and where they could be bought, and we can perceive our readers – Lubbock's imagined public – in the lump. What, then, of individual choice and experience, the activities of readers and their contribution to the overall development of taste?

Readerly traces: the evidence of commonplace books and annotated copies

Like many nineteenth-century readers, Charlotte Robinson, living at Hull in Yorkshire, kept a commonplace book in which she recorded affecting passages of poetry and scripture, and to which a number of friends – known only by their initials – have added mementoes and sketches. Leafing through its pages, one finds a sketch of a Gothic ruin, Matthew's Gospel, an extract from the *Christian Minister*, an acrostic and some original verses on the death in childbirth of Princess Charlotte in 1821. Later on comes some conventional oriental imagery: birds and gazelles in *Lalla Rookh*, and Byron's Assyrian coming down like a wolf on the fold in 'The Destruction of Sennacherib'. Then, on 29 April 1824, 'J.M.' has inserted eight neat lines of Tamil – a dialogue, as the translation beneath it indicates, between a Hindu pandit and a Christian. The contributor may have acquired the language in the Madras Civil Service, or perhaps it was conned from a textbook, after the manner of Jane Eyre and St John Rivers preparing for their Indian ministry. In any case, what may appear initially to be a mere curio in fact palpably illustrates the propagation of oriental letters, even in regional England, via the imperial connection.[33]

Along with official surveys, diaries, autobiographies and marginal annotations, commonplace books were one of the major sources that historians of reading turned to in the 1990s in order, as Stephen Colclough put it, to 'introduce some empirical depth to the theoretical speculation' that then dominated their field.[34] As Colclough points out, a significant drawback of commonplace books is that they do not provide an index of everything their keepers read, but only the choice 'beauties' that they took the trouble to transcribe. Their contents may also tend to represent books that were borrowed, rather than books – possibly important ones – that were purchased and annotated (this was the view of J. T. Hackett, expressed in the prefatory matter to his own published commonplace book,[35] which went through several editions in the 1920s). On the other hand, as Colclough remarks, they are revealing of the 'diversity of reading strategies' that can be employed by one individual for 'diverse genres' of writing, and this quality is helpful for the study of a niche (or not so niche) interest like oriental literature in the nineteenth century.[36] I find that commonplace books afford me a combination of large-scale statistical data as well as evidence of the particular reading practices of individuals and, sometimes, communities of readers. In a survey of eighty-five manuscript books, covering the years 1845 to 1915, I found thirty-six to contain at least one quotation – either in the original or in translation – from Asian literature, philosophy, scripture or proverb. Furthermore, the frequency of occurrence can be seen to rise noticeably across the period. The books represent eighty-five individual readers with no professional or other obvious investment in Asia and its languages, and were consulted in twelve research libraries (four in Britain, two in Ireland, five in the United States and one in Australia). Medical or legal commonplace books and suchlike were not included, but only books primarily dedicated to literature. I also excluded items created by residents of India or other parts of Asia, to prevent these readers' increased exposure to indigenous literary culture (or, perhaps, their prejudice against it) from distorting my results. A word on the Talmud: in my data, it is considered 'Asian literature', but not the Bible, unless (as in one instance) a reader was engaging with the original Hebrew.

Colclough remarks on the interesting mixture of quotations one often discovers in Victorian commonplace books. He does not go into the issue, however, of whether readers are deliberately assembling texts on the facing pages of their albums for the purpose of comparison – a supposition which it is nearly always impossible to prove, but which it may be useful to bear in mind when examining readers with multilingual interests. Incongruous juxtapositions, like that seen in the case of Charlotte Robinson of Hull, certainly abound in my sources and demonstrate the multiple paths that readers of the era were capable of pursuing simultaneously. While a student at Harvard in the late 1870s, the future English professor George Lyman Kittredge patiently compiled a list of oaths and insults culled from *The Shoemaker's Holiday*, *The Knight of the Burning Pestle* and seemingly every Jacobean play in existence. But he also somehow got hold of, almost as soon as it was issued, Part 1 of James Darmesteter's *Zend-Avesta*, the Zoroastrian scripture that constituted the fourth of Oxford University Press's fifty-volume 'Sacred Books of the East'. Particularly interesting to him was the Chinvat Bridge, which the living must cross to enter the realm of the dead, and which, as Kittredge notes, reappears in Islamic tradition.[37] Other juxtapositions, if still perhaps incongruous, are nonetheless deliberate and suggest the analogies that note-keepers may have been drawing between texts far apart in time or place of origin. In the middle of the century, the French governess Amélina Petit de Billier wrote out part of the Spider Surah from 'Le Koran', which urges the faithful not to quarrel with their fellow monotheists the Jews and Christians. The Almighty, it adds, will erase our sectarian differences on the last day and judge us according to our good or ill deeds ('tous les hommes retournent à Dieu'). In the same spirit of humility, she chose on her journal's facing page to copy Southey's 'Imitated from the Persian', a paraphrase of a twelfth-century epigram by Suzani Samarqandi in which the poet, 'a child of dust', offers to God his nothingness, his sins and his contrition.[38] The logic which prompted Lewin Hill's selection is less obvious. An employee of the General Post Office from 1855 to 1898, he grouped on adjacent pages some verses on cleanliness by the Persian mystic Rumi, a Hindu myth about the creation of woman and 'The Palanquin Bearers' by the contemporary Indian poet Sarojini Naidu. However, these are all classed under the heading 'Epigrams' and are probably intended to exhibit sententious gems of Eastern wit.[39] As already mentioned, my survey of commonplace books excluded readers in India. But, as might be expected, such items can reveal diverse medleys and genuine, prolonged study. John Whaley Watson, a political agent in Gujarat from the 1860s to the 1880s, was all too fond of the sort of middlebrow verse (Jean Ingelow and C. S. Calverley) that probably aroused in many colonial exiles a nostalgia for 'Home'. But he also quoted Hafez and the *Anvār-i Suhaylī* in the original, and made a stab at translating Catullus into Persian. His selections derive from a characteristically late-Victorian mixture of erudite and popular sources: if he consumed E. H. Palmer's niche exposition of the medieval Cairene calligrapher Baha' al-Din Zuhair from the point of view of a fellow orientalist, he could also enjoy a commercial success like Edwin Arnold's *Indian Song of Songs* (a rendition of the Sanskrit *Gita Govinda*), from which he wrote out seven stanzas.[40]

In many cases, the quotations in the books I examined evidently did not derive from a published translation in a book or periodical. Some were taken second-hand from books of travel or history. In 1848, the Anglo-Irish aristocrat Mary Louisa Talbot recorded a description of Pompey's Pillar at Alexandria given by the twelfth-century traveller and historian Abd al-Latif al-Baghdadi. But while she credits the original author, her actual reference point is *Eastern Life* by Harriet Martineau, who had read the French translation by Silvestre de Sacy.[41] In the case of many shorter quotations, especially aphorisms and nuggets of sage counsel, the source was probably a periodical or even newspaper. This is particularly clear when examining the commonplace-cum-cuttings book of R. FitzGerald, an Irish immigrant in 1850s Melbourne. During those heady gold-rush years, FitzGerald fortified himself with practical wisdom, including Henry Wadsworth Longfellow and Ben Franklin ('time is money'), the speeches of Charles Gavan Duffy, assorted advice on how to get rich, Pope, Cardinal Newman, Bacon, 'Locke on education', doggerel about socialists and remarks on 'The Degeneracy of the British Aristocracy'. One of the pages contains this: 'Learning without thought is labour lost: thought without learning is perilous. – Confucius'.[42] Probably this is connected with the summary, copied above on the same page, of an article in the *Philadelphia Ledger* about the perspicacity of 'Silent Men' – in this case George Washington and Thomas Jefferson. In the era of mass print, the reprintings and recirculations of such extracts can be so frequent as to present a variety of possible routes of transmission. One consequence is an ever-increasing risk of misquotation or misattribution, or a distortion of meaning brought about by the act of reducing a Chinese philosopher to a handful of pithy sayings. A remark on life after death caught the fancy of Lewin Hill – 'if you do well here you will do well there. I could tell you no more if I preached to you for a year' – turns out not to be Confucius at all, as he supposed, but Longfellow's 'Cobbler of Hagenau'![43] Proverbs in particular, often cited simply as 'Chinese Proverb', 'Indian Saying', 'Turkish', 'Burmese', 'Malay' and so on, sometimes reveal themselves as outright counterfeits. Suspect traffic, however, does not detract from the vibrancy of literary exchange in this period. R. FitzGerald also gives an elegiac image from Firdausi about the decay of empire that seems to have done the round of periodicals. In the course of transmission, the poetic form has been disrupted and the original distich expanded to three lines:

> The spider's web is the royal curtain
> in the palace of Caesar; the owl is the
> sentinel in the watch-tower of Afrasiyab.

These phrases originally entered English literature through Gibbon's *Decline and Fall*, which relates an anecdote given by the historian Cantemir about how Mehmet the Conqueror, after storming Constantinople, stood and recited them in the palace of the Byzantine emperors. William Jones gave an analysis of the lines in his *Persian Grammar*; they were in turn adapted by Byron for *The Giaour*, and by Felicia Hemans in her 1849 poem 'The Last Constantine'.[44] Even today, they frequently crop up in novels and popular histories, and are variously attributed to Firdausi, Sadi or – rather improbably – Rumi. Yet in actuality there is no primary source: the lines are simply, as Edward Heron-Allen remarks, a 'constantly recurring illustration of the vanity of earthly glory in Persian *belles-lettres*'.[45] This, we may presume, is just what FitzGerald valued in them, and while it is vital to interrogate the sometimes dubious provenances of oriental apophthegms, this should not lead us to overlook the seriousness of an individual reader's choices or the variety of factors governing them. By looking elsewhere on FitzGerald's crowded page, we may notice that he has grouped the Persian couplet with a passage from Shelley's *Hellas*, in which a latter-day Ottoman emperor challenges a Jewish magician to conjure up the person of his far greater, and more erudite, precursor Mehmet the Conqueror.

The *Arabian Nights* and *Rubáiyát of Omar Khayyám* were the most frequently occurring texts in the commonplace books I consulted, not even counting imitations, homages, parodies and other spin-offs of the reading culture surrounding them. A poem composed by Benjamin Disraeli during the Christmas holidays of 1829 for the enjoyment of his Grosvenor Gate neighbours, the Dawsons, is indicative. Alluding to the comparatively minor 'Story of Blind Baba Abdallah', the poem assumes a thorough familiarity with the *Nights* that would have been quite usual at the time.[46] Allusions to the *Rubáiyát* likewise often needed no gloss. Another Australian, Private D. H. Jude, kept a scrapbook while stationed in Egypt during the Great War, and inserted a picture of the Nile at sunset. By way of commentary, his friend G. E. Swiman added the well worn lines (slightly misremembered and deprived of punctuation):

> A Book of Verses underneath the Bough
> A Loaf of Bread a Jug of Wine & Thou
> Beside me: singing in the Wilderness
> Oh Wilderness were Paradise enow[47]

Reversing the jug and loaf in line 2, Swiman was evidently quoting from memory. But many other soldiers, such as his fellow Australian private Thomas Ambrose Palmer, will have been carrying their own copies of what was probably among the poems most read by English-speaking combatants. As has often been remarked, the war created a huge demand for portable reading matter; and it is suggestive that the Edinburgh firm of Nimmo, Hay and Mitchell, who had introduced the *Rubáiyát* to its Miniature Series in 1907, decided to reissue it in 1914, in time to occupy the pockets of soldiers like

Palmer, who filled the tiny margins of his rain-damaged, 9 cm × 5 cm Nimmo Miniature with annotations.[48] By choosing to do so, the young Anzac was joining a worldwide community of Omarians who diligently added, alongside each of the poem's quatrains, variant renditions by E. H. Whinfield, Justin Huntly McCarthy, Richard Le Gallienne and others – with particular attention paid to the original translator, Edward Fitzgerald, whose text exists in four versions. A teenage Gertrude Stein, for instance, annotated Fitzgerald's verse with McCarthy's prose in her 1890 copy, while the Shakespearian scholar H. H. Furness bound together Fitzgerald's 1868 and 1872 versions and then added his own comparative assessment of each quatrain: 'better', 'much better', 'worse, worse', 'ugh' and so on.[49] I have seen more than a dozen instances of this tradition of Omarian annotation. In Palmer's case, however, the annotations do not contain translational variants but rather quotations from other works, both Asian and European, which Palmer considered allied in theme or sentiment with the text of the *Rubáiyát*. Omar's remarks on the transience of earthly joy and beauty, for instance, find their echo in a lyric from the classical Japanese poet Fun'ya no Yasuhide:

> Fire of the Autumn turns to
> Red & Gold the greenness
> of the leaves before their
> grave receive them
> but for ever pure & cold
> the white foam blossoms
> on the tossing wave.[50]

If many fin-de-siècle readers celebrated Omar Khayyám as a sceptical hedonist, however, Palmer was a member of another sizeable faction, which claimed him as a mystic or Sufistic allegorist and advocate of religious tolerance. Tennyson's 'Akbar's Dream' and an imitation by Rudyard Kipling of the medieval Hindi poet Kabir both strike an ecumenical note suggesting the essential unity of all religions. The comparative framework that Palmer thus sets up is indicative of many readers, especially in the early twentieth century, who harvested cheap translations and theosophical literature to piece together a private agnostic creed. For Jane Norton Morgan, the wife of the great financier, this came principally through a series of lectures given by Protap Chunder Mozoomdar, the leader of the Brahmo Samaj, a reformist organisation founded during the Bengal Renaissance. The oriental anthology of Charles Mills, mentioned earlier, evidently played an important role, too, in widening her perspective, giving her quotations from Sadi and Rumi, which she added to her commonplace book. But as in so many other cases, Omar Khayyám is present too in one of his various guises: in this case the stoical and serene philosopher as imagined by the translator E. H. Whinfield, and transmitted to her by none other than Sir John Lubbock in his *Pleasures of Life*, the book which contained his revised list of 100 texts.[51] Lubbock had consciously resisted calls to include the *Rubáiyát* among them, which is additional proof – if any were needed – that readers independently made use of the growing body of material at their disposal to interpret, assign value and draw diverse texts into a quasi-curricular formation.

Conclusion: birth and death of an oriental canon

It is essential to bear in mind that, though Jane Norton Morgan and Thomas Ambrose Palmer offer examples of readers seriously engaged with foreign literature and thought in its own cultural particularity, they represent a small reading community in comparison with the much vaster public for travelogues and fictions about the mysterious East. Between 1910 and 1912, only one member of the Leeds Library (a long-established subscription library, separate from the city's public library) borrowed Herbert Giles's *History of Chinese Literature*, one of a series of short guidebooks issued by Heinemann covering the major literatures of the world. In that same period, Robert Hichens's 1904 novel *The Garden of Allah*, which features a decadent Algerian poet and abundant local colour, was loaned thirty-one times.[52] Nonetheless, such readers are exemplary representatives of a substantial branch in nineteenth-century literary culture, and evince a marked contrast with reading patterns today, in which the Western consumption of Sanskrit epics, Persian lyrics or even the perennial *Arabian Nights* is dwarfed by that of contemporary novels from Asian countries.

This brings us finally to a discrepancy which is apparent in almost all of the sources I have cited. Before 1900, translations into English of contemporary Asian authors – that is, anyone living later than the eighteenth century – are very rare, and even rarer if we exclude books and periodical articles published only in India. A strong preference operated for the *classic* literature, especially poetry, of Asia, undergirded by an essentialist rationale that such writing encapsulated the ancient and enduring spirit of these nations, and often buttressed too by the assumption that the contemporary cultures of Persia, China and neighbouring countries were but feeble shadows of what they had once been in golden antiquity. This began to change only in the second decade of the twentieth century, when the writing of the 1913 Nobel laureate, Rabindranath Tagore, charges into the general frame of cultural reference. The popularity of *Gitanjali*, a Bengali collection which Tagore, with the help of W. B. Yeats, recreated for the English reader, marks a watershed in reading history. Gradually, the cluster of assumptions and expectations that lay behind the phrase 'Indian literature' or 'Chinese literature' shifted away from the historic greats, many of which receded into the zone of academic study and specialised publishers – though the nineteenth-century pattern for 'crazes' centred on certain authors persisted. The Omarians who flourished in fin-de-siècle Britain and America, or the Hafez clubs that sprung up in 'Silver Age' Russia, made way for the New Age devotees of Rumi.[53] In many ways, this is all to the good. The flawed thinking behind attempts like Sir John Lubbock's to nominate a canon of oriental 'Great Books' is all too clear to us now. But go to the library of the Working Men's College today, and take down its copy of William Jennings's *Confucian Analects* (a cheap edition issued, along with the other ninety-nine of Lubbock's 100 choices, by George Routledge and Sons in the mid-1890s), and you will find tipped between its sheets a tram ticket. Discolouration of the pages caused by the ticket's acidity testifies to its long presence, and at some date up to 1938 – the year when the tramways near the College were removed – we may picture to ourselves an inter-war student riding home and using his ticket to mark the passage in which the Master discourses on 'The Superior Man': 'The superior man is exacting of himself; the common man is exacting of others.'[54] That this 'common' reader, whoever he may have been, sought self-improvement through Chinese philosophy rather than evangelical tracts or Samuel Smiles (though for all we know he may have enjoyed those too) is a phenomenon that surely warrants sustained attention.

Notes

1. Richard D. Altick, *The English Common Reader: A Social History of the Mass Reading Public, 1800–1900*, 2nd edition (Columbus: Ohio State University Press, 1998), p. 132.
2. Philip Waller, *Writers, Readers, and Reputations: Literary Life in Britain, 1870–1918* (Oxford: Oxford University Press, 2006), pp. 68–9.
3. British Library, London, Add MS 49648, Iddesleigh to Sir John Lubbock, 25 November 1885.

4. Reproduced in the pamphlet *The Best Hundred Books, by the Best Judges* (London: Pall Mall Gazette, 1886), p. 7.
5. Reprinted in *The 100 Best Books: Sir John Lubbock's List* (London: Amalgamated Press, 1899), p. 10.
6. 'Trübner & Co.'s New Publications', *Saturday Review*, 37:964 (18 April 1874), p. 516.
7. John D. Yohannan, *Persian Poetry in England and America: A 200 Year History* (Delmar: Caravan Books, 1977).
8. Hasan Javadi, *Persian Literary Influence on English Literature* (1987; Costa Mesa: Mazda, 2005).
9. Peter L. Caracciolo (ed.), *The Arabian Nights in English Literature: Studies in the Reception of the Thousand and One Nights into British Culture* (Basingstoke: Macmillan, 1988); Marina Warner, *Stranger Magic: Charmed States and the Arabian Nights* (London: Vintage, 2012); Paulo Lemos Horta, *Marvellous Thieves: Secret Authors of the Arabian Nights* (Cambridge, MA: Harvard University Press, 2017).
10. Zhaoming Qian, *Orientalism and Modernism: The Legacy of China in Pound and Williams* (Durham: Duke University Press, 1995); Zhaoming Qian (ed.), *Ezra Pound and China* (Ann Arbor: University of Michigan Press, 2003); Ming Xie, *Ezra Pound and the Appropriation of Chinese Poetry: Cathay, Translation and Imagism* (1999; New York: Routledge, 2015).
11. Michael J. Franklin, *Orientalist Jones: Sir William Jones, Poet, Lawyer, and Linguist, 1746–1794* (Oxford: Oxford University Press, 2011).
12. Norman J. Girardot, *The Victorian Translation of China: James Legge's Oriental Pilgrimage* (Berkeley: University of California Press, 2002).
13. Tejaswini Niranjana, *Siting Translation: History, Post-Structuralism and the Colonial Context* (Berkeley: University of California Press, 1992).
14. Lucy Baxter, *The Life of William Barnes, Poet and Philologist* (London: Macmillan, 1887), pp. 24, 153.
15. The figure of two million is given, in 1927, in the preface to a facsimile of the original 1859 edition of Edward Fitzgerald's translation printed by the Omar Khayyám Club.
16. Accessed 28 February 2018.
17. Box 4, Amherst of Hackney Papers, Thomas Fisher Rare Book and Manuscript Library, University of Toronto.
18. Rogers Collection, R H20, Newnham College, Cambridge.
19. The catalogues for Bernard Quaritch (1887), Henry G. Bohn (1847), Jesse Salisbury (1889) and P. M. Barnard (1907), and the catalogues prepared by the auctioneers Puttick and Simpson for the sale of Alexander Black's stock (on 13–17 February 1851) and F. Horncastle's (on 6–7 July 1852), were all consulted at the library of the Grolier Club in New York.
20. See Yohannan, *Persian Poetry*, pp. 24, 113.
21. Peter France (ed.), *The Oxford Guide to Literature in English Translation* (Oxford: Oxford University Press, 2000), pp. 224–5.

22. Horta, *Marvellous Thieves*, p. 91.
23. Roger Ebbatson, 'Knowing the Orient: The Young Tennyson', *Nineteenth-Century Contexts*, 36:2 (2014), pp. 125–34 (p. 125); Walter Bagehot, 'The People of the Arabian Nights', *National Review*, 9:17 (1859), pp. 44–71; Thomas Cooper, *Life of Thomas Cooper* (London: Hodder and Stoughton, 1872), p. 34.
24. Robert Bell (ed.), *The Story-Teller; or, Table-Book of Popular Literature. A Collection of Romances, Short Standard Tales, Traditions, and Poetical Legends of All Nations* (London: Cunningham and Mortimer, May 1843), pp. 110–17.
25. Annmarie Drury, *Translation as Transformation in Victorian Poetry* (Cambridge: Cambridge University Press, 2015), p. 3.
26. Yohannan, *Persian Poetry*, pp. 31–5.
27. British Library, Mss Eur E301/9, Louisa Stuart Costello to H. H. Wilson, 23 February 1845.
28. Reading University, Records of the Longman Group, MS 1393 1/A5, Divide ledger D4 (1844–61), p. 46.
29. Respectively, *Poetry of the East* (1856), the *Sacred Anthology* (1874) and *Pebbles, Pearls and Gems of the Orient* (1882).
30. Helen Zimmern, *Heroic Tales, Retold from Firdusi the Persian*, 3rd edition (London: T. Fisher Unwin, 1891), p. v.
31. E. J. W. Gibb, *Ottoman Poems, Translated into English Verse* (London: Trübner; Glasgow: Wilson and McCormick, 1882), p. 7.
32. National Library of Scotland, Edinburgh, John Murray Archive, Acc. 13328/13, 'Report on Authors of the Wisdom of the East Series'; and MS.42739, Copies Ledger N, 1905–58.
33. Charlotte Robinson's commonplace book (c. 1817–36) is in my own collection.
34. Stephen Colclough, 'Recovering the Reader: Commonplace Books and Diaries as Sources of Reading Experience', *Publishing History*, 44 (January 1998), pp. 5–37 (p. 6).
35. J. T. Hackett, *My Commonplace Book*, 4th edition (London: Macmillan, 1923), p. xiv.
36. Colclough, 'Recovering the Reader', pp. 12–13, 7.
37. Houghton Library, Cambridge, MA, HUC 8878.315, George Lyman Kittredge, Commonplace book 1878–80.
38. Bodleian Library, Oxford, MS WHF Talbot 123, Amélina Petit de Billier, Commonplace book, 1825–74. The attribution to Suzani is made by Javadi, *Persian Literary Influence*, p. 79.
39. Lewin Hill, *Verse, Prose, and Epitaphs from the Commonplace Book of Lewin Hill, C.B.: 1848–1908* (London: Brown Langham, 1920), pp. 21–2. Since Hill's original manuscript book is not extant, it was not included in the aforementioned survey.
40. British Library, Mss Eur F244/3-4, John Whaley Watson, Commonplace books.

41. Bodleian Library, MS Talbot e. 17, Mary Louisa Talbot, Commonplace book 1847–8.
42. State Library of Victoria, MS 12408, R. FitzGerald, Commonplace book titled 'Patch Work'.
43. Hill, *Verse, Prose, and Epitaphs*, p. 77.
44. Javadi, *Persian Literary Influence*, pp. 81–2.
45. Edward Heron-Allen (ed.), *The Rubáiyát of Omar Khayyám, Being a Facsimile of the Manuscript in the Bodleian Library at Oxford* (London: H. S. Nichols, 1898), p. 303. Recent misattributors of the lines include Ken McClellan, in his 2009 novel *The Last Byzantine* (Denver: Outskirts Press), p. 23.
46. Bodleian Library, Dep. Hughenden 203/1, Benjamin Disraeli, Commonplace books 1826–60.
47. State Library of Victoria, MS 11238, Private D. H. Jude, scrapbook of poems, postcards, and photographs, 1914–15.
48. Jane Potter, 'For Country, Conscience and Commerce: Publishers and Publishing, 1914–18', in Mary Hammond and Shafquat Towheed (eds), *Publishing in the First World War: Essays in Book History* (Basingstoke: Palgrave Macmillan, 2007), p. 12; Ambrose George Potter, *A Bibliography of the Rubáiyát of Omar Khayyám* (1929; Hildesheim: Georg Olms, 1994), p. 15.
49. Beinecke Library, New Haven, Za St34 Zz890P; Bryn Mawr College, Pennsylvania, PK6513 A1 1872.
50. State Library of New South Wales, Sydney, Thomas Ambrose Palmer Collection.
51. Morgan Library, ARC 2235–2236, Jane Norton Morgan, Commonplace book 1875–86.
52. Leeds Library, Borrowing ledgers GI 1908–57 and GA 1910–70.
53. John E. Malmstad and Nikolay Bogomolov, *Mikhail Kuzmin: A Life in Art* (Cambridge, MA: Harvard University Press, 1999), p. 104.
54. William Jennings, *The Confucian Analects: A Translation, with Annotations and an Introduction* (London: George Routledge and Sons, Sir John Lubbock's Hundred Books series, 1895), p. 175. I examined the book in 2017 and photographed the tram ticket.

Chapter 7

Readers and Reading During Russia's Literacy Transition, 1850–1950: How Readers Shaped a Great Literature

Jeffrey Brooks

In 2004 I had the opportunity to lecture at Addis Ababa University on the topic 'The Literacy Revolution in Nineteenth-Century Russia'. The students in the auditorium were the country's elite, fluent in several languages and well integrated into global culture through the Internet. They were also thoughtfully reflective on their own country's experience. By happenstance, Ethiopia was then at a stage in the spread of literacy quite comparable to that of late nineteenth-century Russia, with literacy rates of 39 per cent in the overall population and of 55 per cent among young people. After presentation of brief background on the growth in school attendance and literacy in Russia in the decades after Emancipation, I spent most of the lecture on the explosion of printed materials to meet growing demand; changes in the markets for books, pamphlets, and pictures; and interactions between and among the reading publics that developed. My main message was that literacy had fuelled a transformation of Russian literary culture that encompassed high and low culture and all layers in between.

The Ethiopian students discussed at length the absence of such a cultural transformation accompanying their own literacy transition. Newly literate Ethiopians had, according to their telling, very little to read, and little reason to seek out printed materials for recreation, information or religious purpose. Print culture competed with access to radio and televised soccer games, even in remote villages. Educated Ethiopians switched quite early to an international language, usually English, rather than remaining within and enriching the literary cultures of the local languages.

The brief exchange with Ethiopian students reinforced in my mind the special quality and perhaps uniqueness of Russia's literacy transition, coming as it did when the printed word reigned supreme among media, and when the country entered a period of transformative change. The newly literate joined a culture that had separate audiences but a shared language. Educated Russians had an affinity for the French language, but they were not wooed away from their native tongue for cultural interactions. They engaged with an expanding and diversifying Russian literature that made space for new readers. In addition, literacy conveyed agency, and agency mattered in a society undergoing rapid change. Increased geographic, social and occupational mobility created new opportunities, and the literate were advantaged in capturing them.

The Russian reader of common origins in the late nineteenth century, whether from the village or town, thus benefited from a confluence of circumstances that raised the value of reading. Readers appropriated that value and used the associated agency to change their own lives. In the process, they influenced the evolution of Russian culture during a remarkably creative period from the Emancipation in 1861 through the October Revolution in 1917 and extending approximately to Stalin's death in 1953.

By the time of the October Revolution, Russia was just on the cusp of predominant literacy (i.e. more than 50 per cent). Reading publics were well established and interconnected. Readers were sophisticated enough to have mastered different genres and to read for multiple meanings. The Bolshevik cultural leaders transferred literary agency from readers to the state, as decisions about what to publish and for whom shifted from the market to the state and subsequently to the Party. Yet the strength and depth of the inherited literary tradition and the skill of readers at all levels, honed in the give and take of pre-revolutionary culture, precluded complete control by the Party and the state over literature. Writers and readers preserved channels of communication that partially bypassed the strictures and censorship; the flow was tamped and redirected, but not fully thwarted.

Thus, even under Stalin, Russian readers were a potent force in Soviet culture, giving meaning to works over and above the officially approved messaging. They could do so because they were imbued with a tradition in which reading was sustenance for the intellect, and the written word held power.

Primary schooling was never compulsory under the tsars, but even prior to Emancipation some people of common origins proactively sought instruction for their children, often from itinerant teachers. A rush of change commenced with the liberation of 40 million serfs in

1861 and the Great Reforms under Alexander II. Education expanded at every level. The institutions of local government, the *zemstvos*, and the Orthodox Church opened primary schools that offered rival systems of instruction.[1] The Zemstvo Statutes of 1864 and 1874 contributed to the expansion of schooling, especially in rural areas. The number of rural primary schools throughout the Russian Empire rose from fewer than 30,000 in the 1860s to over 100,000 in 1914. The number of primary school teachers in 1914 in European Russia topped 223,000 and over 300,000 in the Empire. The one-room/one-teacher primary school was common throughout the countryside, and hence the number of teachers closely tracked the growing number of schools.

Although educators decried the deficiencies of the pre-revolutionary school system, schooling became widely available in the last half century of the old regime. By the end of the nineteenth century, most children at least darkened the doorway of a school. The estimated likelihood in 1911 that a child aged seven to eleven years would attend but not necessarily finish the first year of schooling was 88 per cent for boys and 52 per cent for girls, and 72 per cent for boys and 41 per cent for girls for the second year.[2] Literacy rates calculated by census and by the testing of new army recruits rose sharply towards the end of the nineteenth century and into the twentieth. Only 21 per cent of the Empire's population was literate according to the 1897 census (29 per cent of men and 13 per cent of women), but male literacy had reached perhaps 40 per cent by 1913 and had increased still further by 1920.[3] Rates among army recruits rose from roughly 10 per cent in the 1860s to nearly 68 per cent in 1913. According to the census of 1920, the literacy rate in European Russia among children aged twelve to sixteen (that is, the last generation to attend school before the revolutions of 1917) was 71 per cent for boys and 52 per cent for girls.[4]

Schools and their small libraries became local repositories of books. Peasant children commonly read aloud to their parents, and parents responded by buying printed material. Schoolteachers in rural Russia assumed roles parallel to those of the parish clergy – as high priests of a secular culture of books and reading. Maxim Gorky emphasised the importance of reading to his personal success in his autobiographical novels, *Childhood* and *Among People*, which publishing magnate I. D. Sytin serialised from 1913 through to 1915 in his newspaper *Russian Word* (*Russkoe slovo*). At the time, this paper had the largest circulation in Russia.[5]

The ascendant power of the book and reading did not go unremarked by contemporaries. In 1895 M. M. Lederle published a curious compendium, *Opinions of Russian People About the Best*

Books for Reading. Lederle had sent out 200 circulars in 1891 to academicians and correspondents of the Academy of Sciences, as well as to professors, scholars, literati, artists and others, and presented an account of the eighty-six replies he received.[6] Among the responses were warnings that Dostoevsky is not for nervous people and that reading Tolstoy could lead to unhappiness, as well as testimonials to lives changed for the better through reading.[7] The late literary historian A. V. Blium, known for his work on Soviet censorship, introduced a collection of Russian writers' comments on the power of print with a quotation from Pushkin: 'We all think, how can it be stupid or unjust? The thing is that it is printed!'[8]

The influx of new readers occurred fortuitously at a time when Russia's market economy was expanding, entrepreneurs were moving capital into newly profitable endeavours and technical breakthroughs in printing and transport pulled down the costs of producing and distributing printed materials. From the 1860s through to the 1880s, enterprising publishers and authors, often of peasant origin, tested markets catering to new readers. Authors and publishers transformed the old-fashioned literature of the *lubok*, named after the cheap prints with short texts based on old motifs, into engaging popular fiction on a variety of themes that resonated with new audiences. Tales of banditry and rebellion, success and family happiness, science versus superstition, and war and history consistently sold well. Booklets hot off the presses were passed to a network of sturdy local peddlers, who carried them, along with needles, matches and other affordable accoutrements of daily life, into villages and urban neighbourhoods. Readers seized on new stories that addressed pressing issues of mobility, morality and personal identity.

A multifaceted set of interlocked publics arose, driven chiefly by curiosity about changes in society and a growing interest in famous people. As the tsarist autocracy faltered, Russians began to identify with the Empire, the landscape and with the great cultural figures of the day, including the newly minted celebrities of literature and the arts, rather than saints and generals.

Publishers catering to common readers offered a hodgepodge of folklore, transcribed oral literature and reworked old manuscripts in circulation since the eighteenth century. They also borrowed from high literature, revising and adapting to satisfy their growing market. The first genres to accompany the *lubki* were the chivalrous novels (*rytsarskye romany*) of largely medieval origins. The most famous recounted feats of Bova Korolevich (Bova the King's Son), Frantsyl Ventsian, Milord Georg (the English Milord), Guak and Eruslan Lazarevich.

Together they appeared in more than 500 editions from 1820 to 1917.[9] By 1861 these were also familiar as oral tales, which explains how they won an audience despite obscure locations and improbable plots. The titles reveal their archaic quality. Typical was *The Tale of the Glorious, Brave, and Unbeatable Champion Bova Korolevich and about his Beautiful Wife the Princess Druzhevna*, which had circulated earlier in Western Europe in Italian, French and English variants. Folk tales and printed versions of heroic poems called *byliny* were also popular. Stories of Ivan and the Firebird, the Little Humpbacked Horse, the Frog Princess and the feats of Ilya Murometz appeared in some 250–300 editions from 1870 to 1917.[10]

Early *lubok* writers presented upstarts whose efforts to better themselves ended in penury. Typical is P. Tatarinov's *Fomushka in St Petersburg; or, Wealth Is Useless for a Stupid Son* (1852), about a prosperous young peasant whose efforts to become 'Foma the Merchant' spell disaster.[11] Subsequent successful authors appropriated these traditional tales and adapted them to the tastes of their new readers. In many cases this entailed endowing protagonists with agency to connect with the ambitions of the audience. For example, in a *lubok* version of the Frog Princess, the hero refuses to marry the frog until she confirms that she is a princess.[12]

The elevation of agency was a notable turnabout in a peasant society accustomed to validation of the primal powers of religion, nature and fate. Stories of ambitious peasants who overcame difficulties and succeeded in the city soon outnumbered those cautioning against aspiring above one's station. The orphan hero of *Oh Those Iaroslavites, What Fine Folk* (1868), a tale often republished in the 1880s and 1890s, goes to St Petersburg when the village elder rejects his suit to marry his daughter.[13] After exertion and luck, he becomes a bartender at a hotel and returns in a coach to wed the girl, much to the elder's approval. Likewise, in *Masha the Orphan; or, The Sober Lovelace* (1901) a widowed mother finds factory work and fends off a boss's advances until her son lands a job that supports them.[14] A worker saves money and buys a tobacco farm in the Caucasus because he wants to be 'his own boss' in a 1912 novel serialised in the *Kopeck Newspaper* (*Gazeta kopeika*).

The authors created a simplified and effective narrative language to engage readers. New readers could also handle the basic texts that began to appear in the popular prints of the *lubok*, where illustration reinforced the text. For example, the early nineteenth-century pseudo-historical tale *How the Soldier Saved the Life of Peter the Great* appeared in over 100 separate editions, each adapted to common readers of differing skills. The texts that appeared beside the pictures of popular prints ranged from a few lines to a few paragraphs.[15]

Readers were everywhere active in shaping the new literature for common people. The new system of popular commercial publication, including that produced by local government, the central state and the Church reflected the preferences and limits of new readers. According to one late imperial specialist in popular reading, peasants divided books into religious works (*bozhestvennoe*), stories for entertainment (*skazochnoe*) and practical tracts (*zhiteiskoe*).[16] The Psalms particularly were a live presence in peasants' homes. Parents could earn a bit extra by having their children read the Psalms over the dead instead of paying a priest to do so.

The enterprise of literature – including authors, publishers and distributors – proved remarkably flexible over this period, and expanded in many directions to accommodate specialised audiences. While popular literature boomed, journals serving scientists and scholars also proliferated, as did the so-called monthly 'thick magazines' of fiction for elite audiences. Dostoevsky and Tolstoy reached much larger audiences than had their predecessors, with works that pushed the frontiers of fiction. In the process, they confirmed a new authority for the secular written work, assumed authorial moral weight and seized the public podium to influence the evolving identity of the nation.[17] They did so in part through serialising their work in periodicals widely read by the upper reaches of the literary audience.[18]

Serialisation also influenced how readers perceived the work. Readers of Tolstoy's *Anna Karenina* could enjoy Anna's rebellious freedom in extramarital love before facing the expected reckoning at the end. Tolstoy serialised his last big novel, *Resurrection,* in *The Field* (*Niva*) in 1899 for a broad public rather than in a 'thick magazine' with limited circulation.[19] This was a remarkable achievement even for Tolstoy. *The Field* had a circulation of almost 200,000, and since issues circulated among friends and neighbours he likely reached a high proportion of literate Russians.[20] A circulation of 200,000 would have been unsurprising at the time for a leading popular magazine in Western Europe, but it was huge in Russia.

Authors watched in amazement as their publics mushroomed beyond an intimate circle of personal acquaintances to become a vast, anonymous audience of no less serious readers. The shift from 'the reader friend' to the general reader made literature a profitable enterprise, as Abram Reitblat has demonstrated.[21] Although poetry remained poorly paid, the honorarium for prose in the thick magazines nearly doubled from the late 1850s into the 1890s. In the latter period, Tolstoy earned a princely 1,000 roubles per printer's sheet, and Chekhov 500 roubles. The energetic A. F. Marks, owner of *Niva*, bought Dostoevsky's works from his widow for 75,000 roubles. He also bought Chekhov's for 75,000 roubles, leaving the author the right to an additional honorarium that reached 1,000 roubles per signature, the highest price hitherto paid to any author.[22]

Readers' boundless demand for news also meant big rewards for top journalists. For covering the Russo-Japanese War of 1904–5, I. D. Sytin paid star reporter Vas I. Nemirovich-Danchenko 5,000 roubles a month plus expenses,[23] when schoolteachers received 300–400 roubles a year. These increased earnings mirrored the growing influence of the elite public and solidified the intelligentsia's formerly tenuous hold on the public sphere. Beyond the expanded elite public, many middling readers subscribed to new family weeklies, such as *The Field*, and bought satirical magazines at newsstands and kiosks in urban areas. Editors of the family magazines featured the high arts at home and abroad, at a time when knowledge of culture brought prestige.[24] The new humorous magazines joked about the great novels of the day and widened exposure to those works even among people who had not and would not read them. This explains the success of the satirical take on *War and Peace* that appeared in *Little Spark* (*Iskra*) as the novel came out.[25] The left-leaning magazine also poked fun at Turgenev and Dostoevsky. Humorous publications such as *The Alarm Clock* (*Budil'nik*), a stand-out success with a largely male readership, allowed Russian men to vent gently at the inroads that women and national minorities were making against their traditional dominance.[26]

For those who commanded more than a basic ability to read (including many upwardly mobile urban residents and the rural intelligentsia), literacy fuelled an ambition to be recognised as 'cultured': that is, familiar with a basic literary canon. The St Petersburg newspaper *Gazeta kopeika* offered subscribers cheap editions of Tolstoy, Gogol, Pushkin and Lermontov, in addition to novels by authors of the newspaper's own lively serials. Gradually, the canon widened, and the emphasis shifted from the writer's obligation to address social wrongs to an emphasis on spiritual and aesthetic accomplishment. Upon Tolstoy's death, the liberal pundit and early symbolist Dmitry Merezhkovsky asked, 'Who is he? Artist, teacher, prophet? . . . No, more – his face is the face of humanity.'[27] Another commentator opined, 'Our country is poor and lawless, but it gave the world Tolstoy whose death speaks so distinctly of undying life'.[28]

Magazines such as the *Herald of Learning* (*Vestnik znaniia*) and *New Journal for All* (*Novyi zhurnal dlia vsekh*), with circulations of 30,000–40,000 in 1910, catered to the new reader who wished 'to become a developed person' – informed about science, literature and the arts.[29] The slogan of the *Herald of Learning* was 'learn and teach others'. It sponsored a self-help society whose members sought to serve 'the people', and at the same time to acquire learning sufficient to rise above 'the people'. In the first issue of the *New Journal for All* (1911, p. 127), N. A. Rubakin, the maestro of the self-education movement, promised that 'anyone who wishes to can become a really educated person'.

According to a 1910 survey of the readers of the *Herald of Learning*, their preferred authors included Turgenev, Dostoevsky, Chekhov, Gogol and the 'neo-realists' Andreev and Gorky, although Tolstoy was the overwhelming favourite.[30] These authors were recognised as masters at home and abroad, and there would be no confusing substitutions or additions. The nineteenth century was over; the list was agreed upon and closed. When asked about new trends in literature, readers voiced the desire 'to give the decadents and god-seekers the boot!'[31]

The expansion of the reading public and commingling of groups within it generated centripetal forces of differentiation. The disdain of the self-educated for 'the decadents' was mirrored in the way many in Russia's cultural elite, however liberal, looked down on the aspirations of the self-educated: in the liberal daily *Speech* in 1911, the critic Kornei Chukovsky mocked the 'semi-intelligentsia'.[32] The symbolists of the 1890s admired the classics, but chose in their own work to innovate and to separate themselves from the tastes of the broader public. Above all, they espoused aesthetic values and rejected the obligations to societal improvement that had characterised the realist writers of the classical canon. One of the founders of the Russian symbolist movement, Dmitry Merezhkovsky, lamented the pernicious influence of the new mass public of the illustrated press, with its publishers, critics, readers and corrupting honoraria.[33]

After the shock of the Revolution of 1905, even modernist authors acknowledged the presence of the wider public. Alexander Blok, the leading symbolist, began to write about 'the people' even though he did not write for them, while a younger generation of poets abandoned the symbolist aesthetic for a more accessible style under the banner of acmeism. The last pre-revolutionary modernists, the futurists, wrote for an elite audience, but interacted with broader publics through their pursuit of celebrity, outrageous statements, displays and shenanigans of all sorts.

As modernism and symbolism grew around them, activists in the self-education movement clung to the classics. Asked in 1910 to name their favourite writers, readers of the *Herald of Learning*, more than half of whom lacked a secondary education, listed largely classical Russian authors, with the interesting addition of Charles Darwin. The journal's editorial policy and its editor, V. V. Bitner, did not welcome modernist competitors to the classics: 'Why do these unnecessary writers take precedence in literature? Why are their names surrounded by a halo of fame?'[34] Bitner complained in the weekly supplement to his magazine that journalists ignored his movement of self-education and its favourite authors, and instead reported that 'Andreev bought a new suit or returned from abroad, that Kuprin was a referee at a wrestling match, and that one or another of the new poets is ready to issue a little book of his verses (which have already been issued previously in the newspapers)'.[35] A critic in the *New Magazine* (*Novyi zhurnal*), another publication for the self-educated, complained in 1910 about writers who 'live no worse than capitalists and landowners'.[36]

Russians with middling education expressed not only doubt about but active resentment of the new art. The 'people's intelligentsia' – village teachers, medical assistants, clerical workers, local officials and low-level employees in trade and industry, including factory foremen such as the young Nikita Khrushchev – found the latest cultural developments bewildering. Their ambition was for the kind of self-improvement that would grant them entry into the ranks of 'people with culture', but they had an established culture in mind. They venerated the nineteenth-century Russian classics, works that satisfied their demand for a literature that was accessible and amenable to didactic reading. And they admired the art of the Russian realists who seemed to honour their country and civilisation. These motivated consumers carried real weight in the marketplace, unlike the workers who joined Marxist study groups, who sometimes shared their views.

Publishers eager to expand their reach served as de facto peacemakers between and among the literary factions. They offered a variety of formats and genres that softened divisions between high and low literature. Popular detective stories of the early twentieth century as well as novels for and by women appealed to a diverse urban audience. Educated and semi-educated readers alike turned to city newspapers with feuilleton novels and coverage of crime.[37] N. I. Pastukhov, editor of the *Moscow Sheet* (*Moskovskii listok*), attracted an enormous audience with his weekly episodes of *The Bandit Churkin*, a favourite of Chekhov, which he kept up from 1883 through to 1885. Such tales became standard fare in popular fiction, both serialised in the late imperial kopeck dailies and in the new medium of film. In the 1910s, the same diverse public bought detective stories modelled on American dime novels and women's potboilers such as A. A. Verbitskaia's six-volume *Keys to Happiness* (1908–13).[38] By 1914, her public had purchased half a million copies of her various books. V. V. Rozanov, a conservative critic and modernist poet, confessed to a weakness for 'Pinkertons' – forty-eight-page detective adventures.[39]

By the end of the old regime, readers interacting with authors and publishers through the market (and under the watchful eye of the tsarist censors) had shaped an outpouring of literary greatness still appreciated today. New readers made their presence known. Their sheer numbers, as well as their evolving tastes, influenced writers at all levels. Dostoevsky, Tolstoy, Chekhov and countless others enriched their works with traditional themes and motifs shaped in part through cultural dialogue with the new readers.[40] The latter exerted an influence in many ways, but primary among them was the literary market.

The victorious Bolsheviks rejected the legitimacy of the market as an institution and carried strongly held ideological expectations about the tastes and preferences of common people. Lenin and his inner circle moved quickly to dismantle the old cultural system and establish a state monopoly over the printed word. Destruction of the old proved faster than construction of the new. A multidimensional breakdown in the consumption of the printed word resulted. Material and equipment shortages made production difficult. The closing of distribution networks, the shuttering of shops and kiosks, and price and currency fluctuations took a toll. Rural readers were the most affected and the most in need of reliable information. Crisis followed crisis during the Civil War and the first few years of the New Economic Policy (1922–6), and many people dependent on news received little of it.

Even taking into consideration the shrunken dimensions of the Empire, the fall in the production of printed materials was precipitous. By 1920 and 1921, the number of copies and titles produced had fallen by three-quarters relative to 1917.[41] Recovery did not come until the mid- to late 1920s. The Bolsheviks emphasised newspapers rather than literary journals. They replaced the big city dailies that had served diverse readers and smaller papers for specialised audiences with central institutional organs, such as *Pravda* for Party members and *Izvestiia* for government officials and employees. They also began to produce mass newspapers for separate classes, such as the *Workers' Newspaper* (*Rabochaia gazeta*, 1922–32) and *The Poor* (*Bednota*, 1918–31) for rural readers. When the intended audience for the latter chose not to self-identify as 'poor', the paper was replaced by the *Peasant Newspaper* (*Krest'anskaia gazeta*, 1923–39).

The new newspapers carried new content. Readers who had in earlier years avidly consumed stories about floods and disasters or crime were out of luck; journalists pointedly ignored such stories, unless they could be used to teach a political lesson. Among the most successful propagandistic works for peasants were historical stories about revolutionary heroes. These took the place of the pre-revolutionary tales and saints' lives. One reader wrote to the *Peasant Newspaper* in the mid-1920s that biographies of revolutionary heroes 'acted on me more strongly than the suffering of the great martyr Saint George'.[42] Obituaries also provided human interest.[43]

Most of the scarce paper was devoted to producing political volumes, social commentary and schoolbooks. The four authors published 1919–26 in the largest numbers by Gosizdat, the state firm responsible for publishing almost all books, were Lenin (7.5 million copies), Stalin (2 million), Bukharin (1.2 million) and Trotsky (1 million).[44] Publication of belles-lettres and popular fiction plummeted. In 1910, 7.6 million copies of works of belles-lettres were published in Russian, along with nearly 15 million 'people's books' and 2.6 million detective stories. By 1922, only 3.5 million copies of belles-lettres appeared, and the category 'people's books' no longer existed. Unsold books piled up, and after 1922 a decision was made to increase the publication of belles-lettres. Boris Dralyuk has described the efforts in the mid-1920s to create Soviet genre fiction, particularly a 'Red Pinkerton', but these attempts were ultimately abandoned and not renewed until after Stalin's death.[45]

Readers who found the writings of Lenin and Stalin not to their taste had further difficulties with the new politicised vocabulary. Marxist authors used a plethora of specialised terms, foreign words, acronyms and neologisms. Readers of the *Workers' Newspaper* complained in 1924 that they needed ten dictionaries to understand the paper, and requested explanations for foreign and scientific words.[46] Audiences struggled to follow even when activists and Party officials read the newspapers aloud in factories. Soldiers voiced similar complaints when the *Peasant Newspaper* was read aloud to them in 1923. That year, a peasant from Vladimir wrote to the newspaper complaining that it was written 'not in peasant language, and one might even say, not in Russian, but in political language'.[47]

According to the 1926 census, the Soviet Union's literate population numbered nearly 60 million, but only 1 million copies of newspapers were published in 1922 and 2.4 million in 1924.[48] It is likely that ordinary people read less in the decade after the Revolution than in the decade before, limited as they were by lack of reading material, its unappealing quality and its impenetrable language. Though the Bolsheviks initially lost the common readers, they gained an energetic audience of activists, enthusiasts and government employees as well as members of the Party and the Komsomol, the youth organisation. Such readers were eager to understand government policy, to join in official projects and to manifest their loyalty by regularly reading the newspapers. The new information system satisfied the needs of these groups, upon whom the new order depended.

From its earliest days, the new centrally managed press served to signal and shape the attitudes of its readers, rather than, as had been the case earlier, to accommodate its audience's preferences and build readership. The October Revolution thus marked a transfer of agency from readers to the state. The commissars of culture employed three distinct approaches to readers, each with a different kind of discourse. In one approach, political leaders managed a structured dialogue with activists. They conveyed messages and entertained responses through letters and local correspondence. This dialogue between reader-activists (including the worker and peasant correspondents to the newspapers) was controlled and unequal. The staff picked the topics for discussion, chose the letters, edited them and sometimes even wrote them. The interaction was not fully staged, however; the numbers of letters demonstrate the presence of a large and engaged public.[49] In this activist sphere, the authorities also tried to gather information on readers' views.

A second approach to readers entailed conveying information on topics deemed important for general airing. Coverage of foreign affairs fell into this category, since the world abroad was of great interest, and the war scares of 1923 and 1927 stirred fear. A third approach was intended to inspire readers to align with officially promoted goals. Inspirational stories about Bolshevik leaders quickly morphed into the cult first of Lenin and then of Stalin. Patriotic texts and articles, poems and fiction were suitable for reading aloud in schools and other public institutions.

Readers schooled in the diverse pre-revolutionary print media recognised the differentiated approaches and read accordingly. A factory worker reported on reading the various sections of the *Workers' Newspaper* in 1923:

> We rarely read 'In the Trade Unions', 'In the Komsomol', or 'Party Life' – these do not concern us. 'How to Fight Malaria' – it is generally interesting

to read about sicknesses. 'The Life of schools' – I look at it rarely, we don't study anymore; 'Social Insurance' – that is necessary; 'The Book Shelf' is for information, for those who need it; 'During the Day' – this article interests everyone, but there is little in it.[50]

Newspaper editors reported that they valued feedback from readers and acted upon it, not to adjust the content of the publications, but rather to learn about local conditions and (when necessary) to enforce discipline to the new order. The *Workers' Newspaper* in 1923, its first year of publication, stated that it had learned about 'a multitude of defects in our order' from the letters received. In its issue of 24 May 1926, the *Peasant Newspaper* claimed that, on the basis of 80,000 letters received in 1925 and 1926, it had satisfied nearly 60,000 requests, called 673 people to account, brought 948 to trial, fired 769 from their jobs and expelled 139 from the Party or Komsomol. Editors gave special weight to the letters and views of the local worker and peasant correspondents, who initially had some independence, but towards the end of the 1920s they were put under local Party authority. The number of such correspondents for all newspapers rose from 50,000 to a peak of 500,000 in 1928.[51]

The shift in agency from readers to the state corresponded to a shift in the presentation of agency in print. Gone were the old popular narratives in which readers could identify their own ambitions with the exploits of heroes and heroines. Orders from institutions replaced decisions of individuals as motivation for action. Over time, the orders came increasingly from Stalin alone. Journalists presented this logic of human behaviour in such statements as: '*Pravda*, the organ of the Central Committee of the Russian Communist Party, ought to be the leader and friend of each member of the Party'.[52]

As orders from above became the guide to action, the range of legitimate motives shrank to fit the narrowing discourse. The winnowing of diversity and relatively unfettered initiative began in the periodical press, but soon encompassed readers and writers of fiction as well. The codification of change was celebrated at the First Congress of Soviet Writers in 1934, under the banner of Socialist Realism.

Ideological preconceptions about the tastes of workers and peasants had led Bolshevik leaders to assume that their agendas for the press coincided with the preferences of readers. Kornei Chukovsky had in 1910 offered a prescient warning that this might not be so:

> Mr. Lunacharsky [the subsequent early Soviet minister of enlightenment], you ... so often spoke of the 'clear light of proletarian art', that I could not believe my eyes when I saw how the workers were consumed by Nat

Pinkerton. I thought, it's nothing; today they are reading Pinkerton, and tomorrow they will read Pinkerton, but the day after. . . . And the day after? The day after they began to read Verbitskaia [the famous women's author].[53]

Once Lunacharsky and the other Bolshevik leaders discovered the disconnect between what they published and what ordinary people wanted and could understand, they embarked on a series of studies of readers, the first under the auspices of the army.[54] In 1920 the Red Army had provided soldiers – a captive audience – with 20 million pamphlets, leaflets and posters, 5.6 million books and 300,000–400,000 copies of newspapers per day. The Political Administration of the Red Army circulated questionnaires to 11,900 soldiers in 1920–1 to probe what they thought about these materials. Although the sample was not necessarily representative, the study was nonetheless revealing. Respondents demanded information about agriculture, stories about travel and adventure, and fiction, but showed little interest in politics. The overtly political questions were often left unanswered, and when those questionnaire items did get a response, hostile remarks were not infrequent. When respondents were asked to name a favourite author, Pushkin and Tolstoy stood out.

The compulsory survey was suitable for the army but not for the population at large. In the early period of the New Economic Policy, published books included comment sheets, and focus groups convened for trial readings to test responses. In 1925 researchers carried out ambitious studies of the readers of the *Workers' Newspaper* and *Peasant Newspaper*. The results indicated a sharp dichotomy between what readers wanted and what was offered. Such studies paralleled the reports of the worker-peasant correspondents, who felt free at this stage to call for an unmasking of privilege, inequality, favouritism, bureaucratic excesses and immorality. As noted above, this activist public of correspondents was soon subordinated to local Party leaders, after which their criticism was muted.

Surveys confirmed that the readers of the early Soviet press were often not what Soviet cultural administrators actually wanted. The era of surveying the reader ended as Stalin consolidated power. The press took a decided turn away from engaging with readers, and towards signalling the behaviour required for compliance with official policy. The leadership largely abandoned efforts to convince the population through explanation and rational discourse, and turned to threats and compulsion to enforce collectivisation, industrialisation and the other core policies of the 1930s. Librarians continued to study readers, but the results were used largely to assess the views of Party members and others, and to identify suitable candidates for later membership. The increased reliance on exemplary readers in the late 1920s and early 1930s was manifested in the audience of Party activists at the First Congress of Soviet Writers in 1934. They endorsed Socialist Realism and demanded that they themselves and their deeds be the sole appropriate subjects of works of literature.[55]

The evolution of cultural policy traced above pertained to belles-lettres as well as to newspapers. The fluctuation in cultural policy throughout much of the 1920s accommodated the creation of works of literature as products of their times and of the reading skills of audiences in the pre-revolutionary period. Isaac Babel offered his tales of the Civil War and tough-guy Jewish gangsters. Mikhail Zoshchenko presented some of the world's all-time best satire in an environment unsympathetic to direct self-criticism. The consummate jokers Ilya Ilf and Evgeny Petrov loosed the antihero Ostap Bender on an appreciative readership concurrently with official celebration of the Soviet heroic figure. The skill of these and other writers and the sophistication of their readers allowed the simultaneous presentation of multiple storylines, at least one of which was sufficiently in tune with official policy to secure permission to publish.

The space in which these talented writers could operate shrank after the First Congress of Soviet Writers in 1934 and a new wave of terror that extended into the Second World War and thereafter. During these times, readers lost beloved works, and esteemed authors lost their lives or liberty, as did Babel, the great poet Osip Mandelstam and many others.

Works recognised as truly great from the Soviet era were permitted by the state apparatus, but not generated by it. Concurrently, the state embarked on an effort to commission and shape its own popular literature to carry Soviet messages and values. It was designed to appeal to readers and at the same time promote self-sacrifice in the name of the collective, the leader and the Party/state. It is in this light that Nikolai Bukharin's appeal in 1923 for cheap Soviet detective adventure stories can be understood.[56] The most successful such effort was Marietta Shaginian's *Mess Mend* series, which ran from late 1924 to 1926 in 30,000 copies and appeared in thirty-two-page segments, much like the old pre-revolutionary popular novels. Shaginian parodied in three popular novels, beginning with *Mess Mend*, the bourgeois genres of the detective story, science fiction and the colonial travel adventure.[57] Despite exotic settings and situations, the work lacked the excitement of the old popular fiction. Bukharin read *Yankees* (one of the *Mess*

Mend stories) in manuscript and the chief of the state publishing house, N. L. Meshcheriakov, asserted in the introduction that 'the novel's main hero is the collective of the proletariat'.[58] Shaginian was caught in the cross-currents of a changing policy, and became a case study in the limits of melding popular themes with official directives. Her work sold widely, but she was savaged by critics for a lack of seriousness and ideological firmness.

In the 1930s, the official lines and messages of literature became clearer and more readily discerned. Not that Stalin-era books were necessarily unpopular: many of them achieved enormous print runs and wide readership. Some of the best works were never published and reached miniscule audiences until the post-Stalin thaw, but what was published was frequently read. The styles of Socialist Realism concurred with the tastes and values of the self-educated readers who had earlier rejected modernism. That class increased in numbers and prominence during the consolidation of Stalinist power structures, finding in Socialist Realism a literature that they could appreciate.

At the same time, an intellectually engaged public operating under the constraints of tightening censorship retained the skill of perceiving multiple messages in the same works. A simplistic use of language aided and abetted dual messaging, particularly in cases in which counter-stories cried out from the facts. During the first months of the 'Great Patriotic War', for example, Stalin and his colleagues were fearful of revealing the true extent of the disaster at the front.[59] Rather than report straightforwardly about fallen cities and lost territory, they simply noted the places of current fighting. Critical readers could immediately map the captured territory. As the war progressed, the authorities had to change the terms under which journalists communicated with readers. To motivate the population, reporters such as Ilya Ehrenberg and Vasily Grossman stepped in as active voices, moving soldiers, partisans and the civilian population to the forefront of coverage at the expense of the leaders and bosses to whom all achievements had previously been attributed.

This meant, at least before the victory at Stalingrad, the celebration of ordinary people as heroes and heroines. Coverage returned, however briefly, to a kind of journalism driven by an organic connection with readers. Reports from the front by leading journalists in the *Red Star* (*Krasnaia zvezda*) and other newspapers were popular, informative, respected and believed. Little or no irony was to be found in their columns or in the minds of even critical readers until Stalin felt confident enough to put himself forward once again as the sole achiever and planner of every victory. Readers may have regretted the loss of quality journalism, but it was a small price to pay for the end of the war. They fully recognised the shift in voice that had taken place and settled back to prior modes of reading.

Russian and subsequently Soviet literature of the literacy transition – that is, roughly the century between 1850 and 1950 – is a cultural treasure of enduring value. The authors who created it are rightly celebrated, translated and widely read. Their rarely sung partners in creativity were millions of contemporary readers with whom they carried on a complex dialogue. The confluence and interaction of writers, readers and the many other agents in linked reading publics yielded a body of work of peerless value. Readers were not passive beneficiaries of literary greatness, but instead active participants in its creation.

The Russian experience may have been unique in its timing and circumstance, as suggested during my interactions with the students in Addis Ababa. If so, it is a fortuitous uniqueness that continues to enrich.

Notes

1. Jeffrey Brooks, 'The Zemstvos and the Education of the People', in T. Emmons et al. (eds), *The Russian Zemstvo* (Cambridge: Cambridge University Press, 1982), p. 249, p. 274 (for statistics) and pp. 243–78.
2. Jeffrey Brooks, *When Russia Learned to Read: Literacy and Popular Literature, 1861–1917* (Princeton: Princeton University Press, 1985), pp. 43–4.
3. I. M. Bogdanov, *Gramotnost' i obrazovanie v dorevoliutsionnoi Rossii i v SSSR* (Moscow, 1964), pp. 358–9; Jeffrey Brooks, 'Literacy and the Print Media in Russia, 1861–1928', *Communication*, 11 (1988), pp. 47–61.
4. Tsentral'noe statisticheskoe upravlenie, *Gramotnost' v Rossii* (Moscow, 1922), pp. 10–11.
5. *Pol veka dlia knig, 1866–1916. Literaturno-khudozhestvennyi sbornik posviashchennyi piatidesiatiletiiu izdatel'skoi deiatel'nostii I. D. Sytina* (Moscow, I. D. Sytin, 1916), pp. 4–5.
6. *Vestnik Evropy*, October 1895, p. 831; and *Obrazovanie*, September 1895, p. 100.
7. M. M. Lederle, *Mneniia russkikh liudei o luchshikh knigakh dlia chteniia* (St Petersburg: M. M. Lederle, 1895), pp. 41, 104, 109, 119. Lederle cites various published memoirs and other material in this compendium.
8. A. V. Blium, *Ocharovannye kingi: sbornik khudozhennykh proizvedenii (rasskazov, ocherkov, esse), posviashchennykh knige, chteniiu, bibliofilam* (Moscow, 1982), p. 9.

9. Brooks, *When Russia Learned to Read*, pp. 59–108.
10. Ibid., p. 363.
11. P. P. Tatarinov, *Fomushka v Pitere, ili glupomu synu ne v pomoshch bogatstvo* (St Petersburg: Veimar, 1852).
12. Brooks, *When Russia Learned to Read*, pp. 69–70.
13. Ibid., p. 287; my translation appears in James von Geldern and Louise McReynolds (eds), *Entertaining Tsarist Russia* (Bloomington: Indiana University Press, 1998), pp. 135–41.
14. V. A. Lunin (pseudonym Kukel'), *Masha-sirota ili tregubyi volokita* (Kiev: Gubanov, 1901).
15. Jeffrey Brooks, 'How a Soldier Saved Peter I: A Kudzu Vine of Russia's Popular Fiction', *Russian History/Histoire Russe*, 35:2 (summer 2008), pp. 1–19.
16. A. S. Anskii (Shloyme Zanvl Rappoport), *Narod i kniga*, 2nd edition (Moscow, 1913), p. 137.
17. See Dina Khapaeva, *Nightmare: From Literary Experiments to Cultural Project* (Leiden: Brill, 2012); and Jeffrey Brooks, 'How Tolstoevskii Pleased Readers and Rewrote a Russian Myth', *Slavic Review*, 64:3 (2005), pp. 538–59.
18. See William Mills Todd's many works on Russian literature as an institution, including his 'Tolstoy and Dostoevsky: The Professionalization of Literature and Serialized Fiction', *Dostoevsky Studies*, 15 (2011), pp. 29–36.
19. I. I. Frolova (ed.), *Kniga v rossii, 1881–1895* (St Petersburg, 1997), pp. 309–10.
20. Brooks, *When Russia Learned to Read*, p. 113.
21. Abram Reitblat, *Ot Boby k Bal'montu* (Moscow: MPI, 1991), pp. 84–9.
22. *Izvestiia knizhnykh magazinov t-va M. O. Vol'f*, nos 7–8 (1907), p. 167.
23. Ibid., no. 9 (1907), pp. 183–9.
24. Jeffrey Brooks, 'Russian Nationalism and Russian Literature', in Ivo Banac et al. (eds), *Nation and Ideology: Essays in Honor of Wayne S. Vucinich* (Boulder: East European Monographs, 1981), pp. 315–34; Katia Dianina, *When Art Makes News: Writing Culture and Identity in Imperial Russia* (DeKalb: Northern Illinois University Press, 2013).
25. Jeffrey Brooks, 'Laughing with the Count: Humor in *War and Peace* and Beyond', in Inessa Mezdzhibovskaya (ed.), *Tolstoy and His Problems: Views from the Twenty-First Century* (Evanston: Northwestern University Press, 2018), pp. 224–49.
26. Jeffrey Brooks, 'The Russian Nation Imagined: The Peoples of Russia as Seen in Popular Imagery, 1860s–1890s', *Journal of Social History*, 43 (2010), pp. 535–57.
27. *Rech'*, 9 November 1910.
28. *Rech'*, 8 November 1910.
29. Jeffrey Brooks, 'Popular Philistinism and the Course of Russian Modernism', in Gary Saul Morson (ed.), *Literature and History: Theoretical*

Problems and Russian Case Studies (Stanford: Stanford University Press, 1986), pp. 90–110.
30. See A. A. Nikolaev, *Khleba i sveta* (St Petersburg, 1910) on surveying the readers.
31. N. A. Rubakin, 'Zhurnal i chitateli', *Novyi zhurnal dlia vsekh*, no. 37 (1911), p. 120.
32. Kornei Chukovskii, *Litsa i maski* (St Petersburg, 1914), pp. 190–1.
33. D. S. Merezhkovskii, *O prichinakh upadka i o novykh techeniiakh sovremennoi russkoi literatury* (St Petersburg, 1893), p. 20.
34. *Nedelia*, no. 1 (1913), p. 15.
35. *Nedelia*, no. 2 (1913), p. 37.
36. *Novyi zhurnal*, no. 23 (1910), p. 85.
37. Louise McReynolds, *The News Under Russia's Old Regime: The Development of a Mass Circulation Press* (Princeton: Princeton University Press, 1991). See also Brooks, *When Russia Learned to Read*, pp. 109–65.
38. Brooks, *When Russia Learned to Read*, pp. 153–4.
39. V. V. Rozanov, *Opavshie list'ia* (St Petersburg, 1913), p. 341.
40. Jeffrey Brooks, *The Firebird and the Fox: Russian Culture Under Tsars and Bolsheviks* (Cambridge: Cambridge University Press, 2019), pp. 80–92; Brooks, 'How Tolstoevskii Pleased Readers', pp. 538–59; Jeffrey Brooks, 'The Young Chekhov: Reader and Writer of Popular Realism', in Damiano Rebecchin and Raffaella Vassena (eds), *Reading in Russia: Practices of Reading and Literary Communication, 1760–1930* (Milan: Ledizioni, 2014), pp. 201–18.
41. See Jeffrey Brooks, 'The Breakdown in the Production and Distribution of Printed Material, 1917–1927', in Abbott Gleason, Peter Kenez and Richard Stites (eds), *Bolshevik Culture: Experiment and Order in the Russian Revolution* (Bloomington: Indiana University Press, 1985), pp. 151–74.
42. M. I. Slukhovskii, *Kniga i derevnia* (Moscow, 1928), p. 81.
43. Jeffrey Brooks, 'Revolutionary Lives: Public Identities in *Pravda* during the 1920s', in Stephen White (ed.), *New Directions in History* (Cambridge: Cambridge University Press, 1991), pp. 27–40.
44. Brooks, 'The Breakdown', p. 157.
45. Boris Dralyuk, *Western Crime Fiction Goes East: The Russian Pinkerton Craze 1907–1934* (Leiden: Brill, 2012), pp. 83–160.
46. Ia. Shafir, *Rabochaia gazeta i ee chitatel'* (Moscow, 1926), p. 221.
47. A. Meromskii and P. Putni, *Derevenia za knigoi* (Moscow, 1931), p. 169.
48. *Vsesoiuznaia perepis' naseleniia 1926 goda*, 17 (Moscow, 1929), pp. 48–9.
49. Jeffrey Brooks, *Thank You, Comrade Stalin: Soviet Culture from Revolution to Cold War* (Princeton: Princeton University Press, 2000), pp. 3–18; Jeffrey Brooks, 'Public and Private Values in the Soviet Press, 1921–1928', *Slavic Review*, 48:1 (spring 1989), pp. 16–35, and appendix B, pp. 30–1.
50. Quoted in Ia. Shafir, *Gazeta i derevnia* (Moscow, 1924), p. 68.

51. Brooks, 'Public and Private Values', appendix B.
52. *Pravda*, 12 February 1924.
53. Kornei Chukovskii, 'Verbitskaia', *Rech'*, 21 February 1910.
54. The following discussion draws on Jeffrey Brooks, 'Studies of the Reader in the 1920s', *Russian History/Histoire Russe*, 9:2–3 (1982), pp. 187–202.
55. Jeffrey Brooks, 'Socialist Realism in *Pravda:* Read All About It', *Slavic Review*, 53:4 (winter 1994), pp. 973–91; Evgeny Dobrenko, *The Making of the State Reader: Social and Aesthetic Contexts of the Reception of Soviet Literature*, trans. Jesse M. Savage (Stanford: Stanford University Press, 1997).
56. See Dralyuk, *Western Crime Fiction*, pp. 83–97.
57. The original version of *Mess Mend* appears in Marietta Shaginian, *Sobranie sochinenii, 1905–1933* (Moscow, 1938). See also later versions and one in English as *Mess-Mend, Yankees in Petrograd*, trans. Samuel D. Cioran (Ann Arbor: Ardis, 1991). On the film, see Denise Youngblood, *Movies for the Masses: Popular Cinema and Soviet Society in the 1920s* (Cambridge: Cambridge University Press, 1992), pp. 128–34. The 1954 version of the novel also appears in *Mess-Mend, ili Ianki v Petrograde. Roman-skazka* (Moscow, 1979).
58. Shaginian, *Sobranie sochinenii*, 3 (Moscow, 1938), p. 108.
59. See Brooks, *Thank You, Comrade Stalin*, pp. 159–94.

Chapter 8

F. F. Pavlenkov's Literacy Project: Popular Serials and Reading Rooms for the Russian Masses

Carol Ueland and Ludmilla A. Trigos

For almost a century, Russia (and formerly the Soviet Union) has considered itself the 'most well-read nation'[1] because of the successes of its literacy campaigns after the 1917 Revolution. In the Bolshevik understanding, education was inextricably linked with politics and was necessary for the development of class consciousness. The Bolshevik assumption was that the imperial Ministry of Education had little interest in popular education other than to instil a 'monarchist-orthodox ideology' in the masses.[2] Prior to the Bolshevik victory in the 1917 October Revolution, according to N. K. Krupskaia, Lenin contemptuously deemed private philanthropists who tackled illiteracy and adult education specifically as 'do-gooders'.[3] But after the 1917 Revolution, when confronted with the economic and social backwardness of the former tsarist empire, Lenin believed that the cultural level of the people had to be raised in order to secure 'certain economic well-being, industrial and technical accomplishments, modern attitudes to the problems of existence, and certain very basic intellectual accomplishments'.[4] Striving for full literacy among its subjects in all its republics, the Soviet Union in its early years pushed its citizens to master reading as one of the foundations of modern civilisation (among others, such as electricity) and conducted campaigns to eradicate illiteracy, sending workers and peasants to night schools.

Evgeny Dobrenko, in *The Making of the State Reader*, discusses the interaction between the mass reader, writers and the process of reading as a pivotal force in the creation of Soviet culture. Likewise, Stephen Lovell, in *The Russian Reading Revolution*, has explored this phenomenon in the Soviet period, without, however, connecting it to the upsurge of interest in the cultivation of a mass reading public in the pre-revolutionary era. Jeffrey Brooks has tackled the topic of literacy and popular literature in the tsarist period (1861–1917) but focuses primarily on commercial literature, including the *lubok* (chapbook), potboilers, adventure stories and other popular periodical or serialised fiction.[5] This chapter examines the foundation of this myth of the most well-read nation, locating its origins instead in the work of nineteenth-century reformers. We focus specifically on publisher F. F. Pavlenkov (1839–1900) and his efforts to make progressive political, social, scientific, religious and cultural ideas available to the newly literate Russian masses at the turn of the twentieth century.

Florenty Fedorovich Pavlenkov was born into a gentry family in Tambov, Russia. He was the tenth of eleven children born to his father, Fedor Iakovlevich, who gained noble status through military service. His grandfather and great-grandfather came from Ukrainian Cossacks who served in Ostrogoshk. His mother, Varvara Nikolaevna, was the third wife of Fedor Iakovlevich and bore him three children, including Florenty. When Florenty was not even a year old, he and his older brother Vadim were sent to the Tambov Kadet School (his family was overwhelmed with so many children). When Pavlenkov reached age ten, he and his brother were transferred to the St Petersburg Kadet School on government scholarships. He was orphaned at age fifteen, when his father died (his mother having passed away earlier). He was a diligent student, excelling especially in literature and the sciences. Upon completion of the Kadet School, he attended the Mikhailovskii Artillery Academy, receiving his diploma in 1861. Pavlenkov started his service as a lieutenant in the Horse Guards of the Artillery in the Kiev Military Arsenal, but quickly became disillusioned by his colleagues' and superiors' focus on cards, drinking, gossip and bribes. After registering a formal complaint against his superiors, he suffered repercussions and determined that he could no longer continue in the military. Pavlenkov initially hoped that he would become a teacher, but he found that avenue closed to him because of his active campaign against corruption in the military and his progressive/radical political leanings.[6] So he turned to a career in publishing.

He contributed to various magazines and newspapers, including *Artillery Journal* (*Artilleriiskii zhurnal*), *The Photographer* (*Fotograf*), *The Torch* (*Svetoch*), *Russian Word* (*Russkoe slovo*) and *Russian Veteran* (*Russkii invalid*).[7] He translated a booklet on popular photography and published it himself in Kiev.[8] But his real breakthrough as a publisher came with his 1864–5 translation of two bestselling French physics textbooks by Adolphe Ganot, *Traité élèmentaire de physique expérimentale et appliquée* and *Cours de physique purement expérimentale* (Figure 8.1). The first edition of the

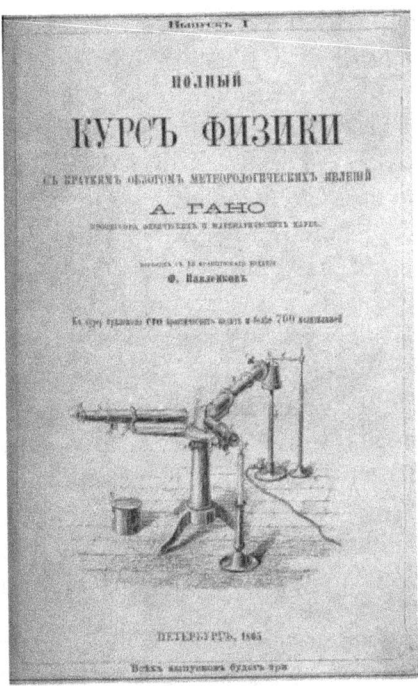

Figure 8.1 The Pavlenkov 1865 Russian-language edition of A. Ganot's *Complete Course of Physics with a Brief Review of Meteorological Phenomena*, translated from the French (12th edition) by F. F. Pavlenkov and V. Cherkasov (St Petersburg: F. F. Pavlenkov Publishers, 1866), part I of IV

former had a print run of 4,000 (priced at 3 rubles 50 kopeks), which sold out by 1867. It was followed by nine more editions of 6,000 copies each, the last in 1898.[9] Capitalising on the success of the first work, he later translated Ganot's 'Course' into Russian as *Popular Physics* (*Populiarnaia fizika*), which went through four editions.[10] Pavlenkov obviously had his finger on the pulse of the Western European book market, especially in popular scientific publications. He saw the educational value as well as the market success of Ganot's textbooks in Europe, and he appreciated their understandable language and use of illustrations, two features which later became hallmarks of Pavlenkov's own publications. Another reason that Pavlenkov may have chosen Ganot's physics textbook was that it featured in Ivan Turgenev's *Fathers and Children* (1862). In a key scene in the novel, it is deployed as a symbol of materialist psychology and the privileging of physiology over spirit in a debate between Turgenev and Pavlenkov's idol, the revolutionary critic Dmitri Pisarev. As Josep Simon suggests, the popularity of Ganot's physics course was confirmed by its use in Turgenev's as well as other Western European authors' works 'to display the tense relations between the two sexes'.[11]

The proceeds from these very successful translations of Ganot's textbooks allowed Pavlenkov to go into the publishing business in earnest. At the end of 1866, he officially retired from military service and purchased a bookstore from P. A. Gaideburov on the fashionable Nevsky Prospekt in St Petersburg. It became known as the 'Out of Towners' Bookstore' and was very popular.[12] Pavlenkov no longer had to rely only on subscription sales and other booksellers now that he had obtained an outlet for his books and a space for propagating scientific knowledge and culture to a broad urban audience.

Pavlenkov absorbed the ideas of celebrated Western thinkers such as Thomas Carlyle, Jeremy Bentham, Adam Smith and John Stuart Mill, all of whom he would later include in his famous biographical series, the 'Lives of Remarkable People'. Mill emphasised the central societal role of publishers who are not merely focused on commercial success:

> It is necessary to look at a publisher as an enlightener of the people, since we are obliged to him for the appearance of many compositions which never would have otherwise seen the light; publishers, imparting a particular direction to their activities develop, so to speak, a taste for one or another branch of science or literature, create readers, enable the dissemination of literacy.[13]

Pavlenkov also looked to Western advocates of popular literacy such as Jean-François Macé, the founder of the Ligue de l'Enseignement in France, who created free public libraries in remote regions. However, Pavlenkov's championing of the mass reader's right to books stemmed more directly from the lectures of Petr Lavrov, his mathematics and theoretical mechanics teacher at the Mikhailovskii Artillery Academy, who would later become the ideologist of revolutionary populism (*narodnichestvo*). The police noted the relationship between teacher and student in an official report: 'The young officer was a collaborator on the *Encyclopedic Dictionary* published under the editorship of the famous Colonel Lavrov, though his work was brief'.[14]

However, the most important influence on Pavlenkov's career came from the literary critic and revolutionary activist Dmitry Pisarev (1840–68), whose articles gained great popularity in the early 1860s and whose work, even after his untimely death, continued to inspire an entire generation of Russians to radical action. Peter Posefsky shows that Pisarev 'caught the attention of the reading public as a radical materialist popularizing science'. In his role as a literary critic, he acted essentially as a professional reader, instructing his youthful public on what to read and how. . . . The experience of reading, moreover, helped to unite radical readers into a community, as their favorite journalists provided them with a kind of core curriculum as well as a common set of interpretive skills.[15]

Pisarev's ethos served as an inspiration for much of Pavlenkov's work, so much so that Pavlenkov took on the challenging and risky project of publishing a compilation of Pisarev's journalistic writings despite the fact that Pisarev was at that time imprisoned by the tsarist authorities because of an incendiary article he had written in 1862. Pavlenkov became acquainted with Pisarev's family sometime at the end of 1865 or the beginning of 1866, gaining their assistance in negotiating a contract with Pisarev while he was still imprisoned in the Peter and Paul Fortress. He engaged in a lengthy battle with the Russian censors in order to achieve his goal to publish the collected works.[16] Pavlenkov acted as his own defence lawyer in the court proceedings blocking the publication of Pisarev's collected works. The trial was 'one of the first open court proceedings on publishing' and was watched by all 'cultured Russia'. Pavlenkov knew this, and brought his own stenographer to record the testimony, which was subsequently published in *Saint Petersburg News* and the *Court Herald*.[17] Prosecutor N. O. Tizenhauzen took Pisarev to task for mocking the Orthodox Christian views expressed by I. V. Kireevskii in his article 'Russian Don Quixote' (first published in *Russkoe slovo* in 1861) and for Pisarev's offhand remark (in his article 'Poor Russian Thought' also published in *Russkoe slovo* in 1862) that the life of the Russian nation would not have changed if Peter the Great had been assassinated in his youth. Not only did Pavlenkov trip up the accuser in logical fallacies and contradictions, but he also showed the court his recently printed brochure containing the two articles in question (which had been approved by the censor in Moscow) without the name of Pisarev on the front cover. At that point, charges were dropped against Pavlenkov and the ban on the publication of the second part of Pisarev's works was removed. One biographer remarked:

> With this trial, Pavlenkov created his popularity. From that time on, the censor began to consider him a serious opponent, with whom it was challenging and unpleasant to do business. Pavlenkov's speech for the defence, appearing as an indictment against the censor and censorship – the prosecutor and the judges sympathized with him – revealed his political face as an enemy of the autocracy.[18]

After Pisarev's release in 1866, Pavlenkov became an intimate of the family, and in 1868 escorted Pisarev's body back from Dubbeln, Latvia, after his death by drowning. Pavlenkov arranged Pisarev's funeral and took up a subscription to establish a scholarship in Pisarev's memory and to erect a monument on his grave.[19] For printing unauthorised leaflets asking for donations and planning to distribute them in his bookstore, Pavlenkov was prosecuted by the tsarist authorities, sent into indefinite exile from St Petersburg to Viatka in central Russia, and banned from publishing. Though Pavlenkov's first publishing projects had been motivated by his sense that the Russian reader needed exposure to contemporary sources of scientific knowledge and socio-political thought, it was only during his exile in Viatka that he realised how much basic information the mass reader needed to start on the path to enlightenment.

To borrow a line from Richard D. Altick, 'The history of the mass reading audience is, in fact, the history of English [insert "Russian" here] democracy seen from a new angle'.[20] Altick asserts that in England the struggle for political democracy did not normally focus on the right of the common man to literacy. But in Russia, it actually became a part of the programme of social and political activists during the 1860s. After the abolition of serfdom in 1861, 'landmark legislation' in 1864 set forth rules for the establishment of primary schools throughout the Russian Empire, giving local groups the opportunity to participate in their construction and support. Known as *zemstvos*, these local groups were partially self-governing institutions in the provinces, in essence an early form of local government; however, the Ministry of Education still oversaw the *zemstvos*' efforts. Yet, as Ben Eklof has pointed out, prior to the 1890s the primary impetus for schools and literacy came from the peasants and not the *zemstvos* or the elite landowners, for several reasons. First, most *zemstvos* were dominated by local gentry, whose own children were educated by private tutors or in existing urban schools, and had no need of the institutions; second, funding a large number of primary schools would necessitate an increase in taxes on the gentry's lands; and third, there still remained 'strong vestiges of traditional elite hostility to mass education even after the Emancipation of the Serfs'.[21] Eklof charts three distinct phases of literacy campaigns in Russia: the first based on peasant initiatives in the 1860s; a second phase when local organisations (*zemstvos*, *dumas* and private elite initiatives) expanded the peasant 'free schools' (*volnye shkoly*); and a third phase when private and governmental efforts jointly developed a broad network of primary schools. Eklof thus confirms that popular literacy began to rise 'before large scale elite intervention which began in the 1890s',[22] though Pavlenkov was already at the forefront of the mass education movement, having been active since the mid-1860s. Pavlenkov's involvement in the development of materials for mass readers coincided with the second and third phases sketched out by Eklof, peaking in the third phase, and greatly facilitated the growth of the mass reading public.

Moreover, Pavlenkov's trajectory as a publisher and activist in mass education and literacy parallels the one Altick describes in England, where initially the growth of the reading public was viewed with concern. Reading was thought to interfere with the common man's morality and ability to work; after 1790, the figure of the common reader became a threat to the nation's security (that is, as a spur to social unrest), which the authorities tried to control by institutionalising Sunday schools for poorer children to keep them in line on their sole day off.[23] Something similar took place in Russia in a more condensed fashion over a half century later, beginning in the 1860s. Jeffrey Brooks notes that the educated elites expected that the lower classes would come to share in a common Russian culture, which would be created and controlled by the elites: 'the proper goals of literacy and education were to enable people of lower-class origin to share in this general culture', which would not be primarily focused on popular commercial literature. Some educated Russians who rejected popular commercial literature became activists who strove to create and sponsor a 'people's literature' and went on to produce non-commercial publications to carry their cultural values to the mass reader. Though Brooks comes to the conclusion that the activists were not successful in trying to turn the mass reader away from popular commercial literature, he does not discuss the very important category of what we would call popular educational or self-improvement reading that Pavlenkov produced, and which mass readers increasingly demanded.[24]

Pavlenkov's exile in Viatka (from 1868 to 1877), a large provincial town in central Russia, put him into touch with how life was experienced not just by the urbanised population, but also by the provincial middle and lower classes and especially the peasantry. Viatka was unique as a provincial capital in that its local *zemstvo*, formed only in 1867, was not dominated by the nobility – its membership included peasants, merchants and middle-class citizens.[25] Viatka also brought him into direct contact with a circle of radical and progressive *intelligenty,* many of whom had themselves been sent into exile for their political activism and who sympathised with his own beliefs. These Viatka inhabitants provided him with a social network and support, eventually assisting him in his publishing efforts despite the official prohibition. His circle included the exiled teacher V. I. Obreimov, the publicist and local historian N. Ia. Agafonov, the writer M. E. Selenkina and her husband A. N. Selenkin, V. A. Krasovskii (a local civil court judge) and his brother, A. A. Krasovskii (who owned a printing press and bookshop) and the exiled doctor V. O. Portugalov. Pavlenkov also became acquainted with a local priest, Nikolai Nikolaevich Blinov, whose two primers had been published in Viatka by the local *zemstvo*: *Alphabet for Udmurt Children* (*Azbuka dlia votskikh (Udmurtskikh) detei*, 1867)[26] and *A Grammar* (*Gramota*, 1868) for Russian schools. Pavlenkov was taken by Blinov's approach and felt that his work deserved to be known beyond the confines of the Viatka region, so he had Blinov's textbook, *On Methods of Teaching People's Elementary School Subjects at Home and in School* (*O sposobakh obucheniia v sem'e i shkole predmetam uchebnogo kursa v nachal'nykh narodnykh uchilishchakh*)[27] republished by V. D. Cherkasov, Pavlenkov's oldest childhood friend, who was running his publishing business while Pavlenkov was in exile.

Pavlenkov realised that the mass reader needed to start at the very beginning, with the ABCs, so he began with the basic tools for elementary education. He studied the theories of pedagogue Konstantin Dmitrievich Ushinskii (1824–70), especially two foundational concepts: first, if reading or study 'touches the heart' then it will leave a mark and 'will arouse in the child not only an idea, but also a wish, a striving and feeling'; and second, that the use of visual aids was 'necessary for a child for the independent understanding of one or another idea'.[28] Following these principles, Pavlenkov began work on his *Illustrated Alphabet Primer* (*Nagliadnaia azbuka*) (Figure 8.2), which would allow students to teach themselves to read after only minimal contact with and instruction by a teacher. Pavlenkov developed a unique methodology where it was necessary to teach the students only the letters which corresponded to the few vowel sounds of Russian and then the letters for four to six consonants, after which the students could learn to read on their own. In his note appended to the primer (which was taken from a separate book, *A Guide to the Illustrated Alphabet Primer* [*Ob'iasnenie k 'Nagladnoi azbuke'*]), Pavlenkov explained that the self-teaching process was founded on a 'simple mathematical principle: Knowing the sum of two numbers and then having a third added, we can easily guess what the third is'.[29] Pavlenkov's primer was sold for the low price of twenty kopecks and included 600 illustrations, mainly taken from rural life.

Figure 8.2 F. F. Pavlenkov's *Illustrated Alphabet Primer for Learning and Self-Taught Literacy*, with 600 illustrations (St Petersburg: V. D. Cherkasov Publishers, 1873). Price 10 kopeks. Typography of A. M. Kotomin, p. 3

The title page featured a quotation from the German pedagogue Friedrich Fröbel (1782–1852) and a dedication to K. D. Ushinskii.[30] But Pavlenkov's authorship remained unknown, due to the imperial ban on his publishing activities during his exile. The book was printed without an author's name on the title page, and was attributed to Pavlenkov's Viatka colleague and friend Blinov. According to Blinov's memoirs, he played a prominent role in shaping the text by discussing the manuscript with Pavlenkov and helping to finalise what would appear in the published book.

After publication, Pavlenkov arranged for 2,000 free copies to be sent to specific teachers at village schools (whose addresses Blinov acquired while he was in Moscow organising the publication of supplementary materials).[31] The books were sent along with a request for practical feedback about the teaching methodology and content, both positive and negative; Pavlenkov later published these remarks in a separate volume to promote the textbook.[32] Blinov willingly lent his cachet as an already published pedagogue to the project and attended the 1873 International Conference on Pedagogy in Vienna, where the famous Russian educator and pedagogue N. A. Korf presented the book to a large audience. The book received an honourable mention and created a sensation among the pedagogues who attended, as well as among progressively inclined Russian pedagogues. The Kharkov pedagogue, Sunday school teacher and activist Kh. D. Alchevskaia, at a meeting with Lev Tolstoy in April 1884, told him how quickly and easily schoolchildren learned to read and write with the help of Pavlenkov's primer.[33]

Pavlenkov came up with a plan to facilitate the use of the book by the largest number of teachers and students. Viatka, like many other provinces of Russia, did not have enough teachers, especially for free public schools. With the assistance of the local Viatka *zemstvos*, he set up an experimental 'mobile' school, where a teacher would travel around the region to teach groups of ten people – peasant children but also adults – the rudiments from the textbook over the course of two weeks, which they could then continue working on at their own pace for the next three weeks. The results were beyond what they imagined could be achieved in such a short time. More than eighty itinerant schools were established, which greatly worried the Ministry of Education.[34]

At this point, despite the fact that the reader and other materials had gone through two separate rounds in the censors' office and received accolades (even from those educators who pointed out some shortcomings), the censorship committee took issue with some juxtapositions of the illustrations, which they felt placed the sacred and the profane in too close proximity, or in other cases appeared to be propagandising Darwinism. The book was banned in 1874, withdrawn from all schools and libraries, and destroyed. Even the title was prohibited. Pavlenkov cleverly devised tactics to make sure that his alphabet book would be republished. He made insignificant changes in the order and layout of the illustrations, changed the title to *Reading and Writing According to Illustrations* (*Chtenie i pis'mo po kartinkam*) and sent copies to censors' offices in Kazan, Moscow, Kiev and Riga. He received approval to publish without any problems and in early 1876 issued 30,000 copies of practically the same book. Another sly tactical move was his introduction to the new book, which included a critique of the earlier 'Pavlenkov publication'. In the end, his ruses were discovered, but after his return to St Petersburg from exile in 1877, he was, nonetheless, able to return the original title to the work. The work went through twenty-three editions in all.[35] These tactics were commonly used by other authors and publishers to get around censorship restrictions, but Pavlenkov was especially masterful at achieving his goals despite restrictions.[36]

At the same time that Pavlenkov was publishing teach-yourself-to-read primers, he continued to translate and publish textbooks on chemistry, physics, arithmetic, geometry, geography and pedagogy, for use by the self-taught learner and for the use of teachers at various levels. In the 1860s and 1870s, publishing books about the natural sciences increased nationally, representing 12.8 per cent of all publications in 1876, with an average print run of 2,500.[37] Seven of the thirteen titles that Pavlenkov published during that era (including while he was in exile) were related to the natural sciences. His print runs were between 4,000 and 6,000, which meant that the books were in high demand. Even when he had been prohibited from publishing, he still managed to publish thirty-four individual titles, plus the republished Pisarev collection, during his exile.[38]

Pavlenkov's output only increased after he returned from exile in Viatka and received official permission to resume his publishing business, but he remained under police surveillance, and in February 1879 his publishing career was cut short again by another arrest. He was incarcerated and exiled to Siberia until his release and return to Petersburg in April 1881. Then the real expansion of his publishing empire began.

The last two decades of Pavlenkov's life saw an explosion in the market for publications for the newly literate readership, one which Pavlenkov helped create. From 1880 to 1900 he published more than 700 titles.[39] This new market filled the gap between works for an elite readership and the simplest forms of mass market literature. Over the course of his later career, Pavlenkov produced and published more than ten popular serials, which reflected his ongoing interests in science, literature and progressive thought.[40] These serials became the financial backbone of his success. Following the precepts of Pisarev – 'the popularizer must be an artist with words, and the highest, most beautiful, most humanistic task of art lies specifically in merging with science and through that combination, to give science such practical power, which it cannot obtain exclusively by its own means'[41] – Pavlenkov sought out and cultivated authors who could popularise.

V. V. Lunkevich (1866–1941), a young biologist who had just completed a degree at Kharkov University, offered Pavlenkov his manuscript 'The Science of Life: Popular Physiology' (*Nauka o zhizni. Populiarnaia fiziologia*) and Pavlenkov immediately offered him a contract. Lunkevich became the author of several books in Pavlenkov's catalogue, as well as a very successful series of illustrated booklets, 'Popular Science Library for the Masses' (forty titles, 1890–1913), which went through five editions. The series included brochures on the earth, stars and sky, on the human body and on other animals, and volumes on 'miracles of science and technology'. When he had fulfilled his contractual obligations and sent in the last manuscript for the series, Lunkevich wanted to undertake a trip to Europe to improve his knowledge of foreign languages so he could better work with primary scientific sources. Pavlenkov offered to send him a monthly honorarium rather than buying the rights to the Popular Science Library, so that Lunkevich could retain them and 'have his library "feed" him for the rest of his life'.[42] Pavlenkov garnered a reputation for treating his writers with integrity and respect, paying them well and subsidising their research and travels. Several of Lunkevich's works (including those from the Popular Science Library) continued to be published well into the Soviet era. Reader surveys from the 1920s found that the works of pre-revolutionary popular science authors like Lunkevich were preferred by worker and peasant readers to those produced by Soviet and Marxist science writers because the earlier writers rendered scientific arguments in simplified language which emerging readers could understand.[43]

The impetus for another series, the Popular Law Library, undoubtedly originated in Pavlenkov's own courtroom experiences. Given the notoriety of his trial in St Petersburg, local inhabitants in Viatka asked him for help with their judicial problems, and he acted as a public defender for several court cases there. Edited by Ia. A. Abramov (1858–1906), the series consisted of eleven booklets, ranging in topic from 'Marriage and Family' to 'Divorce' to 'How to Research and Answer in Court' and was published from 1896 to 1903.

Prior to the 1880s, Pavlenkov focused his efforts on fostering literacy through his innovative alphabet primers. Yet Pavlenkov also saw the need for accessible works of children's literature, which had been dominated by the publishing houses of M. O. Vol'f, A. F. Marks and Alfred Devrein, who produced lavishly illustrated, expensive editions of fairy tales and other stories.[44] In the 1880s, Pavlenkov filled that gap by producing inexpensive illustrated libraries of not just fairy tales but also of literary classics. Though Pavlenkov had produced individual books oriented towards children (including accounts of worldwide exploration and several biographies written specifically for children by A. O. Ostrovinskaia), he now began several series geared towards children.

The tsarist cooptation of Russia's greatest writers began in the late 1880s, coalescing around the official celebrations of the anniversaries of Pushkin's and Gogol's births and deaths. As a result, publishers began to reprint collections of their works and other related materials. Taking advantage of the imperial authorisation of Pushkin, Gogol and Lermontov as appropriate literature for the masses, and of the lapse of their original copyrights, Pavlenkov published several volumes and serials, including the Illustrated Pushkin Library (forty books) in 1888, as well as collections of approved foreign authors: the Illustrated Novels of Dickens (1890–1, twelve books), and the Illustrated Novels of Walter Scott (twenty-five books, 1892–5, which went to two editions).[45] Notable as well is Pavlenkov's Illustrated Fairy Tale Library, published in two editions (1894–6 and 1895–9), which comprised 110 separate volumes, including works by Hans Christian Andersen, the Brothers Grimm and E. T. A. Hoffman, as well as collections of national fairy tales.

These publications were geared towards the mass reader because of their length (less than 100 pages), their copious use of illustrations, their soft-cover format and their price. The majority of Pavlenkov's booklets cost only a few kopeks, and an entire series often cost less than 100 kopeks, while his *ABCs for a Kopek* (*Azbuka-kopeika*) really did cost only one kopek each. The books were printed on good paper with professional illustrations even though they had paper covers. Publishers who competed with Pavlenkov for the emerging market for the newly literate reader complained that he frequently undercut their pricing and offered the lowest-cost books with the highest-quality production values. Sociologist of reading Nikolai Rubakin recalled that when he was working in his mother's rental library, readers would ask for books not by author or title but by the name of the publisher, Pavlenkov.[46]

The crowning achievement of Pavlenkov's serial publications was 'The Lives of Remarkable People', which became the longest-running biography series in the history of world literature.[47] It consisted of the biographies of 200 'remarkable people' in ten categories of profession: (1) representatives of world religions, (2) political and national heroes, (3) scientists, (4) philosophers, (5) philanthropists and enlighteners/educational activists, (6) explorers, (7) inventors and people with broad social initiatives, (8) writers, (9) artists and (10) musicians and actors. It was designed to commemorate important figures in both Russian and world history, and to introduce Russian readers to proponents of diverse philosophical, political and religious ideas. It is the one series by Pavlenkov that survived during the Soviet era, when it was taken over by Maxim Gorky. It continues to be published to the present day by Molodaia Gvardiia press, which has released almost 2,000 individual biographies.

In the last year of his life, Pavlenkov completed a project that he had been working on for thirty years, continually writing down information, descriptions and definitions in a notebook. Like his teacher Lavrov, he felt the most urgent need, especially for teachers in village schools, was for an encyclopaedic dictionary, which he finally published in 1899. It contained 2,224 drawings, including 813 portraits and 37 maps; all the plates were made in Paris. 'Until the appearance of Pavlenkov's dictionary, there wasn't anything in the Russian language of equal value', according to Rubakin.[48] It was republished seven times until 1923, in a total print run of close to 160,000.[49] In sum, over a lifetime Pavlenkov's enterprise published more than 750 titles, with a total print run of more than 3.5 million copies.[50]

Pavlenkov's will distributed a small bequest to a family member and larger amounts to two literary funds for writers and scholars, but the bulk of his estate, more than 100,000 roubles, was to be used to establish reading rooms in remote areas of the Russian provinces to serve the lower classes, both adults and children. The three executors of the estate were Pavlenkov's assistant, N. A. Rosenthal, his colleague and close friend V. D. Cherkasov, and V. I. Iakovenko (1850–1915), who was also one of Pavlenkov's co-workers. Iakovenko became his main executor until his own death in 1915 and was responsible for the continuation of his publishing enterprise as well as the fulfilment of his reading room legacy. The tsarist authorities never displayed any desire to help the organisation of free public village libraries. The minister of internal affairs, Peter Durnovo, himself exhorted Iakovenko to give up Pavlenkov's allotment for the founding of 2,000 free libraries in the Russian Empire's far-flung regions in favour of establishing and maintaining ten to twenty large urban libraries.[51] Iakovenko objected that this would violate the terms of the will, which specified that 'the books were to be distributed to the poorest and most remote places and as much as possible across the greatest expanse of Russia'.[52] Iakovenko was aware that there was a great disparity in the development of literacy in urban areas versus rural regions, as he had worked as a statistician for the Moscow province *zemstvo* in the early 1880s.[53]

At the time of Pavlenkov's death, the value of his book stock if liquidated was enough to open the specified 2,000 village reading rooms, but his executors took another path: they decided to complete the unfinished work of the publishing house in order to generate more income to fund and maintain the reading rooms. The founding of each Pavlenkov library/reading room cost approximately 106–55 roubles.[54] Each reading room was to receive fifty roubles' worth of books from Pavlenkov's publishing house and another 100 roubles' worth of books from other publishers. The book donations continued something Pavlenkov had done throughout his life. In Viatka he gave books to prisons, schools and libraries. He was also a major contributor to the book collection Anton Chekhov gathered for Sakhalin Island schools after visiting the prison colony there.[55] Like Jean Macé and Andrew Carnegie before him, Pavlenkov expected local organisations and/or private individuals to make financial contributions to the foundation and maintenance of the reading rooms.[56]

Iakovenko sent letters with the conditions for opening the libraries and a catalogue of books to all the provincial *zemstvos*. Four libraries were opened in 1900, 22 in 1901, none in 1902, 337 in 1903, 313 in 1904, 215 in 1905, in 338 in 1906, 272 in 1907, 178 in 1908, and 112 in 1909.[57] Most often libraries were opened in educational institutions. Every reading room had a set of rules and a council of trustees. The librarians were teachers, literate peasants or workers from churches. In the course of 1901–11, more than 2,000 Pavlenkov libraries were opened in fifty-three Russian provinces, the majority of which (1,547) were formed with the help of local (*uezd*-level) *zemstvos*. In areas where there were no *zemstvos* (about half of the Empire's provinces) literacy societies and people's temperance organisations often served this role.[58] Pavlenkov libraries opened and were replenished until March 1915, when Iakovenko died.

Unlike in England with its history of village reading rooms, which reached a peak but then essentially had died out by the turn of the twentieth century due to the widespread availability of cheap books,[59] in Russia there was no organised system of funding free public reading rooms prior to Pavlenkov's bequest, due to the lack of financial support from the tsarist government. The spread of reading rooms greatly facilitated the progress of literacy in pre-revolutionary Russia, as well as making the book a 'permanent element of village life'.[60] One source claims that Iakovenko may have been responsible for the creation of tens of thousands of reading rooms.[61] Iakovenko greatly contributed to the 'vast adult educational infrastructure . . . of over 14,000 public libraries, 1,000 cultural clubs and numerous literacy centers' created prior to the Bolshevik revolution, as Boris Raymond summarised.[62] Writing in the 1930s, book scholar Olga Kaidanova noted that the Soviet government inherited 'the rich spiritual content that filled the whole of the pedagogical work of the pre-revolutionary period'.⁶³ The names of Pavlenkov and Iakovenko, however, fell out of the annals of book history until the later years of the Soviet era.

The rediscovery of Pavlenkov and his legacy began in the late Soviet period and has taken two parallel but substantially different directions. Renewed scholarly interest in his life and legacy was initiated in 1960 by N. Rassudovskaia, who wrote the first comprehensive biographical essay on the publisher, based on access to his archives. Since 1979, the Russian National Library in Leningrad/St Petersburg has held 'Pavlenkov readings' – scholarly conferences on the history of the book in Russia in the late tsarist period – once every two years.⁶⁴ After the collapse of the Soviet Union and the end of state-subsidised publishing, several publishers reprinted the original Pavlenkov 'Lives of Remarkable People' series. As part of a re-publication of Pavlenkov's series by Ural Press in Cheliabinsk, one of Pavlenkov's earliest and foremost scholars, Iunii Gorbunov, wrote the first comprehensive biography of the publisher in 1999. Eventually, the Molodaia Gvardiia publishing house, which had continued the series during the Soviet period, successfully reclaimed its rights to the series, restored Pavlenkov's name as the series' founder, and in 2006 published its own biography of him, by Vladimir Desiaterik.⁶⁵

However, the more important aspect of the rediscovery of Pavlenkov has been the grassroots revival of the reading rooms and libraries established after his death in the Russian provinces, now widely referred to as the 'Pavlenkov movement'. Gorbunov, the principal scholar of Pavlenkov, also worked as a journalist for the *Ural Tracker* (*Uralskii sledopyt*), a regional local historical studies magazine which in December 1990 began searching for Pavlenkov reading rooms all over Russia. Another journalist at the magazine, L. A. Shirinovskaia, was director of the library in Verkhnii Tagil, one of the oldest of the original reading rooms, and in 1991, through her efforts, it was the first to be renamed after Pavlenkov.⁶⁶ In 1995–6 the Community of Pavlenkov Libraries (Sodruzhestvo Pavlenkovskikh bibliotek) was founded: its aim is to identify those facilities that survived through the Soviet era and restore Pavlenkov's name to them.⁶⁷ The Community is organised under the auspices of a large research library in each region, to which the smaller reading rooms/libraries in more rural areas are affiliated. By 2004 there were 340 Pavlenkov libraries in six regions of Russia: Sverdlovsk, Perm, Cheliabinsk, Kirov, Komi and Udmurtiia.⁶⁸ According to the current president of the Community, Nataliia Iaroslavtseva, in 2018 there were twelve such regional affiliates with a total of 462 libraries in this expanding movement.

In addition, the Community has the overall aim of raising standards for libraries all over provincial Russia and adding new libraries/reading rooms, which have to meet a common set of standards in terms of book holdings, level of facilities, training of librarians and access to current technology. The aim of the Community is to keep the book as the centre of village life but expand the notion of literacy to one appropriate to the age of electronic access. The charter of the Community lists an affiliation with UNESCO and adherence to its guidelines. It holds annual meetings to add new member libraries/reading rooms and update historical information about their origins and survival. A typical example is given in the report of I. A. Ushakova in 2013 on the Svetitskaia village library. It serves a local population of 420, of whom 402 residents used the library a total of about 5,000 times, taking out 9,500 items on loan from a collection of 6,843. Visitors to this library, and many others like it, see a 'Pavlenkov corner', containing albums, archival findings, photographs and other materials relating to the history of the restoration of the library and its current development.[69] The 'Pavlenkov corners' often feature an image of the publisher, sometimes done by local artists, a tradition dating back to the 'red corner' (*krasnyi ugolok*) of the tsarist period, and the subsequent 'Lenin corner' of the Soviet period. Many of these rural libraries have undertaken to establish annual commemorations in Pavlenkov's honour, usually centred on his birthday. A museum in Pavlenkov's honour, with rare holdings of his original works, is presently under construction in the library at Nolinsk in Kirov (formerly Viatka) province (Plate 5). Pavlenkov's combination of service to the public good and success in the marketplace makes him a seemingly ideal role model for today's post-Soviet Russia.

Notes

We wish to express our gratitude for the assistance that Carol received while in Russia in obtaining materials for this article from Nataliia N. Iaroslavtseva of the Herzen Library in Kirov/Viatka and current president of the Confederation of Pavlenkov Libraries, as well as Ekaterina N. Kudriashova, director of the Nolinsk Library.

1. The term in Russian is *samyi chitaiushchii narod* or *samaia chitaiushchaia strana*, depending on the speaker. S. S. Vishnevskii, 'The Most Well-Read Country in the World' (1986), in Adele Barker and Bruce Grant (eds), *The Russia Reader: History, Politics, Culture* (Durham:

Duke University Press, 2010), p. 627. In the original Russian in Vishnevskii's article, it is the latter term.

2. For more on Bolshevik views on education and literacy, see Peter Kenecz, 'Liquidating Illiteracy in Revolutionary Russia', *Russian History*, 9:2–3 (1982), pp. 173–86.
3. N. Krupskaia, *Memories of Lenin* (London: Lawrence and Wishart, 1942), p. 2, cited in Kenecz, 'Liquidating Illiteracy', p. 174.
4. Kenecz, 'Liquidating Illiteracy', p. 173.
5. Evgeny Dobrenko, *The Making of the State Reader: Social and Aesthetic Contexts of the Reception of Soviet Literature*, trans. Jesse M. Savage (Stanford: Stanford University Press, 1997); Stephen Lovell, *The Russian Reading Revolution: Print Culture in the Soviet and Post-Soviet Era* (London: Palgrave Macmillan, 2000); Jeffrey Brooks, *When Russia Learned to Read: Literacy and Popular Literature, 1861–1917* (Princeton: Princeton University Press, 1985). See also Chapter 7 of the present volume.
6. Pavlenkov's principal biographies are: Iu. Gorbunov (ed.), *Florenty Pavlenkov. Ego zhizn' i izdatel'skaia deiatel'nost'* (Cheliabinsk: Ural Ltd, 1999), and in particular the chapter by V. D. Cherkasov, 'F. F. Pavlenkov. Otryvki iz vospominanii', pp. 193–221; N. Rassudovskaia, *Izdatel' F. F. Pavlenkov (1839–1900). Ocherk zhizni i deiatel'nosti* (Moscow: Izd. Vsesoiuznoi knizhnoi palaty, 1960); and V. Desiaterik, *Pavlenkov* (Moscow: Molodaia gvardiia, 2006).
7. 'Nachalo izdatel'skoi deiatel'nosti F. F. Pavlenkova', in I. I. Frolova (ed.), *Kniga v Rossii 1861–1881* (Moscow: Kniga, 1988), vol. I, p. 138.
8. B. P. Mandel, *Knizhnoe delo i istoriia knigi* (Moscow: Direct Media, 2014), p. 30.
9. A. V. Blium, *Pavlenkov v Viatke* (Kirov: Volgo-Viat. kn. izd-vo, Kirov. otd-nie, 1976), p. 8. See Gorbunov, *Florenty Pavlenkov*, p. 240, for information on editions. See also V. B. Pomelov, 'Vklad F. F. Pavlenkova v rasvitie prosveshcheniia v Viatskoi gubernii', *Vestnik Viatskogo gosudarstvennogo universiteta* (2015), p. 125, at <https://cyberleninka.ru/article/n/pavlenkova-v-razvitie-prosvescheniya-v-vyatskoy-gubernii> (last accessed on 11 April 2018).
10. Pavlenkov later published another book by Ganot, on magnetism and electricity (1885). See Gorbunov, *Florenty Pavlenkov*, p. 240.
11. Josep Simon, *Communicating Physics: The Production, Circulation, and Appropriation of Ganot's Textbooks in France and England, 1851–1887* (Pittsburgh: University of Pittsburgh Press, 2011), p. 191. In *Fathers and Children*, Bazarov, a young nihilist associated with materialism and positivism, offers to discuss the textbook with Anna Odintsova, a provincial noblewoman to whom he is romantically attracted despite his own materialist values. August Strindberg also cited Ganot's *Traité* in his work *Miss Julie*, to illustrate marital incompatibility.
12. Cherkasov, 'F. F. Pavlenkov', p. 200. When Gaideburov owned it, the

bookstore had a reading room and was already under police surveillance. See 'P. A. Gaideburov', in Frolova (ed.), *Kniga v Rossii*, vol. I, p. 131.
13. John Stuart Mill, quoted in E. A. Dinershtein, *I. D. Sytin* (Moscow: Kniga, 1983), p. 3. All translations are by the present authors except where noted.
14. Citation from V. E. Barykin, 'F. F. Pavlenkov and D. I. Pisarev', *Zhurnalistika i literatura* (Moscow, 1972), p. 222, in Frolova (ed.), *Kniga v Rossii*, vol. I, p. 138.
15. Peter C. Posefsky, *The Nihilist Imagination: Dmitrii Pisarev and the Cultural Origins of Russian Radicalism (1860–1868)* (New York: Peter Lang, 2003), pp. 19–21.
16. Pavlenkov commissioned a stenographer to transcribe the trial proceedings against him for the publication of Pisarev's collected works and then published them along with the approved subsequent volumes. See P. F. Alisov, 'Protsess Pavlenkova', *Sbornik literaturnykh i politicheskikh statei* (Geneva: H. Georg, 1877).
17. Gorbunov, *Florenty Pavlenkov*, pp. 54–5. The censors prohibited the re-publication of the stenographer's record in later editions of the second volume of Pisarev's collected works (only reappearing in the addenda to the sixth volume of the 1907 edition), but it did appear in the original 1866 volume. See Rassudovskaia, *Izdatel' F. F. Pavlenkov*, p. 12, note 3.
18. Rassudovskaia, *Izdatel' F. F. Pavlenkov*, p. 12.
19. Ibid., p. 13; see also Cherkasov, 'F. F. Pavlenkov', p. 198; Desiaterik, *Pavlenkov*, p. 93.
20. Richard D. Altick, *The English Common Reader: A Social History of the Mass Reading Public, 1800–1900*, 2nd edition (Columbus: Ohio State University Press, 1998), p. 3.
21. Ben Eklof, 'Schooling and Literacy in Late Imperial Russia', in Daniel P. Resnick (ed.), *Literacy in Historical Perspective* (Washington, DC: Library of Congress, 1983), pp. 105–6.
22. See Ben Eklof, 'Russian Literacy Campaigns 1861–1939', in R. F. Arnove et al. (eds), *National Literacy Campaigns* (New York: Springer, 1987), p. 126; and Boris N. Mironov, 'The Development of Literacy in Russia and the USSR from the Tenth to the Twentieth Centuries', *History of Education Quarterly*, 31:2 (summer 1991), p. 251. See also Brooks, *When Russia Learned to Read*, pp. 35–58 on the different primary schools, ranging from *zemstvo*-supported, church parish and peasant schools to state schools controlled by the Ministry of Education.
23. Altick, *The English Common Reader*, pp. 66–7.
24. Brooks, *When Russia Learned to Read*, pp. 295–6.
25. N. D. Doronina, 'Brat'ia Vasnetsovy: stanovlenie', in Iu. A. Gorbunov (ed.), *Knizhnaia provintsiia: sbornik statei* (Kirov: Izdatel'skii dom Gertsenka, 2017), p. 14.
26. The Udmurts were a non-Russian ethnic group residing in the Viatka region.

27. The textbook was published in 1870, at the St. Petersburg typography of A. M. Kotomin, where the majority of Pavlenkov's earlier publications had been printed.
28. Ushinskii quoted in Desiaterik, *Pavlenkov*, p. 127.
29. 'Kak uchit' po etoi azbuke', excerpted from *Ob'iasnenie k 'Nagliadnoi azbuke'* (St Petersburg, 1872), on frontispiece, *Nagliadnaia azbuka dlia obucheniia i samoobucheniia gramoty* (St Petersburg, Izdanie V. D. Cherkasova, tip. A. M. Kotomina, 1873).
30. An English translation of the quotation is: 'In my opinion, the most urgent task of children's upbringing is to stimulate children to think as early as possible'. For a contextualisation of Pavlenkov's work in the larger arena of children's publishing, see Ben Hellman, *Fairy Tales and True Stories: The History of Russian Literature for Children and Young People, 1574–2010* (Leiden: Brill, 2013), pp. 169–70.
31. Blinov also worked on two supplements/appendices to the book: *Learning Is the Light* (*Uchenie–Svet*), a book of readings for school and home, and *The Little Bee* (*Pchelka*), a collection of poetry, riddles and aphorisms, both of which were illustrated by the Viatka artist Vasilii Porfir'ev. These books were published by the Moscow printer A. I. Mamontov, along with a brochure, 'Notes for Teachers About Classroom Exercises for the Book *Learning Is the Light*'. All three publications were presented in Moscow at the polytechnic exhibition for teachers at village schools, along with a demonstration of how to use the reader for self-teaching. For more details see V. B. Pomelov, 'Prosvetitel' i metodist nachal'noi shkoly F. F. Pavlenkov. K 175-letiu izdatelia, prosvetitelia i pedagoga-metodista', *Nachal'naia shkola*, 10 (2014), pp. 6–7; and Desiaterik, *Pavlenkov*, pp. 129–30.
32. *Otzyvy narodnykh uchitelei k 'Nagliadnoi azbuke'* (St Petersburg, 1880).
33. Kh. D. Alchevksaia, *Peredumannoe i perezhitoe: Dnevniki, pis'ma, vospominaniia* (Moscow: I. D. Sytin, 1912), p. 112, quoted in 'Nachalo izdatel'skoi deiatel'nosti F. F. Pavlenkova', in Frolova (ed.), *Kniga v Rossii*, vol. I, p. 142; see also Desiaterik, *Pavlenkov*, p. 330.
34. Pomelov, 'Prosvetitel' i metodist nachal'noi shkoly F. F. Pavlenkov', p. 9.
35. Ibid.
36. See I. P. Foote, 'Counter-Censorship: Authors v. Censors in Nineteenth-Century Russia', *Oxford Slavonic Papers*, 27 (1994), pp. 62–105, especially pp. 97–104.
37. M. V. Muratov, *Knizhnoe delo v Rossii v XIX i XX vv.: Ocherk istorii knigoizdatel'stva i knigotorgovli 1800–1917 gody* (1931), p. 106, cited in James T. Andrews, *Science for the Masses: The Bolshevik State, Public Science and the Popular Imagination in Soviet Russia, 1917–1934* (College Station: Texas A&M University Press, 2003), p. 181, note 38.
38. Blium, *Pavlenkov v Viatke*, p. 25. The total is fifty-two titles counting Pisarev's republished works.
39. Blium, *Pavlenkov v Viatke*, p. 26.

40. A full discussion of all the series is beyond the scope of this chapter. We do not discuss the *Library of Useful Knowledge*, the *Cultural History Library* (which was initiated after Pavlenkov's death) and a second *Popular Science Library* series (Populiarno-nauchnaia biblioteka).
41. D. I. Pisarev, cited on <http://infolib.crimea.ua/infolib/lunkevich.htm> (last accessed 12 April 2018).
42. Desiaterik, who had access to much of Pavlenkov's correspondence, details the communication between Pavlenkov and Lunkevich, without, unfortunately, providing archival citations for the letters he quotes. See Desiaterik, *Pavlenkov*, pp. 268–73. The quoted letter is on p. 273.
43. Andrews says that the most popular natural science books in the Soviet era were those on the origin of the world, land and mankind. He cites surveys by E. Vinogradova (1924) and popular science journals. Andrews, *Science for the Masses*, pp. 70, 126–7. See Brooks in Chapter 7 of the present volume on popular attitudes to the language used in Party publications.
44. For a summary of children's literature of the era, see Hellman, *Fairy Tales and True Stories*, especially pp. 169–293.
45. Pavlenkov published Pushkin's works in three different editions. An eight-volume collection, which was shortly increased to ten volumes (1887), was meant for a broad intelligentsia audience. The one-volume illustrated collection (1887) included almost all the poet's literary works and was aimed at teachers at public schools and gymnasia. The forty booklets of the Illustrated Pushkin Library were addressed to students, peasants and the working poor, and sold at prices ranging from two to twenty-five kopeks each. See <https://expositions.nlr.ru/ex_rare/pavlenkov/1880.php> (last accessed 25 April 2018). The Illustrated Gogol Library (1901–2, six editions) and the Illustrated Lermontov Library (1901–13) were published after Pavlenkov's death by his literary executors based on the example and success of this earlier library of classics.
46. Desiaterik, *Pavlenkov*, p. 329.
47. For an account of the deliberate effacement of Pavlenkov as the series founder and his restoration, see Ludmilla A. Trigos and Carol Ueland, 'Creating a National Biography Tradition: F. F. Pavlenkov's *Life of Remarkable People 1890–1924*', *Slavonic and East European Review*, 96:1 (2018), pp. 41–66.
48. Desiaterik, *Pavlenkov*, p. 342.
49. Rassudovskaia, *Izdatel' F. F. Pavlenkov*, p. 76.
50. V. E. Barykin and V. A. Fokeev, 'F. F. Pavlenkov', in *Bibliotechnaia entsiklopediia* (Moscow: Pashkov dom, 2007), p. 778.
51. V. V. Sarbei, 'Populizator Shevchenka V. I. Iakovenko', in *Zbirnyk prats' chotyrnadtsiatoï naukovoï shevchenkivs'koï konferentsiï (9–10 bereznia 1965 v. Poltavi)* (AN URSR. In-t lit. im. T. H. Shevchenka, Kyïv, 1966), p. 221.

52. V. I. Iakovenko, 'O pavlenkovskikh bibliotekakh, Doklad prochitan na 2-m publichnom sobranii 7 June 1911', in Vserossiiskii s"ezd po bibliotechnomu delu, *Trudy pervogo vserossiiskago s"ezda po bibliotechnomu delu, sostoaivshagosia v S-Peterburge s 1 po 7 iunia 1911 g. v 2-chastiakh* (St Petersburg, 1912), p. 25. Iakovenko's success in establishing the reading rooms in the farthest reaches of the Empire must also have been due to his prior experience as a *zemstvo* statistician and consequently to his deep understanding of the populations that needed to be served by the reading rooms as well as the challenges that would be faced in establishing them. As early as 1894, Iakovenko authored an article about how books actually got into the hands of the provincial masses. V. I. Iakovenko, 'At the Market Fairs with Books: A Letter from Poltava Guberniia' (*S knigami po iarmarkam: pis'mo iz poltavskoi gubernii*), *Vestnik Evropy*, 9 (September 1894), pp. 401–19.
53. Sarbej, 'Populizator Shevchenka V. I. Iakovenko', p. 213.
54. V. Iu. Sokolov, 'Otkrytie i organizatsia deiatel'nosti pavlenkovskikh bibliotek Kievskim obshchestvom gramotnosti v 1900–1907 gg.', in Iunii Gorbunov (ed.), *Knizhnaia provintsiia*, p. 104.
55. Desiaterik, *Pavlenkov*, p. 330.
56. Jean Macé (1815–94) was an inspiration for reading rooms, according to L. A. Shirinovskaia, 'F. F. Pavlenkov i Pavlenkovskie biblioteki', *Chtenie v bibliotekakh Rossii vyp 4* (St Petersburg: Rossiĭskaia natsional'naia biblioteka, 2004), p. 122. Shirinovskaia does not provide any direct reference to possible sources of influence from Macé; however, Pavlenkov was certainly aware of his work, since he includes him in his *Entsiklopedicheskii slovar'* (1899), p. 1348.
57. These statistics were cited by Iakovenko, 'O pavlenkovskikh bibliotekakh'.
58. For detailed information about number of readers, their gender, ages and the percentages of borrowings, see Sokolov, 'Otkrytie'.
59. Carole King, 'The Rise and Decline of Village Reading Rooms', *Rural History*, 20:2 (October 2009), pp. 163–86.
60. Charles E. Clark, *Uprooting Otherness: The Literacy Campaign in NEP-Era Russia* (Selinsgrove: Associated University Presses, 2000), p. 16. Clark traces the appropriation of such facilities by the Bolsheviks for their own ideological purposes. The quote comes from A. I. Reitblatt, 'Zemskie sel'skie "narodnye biblioteki" i ikh auditoriia', in A. I. Reitblatt, *Ot Bovy k Bal'monty i drugie raboty po istoricheskoi sotsiologii russkoi literatury* (Moscow: Novoe Literaturnoe Oborzrenie, 2009), p. 169.
61. Desiaterik, *Pavlenkov*, p. 361.
62. Boris Raymond, 'Libraries and Adult Education: The Russian Experience', *Journal of Library History*, 16 (spring 1981), pp. 396–7.
63. Olga Kaidanova, *Ocherki po istorii narodnogo obrazovaniia v Rossii i v SSSR* (Brussels: Imp. E. Gelezniakoff, 1939), vol. I, part 2, p. 106, as cited in Raymond, 'Libraries and Adult Education', p. 397.

Plate 1 William Nicol, *Quiet*, 1860. Image courtesy of York Museums Trust: http://yorkmuseumstrust.org.uk/Public Domain

Plate 2 John Callcott Horsley, *A Pleasant Corner*, 1865. © Royal Academy of Arts, London; Photographer: John Hammond

Plate 3 Alexander Rossi, *Forbidden Books*, 1897

Plate 4 William Powell Frith, *Ramsgate Sands*, 1854. Royal Collection Trust / © Her Majesty Queen Elizabeth II 2018

Plate 5 Nolinsk Library, memorial exhibition dedicated to F. F. Pavlenkov. Photograph by Carol Ueland

Plate 6 The Penguin Books edition of *Lady Chatterley's Lover*, at its affordable cover price

Plate 7 Though an undisputed architectural wonder, the Tianjin Binhai Library of China utilises more fake books than real

Plate 8 Simon and Schuster book clubs newsletter web page, 11 December 2013

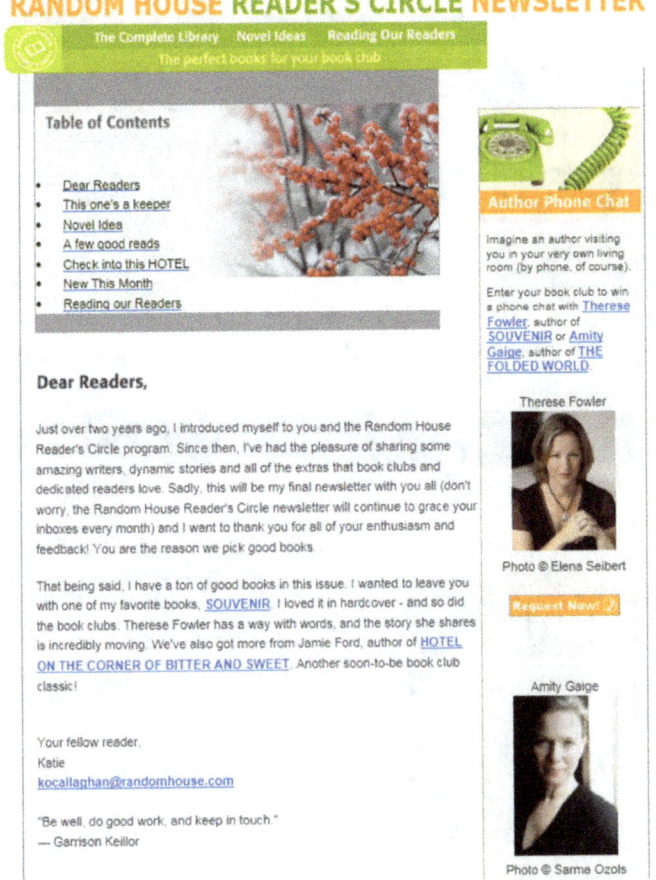

Plate 9 Random House 'Reader's Circle' newsletter, 12 February 2009

Plate 10 Video Spotlight from HarperCollins CA, 'The Savvy Reader', 24 September 2012

Plate 11 Random House CA, BookClubs.ca, 'Books Buzz', 15 June 2011

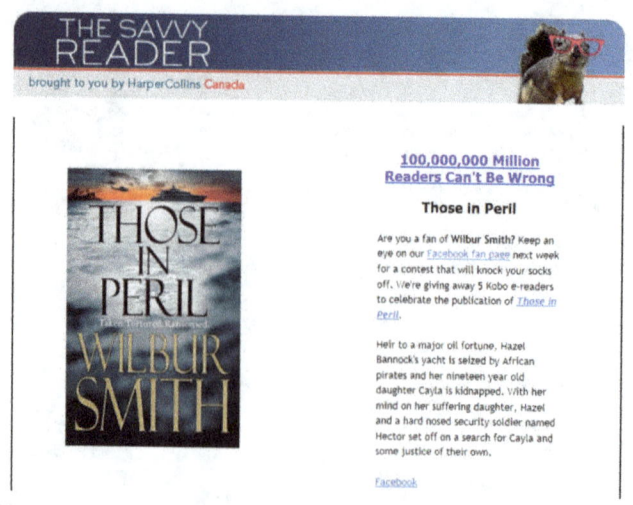

Plate 12 Harper Collins Canada, 'The Savvy Reader', 28 April 2011

64. Florentii Fedorovich Pavlenkov, in *Bibliotechnaia entsiklodepiia* (Moscow: Izdatel'stvo 'Pashkov dom', 2007), p. 778.
65. For more details on this process of deliberate effacement of Pavlenkov from Russian print culture, see note 47.
66. See 'Khronika sodruzhestvo' on the Herzen library website. <http://www.herzenlib.ru/community_pavlenkova/pavlenkov_motion/index.php?SECTION_ID=1764> (last accessed 30 August 2018).
67. Iu. A. Gorbunov, 'Pavlenkovskie biblioteki', in *Bibliotechnaia entsiklopediia* (Moscow: Izdatel'stvo 'Pashkov dom', 2007), p. 779.
68. Shirinovskaia, 'F. F. Pavlenkov i Pavlenkovskie biblioteki,' p. 125.
69. I. A. Ushakova, 'Svetitskaia sel'saia biblioteka im. F. F. Pavlenkova – filial MKUK "Falenskaia TsB"', in *Vestnik Kirovskogo filiala Kluba IuNESKO Sodruzhestvo pavlenkovskikh bibliotek* (Kirov: Gertsenka, 2014), pp. 48–50.

Chapter 9

Formal and Informal Networks of Book Provision for Rural Children in Australia and New Zealand, 1900–60

Bronwyn Lowe

> Gran [grandfather] taught her lessons in the evening, even brushing up his Latin for her benefit; and during the long days . . . she read her father's books and acquired a knowledge beyond her years. But there were other things she sought after too; from novels and from a book on etiquette which she had persuaded Gran to buy her, she was storing up a fund of peculiar information about the way ladies spoke and acted. (Constance Mackness, *Gem of the Flat*, 1914)[1]

In the 1914 children's novel *Gem of the Flat* by Australian author Constance Mackness, a striking portrait of a rural child reader is found. Twelve-year-old orphan Gem lives with her gold-fossicking grandfather Gran on the central tablelands of New South Wales. Isolated from other people and children but knowing there is a wider world beyond their shack for which she should prepare, Gem learns all she can about it from old novels and the few books she has persuaded her grandfather to buy for her. In *Gem of the Flat* Mackness depicts a reader of limited resources but considerable intelligence and agency, showing an awareness of the plight of rural and regional children that had been growing across Australia and New Zealand since the late 1800s.

In the first half of the twentieth century, children of these new nations of the British Commonwealth occupied a special position: as future soldiers or mothers of Empire. For rural children, this position was compounded by the idea that frontier or outback Australians and New Zealanders embodied their new nations' spirits. Yet such romantic ideas often hid the challenges that these children experienced. Children in the most remote areas had limited schooling, being taught either intermittently by farming parents or through a correspondence school. Rural children also experienced limitations when it came to reading. While most children had limited agency in reading choice, which was restricted by parents or teachers or by a lack of purchasing power, remote children's challenges were compounded. Shops were sometimes multiple days' drive away, and few families had disposable income to spend on books. In addition, friends and neighbours could be remote, making it difficult to swap books. Children were also less likely to receive books through other avenues, such as Sunday school 'reward books', which across this period were becoming one of the fastest-growing genres of juvenile publishing.[2] Such factors served to shape the reading habits of remote Australians and New Zealanders in particular ways: Martyn Lyons shows that bush readers cherished books for their rarity, they reread books and read books aloud more than urban readers did, and borrowed books from neighbours more readily when they could.[3]

By the early twentieth century, more and more urban Australians and New Zealanders were starting to become aware of the difficulties such remote women, men and children faced in accessing reading material. State libraries began to create mobile branches and book delivery services, and bush book clubs were set up in New South Wales, Queensland and New Zealand to provide families with regular packages of reading material. Such initiatives were based on the idea that urban Australians and New Zealanders owed a great debt of thanks to rural families for their hard work and sacrifice in working on their new nations' frontiers. Yet this gratitude also came coupled with concern: that if such families were forgotten, their drive, intellect and even moral integrity might be eroded by a lack of entertainment or intellectual engagement. This led to libraries and bush book clubs engaging in strict censorship to ensure that rural families were provided only with 'healthy' literature.

This chapter first examines how children in these areas experienced rural life and accessed education and reading material. It then discusses the particular ways that libraries and bush book clubs imagined the rural children for whom they created reading programmes. Finally, it addresses questions of agency by exploring children's more informal networks of literature provision, pointing out two particular areas in need of further research.

For most of the period 1900–60, children generally stayed in school until around the age of fourteen, when most left to help their families, either by working on the family farm or by gaining other employment. This chapter therefore investigates the varied experiences of children aged between approximately ten and fourteen years. While some of these children attended small bush schools, others lived so remotely that they participated in correspondence schooling. Children who came from wealthy families on large station properties were often sent to boarding school from a young age. Most farming families, however, experienced financial hardship. While some parents were illiterate, others involved themselves heavily in their children's education and reading.[4]

Class was an important factor in the reading habits of rural children. In her work on family and community in New Zealand, Claire Toynbee establishes two categories of rural families. The more prosperous farmers were descended from pioneers, often had family living in the district, lived closer to towns and had better access to transport; but families who had travelled from other regions to settle often struggled to make a living and tended to live in more isolated areas.[5] Families in this second category would have much more difficulty in finding reading material, having neither the financial resources to buy books nor, being more isolated, the same ability to borrow from family, neighbours or library services in the district.

Children themselves were often aware of this class difference. In her work on the history of New Zealand childhood, Jeanine Graham interviewed one man who, as a child growing up near Rahotu, never mixed with the Irish settler children living nearby because they had limited education. 'Although we had these people all round us we were completely segregated from them', he explained. 'We had our culture and education and a family background that didn't exist in those settlers.'[6] Here, class differences served to limit the sharing of literature, or indeed any life experience, between the young boy and the settlers. Such accounts illustrate the wide range of life experiences that existed within the same small region.

Children's backgrounds also affected how they responded to books. The oral history of Australians' reading habits recorded by Martyn Lyons and Lucy Taksa shows, for example, that children from rural areas had a particular affinity with Norah Linton, the protagonist in the 'Billabong' novels by Australian author Mary Grant Bruce (published from 1910 to 1942). Despite the focus in those novels on a family of upper-middle-class station owners, where, according to Lyons and Taksa, 'the interests of Australian rural capitalism' were well defended, children of all rural backgrounds appeared to appreciate rural Australia being featured in such a positive light in the novels that they read – as opposed to the British or American novels that were far more common at the time.[7] 'It was country life', they quote one respondent as saying, 'the theme was rural, and station life was always a subject that appealed greatly to me'.[8] 'I could always relate to her', explained another fan of Norah.[9] The 'Billabong' books were remembered by far more girls than boys; in fact, there were few popular Australian books for boys in this period.[10]

Books that depicted Australian and New Zealand child protagonists showing independence and confidence in the bush were, in fact, relatively new, Michelle Smith says, having developed only in the twentieth century. Nineteenth-century children's books that depicted the Australian bush, such as J. E. Aylmer's *Distant Homes; or, The Graham Family in New Zealand* (1868) or Molly E. Jamieson's *Ruby: A Story of the Australian Bush* (1898), had tended instead to focus on the bush as a fearful or dangerous place for British children.[11]

The later idealisation of rural Australia appealed to urban Australians. In fact, Judith Bessant argues that an Australian 'nationalist arcadian myth' posited that children growing up in the country were not exposed to the detrimental effects of boredom and lack of space in the same way that city children were.[12] Instead, they were free to breathe fresh air and develop their imaginations. This idea greatly influenced the bush book clubs, and was often picked up in the autobiographies and memoirs of rural men and women. In her memoir of growing up in New Zealand, for instance, Lauris Edmond positions her rural upbringing as central to her memories, and differentiates her life from the lives of urban children: 'For city children there must have been other textures and smells and colours', she imagines, but for her it was 'the wrenching, piling, caressing heaps of grass, picking the slender stems of wood daffodils'.[13]

Autobiographies and memoirs provide fascinating insights into children's reading habits in this period – although they do require cautious analysis. Katherine Tinsley and Carl F. Kaestle admit that 'faulty memory, selective rendering of the facts, exaggeration, modesty, and hypocrisy all can come between an autobiography and the life actually lived', although they also argue that 'except for a possible tendency to exaggerate the amount of reading they did or to over-emphasise their appreciation for high culture, there is little reason to suspect distortion in autobiographers' descriptions of reading activities'.[14] Similarly, men and women's depictions of rural life can be understood as coloured by their life experiences and their ongoing reading habits at the time of writing.

In such texts many Australians and New Zealanders used memories of their childhoods to represent the freedom that rural life offered. Australian Molly Keys recalled:

> I could, in summer time, work for two hours before breakfast at 7 a.m., and have most of the day to pursue enthralling outdoor interests. . . . Another three hours of lessons at night, and posting a set of completed work once a week was easy.[15]

This shows that her correspondence education did not interfere with the outdoor adventures she engaged in around her family's property. Poet and activist Judith Wright had similar memories of the freedom of correspondence education at her family's New South Wales property.[16] 'I don't think I ever had so much time for reading when I finally went to boarding-school', she reasoned, 'the days were too full of people and routine for that. So those early days certainly did a lot to turn me into a poet and a writer.'[17] Such authors showed themselves eager to connect their childhoods to the 'arcadian myth' outlined by Bessant.

This myth had particular potency during a period of intense rural development in Australia and New Zealand. Between 1890 and 1925, the number of farms in the state of Victoria alone had grown from around 36,000 to more than 80,000; in Western Australia, the number increased from around 5,500 farms to 19,000.[18] A growing number of children, then, were living in this myth. Correspondence education also played an increasing role in children's lives. Due to the large number of rural families, Australia was the first nation to provide complete primary and secondary education for children who had never been to regular school.[19] Correspondence schools were governed by the state education departments, and generally employed specialised teachers in cities to send printed lessons to the children, who would then send back their completed lessons to receive assessment and feedback.[20] By 1922 some 1,500 children were receiving lessons by mail in New South Wales alone.[21] In New Zealand a correspondence school opened in 1922 to which 200 primary school students had enrolled by the end of that year. A secondary division was opened in 1929.[22]

For some children, correspondence education was the only exposure they received to the outside world, and the only attention they received from adults who were not their parents, who were often preoccupied with farm life or raising younger children. In her recollections of correspondence education, Barbara York Main recalls being particularly encouraged in her interest in natural history by a teacher who would send her such books from the correspondence school's library.[23] Such recollections show the importance of these organisations in assisting in the development of individual children's personal thoughts and ideas outside of their own family unit.

Not all rural children, however, were caught by the net of correspondence education. In 1933 the Adelaide *Advertiser* reported the story of one illiterate boundary rider in the South Australian outback with five children who had never received any education; the children's mother was suffering from paralysis and could not speak or educate them. 'The Australian Inland Mission obtained the approval of the department to send a college girl to the station after she had received a fortnight's training in the Correspondence School', the paper reported. 'She stayed with the children for three months and gave them an elementary education', after which three of the children received a correspondence education.[24]

Other children's education came in the form of 'swaggie teachers', such as Ernest Tambling, who travelled down a central train line of the Northern Territory teaching individual families at their homes. Tambling recalled that while most parents welcomed the chance to have their children taught, he also met with resistance. One father shouted, 'I don't want any bloody school teacher hanging round my place. My wife can teach my children all they need.' Tambling reported that 'I later found out he had seven daughters and wasn't going to trust no rattler-jumping foot-loose school teacher with them'.[25] Children often missed out on the experience of reading or education due to particular fears of their parents. Many children growing up, particularly in the earlier decades of the twentieth century, received very limited formal education.

Even if children did have the ability to read, many spoke of simply not having the time to do so, because they had to help their families around the property. At the beginning of the twentieth century, school inspectors in New Zealand reported country children turning up to school too tired to learn, having already spent three hours in the morning working on the farm.[26] Some parents, such as Patsy Adam-Smith's, put a ban on their children reading, seeing it as frivolous or useless. Adam-Smith, who grew up in rural 1930s Victoria, remembers that she and her sister used to hide books and magazines in the outdoor washhouse.[27] In this instance the parental prejudice against reading was possibly explained by the illiteracy of her father – this factor often explained the behaviour of parents who did not support their children's reading.[28]

Other children, however, recalled great parental interest in their reading. In her memoir of growing up in rural New South Wales in the 1920s and 1930s, Barbara Corbett remembered her entire family being real aloud to by her father. 'Such old delights as *Tom Sawyer, Huckleberry Finn, The Three Musketeers*. . . . How vivid were the pictures.

How shared the chuckles. If we enjoyed a paragraph, we'd insist that he read it again.'[29] Lauris Edmond fondly recalled her father reading *Alice in Wonderland* to her in New Zealand.[30] Reading aloud, Lyons and Taksa argue, was an important feature of family life in the early twentieth century.[31] The practice was often necessary in rural areas because of a lack of lighting at night-time, meaning that only one member of the family could receive enough light to read. However, it also had the effect of reducing children's reading material to the books that their parents selected.

In choosing books to read to their children, or for their children to read themselves, parents were often influenced by ideas in the media about the vulnerability of children's minds. In the media, parents, particularly mothers, were positioned as the first point of defence to stop the flow of nefarious messages in the 'dangerous' books and comics. Parents were told that it was their responsibility to provide children with books that would improve their minds. In 1932 Australian journalist Linda Littlejohn posited that the provision of a large variety of literature was key here: 'if we see that children have a collection of books to suit varying tastes and moods', she argued, 'it must follow those brought up in a reasonably fair environment will automatically censor their own literature'.[32] In 1930 the chief inspector of the Victorian Education Department, Mr J. McRae, on the other hand, had contended that poetry was the solution. He argued that children were being bombarded with 'sensation mongering newspapers, novels that offend against good taste, and moving pictures which are frequently vulgar in tone and at times positively indecent' and went on to assert that the 'best way to deal with such evils is . . . by filling their hearts and minds with a love and appetite for good poetry'.[33] Such articles, while negating the intelligence of children in choosing their own reading to suit their mood and context, also show the pressures on parents to provide their children with the 'right' kind of reading material. Such pressures on parents would have only intensified the already significant pressures of running a family and a farm in a remote location.

While British children's magazines, which were read widely in Australia, enforced strict editing and self-censorship of their content, British and American comics were more varied in language and theme, so they were often the target of parental censorship.[34] Many parents banned them from entering the house: Lauris Edmond in New Zealand explained her parents' attitude by saying that while 'other children might wallow, we must not'.[35] Nevertheless, she still recalled the names of such popular children's comics as *Tiger Tim* and *Beano*, showing a close awareness of what other children around her would have been reading.

Other parents chose not to censor their children's reading but still showed concern about their children's 'taste'. Australian children's author Eleanor Spence remembers the choice in reading that was opened up to her once the local Country Women's Association library was installed on her family's veranda. She recalls that some of the books 'my mother viewed with a doubtful eye – but mostly on grounds of literary criticism, not unsuitable content'.[36] Another Australian children's author, Hesba Brinsmead, recalls:

> when I was about nine years old I was suddenly and violently hooked on the works of a writer, best unnamed, who was incredibly prolific, luridly romantic and pukingly bad. My parents wrung their hands in horror and despair; not that I should be sullied by their content, but that my taste should prove so execrable.[37]

The memories of Spence and Brinsmead show that not all country children were subjected to intense censorship or the fear that children would take on the wrong message from their reading material. Indeed, such memories show that concerns about taste were prominent in the country as well as in the city.

Even when children did not have to worry about parental censorship, choice was often limited by a simple dearth of material. However, some memoirists sought to negate the idea that their reading had suffered for it. Mary Turner Shaw, who grew up on a country station, did complain that her country 'school "library", a double cupboard two metres wide, contained only the stories of Ethel Turner and Mary Grant Bruce and for the seniors the novels of Zane Grey, Anthony Hope and the Baroness Orczy'.[38] However, Max Fatchen, whose South Australian bush school library consisted of 'kerosene cases stacked one on the other' containing 'brown-covered paperbacks so dull looking they would send any cover designer of a modern publisher swooning', chose to engage with this lack positively. 'Here were stories of the Aztecs, stories of *Robinson Crusoe*, *The Little Black Princess* and *Westward Ho*', he wrote, showing that the joy of discovery could still be experienced even through this meagre collection – should one choose to look.[39] Such memories show that, despite the limited agency that was offered them through meagre school libraries or parental censorship, this sense of ownership and choice over their reading was still important to young people.

While less remote children could access books in school libraries, even if they were meagre, not everyone had this luxury. In the early twentieth century, many organisations and initiatives were set up to improve Australians' and New Zealanders' access to books. Prominent in regional towns were School of Arts or Mechanics' Institute libraries, which were of vital importance to less remote rural Australians, or those who could at least travel. These libraries, which took after their Scottish and British counterparts in their aim to educate working-class people towards self-improvement, had been established across Australia in the nineteenth century.[40]

The Eurunderee School of Arts library in central New South Wales was integral to John Tierney's self-education. Tierney recalled his family at home after supper, when 'a roaring fire would be put on and the family would sit round while my oldest sister and my brother would take turns at reading all manner of books from the School of Arts Library or from our own stock'. Marcus Clarke's *For the Term of His Natural Life*, Rolf Boldrewood's *Robbery Under Arms* and Ellen Wood's *East Lynne* and *Pomeroy Abbey* were particular favourites.[41] That Tierney remembered and recorded so many titles by name, and that his family was also involved in running the local School of Arts library, illustrate the love of literature that enabled Tierney to develop wide reading tastes.

State libraries also became involved in the provision of literature to rural families. In South Australia children were particularly encouraged to join the Public Library's lending service for country people, which sent two children's books at a time.[42] In Tasmania, the Australian Council for Educational Research wrote:

> the library has always been a popular feature of the school work. . . . At present, a circular is sent with each parcel of books. On this the children name the book they liked best and the type they would prefer to be sent next time.[43]

In setting up a plan to send library books to children in remote areas in 1920, W. H. Ifould, the principal librarian of the Public Library of New South Wales, ensured that choice was restricted to suitable themes: 'on no account should children be introduced to stories dealing with sex problems, passionate love stories, tales of dishonesty and dishonour, and books calculated to provoke discontent'.[44] Only appropriate, moralistic and patriotic books were permitted.

But such institutions also began to employ specialised children's librarians, who understood the sorts of books that children might like. Speaking of her experiences working with a travelling children's library in Hornsby Shire, north of Sydney, Eve Pownall wrote that 'books in bulk were definitely a new experience' in the lives of country children, who were used to irregularly receiving one book at a time through the post. She went on:

> In some districts reading was less mature than in others . . . they were all, openly or surreptitiously, interested in books for the younger age groups. . . . In such districts, the School Magazine is one of the few links with the world of children's literature.[45]

School magazines usually contained articles, literary excerpts and poems and for many children they formed their first experiences with the British 'canon'.

Charitable organisations which became involved in the provision of literature could often ignore the subtlety of children's reading experiences in service of their own aims. John Flynn, who established the Australian Inland Mission to provide medical, social and educational services to inhabitants of the remote Northern Territory, believed that he was spreading a protective 'mantle of safety' over the white women and children of the outback. He was consciously advancing the cause of white Australia, making sure that thinly populated Australia could be settled so that it could never be taken away from Europeans.[46] This was a common concern in the early twentieth century, and framed the types of books that were considered appropriate to provide to frontier Australians.[47]

Throughout this period, it was the New South Wales Bush Book Club and Queensland Bush Book Club that saw the greatest success. The former was established in 1909 to provide literature to the most remote families, who lived out of reach even of School of Arts or travelling libraries.[48] It aimed particularly to provide the sort of leisure reading that might keep participants company in the lonely bush, where novels were seen as particularly difficult to obtain. The *Sydney Stock and Station Journal* reasoned in 1912:

> Book-buying comes expensive and there are so many things to buy. Besides, who wants to keep a stock of novels? The novel is read, then thrown away or leant to a friend which comes to the same thing in the sense that the original buyer sees it no more.[49]

The club relied on donations of books from urban Australians, and aimed to send a package of books and magazines to a rural family every three months. From the start, children's books were included in every package that was sent out.

In New Zealand, a bush book club was established through the Women's Division of the Farmers' Union around 1927 as part of its broader remit of 'providing nursing service and domestic assistance for those living in the backblocks; collecting and distributing literature to country dwellers; promoting the interests of immigrant settlers; and generally making country life brighter'.[50] While it was successful in circulating 600 different books in parcels of ten to the rural districts of New Zealand, it does not seem to have achieved the same reach or publicity as the Australian versions – perhaps as a result of being part of a wider organisation rather than an independent institution.[51] In 1938 the service was augmented considerably by the establishment of the Country Library Service, which began outreach specifically to country school children in 1942. In gaining the ability to import books directly from the United States, this visionary service widened rural children's reading to books that even urban children had not yet had the chance to read.[52]

The Queensland Bush Book Club was inaugurated in 1922, modelled closely on the older New South Wales Bush Book Club. The inaugural members came from the Lyceum Club in Brisbane, a club of upper-class university-educated women dedicated to the arts. They had been inspired by a series of newspaper articles in 1921 dedicated to women of the outback, one of which had hoped that

> women of leisure who need an outlet for their money and sympathy may learn that an effort to ameliorate the condition of their sisters in the bush may be quite as laudable an object as equipping and maintaining religious missions for the conversion of the heathen in China or elsewhere.[53]

In its first annual report the Club proclaimed that

> our aim is simply to brighten the lives of the men, women and children whose work in the country is of such great national importance to Australia. . . . If an association such as the Bush Book Club does a little to alleviate the loneliness and dreary monotony of the bush, it really seems just a matter of ordinary gratitude on the part of the town for benefits received.[54]

This exemplifies the tone of noblesse oblige that so often characterised discussions of rural Australians.

The Club was eager to distance itself from more religious or political organisations, such as the Australian Inland Mission. 'The Bush Book club has no axe to grind', it maintained. 'It is simply an association of men and women who are near enough to the pioneering days to know something of the loneliness of the bush. . . . We are non-sectarian and non-political[;] we spread no propaganda of any kind.'[55]

Yet despite such claims, both state clubs did see themselves as defending and maintaining the moral aptitude of bush Australians, and could not help but respond to the social issues of the time. In July 1919, New South Wales's *Red Cross Record* reported that at the club's annual meeting, member Mrs Gordon Wesche reasoned that 'if people have nothing to read, they must find someone to talk to. And, for a man, that often is at the public house. It is just the necessity for some kind of company.' The *Record*, framing 'our claim to national sobriety', concurred with this fear.[56]

The fact that the bush book clubs engaged in political and social issues such as temperance is indicative of their general attitude towards the inhabitants of the bush. While these people were hailed as 'the Soldiers who are holding the front line trenches of Australian civilization', they were also considered to be at risk due to the challenges that loneliness and boredom presented.[57] Although the Queensland club's 1927 annual report pronounced that 'books of all kinds are needed' as donations, it also reasoned that 'because Books are often the only glimpse of life many of the Out-back get, the Bush Book Club appoints a censoring committee which sees to it that the pictures of life supplied are healthy and wholesome'.[58] For children particularly, these attitudes meant that the books that were sent to them were carefully considered: 'our books must pass the test of mother and father, and growing boys and girls', the 1924 annual report had stated.[59] This test would have precluded bad language, intense romantic relationships or excessive violence.

While the Queensland club had started off including children's books in every package that it sent out, this practice was soon deemed unsatisfactory, as not all families had children. Instead, children in individual families received Christmas packages of books and magazines.[60] 'We have sent innumerable parcels of children's books up and down the State', the 1936 report stated, 'and the delighted clamour of the little ones, must have been heard for miles. "I thought Santa Claus would have to miss us this year" said one mother "and then your parcel came".'[61] The Queensland club also realised that book reading provided a sense of community to readers, and particularly to children. In regions where there were three or more children in close proximity, children's groups were set up so that they could exchange books between them.[62] Sometimes children ended up doing this themselves anyway – requesting particular books alongside illustrated magazines and papers, as well as encyclopaedias.[63]

While the records of the bush book clubs contain many notable letters of thanks from grateful families desperate for books, such organisations were not the only way that children received books. In creating their own networks to share reading material around, children found ways to exercise choice that sidestepped parental supervision and organisational censorship. This desire to be independent readers was especially important for children who did not have physical access to a library – in contrast to urban children, who used libraries to choose their own books.[64]

The importance of libraries to children can be seen in the sociological surveys of reading habits that began to be conducted in Australia and New Zealand in the 1940s. In 1947, New Zealand educator W. J. Scott published his survey of the reading habits of nearly 4,000 students aged thirteen to fifteen, from both urban and rural schools. The boys' favourite books were *Treasure Island* (Stevenson), *Coral Island* (Ballantyne) and *Tom Brown's Schooldays* (Hughes), whereas *Little Women* and *Good Wives* (Alcott) and *Anne of Green Gables* (Montgomery) led among the girls. These books were all children's classics that would have been widely available in school libraries. Scott concluded that access to libraries was integral to helping develop young people's reading habits, putting the onus on school libraries to broaden their selections to more modern texts as well as the classics.[65]

By the 1940s and 1950s, when school attendance was common even for more remote children, sociological reading surveys started to record the great importance of informal school reading networks in making books available to individual children.[66] For many children, the reading communities that they developed among themselves were their prime source of books. Marjorie Roe, who interviewed 326 children from six different schools in the rural Mittagong area of New South Wales in the mid-1950s, noted the runaway popularity of Enid Blyton: she was the favourite author of 53 per cent of girls and 31 per cent of boys.[67] But Roe also found that 'for individual schools the figures ranged from 68 per cent for Blyton down to *nil*'. That wide variation suggests that schools and peer groups played a large role in how children chose their reading matter, particularly in country areas, where access to libraries and bookshops would have been more difficult.[68] In her work on American young people's reading in late nineteenth-century Iowa, Christine Pawley notes that this sharing of 'unofficial' reading is an area worthy of further research.[69]

Similarly, in their survey of rural readers from 1930 to 1970, Denis Cryle and Betty Cosgrove mention pen-friends as a way that rural children were able to develop reading communities.[70] It was also a common practice to write in to children's pages of newspapers to find others with similar reading interests with whom to exchange literature: Doris Page, for example, wished 'to hear from a girl clubmate, 13 years of age, and who is interested in "The Schoolgirls' Own"'.[71] Some children became lifelong friends with the correspondent whom they had discovered in this way – another aspect of the history of reading that needs more research.

In its 1966 annual report, which turned out to be its final one, the Queensland Bush Book Club mentioned its dwindling subscription rates:

> possibly the years of our usefulness to the country people will come to an end. Better roads, the establishment of many Regional libraries in the country, as well as cars, radio and telephone all help to remove the isolation of earlier years, and though loneliness will still exist, communication in most areas is becoming easier and more frequent.[72]

The report expressed both regret in losing subscribers who had almost become friends through years of correspondence, and pride in all that the organisation had achieved.

In memoirs of childhood and letters sent by grateful parents, the writers often expressed the belief that they or their children would not have gone on to be readers, authors, broadcasters or academics had it not been for the literature provided through the bush book clubs and correspondence schools. As one mother wrote to the Queensland Bush Book Club:

> many thanks for the books . . . which taught the children the King's English much better than any local association could do. One of them has done a lot of broadcasting and another has written poetry – and been paid for it too! I do not think their literary tastes could have been fostered in the bush, had it not been for the parcels of books.[73]

As noted above, Judith Wright believed that it was her correspondence education that turned her into a writer.[74]

Nevertheless, the bush book clubs and similar organisations were not all positive in motive or outcome. If men and women, in their autobiographies and memoirs, spoke of the importance of developing a sense of agency and choice in reading, such institutions curbed their choices. This was the inevitable result of the idealised conceptions of rural children and the belief that they were particularly susceptible to moral erosion and not really capable of making up their own minds about the messages that they took from books. The bush child, straddling class, gender and geographical divides, was far more complex than urban organisations ever liked to imagine.

Notes

1. Constance Mackness, *Gem of the Flat* (Sydney: Angus and Robertson, 1914), p. 13.
2. Joseph McAleer, *Popular Reading and Publishing in Britain 1914–1950* (Oxford: Clarendon Press, 1992), pp. 134–5.
3. Martyn Lyons, 'Reading Practices in Australia', in Martyn Lyons and John Arnold (eds), *A History of the Book in Australia 1891–1945: A National Culture in a Colonised Market* (St Lucia: University of Queensland Press, 2001), p. 349.
4. For further discussions on country childhoods, see for example Catherine Driscoll, *The Australian Country Girl: History, Image, Experience* (Farnham: Ashgate, 2014); Kathryn Hunter and Pamela Riney-Kehrberg, 'Rural Daughters in Australia, New Zealand, and the United States: An Historical Perspective', in Ruth Panelli et al. (eds), *Global Perspectives on Rural Childhood and Youth: Young Rural Lives* (New York: Routledge, 2007).
5. Claire Toynbee, *Her Work and His: Family, Kin and Community in New Zealand 1900–1930* (Wellington: Victoria University Press, 1995), p. 137.
6. Quoted in Jeanine Graham, *'My Brother and I . . .': Glimpses of Childhood in Our Colonial Past* (Dunedin: Hocken Library, University of Otago, 1992), p. 16.
7. Martyn Lyons and Lucy Taksa, *Australian Readers Remember: An Oral History of Reading 1890–1930* (Melbourne: Oxford University Press, 1992), p. 98–9.
8. Ibid., p. 99.
9. Ibid., p. 98.
10. For further discussion of this issue see Brenda Niall, *Australia Through the Looking-Glass: Children's Fiction 1830–1980* (Carlton: Melbourne University Press, 1984).
11. Michelle Smith, 'Transforming Narratives of Colonial Danger: Imagining the Environments of New Zealand and Australia in Children's Literature', in Shirleene Robinson and Simon Sleight (eds), *Children, Childhood and Youth in the British World* (Houndmills: Palgrave Macmillan, 2016), p. 197.
12. Judith Bessant, '"Ferrets to Look After and Rabbits to Chase": The Rural Myth and Experiences of Young Country Australians', in R. C. Petersen and G. W. Rodwell (eds), *Essays in the History of Rural Education in*

Australia and New Zealand (Casuarina: William Michael Press, 1993), p. 119.
13. Lauris Edmond, *Hot October: An Autobiographical Story* (Wellington: Allen and Unwin, 1989), p. 39.
14. Katherine Tinsley and Carl F. Kaestle, 'Autobiographies and the History of Reading: The Meaning of Literacy in Individual Lives', in Carl F. Kaestle et al. (eds), *Literacy in the United States: Readers and Reading Since 1880* (New Haven: Yale University Press, 1991), p. 226.
15. Molly Keys, *Bellbirds and Blowflies: A Bush Girl's Diary 1942–46* (Armidale: M. Keys, 1990), p. 8.
16. Judith Wright, 'Seven Years of Correspondence School', in Geoffrey Dutton (ed.), *Snow on the Saltbush: The Australian Literary Experience* (Ringwood: Viking Press, 1984), p. 77.
17. Ibid., p. 78.
18. Graeme Davison and Marc Brodie, *Struggle Country: The Rural Ideal in Twentieth Century Australia* (Clayton: Monash University ePress, 2005), p. xii.
19. S. A. Rayner, *Correspondence Education in Australia and New Zealand* (Melbourne: Melbourne University Press, 1949), p. 12.
20. Elizabeth Stacey and Lya Visser, 'The History of Distance Education in Australia', *Quarterly Review of Distance Education*, 6:3 (2005), p. 254.
21. Craig Campbell and Helen Proctor, *A History of Australian Schooling* (Crows Nest: Allen and Unwin, 2014), p. 112.
22. Rayner, *Correspondence Education in Australia and New Zealand*, p. 97.
23. Barbara York Main, as quoted in Dutton (ed.), *Snow on the Saltbush*, p. 79.
24. 'Value of Correspondence Education', *Advertiser*, 15 December 1933, p. 28.
25. Patsy Adam-Smith, *Outback Heroes* (Sydney: Lansdowne Press, 1981), p. 43.
26. Mary Trewby, *The Best Years of Your Life: A History of New Zealand Childhood* (Auckland: Viking, 1995), p. 64.
27. Patsy Adam-Smith, *Hear the Train Blow: An Australian Childhood* (Sydney: Ure Smith, 1964), p. 38.
28. McAleer, *Popular Reading and Publishing in Britain*, p. 150.
29. Barbara Corbett, *A Fistful of Buttercups: Glimpses into a Country Childhood of the 1920s* (Kenthurst: Kangaroo Press, 1983), p. 116.
30. Edmond, *Hot October*, p. 43.
31. Lyons and Taksa, *Australian Readers Remember*, p. 28.
32. Linda Littlejohn, 'Can Parents Censor Their Children's Reading?', *Sunday Mail*, 27 November 1932, p. 14.
33. J. McRae, 'Urgent Reforms in Victorian education', *Teachers Journal*, 13:10 (1930), p. 368.
34. McAleer, *Popular Reading and Publishing in Britain*, p. 145.

35. Edmond, *Hot October*, p. 43.
36. Eleanor Spence, 'A Special Sort of Dreaming', in Michael Dugan (ed.), *The Early Dreaming: Australian Children's Authors on Childhood* (Milton: Jacaranda Press, 1980), p. 98.
37. Hesba Brinsmead, 'Longtime Childhood', in Dugan, *The Early Dreaming*, pp. 5–6.
38. Mary Turner Shaw, 'Education of a Squatter's Daughter', in Patricia Grimshaw and Lynne Strahan (eds), *The Half-Open Door: Sixteen Modern Australian Women Look at Professional Life and Achievement* (Sydney: Hale and Iremonger, 1982), p. 291.
39. Max Fatchen, 'Haystacks and Printer's Ink', in Dugan (ed.), *The Early Dreaming*, p. 27.
40. Joe Beddoe, 'Mechanics' Institutes and Schools of Arts in Australia', *Australasian Public Libraries and Information Services*, 16:3 (2003), pp. 123–4.
41. Tierney quoted in Janet Doust, 'British Literature and Australian Identity', in Kate Darian-Smith et al. (eds), *Exploring the British World: Identity, Cultural Production, Institutions* (Melbourne: RMIT Publishing, 2004), p. 506.
42. Rayner, *Correspondence Education in Australia and New Zealand*, p. 55.
43. Ibid., p. 56.
44. Quoted in David J. Jones, 'William Herbert Ifould and the Development of Library Services in New South Wales, 1912–1942', PhD dissertation (University of New South Wales, 1993), p. 141.
45. Eve Pownall, 'Books and the Open Road', *Australasian Book News and Library Journal*, 1:9 (1947), p. 407.
46. Graeme Davison, 'Religion', in Alison Bashford and Stuart Macintyre (eds), *The Cambridge History of Australia, Vol. II: The Commonwealth of Australia* (Melbourne: Cambridge University Press, 2013), p. 222.
47. Davison and Brodie, *Struggle Country*, pp. x–xi.
48. Martyn Lyons, 'Case-Study: The Bush Book Club of New South Wales', in Martyn Lyons and John Arnold (eds), *A History of the Book in Australia 1891–1945: A National Culture in a Colonised Market* (St Lucia: University of Queensland Press, 2001), p. 204.
49. 'Bush Book Club: Books for the Asking', *Sydney Stock and Station Journal*, 17 December 1912, p. 8.
50. 'Women's Division Farmers' Union', *Manawatu Times*, 24 September 1927, p. 3.
51. See, for example, 'Women's Division of Farmers' Union', *Manawatu Times*, 2 August 1928, p. 11.
52. Mary Hutton, 'From Millions of Cats to Te Kuia me te Pungawerewere: Children's Reading in New Zealand 1940–1990', in *Fabulous and Familiar: Children's Reading in New Zealand, Past and Present* (Wellington: National Library of New Zealand, 1991), p. 21.

53. 'North–South Line. Real Heroines. The Women of the West, Vivid Story of Their Courage', *Brisbane Courier*, 7 September 1921, p. 8. See also Robin Wagner, '"A Little Bit of Love for Me and a Murder for My Old Man": The Queensland Bush Book Club', in B. J. McMullin (ed.), *Collections, Characters and Communities: The Shaping of Libraries in Australia and New Zealand* (Melbourne: Australian Scholarly Publishing, 2010), p. 123.
54. Queensland Bush Book Club, *Annual Report* (1922). (The National Library of Australia holds copies of the *Annual Reports*.)
55. Ibid.
56. 'The Bush Book Club', *Red Cross Record*, 5:7 (1919), p. 52.
57. Queensland Bush Book Club, *Annual Report* (1925).
58. Queensland Bush Book Club, *Annual Report* (1927).
59. Queensland Bush Book Club, *Annual Report* (1924).
60. Queensland Bush Book Club, *Annual Report* (1953).
61. Queensland Bush Book Club, *Annual Report* (1936).
62. Queensland Bush Book Club, *Annual Report* (1925).
63. 'The Balm of Bush Solitude: Bring Books to Outback Folk', *Australian Women's Mirror*, 10 May 1927, p. 22.
64. For a British examination of this sentiment see Alistair Black, 'The Past Public Library Observed: User Perceptions and Recollections of the Twentieth-Century British Public Library Recorded in the Mass-Observation Archive', *Library Quarterly*, 76:4 (2006), pp. 450–1.
65. W. J. Scott, *Reading, Film and Radio Tastes of High School Boys and Girls* (Wellington: New Zealand Council for Educational Research, 1947), p. 36.
66. Kathleen McDowell points out the need to be cautious with the use of reading surveys, as child readers responded to such surveys with varying motivations to exaggerate or underplay their reading. Nevertheless, surveys provide an important record of children's attitudes and habits. See Kathleen McDowell, 'Toward a History of Children as Readers, 1890–1930', *Book History*, 12 (2009), p. 261.
67. Marjorie Roe, 'The Teen-age Reader', *Australian Library Journal*, 7:2 (1958), p. 20.
68. Ibid.
69. Christine Pawley, 'What to Read and How to Read: The Social Infrastructure of Young People's Reading, Osage, Iowa, 1870–1900', *Library Quarterly*, 68:3 (1998), pp. 276–97.
70. Denis Cryle and Betty Cosgrove, 'The Rural Reader: An Australian Survey (1930–1970)', *Australian Library Journal*, 48:2 (1999), pp. 128–36.
71. Doris Page, 'Mates' Letterbox,' *Mail*, 13 October 1928, p. 23.
72. Queensland Bush Book Club, *Annual Report* (1966).
73. Queensland Bush Book Club, *Annual Report* (1939).
74. Wright, 'Seven Years of Correspondence School', p. 77.

Chapter 10

Putting Your Best Books Forward: A Historical and Psychological Look at the Presentation of Book Collections

Nicole Gonzalez and Nick Weir-Williams

I slipped the brown paper bag to her covertly as we stood amongst the parents in the school pick-up line. As the heft of the contents shifted from my hands into hers, she offered a 'Thank you' so hushed it was barely a puff of air before tucking the package inside her coat. There were sheepish smiles exchanged. Blushing cheeks, quickened hearts, too. We looked around instinctively, bracing for judgment and ridicule. 'You're going to love it,' I whispered to her.

It has often been asserted that our favourite books reflect something about who we are as individuals – everything from our personalities to our political leanings, our integrity to our intellects. So ingrained is this belief that two friends might feel so ashamed to share a copy of Suzanne Collins's *The Hunger Games* in front of their neighbours that they would exchange it with the stealth of seasoned spies. (The book, after all, has two strikes against it: not only is it reading for pleasure only, but it is also young adult fiction.)

Entwined in the very terminology we use to classify our books – 'highbrow', 'lowbrow' and 'middlebrow' – is the history of those words, rooted in the practice of phrenology as indicators of intellectual capacity. Whether we are aware of the historical source of these words, we are mindful – consciously or unconsciously – of the judgements they carry. We know our books define us. Do we, then, carefully craft our public collections to make the best impression? What factors into the books we choose to keep and display versus the books we read (and enjoy!) but quickly usher from sight? Moreover, what significance is there in *how* they are displayed?

This chapter takes a historical journey through examples of specific books and authors and genres of books in the framework of these high-to-lowbrow categories and is accompanied by psychological theories that offer insight into the cognitive roots of these designations. We further explore books from the past and present that have (with bashfulness) titillated populations; evaluate opinions and practices of readers and the art of curating their bookshelves with our own survey; and examine the preconceptions we attribute to readers, framed in the light of psychological foundations such as impression formation. Our final consideration are the displays themselves, where we examine emerging trends of utility, space and aesthetics.

***

'A highbrow is someone who looks at a sausage and thinks of Picasso.' (A. P. Herbert)

When the fingers of Dr Franz Joseph Gall ran across the scalps of his patients, searching for the most subtle of protrusions and indentations, they were likely firm with assuredness in their examination – an assuredness equal to the confidence Gall possessed in his own theory. His hands, finding over- or undergrowths of each cerebral region – *organs of the brain*, as he referred to them – read from them each person's specific abilities and deficiencies, as though each head was a book of Braille. A bump here told him one was gifted in benevolence; a concave spot there revealed weakness in self-esteem. Gall, a Viennese physician, mapped out the entire brain with each division responsible for some human trait, and he gave the 'science' its Greek name: phrenology.

Phrenology provided the elite class of the time with a scientific justification to maintain the hierarchy that benefited them so well. After all, their high positions could now easily be understood as what nature intended. Yet, simultaneously, phrenology offered hope to the growing middle class, for, as Gall explained, the organs of the brain could be developed as any other muscle in the body, with proper training. And from phrenology came the terms 'highbrow' and 'lowbrow', respectively describing intelligence and intellectual deficiency. Today we use these words to describe various genres and styles of books.

The more recent term 'middlebrow' describes all that falls between the very tops and bottoms of the literary scale. And in defining it, Virginia Woolf fully intended to be derogatory:

> But what, you may ask, is a middlebrow? And that, to tell the truth, is no easy question to answer. They are neither one thing nor the other. They are not highbrows whose brows are high; nor lowbrows, whose brows are low. Their brows are betwixt and between. They do not live

in Bloomsbury which is on high ground; nor in Chelsea, which is on low ground. Since they must live somewhere, presumably, they live perhaps in South Kensington, which is betwixt and between.[1]

This article, 'Middlebrow', though published posthumously, was intended originally for publication in response to a very public radio spat in 1932. The Yorkshire playwright and novelist J. B. Priestley (whose early bookshelves we will encounter below) had written a contemptuous review of Woolf's *The Second Common Reader*, calling her out as an elitist, rich and idle snob. The BBC offered him the opportunity to follow up with a radio talk, 'To a Highbrow', and Harold Nicolson (whom Priestley had also attacked) responded a week later with 'To a Lowbrow'. The Battle of the Brows had commenced, with Woolf vigorously and proudly defending her position as a highbrow, who, in order to function intelligently and efficiently, required lowbrows to do actual work for her, but admired their 'vitality'. Scorn and contempt were thrown upon those in between, the Middlebrows, whom Priestley felt he represented and wished to foster and improve; in his words, 'Between the raucous lowbrows and the lisping highbrows is a fine gap, meant for the middle or broadbrows . . . our homely fashion'.[2]

This class-ridden battle, archaic as it may seem, actually carries on to this day with the genres of 'literary fiction' and 'mass market' fiction – the two differentiated not only by publishers' blurbs and marketing but also by binding, size, paper quality and price – and with the middlebrow personified by book clubs conducted by television hosts – Oprah in the USA and Richard and Judy in the UK.

And so two questions present themselves now. Are we today just as apt as a Victorian or Bloomsbury resident to cover up our own lowbrow tendencies? Have our evaluations of intelligence moved from the physical to the symbolic, from our brows to our book choices? We may find the answer in personal bookshelf curation throughout history.

***

Mens cuiusque is est quisque
'A person is what his mind is'
The motto on Samuel Pepys on his bookplates

A quotation attributed to Cicero has become popular on tee-shirts: 'A room without books is like a body without a soul'. In fact, Cicero wrote to his long-time correspondent Atticus that 'since Tyrannio has arranged my books for me, my house seems to have had a soul added to it'.³ The quotation reveals that the arrangement of the books was as critical as the actual content of the books themselves. Before printing, books were not easy to display, though by the fourteenth century some mentions of personal collections can be found. In Chaucer's 'The Miller's Tale', for example, the lodger Nicholas lives in his room alone with his personal items of scholarship, and the collection is described along with its display:

> His Almageste and books grere and smale,
> His astrelabie longynge for his art,
> His augrim-stones layen faire apart
> On shelves couched at his beddes heed.⁴

But the real sea change begins in the century or so following Gutenberg, who transformed the ability of the individual to amass a large collection of books. Samuel Pepys is mostly famous for his diary, but – as that diary lovingly reports – one of his greatest prides lay in how he collected and displayed a personal collection of books, manuscripts and official papers, which amounted to some 3,000 items. All of this was bequeathed to his Cambridge college, Magdalene, with a number of provisos that show the importance Pepys placed on his collection and his desire to maintain it for posterity. That bequest has been rigorously adhered to, with the result that visitors can vividly and accurately imagine themselves in his house, viewing his books in the order and in the bindings – and even in the bookcases – that he desired. Not only that, but through his diary one can trace his regular trips to booksellers and bookbinders as he amassed his collection and see something of his motivation both in assembling the library and in bequeathing it.

Pepys was picking up on a concept of the private library which had been strongly encouraged by the emergence of Dutch booksellers. In 1599 Louis Elzevier (founder of what is now the largest publisher in the world, the eponymous Elsevier) pioneered the concept of book auctions via a printed catalogue. The catalogue could be mailed widely and thus introduced the possibility of buying a whole and unique collection of books for personal display. Pepys himself had several books in his collection from the Elzevier catalogue. He also took much delight in visiting London booksellers:

> Thence to St. Paul's Church Yard, to my bookseller's, and having gained this day in the office by my stationer's bill to the King about 40s. or 3l., I did here sit two or three hours calling for twenty books to lay this money out upon, and found myself at a great losse where to choose, and do see

how my nature would gladly return to laying out money in this trade. I could not tell whether to lay out my money for books of pleasure, as plays, which my nature was most earnest in; but at last, after seeing Chaucer, Dugdale's History of Paul's, Stows London, Gesner, History of Trent, besides Shakespeare, Jonson, and Beaumont's plays, I at last chose Dr. Fuller's Worthys, the Cabbala or Collections of Letters of State, and a little book, Delices de Hollande, with another little book or two, all of good use or serious pleasure: and Hudibras, both parts, the book now in greatest fashion for drollery, though I cannot, I confess, see enough where the wit lies. My mind being thus settled, I went by linke home, and so to my office, and to read in Rushworth; and so home to supper and to bed.[5]

Pepys was privileged, Cambridge educated, and an important government official, living in the metropolis, eager to take full advantage of the availability of books and affluent enough to do so. But by the end of the nineteenth century, books were generally accessible to all classes, opening the door to important learning opportunities. The original self-help book, the runaway bestseller *Self-Help* by Samuel Smiles, published in 1859,[6] extolled the virtues of hard work, persistence, science and self-improvement, not least through lifelong learning and the careful perusal of books, illustrated by the brief inspirational biographies that run throughout the book. Its contemporary impact was considerable, with a quarter of a million copies sold by the time of Smiles's death in 1904.

Though book collecting and display was still seen at the end of the century as the province of the 'bookman', some progressive publishers saw an opportunity to make books – the classics especially – available to an increasingly political, aware, ambitious and angry working class. The home library was about to migrate from the province of the rich to the average family. By 1906 there were several cheap uniform editions of the great books, selling for a shilling or less. The Dent/Dutton Everyman's Library was one of the most successful series, its high-mindedness displayed in the epigraph in each volume from the medieval morality play:

Everyman, I will go with thee
And be thy guide
In thy most need to go by thy side

J. B. Priestley, the writer who defended the middlebrow, was asked to edit for the Everyman Diamond Jubilee in 1966 an anthology of selections from Everyman volumes, which by then numbered more than 1,000, with sales of some 50 million worldwide. In his introduction, Priestley portrayed himself as just the sort of eager, bright, working-class young man concerned not just to better himself but determined to both purchase and display the purchases he scrimped and saved to buy every week, by 'walking instead of taking trams and cutting down lunch from ninepence to threepence, to find the shillings. . . . I managed to turn some crates into passable bookshelves and filled those crates and orange boxes with books'. Significantly and deliberately, he referred to his acquisitions as 'a "collection of books" and not a Library', a term he considered suitable for collectors of first editions or 'special fancy' editions. His collection was organised for ease of finding much-loved books, and for utility as a professional writer working from home: 'I may need only a few books for reference, but I like to think those books are somewhere in the house'.[7]

***

> Would you approve of your young sons, young daughters – because girls can read as well as boys – reading this book? Is it a book you would have lying around your own house? Is it a book that you would even wish your wife or your servants to read? (Prosecutor Mervyn Griffith-Jones, November 1960, *Regina v. Penguin Books Ltd*)

The invention of the novel – usually dated from Samuel Richardson's *Pamela* (1740) or Henry Fielding's *Tom Jones* (1749) – soon aroused the ire of the clergy, among others. An early review described *Tom Jones* as 'a motley history of bastardism, fornication, and adultery'.[8] And attitudes toward the novel inevitably affect what people decide to display in their homes for public view. Protestants especially were appalled at what they considered lowbrow smut in early novels and the dreadful moral turpitude that could overtake women and children should they get their hands on these books. Even more, the novel represented a terrible threat to the Protestant work ethic: those who should be studying the Bible and doing good works might instead be enthralled and distracted by the ribald antics of Tom Jones. Reading for anything other than learning, then, was a shocking affront to the Protestant way of life.

The Protestants were not alone in denouncing the novel and reading for pleasure, nor was theirs an antiquated viewpoint left in the far past. Just as the terminology of 'highbrow' and 'lowbrow' has persisted, so too has the Protestant disdain for pleasure reading. In 1954 the Comics Code was promulgated to protect the post-war youth of America from being led astray both by the content and advertisements. As an example, Part B, point 4 reads:

> Inclusion of stories dealing with evil shall be used or shall be published only where the intent is to illustrate a moral issue and in no case shall evil be presented alluringly nor so as to injure the sensibilities of the reader.

The leading light behind this moral crusade was not a member of the clergy but a psychiatrist, Fredric Wertham, who specialised in issues with young children in Harlem. Even the name of his book *Seduction of the Innocent* echoed fears of the lowbrow from centuries before:

> Comic books are definitely harmful to impressionable people, and most young people are impressionable. I think Hitler was a beginner compared to the comic book industry. The time has come to legislate these books off the newsstands and out of the candy stores.[9]

A few years later, the British Crown unwisely launched a prosecution under the new Obscene Publications Act against the publisher of *Lady Chatterley's Lover* in late 1960. (An American court had just the year before ruled the book not obscene.) The novel itself was hardly new – published originally in 1928, it had survived a number of trials, bannings, seizing by police and customs officials – but what was critical this time was that Penguin had published an unexpurgated paperback edition at the shockingly low price of 3s.6d (roughly equivalent to 99p or $1.50). Penguins were admired for their innovative format, for their striking cover designs (which made them highly collectable and displayable both in bookstores and at home), for their editorial perspicacity, but most importantly for their price. Now, not only was the content of the book titillating, but the exterior design garnered additional appeal (Plate 6) – and all at a cost that made the book widely accessible to the masses.

Although the notorious quotation at the top of this section is always treated with mirth, as the last-ditch effort of the old class-ridden English establishment to hold off the permissive society, Griffith-Jones's opening remarks got to the point of the complaint. Obscenity trials had already come and gone in the UK and the USA, but this one moved lurid material out of the intellectual or beatnik milieu (e.g. Allen Ginsberg's *Howl*) and brought it straight into the home. Children, wives, servants, all had access now to rude words and, indeed, a direct challenge posed by Lawrence to both class and male supremacy. That, much more than obscenity, was what this prosecution was really about. Priestley and Dent may have wanted Everyman to own the great classics; Penguin made dirty books available and cheap. But would that make them any more acceptable to put in your home on display for visitors to see and, more importantly, form an impression? Would the court rulings erase or, at the very least, ease from our conscious minds the association of disdain with pleasure reading?

With his call for volunteers proclaiming 'Bookworms required. If you read a lot of light fiction and enjoy it very much, please volunteer to advance the cause of science', author and psychologist Victor Nell began an empirical investigation into these very lasting associations people have with reading for pleasure. His experiments studied what he termed 'ludic reading', a practice he associated with terms like 'pleasurable', 'spontaneous', 'unproductive' and 'getting lost in a book'. Asking participants to rank excerpts of books on the three dimensions of preference, merit and difficulty, Nell found a significant positive relationship between evaluations of merit and difficulty. Simply, his study found that content deemed intellectual in nature and difficult grammatically was weighted with more esteem. However, Nell also found that esteem for a book did not equate with enjoyment. In fact, a clear inverse relationship was found between the two, affirming Nell's thesis question: 'Does the best medicine taste worse?'

Are these judgements also with us as we curate our own bookshelves, driving our efforts to make certain that the contemptible lowbrow books we own (and love so much) are hidden from public view? Indeed, the poor paper quality, the lurid covers, the derogatory term 'pulp fiction' all seem to connote a genre not worth saving, let alone displaying. Ironically, their very destructibility has made some early lowbrow books highly valuable as collectables – but perhaps still not displayable. A neighbour once covertly showed to one of the authors the pride of his collection, not the art books or middlebrow novels but, tucked away in drawers, every first edition paperback of the 'Tarzan' series, worth more than the rest put together.

For our own survey, friends, family, colleagues, acquaintances and persons unknown were invited to participate. We compared their personal bookshelving practices in places with visitors (e.g. living rooms or office space) with those in their private spaces (e.g. bedrooms or e-readers).[10] Eighty-one people of various backgrounds and ages were kind enough to offer their thoughts. And while our survey cannot suss out the specific psychological motivations (particularly the unconscious ones we will consider in a moment), the results do clearly demonstrate that our respondents curate their public and private shelves differently.

In response to the question 'What percentage of the books on your public shelves would you estimate to be "highbrow"?', 57 per cent answered 'more than half', while 35 per cent answered 'less than half'. When the same question was asked about their private shelves, we found a near reversal of these responses, with 44 per cent estimating 'more than half' as highbrow and 56 per cent 'less than half'. As an added dimension to this survey, respondents were also asked to estimate the percentage of highbrow versus lowbrow books on any e-readers they might own. Of the forty-seven respondents who affirmed they owned an e-reader and used it for reading books, only 15 per cent estimated that it included many highbrow works at all. The results offer us a clear linear relationship between the type of collection (public, private or e-reader) and the number of highbrow books displayed: the more public the collection, the more highbrow the books; the more private the collection, the more lowbrow the books. Certainly this survey represents only a preliminary investigation and is limited in scope, but the written open responses our survey-takers offered confirm this general pattern, as the following examples show:

> My public bookshelves are full of classic literature, non-fiction (mostly science and history), and popular works that I enjoy and occasionally re-read. My less-visible collection is much larger and contains about 50% paperbacks from popular fiction authors that I'm not especially fond of. There are a number of non-fiction books on subjects in which I may have had a passing interest. Most are second-hand and very worn.

> My book shelf is almost a testament to my university degrees filled with all the literature I read during my course which I sometimes read again. I also have books about emotional intelligence as well as improving business and sales. For my private reading, which I do on my Kindle, this is mostly filled with best-sellers and other works I find on Amazon which look interesting. None are 'highbrow' but more like a collection of entertainment movies to book form.

> I have a few public shelves that are collectibles, i.e. books that are 100 years old or older. Many (75%) of these would be considered highbrow. These do not necessarily represent my tastes as a reader.

> Our bookshelves in our living room represent our interests and books we are proud to talk about/'show off'.

If indeed we are more apt to 'show off' our highbrow books to others, do we do so with intention? Are we aware of the choices we make as we arrange our display? Moreover, is it significant that a majority of our survey's respondents said, of the three areas in which they collect their books – public, private and e-readers – the privately shelved books most represented them as readers? As one respondent wrote:

> Books on my 'public' bookshelves remind me of times and places, and are evocative in those dimensions, rather than resonant for their content. Books on display on 'private' shelves are well-loved books, many that I know I will or hope to read again. Books (and periodicals) on my eReader are 'fluff' – basically anything I know doesn't require a big investment in time or bandwidth. 'Private' shelves best represent my reading taste, but [the] eReader probably best represents my current ability to engage with content!

Psychological theories and history will offer some insight into these behaviours.

***

Being entirely honest with oneself is a good exercise. (Sigmund Freud)

Sigmund Freud alerted us to the importance of the subconscious, the mental workings that happen without our awareness. And below the surface of our awareness is a constant battle within the human mind, a daily struggle between the primal urges that demand immediate satisfaction and the ingrained moral code that shames us and scolds us for these animalistic tendencies.

Freud himself applied his unconscious theory to the novel. In 'Creative Writers and Daydreaming' (1908) he traced the inspiration of creative writers to their 'phantasies' of childhood, once enacted in their play. Rhetorically, Freud asked, 'May we really attempt to compare the imaginative writer with the "dreamer in broad daylight" and his creations with daydreams?' This expression of childish play is no longer acceptable in the adult world, so the fantasies that play expressed – these daydreams – are now instead translated onto the page as creative expression. Writes Freud, 'a piece of creative writing, like a daydream, is a continuation of, and a substitute for, what was once the play of childhood'. The creative novel, then, offers writers once again the opportunity afforded them as children at play, unburdened by the desire-repressing and shaming constructs of the adult world. As evidence, Freud offers the German language, pointing out the attachment of the word 'Spiel' (meaning 'play') to various literary genres. 'Lustspiel', a comedy, is literally translated as 'pleasure play'; 'Frauerspiel', or tragedy, is 'mourning play'.[11] A respondent from our survey touched upon this sentiment:

> I am more of an avid reader of novels based on the plot of the story. More so often, the less acclaimed books are a lot more worthy to be read and relished. The highly acclaimed books are more for reference use rather than for pleasure reading.

With this attitude, the strikes against the lowbrow book add up. Could our unconscious mind hold the explanation for how we display our books and (more importantly) to whom we display them, so that those that represent our deepest desires – the unrefined urges so openly splayed out on the pages of novels – are hidden from society's condemning judgement?

Conversely, do we put our highbrow books forward out of a need to make a good impression on others? As one respondent wrote, 'We don't want people to expect too much from us but we do own at least 100 books on shelves (not including the children's).' But another, perhaps guessing the survey's aim, was quick to refute this explanation: 'My shelves are about making books easy for me to find, when I want to find them, and about reading. They are not about ego.'

Impression formation is simply defined as the evaluation people make of others' personality characteristics based on observable external cues, cues that include physical appearance, mannerisms and the material items they possess, wear or surround themselves with. Arguably an evolutionary adaptation designed to help humans make quick assessments for their safety and social comfort, these heuristics work primarily outside of awareness. These evaluations of others, then, are rapid and unconscious, and based on both verbal and non-verbal behaviour. Moreover, they tend to be surprisingly accurate. Psychologist Nalini Ambady and Robert Rosenthal named these judgements 'thin slices', to suggest the quick pace and little information used in drawing conclusions about others.[12]

Important to note here, social psychologists suggest that impressed characteristics often come bundled together. In one example, termed 'the halo effect', people judged to be physically attractive by others are also rated significantly higher in positive qualities such as intelligence, success and happiness. Similarly, when children in their study were asked to depict an intelligent person, Hannu Raty and Leila Snellman found that they were most likely to illustrate an individual of high status.[13] In vignettes describing either an affluent or a not so affluent person, Andrew Christopher and Barry Schlenker found 'the affluent target was evaluated as having more personal ability (e.g. intelligence, self-discipline), more sophisticated qualities (e.g. cultured, successful), and a more desirable lifestyle than the not so affluent target'.[14] Nora

Murphy, too, found intelligence ratings to be positively correlated with qualities of maturity, common sense, goodness, likeability and social happiness, as well as status. Presenting a display of even one of these qualities, then, triggers additional associations, creating a fuller impression on other dimensions.[15]

Both the observer and the person being observed use the ownership of material objects to assess and convey information about the self. Christian Jarrett, in 'The Psychology of Stuff and Things', writes:

> More than mere tools, luxuries, or junk, our possessions become the extensions of the self. We use them to signal to ourselves, and others, who we want to be and where we want to belong. And long after we're gone, they become our legacy.[16]

If people make quick judgements of others, putting together a composite sketch of others' personalities based on their visible attributions and possessions, it stands to reason that curated public bookshelves, too, are used in these adaptive, automatic, natural assessments. Psychological research has yet to tackle the examination of bookshelf presentation as it relates to thin-slice judgements, but in his 2008 book *Snoop: What Your Stuff Says About You*, psychologist Sam Gosling draws the connections between the way people set up their personal spaces (bedrooms, offices, bathrooms) and their personality characteristics. As he writes:

> In the years we've been doing this, my teammates and I have learned to be super snoopers, we have trained our eyes to exploit clues that will tell us what a person is really like. Did the Virginia Woolf volume mean my friend was an ardent feminist? Or perhaps the book was merely one of many she was assigned for her course on British literature.[17]

Gosling's findings stress the significance of the placement of objects in personal spaces as much as the objects themselves. In an interview on 'Talk of the Nation' on NPR in May 2008, Gosling said:

> It's really crucial to combine not only what they are, but how they have been placed. Because how they have been placed gives us good information on the psychological function that they serve. So if we have a photo of our beautiful spouse facing us, that shows it's for our benefit. It's what you might call a social snack, something we can snack on to make ourselves feel better over the day. If it's turned the other way, then it's more for the benefit of others.[18]

Thus the question can be asked: Who is meant to benefit if certain books are placed in public view while others are kept in more private, less trafficked areas? Are books displayed in public a form of conspicuous consumption – purchases meant for the show of status or intelligence? While psychological research has yet to investigate the relationship between the content of people's bookshelves and resulting judgements specifically, the Internet is awash with laypeople who admit to just that. For example, a Reddit survey asked, 'Librarians of Reddit, do you judge people based on their books?'[19] 'Count on this: If you invite me to your home, I'm going to peruse your bookshelves', posted one blogger,[20] while Beth Carswell admits that snooping through others' bookshelves is one of her 'favourite things to do', a way of 'ferreting out information about people'. She goes on to lament the rise of the e-reader: 'How can we weed out ill-advised love partners if their stacks of Tom Clancy, John Grisham, and Dean Koontz aren't on display?'[21]

Sociologist Erving Goffman, who coined the term 'impression management' to describe people's tendency to control perceptions of themselves by regulating the information provided, offered a simple sequence: humans work to convince others of their best traits and, in turn, convince *themselves*. As a result, Goffman included the admonition to 'choose your self-presentation carefully, for what starts out as a mask may become your face'.[22]

Along with examining the unconscious psychological motivations behind bookshelf display, this investigation would be remiss not to acknowledge simpler, more obvious and entirely conscious factors: aesthetics and utility. Some of the responses to our survey suggest that sometimes books are shelved with less emphasis on their contents and more on their exterior design, colour or size. Here, books are stripped of their contents and turned into artefacts. An Edinburgh bookseller reported a customer who insisted on buying only books with blue covers.[23] A Melbourne remainder dealer in the 1990s found a great market in selling books by the metre.

Indeed, publishers have long understood the need and desire for uniformity in their choice of size and the desire for collectability among their readers. Books in a series are numbered, of similar size and uniform design, and often care is taken that spines contain not only bibliographic information but serial numbering and even design elements that follow in sequence along the shelf, tempting and even demanding that the buyer have the complete set. One of the authors was castigated by a sequence of philosophers at a convention for having the temerity to change the design of an established series in phenomenology, thereby ruining the look of the collection on the shelf.

In an *Ideal Home* magazine article that has since been said to have divided the Internet,[24] interior decorator Lauren Coleman included a photo of her bookshelves with all of the spines of the books facing inwards, towards the wall. She offered the following rationale:

> I was just trying to make a nice backdrop to display some of the other items on the bookshelf. Too many books of different colours can make a shelf look cluttered. They were mostly chick lit and the colours can be garish. It was better than storing them in a cupboard.

So though Coleman was hiding her lowbrow books, her conscious intent was purely in creating a design. Her efforts, however, were met with a wave of insults that ranged from the sarcastic to the physically threatening: 'I know books are very emotive and do carry a huge amount of meaning for people, but it is going a bit too far to threaten to beat me up about it.'[25]

While inverting books on shelves is perhaps extreme, arranging a bookshelf to make it an aesthetic feature of a living space for mood effects is certainly not new. One of our survey respondents noted:

> I put care into the arrangement of books on the shelves in my living room (what I would consider a 'public space') to help create a mood for myself and my visitors. For me, that's a sense of warmth and coziness – a hygge[26] atmosphere, if I may borrow the term from the Danish. I have friends, though, who utilize their books for a very different feel, such as a modern, sleek sort of feeling. It's all very personal.

History offers up examples of book display both for aesthetic sensibility and for the desire to create a false impression for egotistical reasons. Populating your library with 'faux' books is not simply an affectation of the nouveau riche or of a corporation seeking to impart an image of gravitas. The creation of a false impression has a long historical lineage and can be found in unexpected places. Social media buzzed in 2017 with the extraordinary architectural grandeur of the Tianjin Binhai Library, a wonderful building with room for a million books. As it turns out, they only have 200,000 and the rest of the extraordinary display is in fact largely images of spines (Plate 7).[27]

But the concept goes back further, with a twist. In 1851 Charles Dickens ordered a set of fake books for his new abode, Tavistock Hall:

> I send you the list I have made for the book-backs. I should like the 'History of a Short Chancery Suit' to come at the bottom of one recess, and the 'Catalogue of Statues of the Duke of Wellington' at the bottom of the other. If you should want more titles, and will let me know how many, I will send them to you.

He then added a list of fake but amusing titles: Kant's *Ancient Humbugs* in ten volumes, for instance.[28] The list was not purely random jokes – some were puns on his own titles and characters, some pointed comments on his own pet peeves and dislikes, all intended to amuse both himself and visitors. Ironically, it is easy now to purchase a panel of fake leather-bound book-backs of Dickens's complete works. And Dickens was offering a twist on a library aesthetic that had started a century earlier. When neo-classical Palladian architecture was fashionable, symmetry was all important, inside as well as outside the house. So, oddly shaped doors or corners were best hidden by a uniform look, and fake books became a trend which could be ordered 'by the yard'. Georgiana Verney, the mistress of Compton Verney in Warwickshire (which boasted a Capability Brown landscaped garden), ordered for her panels a selection of books written only by women.[29]

While suggesting different motivations and strategies, all of these psychological perspectives emphasise the affective consequences of an artistic display. This conception of book display as creating a particularly desired atmosphere was put into words by a survey respondent: 'I have a lot of books. More than I could ever read, so I end up putting a lot in boxes in the basement. The ones on display are the ones I feel comforted by.'

That said, bookshelves can of course function purely as storage, simply a space to place things. Said one survey respondent, 'As I have gotten older, I am less interested in the appearance of my bookshelf to others and more interested in its functionality to me.' Another stated bluntly, 'They are not "on display" as such; more in bookshelves for the purpose of storage.' The most intriguing manifestation of utility revealed by the survey was the emergence of shelves shared between partners and family members, creating a montage of reading interests, tastes and abilities. 'The living room is shared with family and represents all tastes within the family', said one respondent, while another agreed that 'Our bookshelf – which is in the hallway – is a collection from all the family so it contains books from the kids to the adults. It's a real mix. It reflects our family unit rather than the individual.'

Even the great British prime minister William Gladstone wrote in late life a short pamphlet *On Books and the Housing of Them*, with practical advice on the construction, dimensions and placement of bookcases. He called for economy, good arrangement and accessibility, and condemned the contemporary fashion for ornament on the bookcase itself:

Now books want for and in themselves need no ornament at all. They are themselves the ornament. The man who looks for society in his books will readily perceive that, in proportion as the face of his bookcase is occupied by ornament, he loses that society.[30]

The short book provided diagrams, calculations of the number of volumes that a reasonable home library could hold and even calculated the maintenance and housing cost per book that should be added to the price of the volume itself.

Probably the prime minister would have approved of the Billy. Once every five seconds, IKEA claims to sell its bookcase by this

Figure 10.1 The IKEA 'Billy' bookcase

name somewhere in the world. First developed in 1979, total sales are now around 60 million worldwide. It is so ubiquitous that there is a Bloomberg Billy Bookcase Index which compares the prices of the Billy around the world. As it is a standard object made identically and sold in only one store, the Billy serves as a yardstick for price comparison (it is cheapest in Slovakia and most expensive in Egypt).[31] It is not ornate or even pretty, but it is decidedly utilitarian (Figure 10.1). Gladstone, Smiles and Priestley would have approved; Woolf and Pepys perhaps not.

In this chapter, we have presented two foundational arguments:

1. Books have, throughout history, been assigned a value of esteem, from the highest highbrow to the lowest lowbrow, based on qualities such as their genre, style and intended audience, and the evaluations of these books then transfer to their owners as well, as badges of honour and esteem, or as stigmas of low intellect and whimsy.
2. Book collections, like other material possessions, are extensions of the self – symbols of who we feel we are, who we would like to be and how we would like others to see us.

In putting these two theses together, we posit, then, that just as we craft our 'public self' as an edited version of our true self, our book displays vary in content to help convey our appropriate 'self' to possible viewers. None of this is to discredit or underestimate the true value books have for people. Rather, it confirms the role books have in our lives, roles electronic versions cannot replace. The physical book serves as a souvenir, both of the journey or adventure its words can take us on and as a time-stamp of the moments surrounding our lives when it came into our possession, when we first held it in our hands. Indeed, we often take steps to establish our ownership of the specific volumes, to indicate that the item is treasured and is ours, not just one copy in a vast print run – from the child putting her name on the first page of a book to an elaborately printed 'ex Libris' bookplate. Our shelves, very often, are a display case of memories and their location – public or private – an indication of whom we are willing to share these with. The response to our survey, the continued strength in sales of 'ink on paper', the resurgence of the independent bookstore all point to a tangible desire of the individual book purchaser and reader to own and cherish and display the printed version of the literature they have purchased.

The biggest shift in sales to the e-book reader has been precisely in the lowbrow genre. The mass market has all but disappeared from the print portfolios of publishers and the bookstores: the romance novels led the way in the 'e-book revolution', the very books our survey suggests would not be out there on display, the books that readers would still rather not be seen reading. E-book sales have levelled out at around 30 per cent of the overall market, as audiobooks have levelled out at 10 per cent. To the consternation of the pundits and the befuddlement of many publishers who started to close warehouses and terminate contracts with printers, people clearly want to buy and display their books no less than Samuel Pepys did.

Our bookshelves are – whatever motivation underlies their design – connections with the people whom we permit to see them. One of the biggest social media trends at time of writing (spring 2018) was #shelfie – people posting photos of themselves in front of their bookshelves.[32] The trend has given people the ability to share their books and, by extension, their tastes, their experiences, *their selves* – and to forge connections with a world of people who are not able to walk through their living rooms. Though of course they are likely putting their best books forward.

Notes

1. Virginia Woolf, *The Death of the Moth and Other Essays* (San Diego: Harcourt, Brace, 1974), 'Middlebrow'.
2. J. B. Priestley, quoted in Melba Cuddy-Keane, *Virginia Woolf: The Intellectual and the Public Sphere* (Cambridge: Cambridge University Press, 2003), p. 16.
3. *The Letters of Cicero, Vol. I*, trans. Evelyn Shuckburgh (London: George Bell, 1904), letter to Atticus, Antium, April–May 66 BC.
4. Geoffrey Chaucer, 'The Miller's Tale', in *The Canterbury Tales*, ed. William Skeat (Oxford: Clarendon Press, 1900).
5. Samuel Pepys, *The Diary of Samuel Pepys*, ed. Henry B. Wheatley (London: George Bell and Sons, 1893), 10 November 1663.
6. Interestingly, and perhaps appropriately, Smiles originally published the book himself, after well known publishers had rejected it and he had refused to make changes.
7. J. B. Priestley, *An Everyman Anthology* (London: Dent, 1966), p. 7.
8. Henry Fielding, *Tom Jones*, ed. John Bender and Simon Stern (Oxford: Oxford University Press, 2008), introduction, p. 3.
9. David Hadju, *The Ten Cent Plague: The Great Comic-Book Scare and How It Changed America* (New York: Farrar, Straus and Giroux, 2008), p. 6.

10. For our survey, 'public shelves' were defined for participants as bookshelves in which the books were visible and accessible to guests, such as a living room, whereas 'private shelves' were bookshelves in locations where guests were not likely to view, such as a bedroom.
11. Sigmund Freud, 'Creative Writers and Daydreaming', in *The Standard Edition of the Complete Psychological Works of Sigmund Freud*, trans. and ed. James Strachey et al. (London: Hogarth Press, 1959), vol. IX, pp. 141–54.
12. Nalini Ambady and Robert Rosenthal, 'Half a Minute: Predicting Teacher Evaluations from Thin Slices of Nonverbal Behavior and Physical Attractiveness', *Journal of Personality and Social Psychology*, 64:3 (1993), pp. 431–41.
13. Hannu Raty and Leila Snellman, 'Children's Images of an Intelligent Person', *Journal of Social Behavior and Personality*, 12 (1997), pp. 773–84.
14. Andrew Christopher and Barry Schlenker, 'The Impact of Perceived Material Wealth and Perceiver Personality on First Impressions', *Journal of Economic Psychology*, 21:1 (2000), pp. 1–19.
15. Nora A. Murphy, 'Appearing Smart: The Impression Management of Intelligence, Person Perception Accuracy, and Behavior Social Interaction', *Personality and Social Psychology Bulletin*, 33:3 (2007), pp. 325–39.
16. Christian Jarrett, 'The Psychology of Stuff and Things', *Psychologist*, 26:8 (August 2013), pp. 560–5.
17. Sam Gosling, *Snoop: What Your Stuff Says About You* (New York: Basic Books, 2008), p. 4.
18. Sam Gosling, 'What Your Stuff Says About You: Author Interview', NPR, at <https://www.npr.org/templates/story/story.php?storyId=90829875> (accessed May 2008).
19. 'Librarians of Reddit, do you judge people based on their books?', at <https://www.reddit.com/r/AskReddit/comments/19o4ne/librarians_of_reddit_do_you_judge_people_based_on> (last accessed October 2019). As of this writing, the post had garnered 583 comments, with the majority of librarians, bookstore clerks and circulation desk employees responding emphatically 'No'. One response, in particular, cited ALA privacy and patron rights guidelines learned in graduate school.
20. Ann Bogel, 'Other People's Bookshelves', 6 November 2013, at <https://www.modernmrsdarcy.com/other-peoples-bookshelves> (last accessed October 2019).
21. Beth Carswell, 'Undercover: Judging People By Their Books' See <https://www.abebooks.com/books/shelves-shelf-physical-paper-snoop/judge-people-cover.shtml> (last accessed October 2019).
22. Erving Goffman, *The Presentation of Self in Everyday Life* (New York: Anchor, 1956).
23. Terry Belanger, *Lunacy and the Arrangement of Books* (New Castle: Oak Knoll, 1982), p. 2.

24. See Sarah Young, 'Backward Bookshelves: Impractical Trend for Stacking Books with Spines to the Wall Divides the Internet', *The Independent*, 11 January 2018, available at <https://www.independent.co.uk/life-style/backwards-bookshelves-trend-spines-wall-stacking-spines-ideal-home-twitter-reaction-a8153726.html> (accessed October 2019).
25. See Andrew Ellson, 'Backwards Books Earns Spineless Abuse for Interior Designer Lauren Coleman', *The Times*, 16 January 2018, available at <https://www.thetimes.co.uk/article/backwards-books-earn-spineless-abuse-for-interior-designer-lauren-coleman-78wc5t7v5> (accessed October 2019).
26. Pronounced *hue-guh*, this Danish term used to describe a moment, an atmosphere, or a feeling of coziness and charm. See <http://www.hyggehouse.com> (accessed October 2019).
27. Atlas Obscura, 'Tianjin Binhai Library: China's Breathtaking Futuristic Library Is Lined Floor to Ceiling with Fake Books', 14 January 2018, at <https://www.atlasobscura.com/places/tianjin-binhai-library> (accessed October 2019).
28. Mamie Dickens and Georgina Hogarth (eds), *The Letters of Charles Dickens: Vol. I, 1833–1856* (London: Chapman and Hall, 1880), letter to Mr Eeles, 22 October 1851.
29. There is more information on the unique Compton Verney library at <https://www.unsilencingthelibrary.com/story-of-this-library> (accessed October 2019).
30. W. E. Gladstone, *On Books and the Housing of Them* (New York: Dodd Mead, 1891), p. 26.
31. Tim Harford, 'How Ikea's Billy Bookcase Took Over the World', 27 February 2017, BBC News, at <https://www.bbc.com/news/business-38747485> (accessed October 2019).
32. Authors' observation. A set of examples can be found at <https://www.instagram.com/explore/tags/shelfie/?hl=en> (accessed October 2019).

Chapter 11

In Search of the Chinese Common Reader: Vernacular Knowledge in an Age of New Media

Joan Judge

Model readers were central to China's twentieth-century revolutions. Leaders of the political, literary and social movements that drove these revolutions enjoined 'the people' to read new media, from newspapers to textbooks, and new genres, from 'enlightened' fiction to translated treatises. These new reading practices would introduce the benighted to critical forms of political and scientific knowledge that would hasten their transformation from the unruly masses of China's ungovernable past to the informed citizenry of its national future. What was most actively occluded in these elite urgings, however, was the actual lifeworld of those interpellated to become the new masses: their beliefs, texts and modes of thinking, which were systematically relegated to the dustbin of superstitious and backward 'Old China'.

This chapter is an effort to recover something of that neglected lifeworld through an ethnography of as yet little-explored practices of reading and modes of knowing. Rather than focus on the discursive production of the model reader, it searches for traces of actual common readers. Challenging elite condemnations of vernacular books as crude and ignorant, it subjects these materials to careful observation and close reading. The chapter works from the assumption that alternative ways of interacting with texts, organising information and relating to the natural world are inherently valid topics of enquiry. At the same time, it argues that the common readers' divergent ways of knowing did not constitute a hermetic field of non-knowledge: their epistemic world was integrated into and integral to the circuits of China's broader twentieth-century knowledge culture.

The pages that follow are concerned both with the why of investigating Chinese common readers, and with the difficult methodological question of how. I search for the Chinese common reader in three distinct places: in the materiality of cheaply produced string-bound texts – books as objects; in the usable (and wondrous) information packaged in their crowded pages – texts as meaning; and in the physical spaces where this knowledge was consumed – reading as cultural practice.[1] I begin, though, with a preliminary sketch of the Chinese common reader.

Chinese common readers, like all common readers, are elusive. They rarely left records of or reflections on their own reading and the kinds of materials they consumed have not been carefully preserved or studied. They can initially be defined by what they were not.

Common readers were not among those who read books for a living.[2] In the Chinese case, this meant they did not devote their lives to study for the civil service examinations in pursuit of bureaucratic office. Nor were they members of the new intellectual elite that began to emerge even before the examination system was abolished in 1905. They had neither the luxury nor the inclination to become ideal Confucian readers, for whom moral cultivation was the ultimate goal of study.[3] Nor were they model readers of the various forms of new media promoted by successive reform movements from the turn of the twentieth century through to the 1940s. While their modest literacy and modest means made it possible for them to consume common reading materials, this did not make them, in the words of one group of educational reformers, 'true readers'.[4]

We can gain some insight into who these readers (who were 'not true readers') were by canvassing a disparate array of sources. These include materials that sought either to market texts to common readers for commercial purposes or to survey their reading habits for political purposes. Such sources are suggestive of the common readers' motives, social demographics, level of literacy and even (very tentatively) their aggregate numbers.

The paratexts – titles, prefaces and advertisements – to compilations that targeted common readers reveal how editors and publishers imagined – and attempted to construct – what these readers wanted and who they were. The titles suggest that the practice of common reading was consultative rather than contemplative, pragmatic rather than abstract or political. This is evident in the phrase 'no need to ask' (*bu qiuren* 不求人), which served as the alternative title to one of the earliest genres of texts that directly targeted common readers, *wanbao quanshu* 萬寶全書 (*comprehensive compendia of myriad treasures*).[5] Readers, the title implies, turned to these texts in order to achieve a certain epistemological autonomy by liberating themselves from the need to personally consult experts. The matters about which the reader no longer had the need to ask include, as 'myriad treasures' in the title suggests, the fantastical. At the same time, the genre offered various forms of practical information. This pragmatic content is highlighted in the titles given to the categories of materials that both encompassed and succeeded the *wanbao quanshu*: daily-use (*riyong* 日用) texts. The twentieth-century Chinese book market was flooded with titles such as *Treasury for Daily Life*, *Science for Daily Life* and *Daily-Use Encyclopaedia*.

The plethora of editions of such texts is one indication of the increasing prominence of common readers in the twentieth-century print market. Another is the increasing directness with which publishers appealed to this demographic of readers. In late imperial compilations, the common reader was addressed in code. Texts that announced their 'usefulness for all four groups of people' actually targeted the less educated segments of the population. No self-respecting littérateur would want to put his hands on a book that appealed to the commoners below him.[6]

The conceit that literati and officials read *wanbao quanshu* is slightly tempered in the preface to one edition of these texts, which spawned an enduring lineage of expanded compendia. The preface claims that the compilation's main audience would be low-level bureaucrats: 'those who wait on high-ranking officials and run around everywhere [in search of information], bending and scraping to curry favour'.[7] This image of the scurrying minor bureaucrat accords well with a series of advertisements for another edition of *wanbao quanshu* that appeared in the newspaper *Shenbao* 申報 (*Shanghai Times*) in the 1890s. These advertisements depict low-level officials and merchants throughout China clamouring to get copies of the allegedly useful text. They include an employee at the Yangzhou Lisheng Old-Style Bank and an official working in the Hanyang Railway Office in Hubei.[8] As with testimonials in advertisements for pharmaceuticals in this period, the veracity of these demands for copies of the compendium is certainly questionable. The figures depicted in the advertisements nonetheless reflect the profile of readers the publisher hoped to attract.[9]

Advertisements that appeared in the same newspaper in 1894 assert how useful officials and merchants would find the newly expanded editions of *wanbao quanshu*. While they state that the revised edition of the text is 'popular throughout the land and appeals to the masses', they insist that 'officials and merchants all have a copy in their houses'.[10] Advertisements for yet another edition similarly claimed that it was officials and merchants who had urged the publisher to expand the compendia.¹¹

Editors of the newer genre of daily-use materials, in contrast, abandon all references to literati and officials, and explicitly address common readers. The introduction to a 1915 edition of one such text announces that its mandate is to help the common person (*shehui yiban ren* 社會一般人) understand the complexities of contemporary issues which exceed the mental capacity of any one individual.¹² The 1929 *Treasure-House of All Daily Things Necessary for Social Relations* (*Riyong wanshi baoku choushi bixu* 日用萬事寶庫 酬世必需) announces that it offers common knowledge for general social use. Having banished the lofty and profound, it uses clear and transparent language that even those with only a basic knowledge of characters could understand.¹³

The references in these various paratexts to 'common people' with 'a basic knowledge of characters', and an apparent aversion to theoretical pronouncements, suggests a certain level of literacy. The compendia's prospective readers clearly straddled the worlds of 'full' and 'fragmented' literacy and could best be described as possessing basic general literacy.¹⁴ While we lack the data that would allow us to calculate the precise percentage of the population these basically literate individuals represented, disparate sources defy the most commonly quoted figures we now have of 30–40 per cent literacy for Chinese for males and 2–10 per cent for females.¹⁵ Some of these sources are vague declarations of an overwhelming abundance of daily-use texts – enough to 'make a packhorse sweat or fill a house to the rafters' in the familiar idiom – which suggests an abundance of readers who consumed them.¹⁶ Other sources are more exacting. They include a 1933 survey conducted by Xu Xu 徐旭 (Yinchu 寅初, fl. 1925), a theoretician and founder of mass libraries (*minzhong tushuguan* 民眾圖書館). According to Xu, the majority of Shanghai residents could read, even if they were only crudely literate. This observation aligns with estimates as high as 80–90 per cent for the literacy rate in larger urban centres in nineteenth- and early twentieth-century China (in sharp contrast with much lower literacy rates in the countryside). Xu estimates that beyond the crudest level of literacy (which would mean knowledge of between several hundred to 1,000 Chinese characters), one in every forty people in the city read a newspaper (which would require knowledge of as many as 4,000 characters). He concluded that this number of Shanghai residents able to read newspapers contested the prevailing figure of 80 per cent illiteracy for this period.¹⁷ Xu's findings also challenge the assumption that ordinary women did not like reading, an assessment that corresponds with my own hypothesis elsewhere that as many as 25–30 per cent of women in Shanghai were literate in the early twentieth century.[18]

Xu further offers one of the most fine-grained breakdowns of the readers who frequented Shanghai bookstalls in the early 1930s – data that can be cautiously extrapolated with further corroboration backwards and forwards in time. They include housewives, store clerks, merchant apprentices, children, workers and prostitutes.[19] A survey from the city of Kaifeng in Henan province for the same period also includes store clerks among bookstall customers. It further identifies rural common readers who bought books to take back to the countryside with them.[20]

Common readers were characterised as 'not true readers' because the books they consumed were not orthodox books. Like their readers, these books can first be defined by what they were not. They were not officially sponsored texts produced to further the aims of the bureaucratic organisation of knowledge – whether the civil service examination system or the new-style formal education system which replaced it. They were not written by essayists or authors seeking either to please the authorities or to make a name for themselves.[21] Nor were they included in standard catalogues, since they did not generally fall under the four categories into which orthodox works were divided: classics, histories, philosophy and belles-lettres.

The genres of texts common readers did 'happily use' included 'old-style primers' such as the *One Hundred Surnames* (Baijia xing 百家姓) and the *Collection of Six-Word Phrases* (Liuyan zazi 六言雜字). The building blocks of commoner literacy, these collections were used in old-style private schools or informally in the home.[22] Unlike the mass reading materials put out by public institutions – which were so flavourless, useless and difficult to chant, according to one critic, that only students forced to read them in government schools would even look at them – these primers were a pleasure to read aloud.[23] When common readers moved beyond these primers, they turned to *wanbao quanshu* and a range of other daily-use texts for information. In addition to the comprehensive *riyong* compilations mentioned above, these included medical primers, letter-writing manuals and merchant handbooks.[24]

These various common reading materials were published, bound and printed differently from government-sanctioned model volumes. They were commercially produced by non-governmental (*minjian* 民間) publishers, rather than by the big three print conglomerates that serviced the new education system and dominated the twentieth-century print market.²⁵ Materially, they were radically distinct from the new-style texts. Generally string-bound in the traditional way rather than Western bound with glue and cardboard, they were softer and more pliable in the hand. Often crudely printed, the characters on their pages were nonetheless generally more pleasing to the eye. Whereas new-style texts were printed in standardised letterpress characters, the characters in string-bound texts were fluidly drawn by the human hand on slabs of limestone and then lithographically reproduced.²⁶ In terms of language register, texts targeting common readers used a simple form of literary prose.²⁷ This language was more accessible than not only high classical prose but even the new-style vernacular that New Culture activists promoted for model readers from the late 1910s.

These linguistically accessible *minjian* texts were also more affordable than their more highbrow letterpress alternatives. A two-volume how-to manual for the abacus cost one *jiao* 角, a quarter of the price of an issue of a new-style periodical published in the 1910s.²⁸ Through the early 1920s, a multivolume compendium of myriad treasures which a household would keep on hand indefinitely cost eight *jiao*, whereas a two-volume new-style encyclopaedia published by one of the leading publishers in 1919 cost over six times as much, five *yuan* 元.²⁹ To put these prices in context, a female labourer who earned a living wrapping cigarettes or working in a textile factory in this period could earn one to two *jiao* or two to three *jiao* a day, respectively.³⁰

Literati and scholars would not deign to look at these cheap string-bound mellifluous texts.³¹ Even 'middlebrow' authors promoted their collections as superior alternatives to the crude and inferior works sold in bookstalls on the streets. This was a strategy editors of each generation of daily-use texts used to distinguish and market their products.³² The preface to the 1919 *Complete Treasury for Citizens* (*Guomin baoku quanshu* 國民寶庫全書) condemned flawed and obsolete 'block-printed editions such as *wanbao quanshu*' occluding the publication of expanded and updated lithograph editions of this genre of texts.³³ The 'Introduction' to the 1929 *Treasure-House of All Daily Things Necessary for Social Relations* similarly declared that the countless daily-use books available in old-style bookstores were essentially useless: filled with platitudes, excessively narrow, poorly organised and outdated.³⁴

There is certainly some truth to these criticisms – sections of the *wanbao quanshu* were woefully outmoded by the 1910s and their original organising logic had long been lost, as worldviews changed and new material was inserted. At the same time, editors who condemned prior or competing genres of daily-use materials often shared content with or even directly borrowed from them. A close examination of these 'outdated' works reveals that they often served not only as a convenient foil for allegedly superior new texts but as a misrecognised source of their content.

Daily-use materials designed for common readers offered economies of knowledge. Just as the alternative title to the earlier *wanbao quanshu* promised to save readers from the need to ask others for information, later daily-use texts promised to save readers from having to buy or to read too many texts. 'This book', the front matter for one 1924 compilation declared, 'will spare you the cost of buying 10,000 others!' and the time of doing 'ten years of reading!'[35] Concerns with managing a surfeit of information were not new in this period, nor were they unique to China. But what constituted the most essential knowledge that early-twentieth century Chinese common readers required?

One strategy for tracing what constituted urgently needed common knowledge is to examine a series of supplements added to the compendia of myriad treasures (*wanbao quanshu*) from 1894 through 1906 and reprinted in only slightly amended form through to the early 1920s. The *wanbao quanshu* genre had first emerged in the sixteenth century to engage a demographic of readers that was largely separate from the office-seeking literati. Over the next 300 years this original mandate of proffering practical daily knowledge was reinforced as information was repeatedly added and deleted *within* the compendia's existing categories.[36] It was not until the turn of the twentieth century, however, that additional sections were added to the core text.

The decision on the part of lithograph publishers to supplement this existing genre, rather than jettison it in favour of some form of new media, does not solely signal the publishers' limitations. It also evinces their market savviness: they calculated that readers who were accustomed to consulting *wanbao quanshu* would continue to turn to them in search of new forms of knowledge. Given the plethora of editions of these supplemented texts put out by different publishing houses into the 1920s, this calculus appears to have been accurate.[37]

The content of the supplements reflects the publishers' projection of the kind of knowledge that would be most relevant to their common readers in this period. While it included some aspects of the 'new foreign learning' that was then rapidly being introduced into China, it was ultimately a curious mix of extracts from longstanding and relatively recent texts. In conformity with all Chinese compilations in this compendia genre, the material in the supplements was not original but was derived from other sources. Most of the source texts were practical handbooks of various kinds, the majority dating from the nineteenth century. There is no clear epistemological link among the six supplements or even among the subsections within a particular supplement – similar to the contents of the main body of the *wanbao quanshu*.

The first three supplements include information on foreign coins, flags, trade, commerce and the city of Shanghai, addressing what would have been merchant concerns. The next two, on plants and animals, and magic tricks, offer instruction on leisure activities and include what could be considered proto-scientific content. The final supplement, which seems to have been added in 1906, includes a short section on prognostication followed by three sections on health: Western approaches to health maintenance, an opium cure, and a series of first aid tips. Much of the content in the supplements foreshadows the subject matter included in subsequent daily-use texts, whether compendia or specialised volumes designed for merchants, home health care or letter writing. The expanded *wanbao quanshu* thus serve as a barometer of the ongoing concerns of common readers in Republican China.

These concerns were manifest in the rich contents of the later daily-use texts, which were often several volumes and hundreds of pages in length. To provide a glimpse into the common reader's preoccupations, I will briefly introduce three topics that resonated across the period – from *wanbao quanshu* supplements in the late 1890s through to the daily-use texts that appeared through the 1940s. They relate to merchant livelihood, plant cultivation, and disease prevention.

The supplement that appears first in most of the compendia concerns foreign coins. Based on my examination of a number of physical texts, this seems to have been one of the most widely used sections of the compendia: it shows the greatest signs of use, with worn pages and loosened string bindings.[38] The supplement was avidly read because it addressed one of the most crucial skills a merchant had to acquire: the ability to distinguish the confusing array of foreign coins and counterfeit 'native-minted' coin in circulation in China. The section includes illustrations and descriptions of various coins, in particular the Carolus peso: among the first foreign coins to enter China in large quantities, it was issued in Spain from the mid-eighteenth century and minted in Mexico. By the early nineteenth century, the Carolus peso had become a new de facto monetary standard in China.[39] The supplement offers detailed analyses of lettering on foreign coins, though the author of the source text apparently had no understanding of Western languages, all of which he collapsed under the general rubric of 'foreign' (literally ghost) language.[40] He nonetheless offered relatively meticulous renderings of the 'ghost language' on the coins. This meticulousness is lost in illustrations in the compendia supplements, in which foreign letters become gibberish or are excluded altogether.

While posing challenging questions about the usefulness of some of its information, the supplement on coins does provides potentially valuable insight into the vocations of its readers. By the time the supplements were added, the prominence of Carolus coins was already in decline in major Chinese markets.[41] This suggests that the targeted readers of these texts would most likely have been low-level merchants active in 'minor' markets – including the retail trade and commerce with interior regions – where the Carolus peso and its imitations continued to have currency through to the early twentieth century.[42]

The fourth *wanbao quanshu* supplement includes a very different genre of material: excerpts from a seventeenth-century text on plants, *Huajing* 花镜 (*Mirror of flowers*), by Chen Haozi 陳淏子 (b. 1612/15). These excerpts are from the most acclaimed section of the book, entitled 'Eighteen Methods for Growing Plants',[43] which offers the common gardener a general introduction to plant cultivation together with details about classifying and grafting plants.[44]

This form of botanical knowledge was clearly attractive to readers beyond the consumers of the *wanbao quanshu* supplements. Similar excerpts were reproduced in recurring sections on plant cultivation in daily-use texts in the 1930s. The *Huajing* also appealed to more learned readers, who valued it for fostering intimacy with nature. They include Zhou Zuoren 周作人 (1885–1967), a prominent intellectual who cherished the text for teaching him not about extraordinary plants but about the ordinary plants he was likely to encounter on his daily walks in the countryside. Astute, articulate and unpretentious, the *Huajing* was, in Zhou's words, a refreshing alternative to the idiocies of intellectual essay writing.[45]

At the same time, the *Huajing* contained scientific insights into relations with the natural world. Its method of taxonomy made it a valuable source text for the first formal Chinese dictionary of botanical nomenclature, published in 1918.[46] Its information on grafting plants is, however, the *Huajing*'s most widely acclaimed contribution. This material was repeatedly reproduced in sections on agriculture or plant cultivation in later daily-use texts. It has also been praised as scientifically advanced by some twenty-first-century scholars in the People's Republic of China.[47]

While the section on plants straddled the realms of science and recreation, the section on first aid in the final supplement addressed what would have been an urgent concern for Chinese common readers from the turn of the twentieth century – epidemic cholera. Shanghai suffered a cholera epidemic in the autumn of 1901, a few years before the supplement was added.[48] This was just one of at least forty-six outbreaks of the disease that ravaged China from 1820 (when records were first kept) through to the mid-twentieth century.[49] At this time, public health institutions were poorly developed in China, making disease management largely the responsibility of individuals, and rendering commercially produced handbooks one of the prime sources to which individuals could turn for information on treatments and cures. The *wanbao quanshu* supplement provided common readers with a simple DIY treatment for dry cholera, one of the more devastating forms of the disease.

In addition to publishing simple prescriptions, later daily-use texts directly or indirectly taught common readers about the nature of the disease and methods of preventing its spread. A 1921 letter-writing manual introduced readers to germ theory in a note appended to a model letter addressed to a fictive friend suffering from cholera. While there is some confusion in terminology – the author uses the term "mould germ" (*meijun* 黴菌) rather than the more commonly used term for germ (*weijun* 微菌) – the text clearly conveys the necessary information: those who come into contact with this germ/mould could become fatally ill.[50]

Once aware of this danger, common readers could turn to daily-use texts for tips about prevention. These included a list of twelve key methods of cholera prevention that was first published in 1905 by a promoter of Western medicine, Hou Guangdi 侯光迪 (fl. 1905).[51] While Hou's 1905 text would not have been immediately accessible to common readers, its list of twelve measures was repeated, with some reordering and changes, in a 1912 newspaper article and then (unattributed) in successive daily-use texts published in the 1910s, 1920s and 1930s. The list of preventative measures included refraining from overwork and abstaining from overindulgence in food, alcohol and sex – all related to the core principle of *qi* depletion in Chinese medicine. It also emphasised the need to avoid unboiled water and milk, food that had been exposed to flies, and infected individuals. By 1934, the first item common readers of a daily-use text encountered on the revised list was immunisation.[52]

Traces of common readers can, thus, be found in the content and materiality of the string-bound objects that were their most affordable source of practical information. They can also be found in visual and textual sources that depict the physical spaces where common readers perused, purchased or rented these materials. The most important of these spaces was the street-side bookstall (*shutan* 書攤). Some 1,300 bookstalls dotted the Shanghai landscape in the early 1930s, and they were also fixtures in smaller cities.[53] Kaifeng, a mid-sized city, had between thirty and forty bookstalls in same period.[54] Serving at once as the common readers' study, public library and classroom, bookstalls offer a sense of how common readers chose to read and what they may have read beyond practical daily-use materials.

A rich avenue of enquiry for the history of reading, bookstalls nonetheless pose significant methodological challenges. They are one of those little-documented and rarely commented upon elements of a public landscape. They do not seem to enter the historical record until the nineteenth century, when they are mentioned in scholars' jottings and, at the end of the century, in missionary sources.[55] By the 1930s, a convergence of political interest in 'the masses' (*minzhong* 民眾), cultural interest in the power of new media, and intellectual interest in social science research led to more focused studies of bookstalls. Together with disparate references that appear in memoirs and in the periodical press, the richest sources are two bookstall surveys, published in Shanghai and Kaifeng in 1933 and 1934, respectively.[56]

The Shanghai survey was conducted by Xu Xu, whose mission was to 'massify reading and to turn the masses into readers' by creating truly usable libraries for the common people. This mission drove him to undertake his bookstall survey: he was convinced that a better understanding of the interests of common readers was essential to compiling effective mass reading materials.[57] Over the course of approximately two weeks in November 1933, Xu investigated twenty-two bookstalls and ten newspaper stalls in three areas of Shanghai. His survey was unprecedented in terms of the questions he asked, the methods he used and his compilation of the results into tables. He gathered information on the publishers and materiality of the books, and on the operators, economics and hours of operation of the bookstalls.[58] The most relevant information for our purposes is the kinds of books available in the bookstalls and the profile of the readers who consumed them.

The motivation for the Kaifeng survey, undertaken by a group of local educational reformers, was more overtly political. The introduction to the report on the survey explained that in order to revive the Chinese nation it was necessary to train the masses, and in order to train the masses effectively, it was necessary to undertake a thorough investigation of their material and spiritual life. Existing mass reading materials, the investigators assumed, would provide access to this material and spiritual world.[59] Due to limited finances and manpower, the Kaifeng team was unable to do a general survey of the city. Instead, they focused on the Xiangguo Temple, which was a prime social nexus, similar to famous temples in other major cities. The investigators used the case method together with actual observation in studying the bookstalls around the temple. The entire survey was carried out over two weeks, followed by four weeks of data analysis.[60]

We learn from these surveys, together with other sources, that bookstalls were not one thing at any point in their history. A full study of the phenomena will have to devise a typology that distinguishes, for example, 'small bookstalls' and second-hand or 'old-book' bookstalls. The writer Mao Dun 茅盾 (1896–1981) described a particularly crude small bookstall he came across in Shanghai in the early 1930s – two planks of wood leaning against a wall next to a public toilet. He would not have even known of its existence if the son of his landlord had not taken him there by the hand, anxious to purchase an illustrated serial book (lianhuantu 連環圖).[61] At approximately the same time in the City God Temple, also in Shanghai, a second-hand bookstall sold a very different inventory: used copies of the classics.[62]

Differences between bookstalls could also depend on their location within a city. This was particularly true in the Shanghai cosmopolis, where illustrated serial books constituted as much as 100 per cent of the stock of books in the relatively poor Zhabei area and as little as 30 per cent in the foreign concessions.[63] At the same time, different customers received different treatment at the same bookstall. Bookstall owners in Kaifeng offered a fixed discount to their savvy city readers but raised the prices for peasants, who had fewer options and certainly inferior bargaining skills.[64]

Bookstalls offer insights not only into who read but how they read. They suggest a radical divide between idealised modes of reading and the common readers' actual reading practices. Ideal literati readers studied texts in tranquil, well appointed studies, while model reformed readers perused them in new public spaces: well equipped classrooms, newspaper reading rooms and mass libraries. In sharp contrast, common readers often read on the fly, in the streets, sitting, standing or leaning (Figure 11.1). This choice of reading space was partly determined by economics. Common readers 'would not set foot in' more formal bookstores that sold textbooks, or print shops that sold old books, because they could not afford (and had little interest in) the books for sale.[65] Bookstalls, in contrast, offered readers low

Figure 11.1 A bookstall in Shanghai in the 1930s

prices and flexible reading arrangements. The cheapest bookstall rate was for reading while standing at the stall. Those who preferred to take books home to their cramped living quarters but could not afford to buy them could rent them instead. The rental price was determined by the original cost of the book, the number of times the reader borrowed it and the length of time it was in their possession.[66]

Cost was far from the only factor that made bookstalls attractive to common readers, however. They were also drawn by the ease and culture of bookstall reading. Public reading rooms which targeted this same demographic with the aim of 'universalising social education' had cropped up in urban centres from early in the century, but these institutions were neither as airy nor as convenient as public bookstalls. A reading room which was established on South Chengdu Street in Shanghai in 1920, for example, was cramped and required all readers to fill out a form before entering. The rewards for these inconveniences were slim: due to financial constraints, the reading room's offerings were limited to journals, newspapers and a few ordinary books.[67]

New mass libraries which the Nationalist government established from the late 1920s were also unable to draw readers away from bookstalls. Common readers who frequented Wenmiao Street in Shanghai gravitated towards its ten bookstalls rather than its municipal library.

While the library aimed to be responsive to readers' needs, common readers found the library procedures onerous. They preferred to pay to casually leaf through a rented bookstall book rather than read a library book for free.⁶⁸

Bookstalls thus served the critical social function that public libraries and reading rooms failed to serve. They were repositories of knowledge for the masses, their prime reading site and their principal source of popular reading material.⁶⁹ A magazine feature in 1934 hailed them as the locus of 'real education'. The pampered sons of wealthy families who attended formal schools only learned to chat about their feelings, discuss love, watch movies, and dance. Poor youths in the city, in contrast, had the discipline to educate themselves. 'In the current period when the right of the masses to education has been stripped away', the article states, life on the streets – including the street side bookstalls – provides them with real education.⁷⁰

Not all assessments of bookstalls were so lofty, however. One of the attractions of at least some of the stalls was that they offered illicit material that more established bookstores did not deign or dare to sell – from cheap illustrated serial novels to 'harmful' sexual histories.⁷¹ According to one Western commentator writing in 1901, they offered books that were 'cheap and nasty as regards paper and printing, and containing subject matter to correspond'. Their influence on readers was 'undoubtedly vicious'.⁷² Similar laments over the harmful effects of these street-side libraries, particularly on schoolchildren, appeared in the periodical press throughout the first half of the twentieth century.⁷³

Polemics aside, bookstall inventories provide a glance into the 'library' of the Chinese common reader. Xu's list of the genres for sale in the bookstalls includes seven-character sentence primers, calligraphy copybooks and letter-writing manuals, as well as various literary genres: play and opera scripts and old and new fiction.⁷⁴ The Kaifeng list is similar: compilations such as *wanbao quanshu* and daily-use materials related to medicine, letter writing, mathematics, couplets and morality. Literature and entertainment also feature highly on this list – fiction, drum songs, poetry, opera and stories – as does fortune telling.⁷⁵

The genre most frequently associated with bookstalls and prominently featured in the surveys is the illustrated serial book. It appears first on Xu's list and was the subject of a separate study by the Kaifeng investigators.⁷⁶ Children were certainly the most avid readers of these illustrated books, but, as Mao Dun noted, adults consumed them as well – though not adults in scholars' long gowns.⁷⁷ The contents of these illustrated books were an exceedingly varied mix of rehashings of old novels together with newly created works.⁷⁸ They include tales derived from the *Romance of the Three Kingdoms* and from recent movies, as well as stories of spirits and demons, of knights-errant and of tragic romances. Some also offered more 'serious' content on history, education and current affairs.⁷⁹

What can we learn about Chinese common readers, the elusive target of reform and the little-understood object of much disdain in the twentieth century? How did they experience the shifts in China's epistemic terrain as notions such as 'science' and 'encyclopaedia' drew sharper fault lines than had cosmology and myriad treasures? Where did these readers situate themselves in the world beyond China's borders, which was increasingly present in the ghost language on circulating coins, the flags in the Shanghai harbour and new disease concepts that reinterpreted old afflictions?

This investigation of books, texts and reading spaces has sketched the contours of a reading world apart, with softer books that were easier to chant and cheap to rent. At the same time, it has uncovered a degree of epistemic integration that was and continues to be overlooked. Daily-use materials helped readers grapple with the very challenges that reformers and bureaucrats claimed necessitated a total overhaul of the material and spiritual world of the masses – from epidemic cholera to opium addiction, from foreign trade protocols to new approaches to nature.

The chapter urges us to understand common knowledge as knowledge rather than ignorance, and to map it in terms of circulation rather than stratification. It also encourages us to seek out common readers not only in the crude books they consulted or the wondrous tales they imbibed but in the reasoned material choices they made – a rhyming primer over an arid textbook, a bookstall stool over a cramped public reading room. Becoming more familiar with these moderately literate seekers of useful knowledge potentially has much to teach us about the politically salient gaps – and overlap – between model and common readers in China's century of revolution.

Notes

1. This method is inspired by the work of Roger Chartier. See, for example, 'Texts, Printing, Readings', in Lynn Hunt (ed.), *The New Cultural History* (Berkeley: University of California Press, 1989), pp. 154–75.
2. Jonathan Rose, 'Rereading the English Common Reader: A Preface to a

History of Audiences', *Journal of the History of Ideas*, 53:1 (January–March 1992), p. 52.
3. Dai Lianbin, 'Books, Reading, and Knowledge in Ming China', PhD dissertation (University of Oxford, 2012), pp. 40, 42.
4. Li Buqing 李步青 and Lian Fang 廉方, 'Xie zai Xiangguosi minzhong duwu diaocha junshou' 写在相国寺民众读物调查卷首 ('Introduction to the Investigation of Mass Reading Materials at the Xiangguo Temple, Section 1), reprinted in Li Wenhai 李文海 (ed.), *Minguo shiqi shehui diaocha congbian: wenjiao shiyejuan* 民国时期社会调查丛编：文教事业卷 [*Compendium of Republican-Era Surveys: Volume on Cultural and Educational Institutions*] (Fuzhou: Fujian jiaoyu chubanshe, 2004), p. 463.
5. The phrase *buqiuren* was also part of the title of a number of related texts: for example, *wanshi buqiuren* 萬事不求人書 (myriad matters you won't need to ask).
6. Cynthia Brokaw, 'Gérard Genette in Late Imperial China: Paratexts in Woodblock Texts', unpublished paper, p. 10.
7. See, for example, Tianji shuju 天機書局, *Zengbu wanbao quanshu* 增補萬寶全書 [*Expanded Comprehensive Compendium of Myriad Treasures*] (Shanghai: Tianji shuju, 1912), vol. I, n.p.
8. *Shenbao*, 1 and 7 March 1895.
9. On testimonials in advertisements, see Joan Judge, *Republican Lens: Gender, Visuality, and Experience in the Early Chinese Periodical Press* (Berkeley: University of California Press, 2015), pp. 27–8.
10. *Shenbao*, 5 June 1894.
11. *Shenbao*, 29 April 1894.
12. 'Riyong yaolan tiyao' 日用要覽提要 [Key features of *A Must-Read for Daily Use*], in *Riyong yaolan* [*A Must-Read for Daily Use*] (Shanghai: Shanghai tongsu bianyishe, 1915), vol. I, p. 1.
13. Saoye shanfeng 掃葉山房, 'Liyan' 例言 [Introduction], in *Riyong wanshi baoku choushi bixu* (Shanghai: Saoye shanfang, 1929), vol. I, n.p.
14. For a discussion of these various levels of literacy, see Cynthia Brokaw, *Commerce in Culture: The Sibao Book Trade in the Qing and Republican Periods* (Cambridge, MA: Harvard University Asia Center, 2007), pp. 562–8.
15. Evelyn Sakakida Rawski, *Education and Popular Literacy in Ch'ing China* (Ann Arbor: Michigan University Press, 1979), p. 23.
16. Saoye shanfeng, 'Liyan'.
17. Xu Xu 徐旭, *Tushuguan yu minzhong jiaoyu* 圖書館與民眾教育 [*Libraries and Mass Education*] (Shanghai: Shangwu yinshuguan, 1941), p. 201. Although Xu's estimate of one in forty newspaper readers in Shanghai (whose population he gives as 3,132,782) would translate to a literacy rate of only 2.5 per cent, he is clearly taking the number of those who had the relatively high degree of literacy required to read a newspaper as an indication of a much broader community of readers with more basic literacy skills. On literacy rates as high as 80–90 per cent among

residents of Chinese cities from as early as the nineteenth century, see: Rawski, *Education and Popular Literacy*, p. 11; Wu Jen-shu and Ling-ling Lien, 'From Viewing to Reading: The Evolution of Visual Advertising in Late Imperial China', in Christian Henriot and Wen-shin Yeh (eds), *Visualizing China, 1845–1965: Moving and Still Images in Historical Narratives* (Leiden: Brill, 2013), p. 252. The general assessment of basic literacy in China is, however, much lower than Xu Xu suggests, as Rawski (*Education and Popular Literacy*, p. 23) has argued.

18. Xu, *Tushuguan yu minzhong jiaoyu*, p. 163; Judge, *Republican Lens*, p. 69.
19. Xu, *Tushuguan yu minzhong jiaoyu*.
20. Li and Lian, 'Xie zai Xiangguosi', p. 464.
21. Ibid., p. 463.
22. On these various primers and their uses, see Wu Huifang 吳蕙芳, '"Riyong" yu "leishu" de jiehe: cong *Shilin guangji* dao *wanshi buqiuren*'「日用」與「類書」的結合 — 從《事林廣記》到《萬事不求人》 [The link between 'Daily use' and 'Category books': from the *Comprehensive Records of All Matters* to *Myriad Matters About Which One Will Not Need To Ask*], in *Ming Qing yilai minjian shenghuo zhishi de jiangou yu chuandi* 明清以來民間生活知識的建構與傳遞 [*The Construction and Transmission of Popular Daily Knowledge from the Ming and Qing Dynasties*] (Taipei: Taiwan xuesheng shuju, 2007), p. 43.
23. Li and Lian, 'Xie zai Xiangguosi', p. 463.
24. I have now collected more than 400 of these various texts from East Asian libraries, informal collections and used-book stores.
25. On the dominant print conglomerates, see Christopher A. Reed, *Gutenberg in Shanghai: Chinese Print Capitalism, 1876–1937* (Honolulu: University of Hawai'i Press, 2004).
26. On the process of lithography, see Joan Judge, 'Science for the Chinese Common Reader? Myriad Treasures and New Knowledge at the Turn of the Twentieth Century', *Science in Context*, 30:4 (winter 2017), pp. 362–3.
27. Li and Lian, 'Xie zai Xiangguosi', p. 463.
28. On the prices of new-style periodicals, see Judge, *Republican Lens*, p. 18.
29. On the price of *wanbao quanshu*, see Zhou Zhenhe 周振鶴 (ed.), *Wan Qing yingye shumu* 晚清營業書目 [*Late Qing Trade Catalogues*] (Shanghai: Shanghai shudian chubanshe. 2005), p. 435. Compare with Wang Yanlun 王言論 (ed.), *Riyong baike quanshu* 日用百科全書 [*Everyday Cyclopedia*] (Shanghai: Shangwu yinshu guan, 1919).
30. Wanxiu 晚秀, 'Shanghai pinnü shengya zhi diaocha' 上海貧女生涯之調查 ['An investigation of the careers of poor women of Shanghai'], *Funü shibao* 婦女時報, 18 (June 1916), p. 26; Qin Huirong 秦蕙蓉, 'Jiading nüzi zhiye tan' 嘉定女子職業談 ['On women's occupations in Jiading'], *Funü shibao*, 3 (26 July 1911), p. 39.
31. Li and Lian, 'Xie zai Xiangguosi', p. 463.

32. See, for example, the advertisement for Bao Tianxiao 包天笑 (ed.), *Gaodeng xiaoxue shiyong nüzi shuhan wen* 高等小學適用女文 [*Girls' Letter-Writing Manual, Upper-Level Elementary School*], in *Funü shibao*, 19 (August 1916), front matter.
33. Haohao zi 皞皞子, 'Xu' 叙 [Preface], in *Guomin baoku quanshu* 國民寶庫全書 [*Complete Treasury for Citizens*] (Shanghai: Zhonghua shuju, March 1919), p. 1.
34. Saoye shanfang, 'Liyan'.
35. *Riyong kuailan* 日用快覽 [*Everyday Knowledge at a Glance*] (Shanghai: Shijie shuju, 1924), front matter.
36. On the sixteenth-century editions of *wanbao quanshu*, see Wang Cheng-hua 王正華, 'Shenghuo, zhishi, yu wenhua shangpin: wan Ming Fujian ban "Riyong leishu" yu qi shuhua men' 生活知識與文化商品：晚明福建版‘日用類書’與其書畫門 ['Daily Life, Commercialized Knowledge, and Cultural Consumption: Late Ming Fujian Household Encyclopedias on Calligraphy and Painting'], *Zhongyang yanjiuyuan jindaishi yanjiusuo jikan* 中央研究院近代史研究所集刊 41 (September 2003), pp. 1–85. On their evolution in the later period, see Wu Huifang 吳蕙芳, *Wanbao quanshu: Ming Qing shiqi de minjian shenghuo shilu* 萬寶全書：明清時期的民間生活實錄 [*Comprehensive Compendia of Countless Treasures: (A Veritable Record) of Popular Life in the Ming and Qing Periods*] (Taipei: Hua Mulan wenhua gongzuo fang, 2005), vol. I, pp. 74, 206, 271, 311.
37. There were well over twenty editions of *wanbao quanshu* in print between 1894 and at least 1928.
38. These editions include Longwen shuju, 龍文書局, *Zengbu wanbao quanshu* 增補萬 [*Expanded Compendia of Countless Treasures*, 8 vols] (Shanghai: Longwen shuju, 1906); Tianju shuju, *Zengbu wanbao quanshu*. Both are held in libraries in Tokyo.
39. Richard Von Glahn, 'Foreign Silver Coins in the Market Culture of Nineteenth Century China', *International Journal of Asian Studies*, 4:1 (2007), p. 53; Eduard Kann, *The Currencies of China: An Investigation of Gold and Silver Transactions Affecting China, with a Section on Copper* (Shanghai: Kelly and Walsh, 1927), p. 297.
40. Liang Sizi, 'Fanli', *Xinjuan yinjing fami* 新鐫銀經發秘 [*Newly Carved Classic of Revealing the Secrets of Silver*], preface dated 1826, p. 1b.
41. See, for example, Shangye yanjiuhui 商業研究會 (ed.), *Shangren wanbao quanshu* 商人萬寶全書 [*Comprehensive Compendium of Myriad Treasures for Merchants*] (Shanghai: Dalu tushuju, 1920), vol. V, pp. 88–96.
42. Von Glahn, 'Foreign Silver Coins', pp. 65, 71–2.
43. See, for example, Yi Qinheng 伊欽恒, *Huajing jiaozhuben* 花鏡校注本 [*Annotated version of Huajing*] (Beijing: Nongye chubanshe, 1980), p. 4.
44. For a more detailed analysis of the place of the *Huajing* in the *wanbao quanshu* and its links to modern notions of science, see Judge, 'Science for the Chinese Common Reader?', pp. 369–71.
45. Zhou Zuoren 周作人, 'Huajing' 花鏡 [*Mirror of Flowers*], in *Yedu*

chao 夜读抄 [*Notes From Night Reading*] (Shijiazhuang: Hebei jiaoyu chubanshe, 2001), pp. 96–7.
46. *Zhiwuxue dacidian* 植物學大辭典 [*Botanical Nomenclature: A Complete Dictionary of Botanical Terms*] (Shanghai: Shangwu yinshuguan, 1918).
47. For an example of later use of this material, see Saoye shanfang, *Riyong wanshi baoku*, vol. XIV, *bian* (chapter) 28.
48. 'Cholera Epidemic in China', *British Medical Journal*, 27 August 1904, p. 458. On cholera in Shanghai, see Wu Lien-te, J. W. H. Chun, R. Pollitzer and C. Y. Yu, *Cholera: A Manual for the Medical Profession in China* (Shanghai: National Quarantine Service, 1934), p. 16.
49. Wu et al., *Cholera*.
50. He Chunshan 賀春珊 (ed.), *Fenlei chidu guanhai* 分類尺牘觀海 [*Vast Manual of Classified Correspondence*] (Shanghai: Guangyi shuju, 1921), vol. II, p. 11.
51. Hou Guangdi, *Yibing weisheng shu* 疫病衛生書 [*On the Prevention of Epidemics*] (Shanghai: Wenming shuju, 1905). On Hou, see Judge, *Republican Lens*, pp. 38, 119, 121, 131, 134.
52. He Yijiu 何一鳩. *(Gejie bibei) Minzhong riyong choushi daguan* (各界必備) 民眾日用酬世大觀 [*[Necessary for All] Grand Perspective on Everyday Social Interactions Among the People*] (Shanghai: Da Shanghai shuju, 1934), p. 8.
53. Xu, *Tushuguan yu minzhong jiaoyu*, p. 176.
54. 'Shuye kaikuang diaocha' 书业概况调查 [Investigation of the Book Business in Kaifeng], in Li Wenhai, *Minguo shiqi shehui diaocha*, p. 466.
55. See, for example, Chen Kangqi 陳康祺 (1840–90), *Langqian jiwen* 郎潛紀聞 [*Chronicles of an Unpromoted Official*] (Beijing: Zhonghua shuju, 1984), *juan* (section) 8; William Arthur Cornaby, *China Under the Search-Light* (London: T. Fisher Unwin, 1901), pp. 195–224.
56. I have also subsequently collected data from the Shanghai Municipal Archives dating from the early 1950s that reflects on the earlier histories of bookstalls but was able to include analysis of that material in this article .
57. Xu, *Tushuguan yu minzhong jiaoyu*, pp. 142–3.
58. Ibid., pp. 146, 143, 181.
59. Li Dongxu 李东旭, 'Jieshao benshu de jihuhua' 介绍本书的几句话 [A Brief Introduction to This Book], in Li Wenhai, *Minguo shiqi shehui diaocha*, p. 462.
60. 'Qianyan' 前言 [Preface], in Li Wenhai, *Minguo shiqi shehui diaocha*, pp. 465–6.
61. Mao Dun 茅盾, 'Shanghai' 上海 [Shanghai], *Zhongxue sheng* 中学生, 41 (1 January 1934), reprinted in *Maodun quanji* 矛盾全集, 第十一卷・散文卷 (Beijing: Renmin daxue chubanshe, 1986), pp. 205–6.
62. Li Shifang 李世芳, 'Cheng huangmiao de xiesheng' 城隍廟的寫生 [Sketches from the City God Temple], *Xianxiang* 現象, December 1935, p. 19.
63. Xu, *Tushuguan yu minzhong jiaoyu*, pp. 156–7.

64. 'Shuye kaikuang', pp. 466–7.
65. Li and Lian, 'Xie zai Xiangguosi', p. 464.
66. Zhang Lüqian 張履謙, 'Xiangguosi minzhong duwu diaocha' 相国寺民众读物调查 (Investigation of Mass Reading Materials at Xiangguo Temple), in Li Wenhai, *Minguo shiqi shehui diaocha*, p. 466.
67. 'Shiwen' 時聞 [Current News], *Tongsu jiaoyu congkan* 通俗教育叢刊 [*Popular Education Collection*] 6 (July 1920), p. 11a.
68. Xu, *Tushuguan yu minzhong jiaoyu*, p. 177.
69. Ibid., pp. 143, 142.
70. 'Shehui daxue: jietou tushuguan' 社會大學:街頭圖書館 [Society as University: Street-Side Libraries], *Pangguanzhe* 旁觀者, 1 (1934), p. 1.
71. 'Shuye kaikuang', p. 466.
72. Cornaby, *China Under the Search-Light*, p. 196.
73. Liu Baoqin 劉葆欽, 'Taihai xuetong zhi "jietou tushuguan"' 貽害學童之 '街頭 圖書館' ['"Street Library" – A Source of Evil Deeds of Schoolchildren'], *Jiankang jiating* 健康家庭, 2:3 (1940), p. 1.
74. Xu, *Tushuguan yu minzhong jiaoyu*, pp. 155–6.
75. 'Shuye kaikuang', pp. 502–3.
76. 'Lianhuantu diaocha' 連環圖調查 [Investigation of Illustrated Serial Books], in Li Wenhai, *Minguo shiqi shehui diaocha*, pp. 503–22.
77. Mao Dun, 'Shanghai', p. 206.
78. Ibid.
79. Xu, *Tushuguan yu minzhong jiaoyu*, pp. 166–7. The Kaifeng survey broke these categories down by percentages. See 'Lianhuantu diaocha', p. 520.

Chapter 12

From 'Bookworms' to 'Scholar-Farmers': Tao Xingzhi and Changing Understandings of Literacy in the Chinese Rural Reconstruction Movement, 1923–34

Zach Smith

In 1923 China's leading advocate of popular education, Yan Yangchu (晏阳初, 1890–1990) called literacy a 'wonder drug' (*wanlingdan* 萬靈丹) that could heal the 'deafness, dumbness, and blindness' of the Chinese nation, if only it were extended to the over 300 million mostly rural Chinese who lacked an education.[1] By 1934, however, Yan had significantly altered his prescription for China's woes, acknowledging that 'literacy alone . . . had little practical value to farmers', and, as such, literacy training should be likened to 'plowing the field . . . for later cultivation' rather than a cure-all.[2] The intervening decade witnessed not only a change in Yan's attitudes towards literacy, but also a fundamental redirection of China's political and social reform energy from the urban coast to the countryside. Around the same time of Mao Zedong's famous 1927 Autumn Harvest Uprising, a broad spectrum of teachers and activists who had previously sponsored urban literacy campaigns and street-corner lectures in cities like Beijing and Changsha now devoted themselves to a sweeping educational, political and economic revitalisation of the countryside, known collectively as the Rural Reconstruction Movement (*Xiangcun jianshe yundong* 鄉村建設運動).[3] This ambitious project required pedagogues to answer an array of questions, not just about how to target new students, recruit new teachers and develop new education strategies, but about what role literacy should play in the education of the masses, and what role the masses should play in China's modern political development. Reading Confucian texts had long been a fundamental prerequisite for entry into Imperial China's social and political elite, but what should be the purpose of literacy for rural citizens of the modern Chinese nation-state?

Among the foremost Rural Reconstruction leaders attempting to answer this question was pedagogical theorist, popular education activist and close friend of Yan, Tao Xingzhi (陶行知, 1891–1946). As editor of the reform journal *Xin jiaoyu* 新教育 (*New Education*), author of popular literacy primers like the *Pingmin qianzi ke* 平民千字課 (*Commoners' Thousand-Character Text*) and chief organiser of the Chinese National Association for the Promotion of Commoners' Education (*Zhonghua pingmin jiaoyu cujinhui* 中華平民教育促進會, known colloquially in English as the Mass Education Movement or MEM), Tao found himself at the epicentre of rural reconstruction efforts. Like several other prominent education reformers of his generation, Tao attended graduate school at Teachers College, Columbia University, where he encountered the progressive educational philosophy of John Dewey (1859–1952) and Paul Monroe (1869–1947). Upon returning to China in 1917, Tao devoted himself to problems of popular education and, especially after 1923, rural education. Throughout his career, Tao was keenly interested in the relationship between knowledge and experience, whether in the form of 'unity of knowledge and action' (*zhixing heyi* 知行合一) as conceived by the Ming philosopher Wang Yangming (王阳明, 1472–1529) or John Dewey's ideas about experiential learning.[4] Tao's belief in the value of experiential education models found its fullest expression in the Xiaozhuang Experimental Normal School, which Tao founded in a rural community outside of Nanjing in 1927. Here, prospective rural teachers spent their time working alongside rural farmers while studying agronomy and running adult education night classes. Ultimately, Tao's preference for action and experience over abstract theory led him to question much of the received wisdom of both his Columbia professors and fellow Chinese education reformers, and his Xiaozhuang school, though short-lived, became a model for a new kind of popular education, dubbed 'life education' (*shenghuo jiaoyu* 生活教育).

In this chapter, I suggest that Tao's views on reading and learning reflected not just a new way of teaching rural communities, but also a fundamental change in how Chinese education reformers thought about popular literacy. Whereas literacy was once viewed, both during the height of China's Imperial period and in the first decade of the Republic, as a self-evident normative good, Tao's pedagogical essays, textbooks and experimental schools reveal an increasing conviction that reading in the new Chinese nation was merely a practical 'tool' with which to do economically productive work. In keeping with this view, Tao's own experimental school took as its focus the transformation of rural masses not into readers, but into ecologically savvy and efficient scholar-farmers. I argue further that this re-evaluation of literacy from a normative good to a practical means heralds an even broader shift in Chinese understandings of citizenship, as reformers who had previously conceived of Chinese citizens as a social and political community defined by access to shared values grew to see citizenship as predicated on an individual's ability to contribute economically to the nation-state. To be clear, given the complex, frequently international and multidirectional dialogue among Chinese pedagogues in the 1920s and 1930s, such a shift cannot be reduced to the influence of any one thinker, even one as widely discussed and debated as Tao Xingzhi. Rather, Tao's pedagogical theory and practice, as well as their applicability to an array of Nationalist and Communist political projects in the following decade, are indicative of the especially broad conditions of possibility for imagining the role of literacy and the meaning of citizenship in China's Republican period.

Tao's influential positions on literacy and reading complicate our understanding of both the history of modern Chinese education and the concept of citizenship in Republican China. Many studies of Republican Chinese education reform have tended to focus on those aspects that are the most 'new' or foreign, such as the increased focus on physical education or the reorganisation of schoolhouses following Japanese and German models, and in so doing they risk reducing transformations in Chinese education to mere products of its semi-colonial encounters with foreign powers.[5] Though these studies highlight many of the most disruptive elements of the education reform movement, they cannot explain how these policies gained relevance for reformers like Tao, who, despite his international education, remained broadly sceptical of uncritically adopting Western norms and policies, which he compared to 'strangers who come inside our house and stay the night' without being vetted.[6] Studies of citizenship and the public sphere in the Republican period have similarly focused on the most novel forms of civic engagement, such as the growth of public speaking, workers' strikes or suffrage movements, without exploring the broader avenues through which Chinese reformers imagined new forms of social and political community.[7] The issue of popular literacy provides a useful lens for investigating emerging attitudes toward education and citizenship precisely because it was *not* new to China and thus engaged the interest of many reformers, from radical Communist organisers to Confucian revivalists. An investigation of Tao Xingzhi's perspective on literacy, then, reveals the degree to which the subject of literacy served as a medium through which new notions of citizenship integrated with existing attitudes about knowledge and the state in ways that became legible to a broad spectrum of teachers, administrators and students. Indeed, Tao's critique of literacy helps illustrate not only the ways popular literacy transformed marginalised rural communities, but also how the capacious concepts of literacy and citizenship were themselves transformed by these inclusive efforts.

The precise meaning of literacy had been a subject of intense debate among Chinese educators in the decades prior to the founding of Tao's Experimental Normal School. In Chinese, the concept of 'literacy' could be expressed in any number of ways. The compound phrase *shizi* 識字 (literally, 'to know characters') might refer to the ability to recognise a few basic words, while *shi wenzi* 識文字 implied an ability to read and understand Confucian texts. Broader still, the phrase *you wenhua* 有文化 (literally '[one] has culture') was used to refer to someone who was literate and by extension understood the norms and values contained within classical texts. During the waning decades of the Qing Dynasty (1644–1911), it is unclear precisely how many people fell into these ill-defined categories, nearly all of which represented political and ideological values rather than empirical descriptions of skill.[8] Though some scholars estimate that during the late Qing period as many as 45 per cent of men (and 2–10 per cent of women) could read and write at least a basic number of characters related to their profession, the formal education system defined literacy in narrow terms of one's ability to read classical Chinese (*wenyan* 文言) and therefore participate in public life.[9] The abolition of the civil service examination system in 1904, and its eventual replacement with a network of public schools designed to 'educate all citizens', fundamentally changed the political and social context for this narrow understanding of literacy, and paved the way for enormous changes in who could read, what was read, and why.[10]

Perhaps the most obvious and most well studied shift in Chinese attitudes towards literacy concerns the steady abandonment of classical Chinese (*guwen* 古文) and its replacement by a standard vernacular (*baihua* 白話).[11] Despite its hand in destroying the examination system, the Qing Ministry of Education initially sought to preserve the value of classical texts; indeed, the 1908 Qing *Principles of the Constitution* declared literacy in classical Chinese to be a prerequisite for suffrage in the new constitutional monarchy.[12] After the Qing fell, members of the 'national essence group' (*guocuipai* 國粹拍), including anti-Manchu activist Zhang Binglin (章炳麟, 1868–1936), continued to insist that classical Chinese remained relevant as an embodiment of national identity.[13] Yet as early as 1909, some popular education advocates, such as Lufei Kui (陆费逵, 1886–1941), cited the difficulty of the classical script as a barrier to mass education, and argued for a new curriculum based on shorter semesters, simpler characters and greater adherence to 'common written style' (*putong wenzi* 普通文字).[14] During the New Culture Movement of the late 1910s, many of China's leading intellectuals and educators questioned not only the form but also the content of the Confucian canon, and increasingly turned to vernacular texts – moral fables, public speeches and Chinese translations of Western science – as the basis for national language (*guowen* 國文) training.[15] By the late 1920s, *baihua* had almost completely overtaken classical Chinese as the primary language of educational instruction and political expression, leading primary school pedagogue Yu Ziyi (俞子夷, 1885–1970) to declare, 'if we take universal education as our objective, then the dead language of classical texts completely lacks a basis for existence'.[16] Under this new educational system, reading classical Chinese was no longer a prerequisite for declaring oneself literate – literacy could be defined merely as the ability to read *baihua*.

Yet within this profound shift in the *kinds* of language that one could read in order for one to be considered literate, there existed a certain continuity regarding the *purpose* of literacy education, as both vernacular reformists and classical defenders viewed literacy as a platform for accessing the shared norms and values of citizens. Early Republican minister for education Tang Hualong (汤化龙, 1874–1918) defended the classical curriculum by arguing that schools should focus on the 'simple words with deep meanings' of the Confucian canon in order to develop proper 'citizenship norms' (*guomin guyou zhi bingyi* 國民固有之秉彜).[17] Even after political reformers rejected Confucian values and the language that conveyed them as impractical and irrelevant, many advocates of popular education continued to argue that mass literacy was the essential means by which more contemporary values would be spread. As one New Culture writer put it, 'illiterate people are truly unprecedented and unrepeatable ... they cannot acquaint themselves with people of the past, but also when it comes to their own time, they cannot mutually circulate or understand each other'.[18] As such, teaching common people to read and write was an important step towards making 'everyone's thoughts draw nearer to each other' and creating a national community capable of self-determination.[19] In editorials, textbooks, morality plays and publicity materials, education leaders signalled their continued attachment to the cultural value of literacy by referring to those who could not read as *wenmang* 文盲 (literally 'blind to literature/culture') and insisting that mass education was necessary to raise 'citizens' cultural level' (*guomin wenhua de chengdu* 國民文化的程度).[20] Thus, while both the form of Chinese language and the values literacy was meant to provide had changed, many educators in the early 1920s still believed that mass literacy was a cultural and moral imperative co-terminous with education itself.

However, within the emerging consensus regarding the necessity of national vernacular language instruction, some reformers for popular education were beginning to offer more radical perspectives on literacy's place within Chinese education. Perhaps the most vocal of these critiques came from the growing cohort of Chinese educators in dialogue with the pedagogical theory of John Dewey, who embarked on a lecture tour of China in 1919.[21] Dewey's own educational philosophy acknowledged the value of literacy but placed special emphasis on experiential learning and the acquisition of practical skills. At one stop on his tour, Dewey defined the ultimate goal of democratic education as follows:

> I want to emphasize the fact that the end of education is not just the cultivation of scholars or 'bookworms' who are satisfied to spend all their time reading, but rather it is to cultivate useful members of society. Ability to read is not enough to make a good citizen, if by good citizen we mean one who must make a real contribution to his society. . . . [The] school should not merely acquaint students with the needs of society, but must also prepare them to meet these needs.[22]

Publications of Dewey's lectures, often translated by vernacular language advocate Hu Shi (胡適, 1891–1962), appeared in both the official Ministry of Education *Bulletin* and journals on popular reform like *Jiaoyu chao* (*Educational Tide*) and *Xin jiaoyu* (*New Education*).[23] Here they joined calls from the advocates of vocational education like Huang Yanpei (黃炎培, 1878–1965) and from Chinese students eager to appropriate Dewey's name to explain their own critiques of Chinese education.[24] One contributor to the journal *Pingmin jiaoyu* (*Democracy and Education*) criticised the existing education system for being too focused on esoteric knowledge, and invoked Dewey before paraphrasing a passage from the Confucian *Analects* to ask, 'What is a person who reads books? Are they not parasites who do not work and are ignorant of common things?'[25] Elsewhere, the reformer of primary education and Columbia graduate Yu Ziyi asserted, 'we teach children in order to expand their experiences, not to recognise a few characters or read a few books'.[26] Consequently, he argued for a primary school curriculum whereby students would learn written characters only after they had encountered new experiences and mastered the ability to speak about them.[27] The growing admiration for learning from experience rather than texts represented a profound devaluation of literacy's place within even the formal school curriculum, and the proposals from Yu Ziyi, Huang Yanpei and others provided educators with the space in which to question the meaning of literacy in fundamentally new ways.

In the years immediately following his graduation from Columbia and return to China in 1917, Tao Xingzhi occupied a rather mainstream position within the popular literacy movement, albeit one clearly closer to the progressive ideas of Dewey. As editor of *Xin jiaoyu*, he provided a platform for the advocates of vernacular language teaching alongside his own articles on democratic classroom management, and he participated in political efforts to reform the public school system.[28] Tao's focus shifted to popular literacy in 1923 when he met Yan Yangchu, who had already spearheaded a series of urban literacy campaigns in Changhsa and Yantai, and the two went on to found the National Association for the Promotion of Commoners' Education (*Zhonghua pingmin jiaoyu cujinhui* 中華平民教育促進會), which took as its slogan 'To eliminate illiteracy and create new citizens' (*yu wenmang, zuo xinmin* 餘文盲, 作新民).[29] In pursuit of this goal, Tao worked with Yan to develop a new literacy primer, *Pingmin qianzi ke* (*Commoners' Thousand-Character Text*), whose organisation and contents capture Tao's ambivalent attitudes toward literacy at the time. On the one hand, the textbook reflected the progressive position that education should draw from everyday experience and train students to fit the practical needs of society. *Pingmin qianzi ke* was edited specifically with so-called 'commoners' in mind, and an early lesson entitled 'Reading Is Good!' emphasised the value of literacy for farming, working and raising children, among other endeavours.[30] But the volumes also included vernacular lessons on patriotic symbols and even brief accounts of moral exemplars like Confucius and Mencius, which implied a moral dimension to literacy as well.[31] Even its title – *Thousand-Character Text* – suggested a certain continuity with the classical Chinese 'thousand-character texts' still in use among many private schools (*sishu* 私塾) in China, and with the moral community of shared values those lessons hoped to create. In sum, the *Pingmin qianzi ke* reveals an editor who was eager to apply progressive ideas about experiential learning to the practical problem of mass literacy training, but who still retained a fundamental faith that literacy was essential to building a national community.

At the same time that Tao turned towards mass literacy, his encounter with Yan also sparked a new interest in what was to become a much more fundamental transformation: a deep engagement with the Chinese countryside. Tao's critiques of rural Chinese education, first published in April 1923, were markedly more pointed than his other education work with Yan, and spoke to a set of pedagogical problems that extended beyond literacy. In his article 'Fundamental Reform in China's Rural Education' Tao argued:

> Chinese rural education has taken the wrong path! It teaches people to leave the countryside and run to the city, it teaches people to eat food but not to plant rice. . . . It teaches them to distribute profit but not to make profit. It teaches the sons and younger brothers of farmers to become bookworms [*shudaizi* 书呆子]. It teaches the rich to become poor and the poor to become even poorer; it teaches the strong to become weak and the weak to become even weaker.[32]

This emphasis on profit and utility over abstract book learning clearly built on the arguments made by contemporary proponents of experiential learning, but over the next several years Tao's critiques went even further than these efforts by fundamentally questioning both the moral and the economic utility of reading itself. To signal his newfound commitment to the countryside and his rejection of the norms and modes of behaviour that had come to dominate elite reform circles, Tao began dressing in simple robes and grass thong slippers.[33] From this point forward, Tao devoted himself almost exclusively to the problem of rural education.

Over the course of the next decade, Tao became extraordinarily harsh in his discussion of 'bookworms', who were well read but had no means of turning their knowledge into productive work. Tao compared such people to a 'false intelligentsia' (*weizhishi jieji* 伪知识阶级), who are 'parasites on society' and 'taint the country with their corruption'.[34] His protégé Cheng Benhai (程本海, 1898–1980) went a step farther, calling China's primary schools nothing more than 'bookworm manufacturing plants that take good sons and younger brothers of farmers and turn them into unproductive good-for-nothings'.[35] Tao was not completely opposed to literacy as an important part of a well rounded education. He conceded that illiteracy was one of the primary factors behind the exploitation of lower classes, and argued that illiterate farmers were little more than 'hayseeds' (*tiandaizi* 田呆子), incapable of developing more efficient farming methods or otherwise improving their political station.[36] But even in this context, Tao argued that 'books are simply tools, in the same manner as a saw or a hoe, which people can use'.37 To this end, Tao argued that rural students should not 'read dead books' (*du si shu* 讀死書) but 'use living books' (*yong huo shu* 用活書).38 Tao later clarified that 'living books' could include many things that were not books at all, such as 'flowers and plants . . . trees, birds, beasts, microbes . . . mountains and rivers . . . the movements of celestial bodies', and that their use formed the centrepiece of a model of experiential learning Tao branded 'life education' (*shenghuo jiaoyu* 生活教育).39

Tao's questioning of the value of reading books signaled a fundamental reconfiguration of the goal of popular education and its relationship to citizenship in China. In an article written in 1926 for the vocational education magazine *Shenghuo zhoukan* 生活周刊, 'Learning to be a Person', Tao suggested that a good citizen must possess three essential traits: 'a healthy body' to take on work, 'an independent way of thinking' to make good judgments, and 'an independent skill' to make a profit.40 When this notion of citizenship was applied to rural education, it meant teaching students above all to be *economically* productive. As Tao argued, 'A living rural education should teach people to make a profit. It should make a barren hill into a grove of trees and a desolate field grow five grains.'41 In his view, it was their inability to produce profit that made 'book readers' such a terrible scourge on the nation. This focus on the economic productivity of rural communities allowed Tao Xingzhi to position his own educational theories against those of other reformers, who seemed overly enamoured with foreign '-isms' and the 'imitative adoption' of Western pedagogical norms.42 Whereas previous popular-education reformers saw literacy as the gateway to membership in a modern political community of shared (and often Western) values, Tao looked to economic skills as the foundation for the construction of new political communities based on the principles of 'self-sufficiency, self-governance and self-defence' (*zili, zizhi, ziwei* 自立, 自治, 自卫).43

Tao got the opportunity to put his theory of living education into practice when he founded the Xiaozhuang Experimental Normal School on the outskirts of Nanjing in March 1927. The School, which focused on training teachers to promote rural education, was intended to be the culmination of the reformist vision that Tao had been developing over the past decade: it shifted pedagogical development from an urban setting to one that was thoroughly integrated in the rural community, it drew inspiration from the practicalities of Chinese village life, and it sought to develop teachers with 'the physical skills of farmers, the minds of scientists, and the spirit of social reformers'.⁴⁴ You can get a sense of the School's mission from the organisation of a typical school day, which focused more on labour than on traditional pedagogy. Every morning, students would hold a ten- to fifteen-minute meeting devoted to planning and delegating work tasks for the day, while the rest of the morning was spent practising martial arts alongside classroom study. Even the School's more formal curriculum was organised around 'using books' rather than merely 'reading books', as the topics studied were always directly related to the School's rural reconstruction efforts and included texts on farming, environmental science and other subjects beyond the classroom.⁴⁵ The entire afternoon was typically devoted to work, as the teachers-in-training at Xiaozhuang committed themselves to agricultural labour, simple craft manufacturing and working among the people. The evening was often spent teaching at the people's night school and journaling about the day's activities.⁴⁶ The goal of the curriculum was not simply to teach peasants how to read, but to train teachers and rural farmers to transform the rural landscape as self-sufficient, economically productive citizens.

Yet, as much as Xiaozhuang represented a culmination of Tao's ideas about 'life education' and rural reconstruction, the school also reflected the ongoing evolution of Tao's attitudes to citizenship. As historian Hubert O. Brown has noted, Tao did not initially see Xiaozhuang as an effort to learn from the peasants, whose brains he compared to 'vacuum tubes', but rather as an attempt to transform its students from simple villagers into cultivated citizens.⁴⁷ Indeed, when Tao first wrote about the concept of student self-government (*zizhi* 自治), in 1919, he likened it to a form of self-discipline and moral cultivation rather than a means of independence.⁴⁸ Yet, after establishing a unity of 'teaching, learning and doing' at Xiaozhuang, Tao began to take the notion of political self-sufficiency more seriously, and throughout the 1930s repositioned 'life education' as the foundation of a new kind of egalitarian society, with no division between school and society and no clear need for a central state. 'In the great school of society', Tao argued, 'anyone can be our teacher, anyone can be our classmate and anyone can be our student'.⁴⁹ In 1934, Tao founded a new journal, simply titled *Life Education*, which outlined what this conception meant for mass mobilisation. Tao suggested that true life education must 'teach the masses to use the work of the people to feed the life of the people, to use the science of the people to enlighten the life of the people, and to use the organized force of the people to safeguard people's livelihood'.⁵⁰ Gone were the notions of moral, political or scientific tutelage that had characterised many earlier attempts at popular education (including some of Tao's own), all of which were predicated on the ability of common people to access shared values through reading. They had been supplanted by an understanding of education that placed rural reconstruction firmly in the hands of 'independent citizens' themselves.

Tao's Xiaozhuang Experimental Normal School generated great interest in the reform community, earning coverage in education journals from Hunan, Shaanxi and Beijing, as well as visits from the Nanjing Municipal Education Department and faculty members from Columbia University Teachers College.[51] Unfortunately for Tao, it also attracted the ire of the nascent Nationalist (Guomindang) state, whose leaders were hostile to the Communist and anarchist rhetoric stemming from Xiaozhuang instructors and perhaps of Tao's personal friendship with a competing warlord. In April 1930 Guomindang troops forcibly closed the School, less than three years after its founding.[52]

Perhaps because Tao Xingzhi had a unique authorial voice, and because of the truncated lifespan of his Xiaozhuang School, he is sometimes presented in the literature as a radical outlier at odds both with the mainstream currents of the reform community and with China's growing political parties. Yet Tao was not entirely opposed to the broader Chinese nationalist project – he encouraged his own students to read selections from Sun Zhongshan's *Three People's Principles*, and the nearby Yaohuamen Experimental Primary School (run by Xiaozhuang students) held weekly Monday morning meetings commemorating Sun Yatsen in a style that mirrored the nationalist rituals and ceremonies encouraged by the Guomindang.[53] Moreover, Tao was not entirely alone in his re-conception of the relationship between literacy, society and economic productivity. By the early 1930s, even Yan Yangchu began to emphasise the importance of creating 'scholar-farmers' for whom literacy was merely a step towards a greater understanding of agricultural science and personal hygiene.[54]

While the Guomindang government may have been wary of Tao himself, many literacy primers edited and published by the Nationalist Ministry of Education drew frequently on Tao's ideas. One government-approved text, Wei Bingxin's *Minzhong qianzi keben* 民眾千字課本 (*Mass Thousand-Character Text*), opens with the claim that 'Good citizens must do work!', while another rejects the label of 'thousand-character text' entirely because its author felt such titles placed undue focus on literacy alone.[55] One Nationalist Party reader even seems to channel Tao himself by claiming 'school should not teach you how to rigidly read books because rigidly reading books is not useful'.⁵⁶ Such rhetoric, though not a direct endorsement of Tao Xingzhi, demonstrates the degree to which Nationalist Party educators viewed Tao's notion of practical literacy as advantageous to the broader Nationalist project, which defined 'useful people' (*youtong de ren* 有用的人) as those who were capable of handling affairs and producing profit on behalf of the nation.

At the same time, Tao's students (and therefore his ideas more generally) found long and meaningful careers within the Chinese Communist Party (CCP), even if Tao himself was intermittently criticised by the CCP as a bourgeois American-style progressive. Though Tao did not personally identify as a Communist, historian Miao Feng has argued persuasively that his forays into rural reconstruction were motivated by an admiration for Communist organising efforts and by a desire to mitigate the damage of urban-centred capitalism on the Chinese countryside.⁵⁷ After the Xiaozhuang School closed down, some of its students and collaborators, including Fang Yuyan (方與嚴, 1889–1968) and Zhang Zonglin (張宗麟, 1899–1976), went on to join the CCP, before eventually serving as deputy directors of primary education and higher education respectively in the government of the People's Republic.⁵⁸ Zhang argued forcefully in the early 1930s that practical literacy and life education could empower poor peasants to take advantage of their own labour and combat 'evil gentry' (*lieshen* 劣绅) in much the same manner as Communist land reform projects in the following decades.⁵⁹ During the decades of intermittent civil war between the CCP and the Guomindang, Tao's practical literacy model of 'mass education' (*dazhong jiaoyu* 大众教育) earned praise in Communist-affiliated journals like *Dushu shenghuo* 读书生活 (*Reading Life*) and from Mao Zedong's own teacher Xu Teli (徐特立, 1877–1968).⁶⁰ Tao's positive reception among Communist educators continued after the founding of the People's Republic, eroding only after a minor intellectual debate over the proper role of individual education leaders within the revolution, rather than as a rebuttal of Tao's fundamental beliefs about citizenship and the value of literacy.

As historian Kate Merkel-Hess has observed, the narrative of the Rural Reconstruction Movement is often one that 'arcs toward failure', not only because many of the projects associated with the Movement were short-lived, but also because the Movement's varied and often liberal visions of a self-sufficient rural political community were seemingly dismissed in favour of the totalising regimes of China's emerging party states.⁶¹ It is certainly true that the Chinese Nationalist and Communist parties found little use for Tao Xingzhi's theory of rural self-governance, and his focus on developing self-reliant rural economic cooperatives stood in contrast to efforts by both party states to appropriate rural labour and material for urban production.[62] Nevertheless, many of Tao's ideas about reading and citizenship, far from being stamped out by the Nationalist and Communist regimes, actually seem to prefigure many of the animating principles that motivated state interest in popular literacy. Moreover, Tao's celebration of experiential learning and of students whose worth was defined by their ability to meet the needs of society in many ways helped lay the intellectual groundwork for widely adopted notions of Chinese citizenship that stressed economic productivity and service to community over abstract individual rights.

Tao's career was in many ways defined by an effort to imagine forms of learning outside of the norms dictated by Western models of modern schooling. But his ultimate celebration of good citizens as economically productive actors rather than literate bearers of shared culture also signals a certain concession to the globalising impulses of capitalism, which ascribed social value to economic utility in a way that transcended the intellectual influence of any one thinker. By redefining the scope and purpose of literacy, Tao made it easier for marginalised groups of rural farmers and workers to claim the mantle of citizenship, but he also helped to ensure that this citizenship would remain contingent on their ability to produce economic results on behalf of the local (and later national) community. Within the broader historical trajectory of citizenship and reading in China, Tao's embrace of life education marks a fundamental shift in Chinese attitudes to literacy, on a par with the ultimate adoption of vernacular text and the rejection of Confucian learning. Viewed in this light, the Xiaozhuang experiment was not simply an aborted alternative, but rather a constitutive element in the discontinuous process by which administrators, teachers, textbook authors and political organisations redefined the political role of the masses.

Notes

1. Yan Yangchu, 'Pingmin jiaoyu' [Commoners' Education], *Xin Jiaoyu* [*New Education*], 7:2 (October 1923); reprinted in *Yan Yangchu wenji* [*Collected Works of Yan Yangchu*], ed. Song Enrong (Beijing: Jiaoyu kexue chubanshe, 1989), p. 3.
2. Y. C. James Yen, *Social Reconstruction Through Education: A Narrative Study of the Ting Hsien Experiment Before 1934* (Dingxian: Chinese

National Association of the Mass Education Movement, 1934), ch 2, p. 12, ch. 3, pp. 1–2. Unpublished. Located in the International Institute of Rural Reconstruction Records, B2, Rare Book and Manuscript Library, Columbia University.

3. For an excellent overview of the Rural Reconstruction Movement and its leaders (specifically Yan Yangchu and Tao Xingzhi), see Kate Merkel-Hess, *The Rural Modern: Reconstructing the Self and the State in Republican China* (Chicago: University of Chicago Press, 2016). For a broader analysis of how interest in rural issues among education reformers coincided with broader political developments in the late 1920s, see Charles Hayford, *To the People: James Yen and Village China* (New York: Columbia University Press, 1990), pp. 60–84.

4. For a fuller discussion of Wang Yangming's influence on Tao, see Yusheng Yao, 'Rediscovering Tao Xingzhi as an Educational and Social Revolutionary', *Twentieth-Century China*, 27:2 (April 2002), pp. 88–91.

5. See, for example: Helen R. Chauncey, *Locality and State During the Chinese Republic* (Honolulu: University of Hawai'i Press, 1992); Huang Jinlin, *Lishi, shenti, guojia: jindai zhongguo de shenti xingcheng, 1895–1937* [*History, Body, Nation-State: The Formation of the Modern Chinese Body, 1895–1937*] (Taibei: Lianjing chuban shiye gongse, 2000); Robert Culp, *Articulating Citizenship: Civic Education and Student Politics in Southeastern China, 1912–1940* (Cambridge, MA: Harvard University Press, 2007); and Elizabeth VanderVen, 'It's Time for School: The Introduction of the New Calendar in Haicheng County Primary Schools, Northeast China, 1905–1919', *Twentieth-Century China*, 32:2 (April 2007), pp. 60–83. It is worth noting that the more limited historiography of Tao himself has similarly focused somewhat narrowly on his relationship to John Dewey, whose progressive education vision competed alongside other intellectual strands like Marxism and anarchism in shaping Tao's outlook. See, for example: Philip A. Kuhn, 'T'ao Hsing-chih, 1891–1946, An Educational Reformer', *Harvard Papers on China*, 13 (1959), pp. 163–95; Barry Keenan, *The Dewey Experiment in China: Educational Reform and Political Power in the Early Republic* (Cambridge, MA: Harvard University Press, 1977); and Hubert O. Brown, 'American Progressivism in Chinese Education: The Case of Tao Xingzhi', in Ruth Hayhoe and Marianne Bastid (eds), *China's Education and the Industrialized World* (Armonk: M. E. Sharpe, 1987), pp. 120–38. Chinese-language scholarship on Tao has been slightly more nuanced in its efforts to place Tao's philosophy in dialogue with other thinkers at the time, and has shifted somewhat based on the historical appraisal of Tao within the Communist Party. See Dong Baoliang (ed.), *Tao Xingzhi jiaoyu xueshuo* [*The Educational Theory of Tao Xingzhi*] (Wuhan: Hubei jiaoyu chubanshe, 1993); and Zhang Kaiyuan and Tang Wenquan, *Pingfan de shensheng – Tao Xingzhi* [*Tao Xingzhi: A Confucius After Confucius*] (Wuhan: Hubei jiaoyu chubanshe, 1992).

6. Tao Xingzhi, 'Guomin yu xiamin' [Citizens and Blind Masses], *Shenbao*, 7 January 1925. Reprinted in *Tao Xingzhi Quanji* [*Complete Works of Tao Xingzhi*] (Chengdu: Sichuan jiaoyu chubanshe, 1991), pp. 227–8.
7. See, respectively: David Strand, *An Unfinished Republic: Leading by Word and Deed in Modern China* (Berkeley: University of California Press, 2011); Elizabeth J. Perry, *Challenging the Mandate of Heaven: Social Protest and State Power in China* (New York: M. E. Sharpe, 2002); and Louise Edwards, *Gender, Politics, and Democracy: Women's Suffrage in China* (Stanford: Stanford University Press, 2008).
8. For a helpful theoretical discussion of literacy as a form of embedded social and political practice, as well as its application to studies of late Qing and early Republican China, see Glen Peterson, *The Power of Words: Literacy and Revolution in South China, 1949–95* (Vancouver: University of British Columbia Press, 1997), pp. 7–11.
9. For the expansive literacy figures, see Evelyn Rawski, *Education and Popular Literacy in Late Qing China* (Ann Arbor: University of Michigan Press, 1979), p. 140. For a discussion of the more narrow and more political category of literacy as understanding classical Chinese, see Alexander Woodside, 'Real and Imagined Communities in the Chinese Struggle for Literacy', in Ruth Hayhoe (ed.), *Education and Modernization: The Chinese Experience* (Oxford: Pergamon Press, 1992), pp. 23–45.
10. For the Qing memorial on the purpose of the new education system, see 'Zou chen jiaoyu zongzhi zhe' [Memorial on the Purpose of Education], in *Da Qing jiaoyu xin faling* [*New Education Laws of the Great Qing*] (1906), vol. I, p. 2; reprinted in Qu Xingui and Tang Liangyan (eds), *Zhongguo jindai jiaoyu shi ciliao huibian: xuezhi yanbian* [*A Collection of Modern Chinese Education History Materials: The Evolution of the Education System*] (Shanghai: Shanghai Jiaoyu chubanshe, 2007), p. 542.
11. The seminal text on this subject is John DeFrancis, *Nationalism and Language Reform in China* (Princeton: Princeton University Press, 1950). For more recent approaches, see: Li Jinxi, *Guoyu yudong shigang* [*A Survey of the National Language Movement*] (Shanghai: Shanghai shudian, 1990); and Elisabeth Kaske, *The Politics of Language in Chinese Education, 1895–1919* (Leiden: Brill, 2008).
12. Kaske, *The Politics of Language*, pp. 277–8.
13. Ibid., pp. 386–9.
14. Ibid., p. 288.
15. For a summary of the accomplishments of the vernacular language movement, see Kaske, *The Politics of Language*, especially pp. 472–3. For a further discussion of *baihua* reforms in the countryside, see Robert Culp, 'Teaching Baihua: Textbook Publishing and the Production of Vernacular Language and a New Literary Canon in Early Twentieth-Century China', *Twentieth-Century China*, 34:1 (2009), pp. 4–41.
16. Yu Ziyi, 'Xiao xuesheng shizi jiaofa' [Primary School Literacy Pedagogy],

Jiaoyu zazhi, 19:5 (May 1927), reprinted in Dong Yuanqian and Shi Yuying (eds), *Yu Ziyi: jiaoyu lunzhu xuan* [*Yu Ziyi: A Selection of Education Treatises*] (Beijing: Renmin jiaoyu chubanshe, 1991), p. 193.

17. Tang Hualong, 'Chi jing neiwai ge xuexiao zhongxiaoxue xiushen ji guowen jiaokeshu caiqu jing xun wu yi Kongzi zhi yan wei zhiguiwen' [An Order That Moral Cultivation and National Language Textbooks in Schools Around the Capital Adopt Classical Teachings and Treat the Language of Confucius as Most Important], *Jiaoyu gongbao*, 1 (1914).

18. Wang Boqiu 王伯秋 in *Pingmin xuexiao jiaoshi zhinan* [*Guidebook for Commoners' Education Instructors*] (Wuxi: Nanjing pingmin jiaoyu cujin hui chubanshe, 1924), pp. 1–2.

19. Ibid.

20. For example, see Tang Maoru, 'Pingmin jiaoyu yundong de jingguo' [The Course of Development of Commoners' Education], *Jiaoyu zazhi*, 19:9 (September 1927), pp. 1–9; *Zhejiang sheng shizi yundong nianbao* [*Annual Report on the Literacy Movement in Zhejiang Province*] (Zhejiang: Zhejiang sheng shizi yundong chuanchuan weiyuanhui, 1929), pp. 1–2; and Gan Yuyuan (ed.), *Xin Zhonghua minzhong jiaoyu* [*New China Mass Education*] (Shanghai: Zhonghua shuju, 1932), pp. 34–5.

21. For a general summary of Dewey's visit and of the contents of his lectures in China, see Keenan, *The Dewey Experiment*, pp. 7–52. See also Robert W. Clopton and Tsuin-chen Ou, 'Introduction', in Robert W. Clopton et al. (eds), *John Dewey: Lectures in China, 1919–1920* (Honolulu: University Press of Hawai'i, 1973), pp. 1–30.

22. Quoted in Robert W. Clopton and Tsuin-chen Oou, 'Cultural Heritage and Social Reconstruction', in Clopton et al. (eds), *John Dewey*, p. 211.

23. See, for example, 'Pingmin jiaoyu zhi zhendi' [The True Essence of Commoners' Education], *Jiaoyu chao*, 1:2 (1919), pp. 27–34; 'Pingminzhuyi de jiaoyu (ji duwei boshi zai jiangsusheng jiaoyuhui yanjiang de dayao)' [Democratic Education (A Record of the Main Points of Dr Dewey's Speech to the Jiangsu Provincial Education Society)], *Jiaoyu chao*, 1:2 (1919), pp. 85–93; 'Duwei boshi yanjiang pingminjiaoyu' [Dr Dewey's Speech on Commoners' Education], *Jiaoyu yu zhiye*, 16 (1919), pp. 55–7; and 'Ji Duwei boshi yanjiang de dayao: Pingminzhuyi! Pingminzhuyi de jiaoyu! Pingmin jiaoyu zhuyi de banfa!' [A Record of the Main Points of Dr Dewey's Speech: Democracy! Democratic Education! Methods for Democratic Education-ism!], *Xin jiaoyu*, 1:3 (1919), pp. 109–14.

24. Huang Yanpei 黄炎培, 'Zhonghua zhiye jiaoyu she xuanyanshu' [Manifesto of the Chinese Vocational Education Society], *Jiaoyu yu zhiye*, 1 (1917), pp. 1–2.

25. 'Jiaoyu de cuowu', *Pingmin jiaoyu*, 9 (December 1919); reprinted in Zhang Yunhou (ed.), *Wusi shiqi de shetuan* [*May Fourth Era Social Groups*] (Beijing: Shenguo, dushu, xinzhi sanlian shudian, 1979), vol. III, p. 20. It is unclear who the author of this article is, but the penname

'Hui' is included in lieu of a byline. The original line from the *Analects* occurs when a student of Confucius asks an old labourer if the older man has seen the student's master, and the old man replies, 'You seem neither to have toiled with your limbs nor to be able to tell one kind of grain from another; who may your Master be?' (For translation, see D. C. Lau, trans., *The Analects* (London: Penguin, 1979), p. 150.

26. Yu Ziyi, 'Xiao xuesheng shizi jiaofa', p. 196.
27. Ibid.
28. Brown, 'American Progressivism in Chinese Education', pp. 131–2.
29. For an outline of the goals of the National Association for the Promotion of Commoners' Education, see 'Zhonghua pingmin jiaoyu cujin hui zai jing kai chengli dahui han' [Letter to the Opening Plenary of the National Association for the Promotion of Commoners' Education], August 1923, reprinted in Zhongguo di'er lishi dang'anguan (ed.), *Zhonghua Minguo shi dang'an ziliao huibian* (Nanjing: Jiangsu guji chubanshe, 1996), pp. 811–13.
30. Tao Xingzhi (ed.), *Pingmin qianzi ke, di er ceng* [*Commoners' Thousand-Character Text*] (Shanghai: Shanghai Commercial Press, 1923), vol. II, p. 2.
31. Ibid., vol. III, pp. 16–21, 40–3.
32. Tao Xingzhi, 'Zhongguo xiangcun jiaoyu zhi genben gaizao' [Fundamental Reform in China's Rural Education], in Tao Xingzhi (ed.), *Zhongguo jiaoyu gaizao* [*Remoulding Chinese Education*] [Shanghai: Yadong tushuguan, 1928), p. 8.
33. Brown, 'American Progressivism in Chinese Education', p. 132.
34. See Tao Xingzhi, 'Weizhishi jieji' [The False Intellectual Class], in Tao (ed.), *Zhongguo jiaoyu gaizao*, pp. 201–3; and Tao Xingzhi, 'Muqian zhongguo jiaoyu liang tiao luxian' [Two Paths Facing Chinese Education], *Jiaoyu zhoukan*, 137 (November 1932), reprinted in Tao Xingzhi, *Huang Yanpei, Xu Teli, Chen Heqin jiaoyu wenxuan* (Hefei: Anhui jiaoyu chubanshe, 1992), p. 37.
35. Tao, 'Weizhishi jieji', p. 201; Cheng Benhai, *Zai Xiaozhuang* [*At Xiaozhuang*] (Shanghai: Shanghai zhonghua shuju, 1930), pp. 8–9.
36. Tao, 'Muqian zhongguo jiaoyu liang tiao luxian', p. 37.
37. Tao, 'Weizhishi jieji', pp. 204–5.
38. Tao Xingzhi, 'Muqian Zhongguo Jiaoyu liang tiao luxian', p. 38.
39. Tao Xingzhi, 'Shenghuo jiaoyu' [Life Education], *Shenghuo Jiaoyu*, 1:1 (1934), reprinted in Tao, *Huang Yanpei*, pp. 50–1.
40. Tao Xingzhi, 'Xue zuo yi ge ren' [Learning to be a Person], *Shenghuo zhoukan* [*Life Magazine*], 1:19 (1926), reprinted in Tao Xingzhi, *Huang Yanpe*, pp. 6–7. Although Tao did not use the phrase 'living citizens' in this particular essay, it is clear from these traits that Tao's 'whole person' encompasses the same qualities as the 'living citizens' referenced in his article 'Fundamental Reforms in China's Rural Education', published three years earlier.

41. Tao, 'Zhongguo xiancun jiaoyu zhi genben gaizao', p. 8.
42. See Tao, 'Guomin yu xiamin', p. 228; and Tao Xingzhi, 'China', in *Educational Yearbook of the International Institute of Teacher's College, Columbia University, 1924* (New York: Columbia University Press, 1925), p. 103.
43. Tao Xingzhi, 'Xuesheng zizhi wenti zhi yanjiu' [Research on the Issue of Student Self-Government], in *Xin jiaoyu*, 2:2, reprinted in Hu Xiaofeng (ed.), *Tao Xingzhi jiaoyu wenji* (Chengdu: Sichuan jiaoyu chubanshe, 2005), pp. 73–81.
44. Tao's description of the ideal Xiaozhuang graduate comes from his 'Aims of Rural Education', published as part of the School's central tenets. See Cheng, *Zai Xiaozhuang*, p. 9.
45. See 'Xiaozhuang xuexiao zhuzhang yongshu bu zhuzhang dushu' [The Xiaozhuang School Emphasises Using Books, Not Reading Books], *Hunan jiaoyu*, 3 (1929), p. 7.
46. Chen, *Zai Xiaozhuang*, p. 17. For a further exploration of morning meetings as an important instance of student self-government, see 'Xiaozhuang xuexiao de "yinhui"' [The 'Yin Meetings' at Xiaozhuang School], *Hunan jiaoyu*, 3 (1929), p. 4.
47. Brown, 'American Progressivism in Chinese Education', p. 135.
48. Tao, 'Xuesheng zizhi wenti zhi yanjiu', pp. 73–81.
49. Tao, 'Shenghuo jiaoyu', pp. 50–1.
50. Tao Xingzhi, 'Chuantong jiaoyu yu shenghuo jiaoyu you shenme qubie?' [What Are the Differences Between Traditional Education and Life Education?], *Shenghuo jiaoyu*, 1:29 (December 1934), reprinted in Tao, *Huang Yanpei*, p. 52.
51. For examples of the journals offering (typically glowing) reportage of the Xiaozhuang project, see 'Wenke tan Xiaozhuang shifan xuexiao shisheng bing gengshi ganfu' [Wenke's Thoughts on Teachers and Students Doing Farm Work Together at Xiaozhuang Normal School], *Jiaoyu yu zhiye* [*Education and Vocation*], 96 (1928), p. 437; 'Nanjing Xiaozhuang xuexiao xuesheng zhi baogao' [A Report on the Students at Xiaozhuang Normal School], *Liaoning jiaoyu yuekan* [*Liaoning Education Monthly*], 1:5 (1929), p. 154; Chen Jianxiao, 'Xiaozhuang xiangcun shifan xuexiao xintiao' [Tenets of the Xiaozhuang Rural Normal School], *Shanxi jiaoyu zhoukan* [*Shaanxi Education Weekly*], 3:32 (1930), p. 34. At the time of his visit to Xiaozhuang, Chen Jianxiao was acting as director of the Nanjing Municipal Education Department, and was accompanied by Chen Heqin. See Cheng, *Zai Xiaozhuang*, p. 15. For details on William Kilpatrick's visit in 1929, including his extended impressions of the School, see Merkel-Hess, 'A New People', pp. 121–9; and Keenan, *The Dewey Experiment*, p. 108. As Merkel-Hess and Keenan both point out, Kilpatrick commented on the strong similarity between Tao's programme and those he had observed in the Soviet Union a few months earlier.

52. For a more detail analysis of the reasons behind the School's closure, see Kate Merkel-Hess, 'A New People: Rural Modernity in Republican China', PhD dissertation (University of California, Irvine, 2009) pp. 108–10. Merkel-Hess suggests that more specific contextual factors, such as Tao's personal friendship with Christian warlord and former vice premier of the Republic, General Feng Yuxiang, ultimately may have played a greater role in the Guomindang's decision to shut the School than Tao's Communist rhetoric. Another reason may have been the efforts of Xiaoxhuan students to block foreign access to the Yangzi River, a policy that the Guomindang opposed.
53. Cheng, *Zai Xiaozhuang*, p. 59. Clearly, Tao Xingzhi did not support the notion of rule by party government but he was nonetheless attracted to the notion of people's rights within Sun's thought. For a broader analysis of the role of political ceremony within modern schools, see Henrietta Harrison, *The Making of the Republican Citizen: Political Ceremonies and Symbols in China, 1911–1929* (New York: Oxford University Press, 2000).
54. See James Yen, *China's New Scholar-Farmers* (Beijing: Chinese National Association for the Mass Education Movement, 1929), pp. 7–8. Such arguments also reflect the broader resonance of the argument equating citizenship with work. In this same pamphlet, Yan Yangchu provides an illustration equating citizenship with agricultural burden. In the illustration, two peasants (a man and a woman) hold up an enormous globe with 'Zhonghua Minguo' (the Republic of China) written on the side and the caption, 'Some Chinese gladly assuming the burden of their citizenship'.
55. See Wei Bingxin (ed.), *Minzhong qianzi keben* [*Mass Thousand-Character Textbook*] (Shanghai: Shijie shuju, 1929), p. 1; and Yang Xiaochun (ed.), *Shizi mingli* [*Reading Made Reasonable*] (Shandong: Shandong xiangcun jianshe yanjiu yuan, 1934), pp. 1–2. Yang's rejection of literacy is unsurprising considering that he worked as a 'political instructor' at Xiaozhuang, demonstrating once again that the Nationalist government was not entirely opposed to the instructional values and methods propagated there.
56. Hu Zhenhui 胡贞惠 (ed.), *Xin shidai guoyu jiaokeshu* 新时代国语教科书 [*New Era National Language Textbook*] (Shanghai: Commercial Press, 1932), vol. V, p. 2.
57. Miao Feng, 'The Politics of Education: Popular Education, Quotidian Experience, and Contention over the Masses in China, 1927–1937', PhD dissertation (New York University, 2013), pp. 113–14.
58. For an overview of the work and career of Fang Yuyan, a particularly strong proponent of Tao's ideas, see Fang Yuyan, *Fang Yuyan jiaoyu wenji: Tao Xingzhi ji qi shenghuo jiaoyu* [*Collected Education Works of Fang Yuyan: Tao Zingzhi and His Life Education*] (Chengdu: Sichuan jiaoyu chubanshe, 1995). For Zhang Zonglin, see Zhang Hu (ed.), *Zhang*

Zonglin xiangcun jiaoyu lunji [*Zhong Zonglin's Selected Works on Rural Education*] (Changsha: Hunan jiaoyu chubanshe, 1987).

59. See, for example, Zhang Zonglin, 'Zhongguo xiancun jiaoyu de weiji' [The Crisis in China's Rural Education], *Zhonghua jiaoyu jie* [*Chinese Education World*], 21:2 (1933), pp. 1–9.
60. Lu Jia, 'Duguo de shu: chuankanhao de "dazhongjiaoyu"' [Book Review: On the First Publication of 'Mass Education'], *Dushu shenghuo* [*Reading Life*], 4:4 (1936), pp. 219–21; and Xu Teli, 'Tao Xingzhi de xueshuo' [Tao Xingzhi's Theories], *Jiefang ribao* [*Liberation Daily*], 12 August 1946. For a brief overview of Tao's positive reception among Communist educators, see Suzanne Pepper, *Radicalism and Education Reform in 20th-Century China: The Search for an Ideal Development Model* (New York: Cambridge University Press, 1996), p. 134.
61. Merkel-Hess, *The Rural Modern*, p. 13.
62. Feng, 'The Politics of Education', pp. 125–6.

Chapter 13

The Voice of the Reader: The Landscape of Online Book Discussion in the Netherlands, 1997–2016

Peter Boot

Book discussion has been deeply influenced by the arrival of the World Wide Web. Especially after the advent of Web 2.0 and social networking sites, it has become increasingly easy to share opinions about books, on a range of sites widely differing in size, sophistication and specialisation. Many of these sites (Amazon, Goodreads, LibraryThing), especially in the English-speaking world, have been the subject of scholarly attention. This chapter provides a history of these sites at a national scale, in this case for the Netherlands.[1]

To begin, we look at online book discussion in the Usenet newsgroup nl.kunst.literatuur. On the (Dutch) Web, large-scale book discussion began with reviews on bol.com, the largest online bookseller in the Netherlands. They were rapidly joined by personal weblogs, bulletin-board-style discussion forums and, later, book-based social networking sites and general-purpose social media.

The different types of platforms are not always easy to distinguish.[2] What a history of these sites will show is that, on the one hand, each of these site types has its own specific characteristics, is suitable for certain types of discussion and attracts a certain type of visitor. On the other hand, there are also many personal connections between these sites. People divide their attention over multiple sites and move between sites as platforms gain or lose favour. All of the sites are to some extent social: users respond to each other, they 'like' each other's posts, they strike up friendships and exchange messages. Online book discussion brings to the foreground the social dimension that has been the focus of much recent scholarship in the history of reading.[3]

In this chapter I characterise a number of paradigmatic sites. I describe their structures, their functionalities and the writing that can be found there, and I focus on a few readers who have made these sites their home. I will not devote special attention to the question of whether these sites offer an extension or replacement of newspaper or academic literary criticism. As Katharina Lukoschek writes, book blogs and social media communities 'are spaces of meaningful communication in areas where literary criticism has no institutional authority, never had, and probably never will have'.[4] Online book discussion should be looked at as an independent phenomenon, not as an impoverished form of literary criticism.

Constraints of space make it impossible to discuss the entire landscape of online book discussion. In this chapter, I focus on discussion platforms for 'ordinary readers', however defined. The readers I study here may have a university degree, perhaps even in literary studies,[5] but I do not consider review sites, weblogs or e-zines that aspire to institutional status or explicitly want to play a role in the national literary landscape. I also cannot cover (sadly) the creative response to books in fan fiction communities[6] or the many genre-specific forums, weblogs and sites.

One problem of writing a history of anything web-related is that the web is a very dynamic environment. Websites come and go and leave few traces after being discontinued. This chapter therefore also draws on the web archive maintained by the Koninklijke Bibliotheek and on a collection of downloaded websites that I have created over the last few years.[7]

Online book discussion before the web

Online book discussion did not start on the web. Before the web became an interactive platform, discussion took place in Usenet groups (later brought to the web by Dejanews and now accessible through Google Groups). In the Dutch language area, the most relevant newsgroup for book discussion was nl.kunst.literatuur.[8] The first posting dates from May 1997. According to its charter, the group discusses literature (in Dutch or in other languages). Posts to the group could contain book reviews, announcements of events and publications, searches for books, language humour, short stories and poems.[9] Commercial postings were allowed if relevant to the group but had to be expressly announced as commercial.

The group took off quickly. After 276 threads in 1997, the group peaked in the years 1998 and 1999, with more than 1,000 threads. Its decline began in 2000 and continued steadily. From 2007 the weekly posting of the group's charter was often the only post in that week.

The subject range of messages in nl.kunst.literatuur was considerably wider than that of later review sites. Interestingly, reviews had to be announced as such in the message header, and other types of submission were typically things like requests for information about books or authors (e.g. 'Who can tell me in which book . . . ?'), announcements of webpages with literary content and students asking for help with their assignments. But besides these paraliterary questions, there was a fair amount of discussion about literature itself, the style and content of books and the merits of certain books or authors. Serious reviews of books often led to discussions at a level not often seen on most of today's book discussion platforms, though some threads did tend to derail into pointless chatter. While the decline in popularity of the newsgroup was partly the result of the availability of alternative platforms, the chit-chat may also explain why some participants moved to those alternative platforms.

The participants in the discussions include some of the pioneers of the Dutch Internet, such as activist and author Karin Spaink. Others were poets (Martijn Benders, Gerard C. Kool), translators (Stacey Knecht, Frank Lekens) or novelists (well known writer Marcel Möring). Linguist Marc van Oostendorp, whom we'll meet again in the section on book blogs, published reviews under the pseudonym Martin Opdop. Many of the discussants maintain or maintained weblogs of their own, such as Jan-Willem Swane and architect Hans Valk.[10] Others maintained sites about other writers, such as Gerrit Jan Kleinrensink about Willem Brakman and Roland Bron about Nescio.[11] The average participant in the newsgroup was clearly more highly educated than those who are or were active on some later platforms, and that may explain the high level of the discussions on nl.kunst.literatuur in its heyday.

Reviews on booksellers' sites

Book reviews on booksellers' sites are probably the best-known form of online reviewing. In the Netherlands bol.com is the largest online bookseller and the only bookseller's site with a substantial number of reader reviews. It was originally part of the German media giant Bertelsmann's attempt to move into the online realm.[12] It is now owned by food retailer Ahold and, like Amazon, sells many things besides books.

Reviewing on the site began in 1999 (1,340 reviews) and in 2016 a total of 50,172 reviews were posted.[13] Reviews on bol.com come with a rating and reviewers can add tags to their reviews, some of them predefined. Reviewers have to choose a nickname and can provide age and place of residence, but there is no option for reviewers to create a personal profile that describes reading preferences or other personal details. As bol.com, unlike Amazon and many dedicated reviewing sites, offers no way of selecting reviews by reviewer, reviewers on bol.com have little opportunity to present themselves, as persons or as readers, to other site users. That makes the bol.com review platform perhaps the least social of the platforms that we discuss in this chapter, though users can (and sometimes do) upvote or downvote reviews.

On its site, bol.com publishes the e-zine *Lees Magazine*,[14] which features interviews, reviews, book fragments and lists of recommended books, sometimes based on a subject (such as World Alzheimer's Day) or on recommendations by a writer or a public personality. The magazine also organises giveaways and a reading club, as well as a workshop in review writing.[15] Editor-in-chief of the magazine is publishing professional Janneke Siebelink; other editors include a thriller writer, a literary scholar and a specialist in reading clubs. Beyond the obvious purpose of selling books, the magazine seems mostly targeted at attracting potential reviewers to the site.

The list of most frequent reviewers is headed by 'clara', who in a period of less than two years (2010–12) contributed more than 700 reviews, mostly about theological and spiritual works. All her reviews are accompanied by ratings of four or five stars. The second most frequent reviewer is 'analetter', who wrote more than 500 reviews, mainly of thrillers.[16] Third in the list is 'ezelsoor' (dog-ear), who reviews mostly literary books. For none of these three have I been able to find traces of their presence on other websites. Mieke Schepens, however, the fourth most frequent reviewer on bol.com, is very active on other book discussion sites. She has a weblog, participates in several Facebook groups and is active on Twitter. She is one of those participants in book discussion who are connected and stay in touch with others through multiple platforms.[17] There are many reviewers like her, such as 'wendy7213' and 'Barnem'.

Scholarship on booksellers' sites often focuses on the question of how these reviews compare to newspaper book reviews.[18] From our perspective, it is more interesting to contrast reviews on booksellers' sites to reader reviews on dedicated reviewing sites. In her comparison of reviews on bol.com with those on Goodreads, M. J. Daniels found reviewers on bol.com use a simple and direct style, and prefer strong positive or negative evaluations.[19] They write more about popular literature and books around which there is a hype, and less about established literature. Sometimes they address the author in their reviews ('Thank you for giving me hope again'). Their reviews often discuss the book's acquisition and the circumstances surrounding its reading. Sometimes they are impatient with other reviewers or with the institution of literature. Stefan Dimitrov et al. found more extreme ratings on Amazon than on Goodreads, but not more extreme language.[20] They argue that reviews at booksellers' sites are targeted at buyers and buying decisions. This might be an explanation for the reviewers' directness and preference for unambiguous language. In the downloads of the Dutch sites, bol.com reviews use many more positive emotion words than do the dedicated review sites but not more negative emotion words.[21] In numerical terms, bol.com reviewers assign much higher ratings than those on other sites (more than half of the reviews are accompanied by five stars). An explanation could be that readers on other platforms write about most or even all of the books they read, while readers on bol.com, being less bookish, perhaps only occasionally write a review, for a book that they especially liked. That would be consistent with their preference for popular and widely discussed books.

Book blogs

A weblog is 'a frequently updated website consisting of dated entries arranged in reverse chronological order so the most recent post appears first'.[22] For the purposes of this chapter, we will limit ourselves to single-author weblogs, as that is where we are most likely to find personal reflections on a reading experience. The word 'weblog' was used first in 1997, but sites that conformed to this definition had been around for some time. The first (proto-)blogs in the Netherlands appeared in 1994.[23] It is hard to say what was the first Dutch book blog, as weblogs come and go without leaving much trace.[24] In a crawl of Dutch book blogs that we performed in April 2017, 'De rode muur' (The red wall) was the blog with the oldest posts, dating back to 2000.[25] In our crawl we found fifteen book blog posts in 2001, 1,057 in 2006, 7,962 in 2011 and 24,219 in 2016, the last full year.[26]

Single-author weblogs may initially appear not to be particularly relevant to the present chapter, which focuses on discussion, but there are many ways in which blogs are in fact part of a network. Many blogs display a list of other weblogs that the blogger is following. Usually there are comments, often from fellow bloggers. Many bloggers have their own group of followers. Beyond these blog-internal networking tools, there are many other ways the blog and its owner may be part of a network, either technically (for instance through a blog aggregator such as Bloglovin') or because the blog owner is active on other platforms as well. Tobias Zeising has investigated German book blogs and found that they are very much networked with each other.[27] That network was evenly distributed: there were no blogs that were exceptionally popular and no strongly connected subgroups.

Here I focus on three book bloggers: Mieke Schepens, Marc van Oostendorp and Femke van der Griendt, a schoolgirl.[28]

We met Mieke Schepens already as a reviewer on bol.com. Her weblog, called 'Graag gelezen' (Read with pleasure), is one of the many platforms that she uses for her reviews. Her weblog has no blogroll, but it can be followed through weblog aggregator Bloglovin (204 followers), Blogspot (89) and Google Plus (183). She is also active on Goodreads,[29] where she mentions that she often receives books from publishers in return for a review, 'honest but with a positive attitude', which she places on the sites she is active on. Her weblog sidebar contains a logo in the form of a picture of a heart-shaped book and the text 'With a heart for stories'. She also mentions that she appreciates receiving comments. Schepens reads in many genres: thrillers, literature, general novels, children's books, psychological thrillers and more. She uses her weblog mostly for publishing reviews, but also for announcing new books (which she may have received in advance from the publisher).

The reviews on her blog often have a similar structure. The review of Johan Zonnenberg's *De schaduwbokser*,[30] for instance, begins with a picture of the cover, then gives some data about the book (title, genre, ISBN). Schepens then mentions she won the book in a raffle and thanks the publisher. Before the actual review she quotes the cover text of the book. The review itself recounts (part of) the story, intermixed with interpretative and evaluative comments. The length of reviews is quite variable. They are often summarised in a single sentence, here for instance (in Dutch) 'Johan Zonnenberg wrote a poignant story, brimming over with emotion, fortunately not without humour'. What generally follows is a paragraph about the author, perhaps a link to more information, links to booksellers where the book can be bought, and finally the publisher's logo.

While for Schepens reading is obviously an occasion for sharing, Marc van Oostendorp writes that 'my reading log is like an allotment garden. . . . It is nice if a passer-by takes a glance at it, but that's not necessary'.[31] Ironically, two fellow bloggers applauded his words. Van Oostendorp's weblog is called 'Read. Books that Marc van

Oostendorp read for fun'. His is the second oldest Dutch book blog in our download. Van Oostendorp is also general editor of another weblog, 'Neerlandistiek' (Dutch Studies), an academic newsletter on Dutch language and literature, where he has been publishing one article a day for some years now.[32] As a newsletter, that blog is obviously targeted at real readers; for the private blogger, however, 'it might be rather embarrassing if they were somehow suddenly discovered by the general public'.[33] Van Oostendorp makes clear he does not want to be judged by the standards of literary criticism: 'On my weblog I do what I want, so if I want to write about a book that wasn't written rather than about a book that was, that is what I do.'[34] Elsewhere he writes, 'it is not my intention to do justice to the writer, but to do justice to my own reading experience'.[35] Like most book bloggers, Van Oostendorp is active on Twitter, but he doesn't usually tweet about the books that he discusses on his book blog.

The books that Van Oostendorp discusses are diverse but 'serious', for want of a better word: mostly literary novels, sometimes poems and also non-fiction, but no genre novels. The non-fiction may be related to literature (like author biographies) but may also be about fields like biology or religion. Unlike many other book bloggers, Van Oostendorp regularly discusses classic authors and works, such as Flaubert or Goethe's *Faust* (which he briefly dismisses). His reviews are usually organised around a few thoughts that struck him during reading. Van Oostendorp does not recount the events in a novel, but he asks, for instance, whether the Tyll character is really the subject of Daniel Kehlmann's eponymous novel, or he focuses on the unrest characteristic of Israel de Haan's life and poetry.

The most characteristic feature of Van der Griendt's reviews is her enthusiasm. Her reviews are full of exclamations: 'So great!' or 'This is a book that leaves you contented, that's so nice! ... Really cool, I'd almost give it five stars.'[36] The posts considered here date from when Van der Griendt was sixteen years old and attending a gymnasium. She started her weblog when she was fourteen. Blogging is attractive to her because of the social benefits, as she mentions in an interview: contact with other readers, an invitation to serve on a jury for young people's books, book friends with whom she visits book presentations.[37] Blogging can also be demanding: time and time again Van der Griendt complains that she lacks the time to write a proper review: 'The idea is that I'll blog about this one day. One day. If I get to it. Which, in the short run, I have my doubts about.'[38]

Like Schepens, Van der Griendt uses a number of other social media platforms in the service of her blog. She is active on Instagram, where she maintains lively exchanges with other booklovers (much more lively than through the comment facility on the blog), she Twitters and her blog can be followed through Bloglovin'. She also places her reviews on Hebban (a book-based social networking site, discussed below), where she was a member of the Hebban Young Adult Club.[39]

Book discussion forums

The largest book discussion forum in the Netherlands is Ezzulia, dating from 2005.[40] The forum uses the familiar bulletin-board format: the discussions are organised in (sub)forums and topics within these (sub)forums. Topics consist of an opening post and replies. As of September 2017, the site in total hosted 556,000 messages on 9,236 topics written by 3,528 users. While books are the forum's raison d'être, somewhat more than half of the exchanges take place within non-book forums: a general chat room and a number of forums related to games, music, film and life in general.[41]

Ezzulia is the creation of Eric Herni, owner of an independent bookshop in Almere. Herni, who also blogs at <http://leeswereld.blogspot.nl> and writes columns on Hebban (see below), had been active on Hebban's predecessor Crimezone and earlier managed a website 'Spanning & Thrillers' (Suspense and Thrillers). He started Ezzulia mainly to create a meeting place for readers and authors,[42] and about 100 members are registered as authors.[43] Among them are Loes den Hollander, Simone van der Vlugt and Corine Hartman, popular Dutch thriller writers who all frequently posted on the site. As the older participants fondly remember, there used to be a Friday night meeting on the forum, in which many Dutch authors (mostly in the suspense genre) participated.[44] One of the favourite guests was Paul Goeken, a friend of Herni, a thriller writer who published under the name Suzanne Vermeer. After Goeken's early death, the Friday night meetings stopped.

The site has 1,900 different posters, but, as on most discussion platforms, the distribution of posts over participants is heavily skewed. Of the 241,000 book-related messages, 90 per cent are written by 10 per cent of the participants, and just three participants (among them Herni) are jointly responsible for more than 30,000 messages. Several members maintain their own book platforms, including a crime novel site and a weblog for suspense novels.[45]

Most of the discussion on Ezzulia is organised around authors. There are also genre-based subforums.[46] The most popular subforum is devoted to thrillers (foreign and Dutch). The next most popular is given to foreign literature in the fantasy and science fiction genres, where the most popular authors are Haruki Murakami, Carlos Ruiz Zafon and J. K. Rowling.

The site also moderates 'Joint reading projects', where a group of members decides to read the same book. One of the more voluminous discussions was about *Anna Karenina*,[47] though most of the participants had trouble finishing it and their judgement was generally negative. A much more positive discussion took place about the novel *Tirza*, by Dutch author Arnon Grunberg. Some of the joint readings involve book giveaways facilitated by publishers.

Ezzulia's popularity peaked in 2011, when more than 40,000 messages were posted; by 2016 this had declined to 15,300 book-related messages. In 2010 more than 500 people posted to the forum, but in 2016 only about 100. Authors' participation on the site seems to have all but disappeared: they posted 2,219 messages in 2008 but just sixteen in 2016. The decline may be related to the rise of other book discussion platforms, notably Facebook groups.

Book-based social networking sites

Book-based social-networking sites (SNSs) combine social networking features with book-based content. Internationally, the best-known example is Goodreads. A fair number of readers from the Netherlands use Goodreads, in either Dutch or English. At the time of writing, by far the largest book-based SNS in the Netherlands is Hebban, which claims to have 139,000 registered users, who write 50 reviews and rate 800 books a day. The users are said to have more than 1.5 million books on their shelves.[48] The site was originally known as Crimezone, specialising in crime fiction, but was redesigned and rebranded into a site catering to readers of all genres in 2014. The oldest reviews date from 2002. Hebban is the only large Dutch book-based SNS still in existence. Earlier similar sites were Dizzie and watleesjij.nu ('what are you reading now'), founded in 2008 and 2009 respectively, but both were discontinued in 2016.

The history of these sites shows how publishers are struggling with the changing environment of the web.[49] Both Dizzie and Crimezone were started by individual booklovers. Dizzie was acquired by newspaper publisher Wegener in 2012.[50] Wegener neglected the site for a while, then tried to revive it in 2014, but when the company was sold to Persgroep, the new owners closed down the site. Crimezone was first acquired by publisher Unieboek in 2005, then sold to another publisher, A. W. Bruna, in 2010, which withdrew in 2014. Watleesjij. nu was started and eventually closed down by publisher NDC/VBK. Boekensalon, yet another similar site, was created by the publishing branch of the library service organisation NBD Biblion, but shut down when that organisation pulled the plug on its publishing activities in 2017. Presumably, all these publishers initially hoped that platforms for direct communication with readers would improve their sales, only to decide later that running sites was too much of a hassle. Hebban is now the property of a commercial company, Book Communities BV, although many users of the site think they are visiting a non-commercial site.[51] Publishers have many ways of publicising their books on Hebban: explicit advertisements, sponsoring giveaways and reading clubs for their books, or having one of their writers made 'author of the month'.[52] For the site's chief editor, Sander Verheijen, growth is very important: 'Our ambition, and my task, is growth, growth, growth. . . . We are already being approached by media companies, but from half a million [visitors per month] we become really interesting.'[53]

Hebban is a complex site. It combines semi-expert reviews with articles, interviews, blogposts and a reading community. All of the contributions can be rated and commented on. Users can follow other users. Authors can also be users and some try to attract large followings. The site hosts 'reading clubs' where members read the same book. Members can also subscribe to challenges to read a certain number of books per year. Hebban 'spots' are subsites within the larger site. They can be used by publishers or booksellers, but many members use the facility to host weblogs of their own or discuss certain genres.

Why do readers visit Hebban? The most important motives reported in a survey[54] were 'Relaxation, fun to talk about books', 'Inspires me to make time for reading' and 'Sociability'. The features of the site that were most important to the respondents were taking part in reading challenges, rating books, receiving newsletters, cataloguing their books and reading reviews, articles and blogs.

Only a small group of participants actually contribute reviews. The most frequent contributors sometimes have their own weblogs, maintain Goodreads accounts and are active on Facebook, such as Mieke Schepens (363 reviews).[55] Cees van Rhienen (804 reviews)[56] has a Facebook page devoted to his reading and is active on thriller platform Thrillzone,[57] bol.com's *Lees* magazine[58] and the weblog Mustreadsornot.[59] However, there are also very frequent contributors who do not seem to feel the need to extend their activities to other platforms, such as Mieke Piersma (821 reviews)[60] or bookshop manager Claar van Lieshout (323 reviews).[61]

The most lively interactions on the site probably happen in the reading clubs. There have been around 300 of them; each one has fifteen members and produces a few hundred messages. This is a good illustration of the fact that even though the tool (a threaded commenting facility) is there, lively interaction does not come about by itself: it must be organised. We will also see that in the Facebook group that we turn to next.

General-purpose social media

Book discussion is not limited to sites dedicated exclusively to books but also takes place on general-purpose social media, such as Facebook, Twitter, Instagram, Tumblr and Pinterest. Facebook is without a doubt the most common platform, though Twitter is used by some to document their reading, for instance @MokumseHuismus (Amsterdam Homebody).[62] @Twitcit used Twitter to share literary quotes;[63] @HetBureau did the same with quotations from a single novel. But Twitter can also be more conversational.[64] In 2012, literary critic Bas Heijne started a book discussion group on Twitter.[65] Leestweeps ('Reading tweeps') was founded the same year and is still alive.[66] Twitter is mainly used, though, for book publicity by publishers or to attract readers to other book sites.

The most lively and informal Dutch-language book discussion on social media is on Facebook. There are active groups with thousands of members, such as Iedereenleest (Everybody reads), Boekenfans! (Book fans), De Perfecte Buren (The perfect neighbours) and Samenlezenisleuker (Reading together is more fun). Iedereenleest is the initiative of an organisation for reading promotion.[67] Samenlezenisleuker[68] had 9,601 members at the time of writing, and posts may draw hundreds of comments or likes. Like many Facebook groups, it is accompanied by a weblog (or the other way around), and the group also has a Twitter and Instagram presence. On the weblog's 'Who We Are' page, the group's founders (Karin Meinen-Benjamins and Corina Nieuwenhuis, a former nurse and a cook) explain how they met on Facebook and became friends based on their shared taste in books. They publish reviews from guest reviewers as well as their own; young adult books are reviewed by a daughter of one of the administrators. They also feature reading club reports, interviews and raffles of books received from publishers. The group's opening message states that conviviality and cosiness are its main aims: 'Everybody is welcome, the more souls, the merrier'. In an interview, Meinen states: 'What we think is important is authenticity, honesty and staying true to yourself. We do this in our own way, full of enthusiasm and passion. That this appeals to others is a mega boost for us.'[69]

Sometimes the administrators take action to protect the group's atmosphere. That was the case when a long-time member with known problems began to use strong language, and issues of foul language also arose around a blog post on the 'pietendiscussie'.[70] ('Pietendiscussie' is a divisive issue in the Netherlands, concerning Black Pete, the black-faced helper of Santa Claus.) In cases like these, the posts that announce the administrators' action draw many positive comments ('happy I missed something').

Though all members of the group can contribute, many of the more lively exchanges are initiated by the group's administrators. They often open a discussion with a 'Thesis of the Week' (such as 'Reviews influence my choice of reading'), or a question ('What are you reading?'). They regularly organise a 'Friday Night Quote Night', and there is also a weekly post where members can reply with references to reviews on their own websites.

International platforms

We have seen that there are no firm boundaries between the different platforms for book discussion within the Netherlands. Similarly, there are no firm boundaries between Dutch platforms and international platforms. Many people from the Netherlands use international platforms, such as Goodreads or LibraryThing, either in Dutch or in English. Others maintain a weblog in English. Some of those who choose to write in English do so because they live in an English-speaking country, but this is by no means the case for all of them.

An example of those who use Goodreads in Dutch only is provided by two people we have already met in this chapter: book blogger Mieke Schepens and the moderator of a Facebook group Karin Meinen. They are friends on Goodreads. Most of their other Goodreads friends are also Dutch or Dutch-speaking. At the other end of the spectrum is 'Annemieke', maintainer of an English-language weblog (A Dance with Books). Most of her reading is in English and so are all of her reviews, even for books that she has read in Dutch. Annemieke has a very international group of friends, including many people from developing countries. 'Annabel' is one of many people who adapt the review language to the language of the book: Dutch books are reviewed in Dutch, English books in English. On Goodreads, speakers of Dutch who read other languages besides Dutch and English are a very small minority indeed, even in bilingual Belgium.

Unlike Hebban, the Dutch site most resembling Goodreads, Goodreads supports book groups. Book groups have a bookshelf, and they can host challenges and polls, but their main function is book discussion. There are a number of Dutch language groups, for example a group for Dutch book bloggers (many members of which also participate in a Facebook group with the same aim), a group of 'United girlscene booknerds', a group of 'Fanatic Dutch readers' and others. But, again, many Dutch Goodreads members also participate in English-language groups. Annemieke is a member of one Dutch group and twelve English ones, which include an *Alice in Wonderland*-inspired group, a group for fantasy fans and a group that discusses the BookTube Science Fiction and Fantasy awards.[71]

Which brings us to BookTube, an informal term for the segment of YouTube devoted to book videos or 'vlogs'. As you would expect, there exists a Goodreads group of Dutch booktubers.[72] While the population of the rest of the book discussion landscape is mostly female, BookTubing is almost exclusively a female occupation. In age, too, booktubers are much more homogeneous than other book discussants: the overwhelming majority is between fifteen and thirty years old. The focus of their reading and vlogging is often on young adult novels. Characteristic topics for book vlogs are: discussion of one or a few books, sometimes in what are called 'wrap-ups' (discussion of a group of recently read books); book hauls, in which the vlogger shows a stack of books which she bought over the last weeks or brought back from a book fair or book shopping spree; showing a pile of TBR (to be read) books; a walk around the vlogger's (new) bookcase; a report from a book event or sometimes a marketing event specifically targeted at book vloggers or bloggers; or an 'unboxing', that is, unpacking a box of books and marketing goodies received from a publisher.

The queen of (originally) Dutch book vloggers is Sanne Vliegenthart, with her English-language channel 'booksandquills'.[73] She has more than 175,000 followers. Vliegenthart studied English literature in the Netherlands and moved to the UK, where she worked with Penguin. On her channel, she notes that she is interested in giving talks about BookTube, about how to be a book influencer and about 'building your personal brand online'. Under the heading 'Sponsorships', she writes 'I'm available to work with brands, both on YouTube and on my other social channels'. For Vliegenthart, what may have been a hobby when she started on BookTube in 2009 has turned into an important component of her personal and professional identity: her Internet and social media skills, not her formal education, landed her a job in publishing. She is very conscious of the new opportunities that the Internet has created:

> We are a new generation that has the opportunity to be friends with people all over the world. We build massive communities online and set up our own projects. We have the Internet, and that is all that you need to start something new. No one needs to give us permission. We make up the rules as we go along.[74]

Much less popular, but still followed by about 8,000 people, is 'Basically Britt', by Britt Alsemgeest. Alsemgeest, who has a bachelor's degree in media and communications, makes English-language videos about books (mostly) and lifestyle. Apart from the typical book vloggers' topics she vlogs about trips and sometimes about clothes, but books are the main fare. When asked in a question session why she decided to vlog in English rather than in Dutch, she answered that she wanted to be part of the English-language BookTube community, compared with which the Dutch-language community is quite small. She also says she loves the English language and that vlogging in English has certainly improved her command of the language; her dream is to live in London. In one video she asks her viewers to say what is so attractive about the BookTube community. The consensus is that booktubers are very friendly, that they are passionate and energetic about books and willing to share their views. Someone writes that she started a BookTube channel because 'I wanted to feel like I am a member of one giant reading family!'[75]

A BookTube channel that is in many respects the opposite of 'Basically Britt' is 'De idioot' (The idiot), by Floris van der Pol.[76] Van der Pol is male, he is studying philosophy and he vlogs in Dutch. As of August 2018, he had only seventy-six followers. His videos always discuss one (staunchly) literary work, sometimes a recent book, sometimes a book by a classic author such as Turgenev, Camus or Kafka. He is unique in his interpretative approach; while most vloggers limit themselves to what they like or don't like about a book, van der Pol delves into the meaning and implications of a story. He also quotes passages that show something of the style of the book. In many ways he is more intellectual than other (Dutch) booktubers. Van der Pol's channel can serve as a warning not to be too quick in thinking all booktubers are similar.

Bringing it together

Having discussed a number of individual sites and site types, let us now look at the bigger picture and briefly discuss quantitative trends, the networking aspects of these sites, their affordances (that is, how their architecture suggests their possible uses) and their bookishness.

Figure 13.1 shows the number of postings over the period 2001–16. The data are not complete: I have no quantitative information about discussions on Facebook, and the reported volume of blog posts in the past is certainly much too low.[77] Still, we can see a number of trends: the increasing volume of reviews posted at bookseller bol.com, Hebban's successful transformation into an all-genre site, the rise and decline of Ezzulia, the disappearance of watleesjij.nu (WLJN) and the persistence of Boekmeter in a landscape dominated by much larger sites.[78] What this also shows is that online book discussion is not a

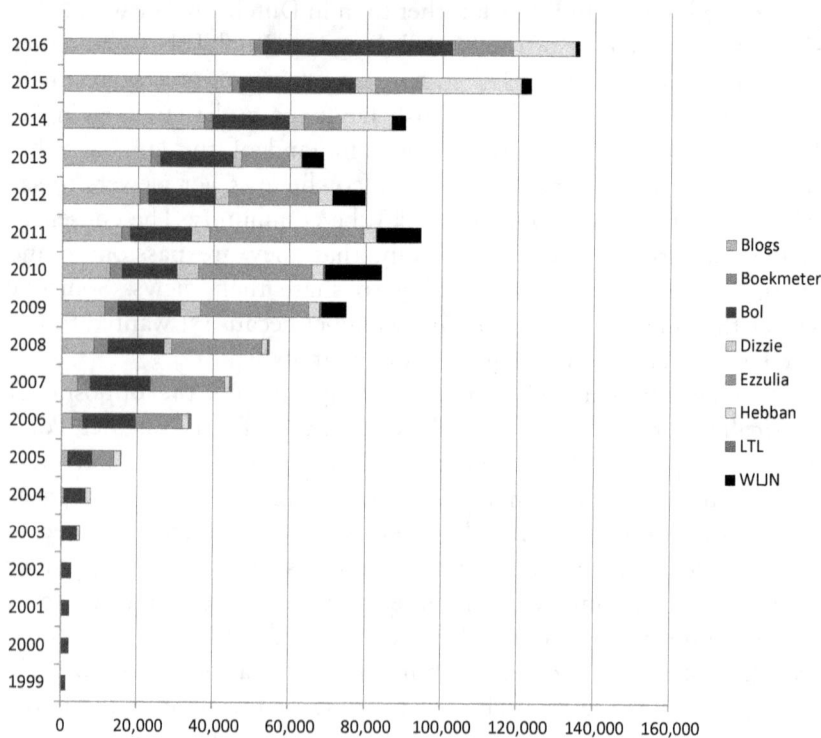

Figure 13.1 Number of posts to Dutch book discussion sites per year, by platform

very large-scale phenomenon. The number of messages in 2016 was about 136,000, one post per 125 inhabitants of the country. Though many more people read these reviews than write them, it should also be clear that people who participate in online book discussion are only a small part of the reading public, and their reading behaviour is not necessarily representative.

Now let us consider networking. The figures above suggest that, over the coming years, the four main platforms for online book discussion in the Netherlands will be Hebban, bol.com, Facebook groups and personal weblogs. However, as we have seen, many readers are active on multiple platforms. From the perspective of many readers, there may be only a single book discussion environment. Even on their personal Facebook pages, friends' lists over and over contain the same names from Hebban and the blog world. For researchers of the phenomenon, this implies that researching a single site can never provide satisfactory answers. As Nancy Baym wrote when researching Swedish music fans:

> For those seeking to study online communities, this sort of social formation poses the methodological challenge of how to bound the object of study. It has long been the norm to go to an online space and study it. . . . We have few studies that explore the connections amongst these disparate online platforms, despite the fact that people's online activities are almost always distributed across multiple sites.[79]

If, for instance, we are interested in the extent to which individuals' reading is influenced by their friends' reading, which seems a very pertinent question to ask, and we cannot just look at friendships on a single site. If we want to understand how people present and define themselves using books, we likewise cannot focus on their profiles and bookshelves on a single site.

This does not imply that different site types do not have different affordances. Discussion is the most essential characteristic for Usenet and for forum sites (although it may degenerate into chatting). Buying advice is the reason for the existence of the reviews at booksellers' sites; discussion is not really relevant here. For the book-based networking sites, discussion is an add-on and nice to have. On weblogs, the culture depends on the blog in question. There are weblogs where every post is hailed by friends; on others, the comment function is hardly ever used. But it is reasonable to ask to what extent comments on weblogs still serve the purpose of discussion. They often seem to be used mostly to create and maintain relationships.[80] On Facebook, discussion is a rarity; there is a lively exchange, but most responses to

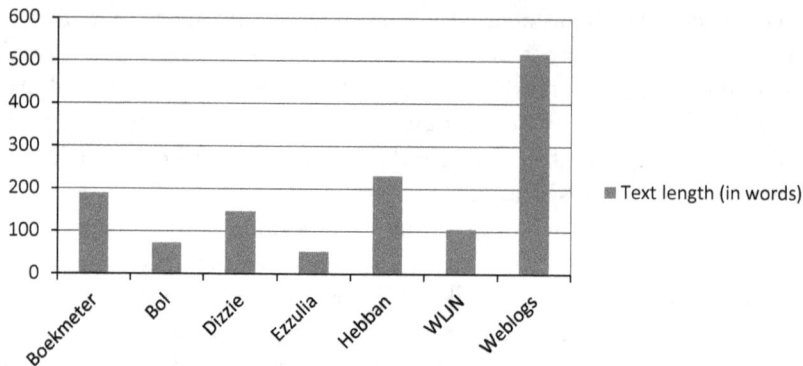

Figure 13.2 Post length (number of words) by platform (all posts on Ezzulia, blog posts on weblogs, reviews on all other sites)

posts are brief, supportive and sympathetic. It is clear that this will attract a different type of person from those attracted by a weblog.

On the other hand, the best platform for writing a longer and more elaborate review is probably the weblog. One would expect the reviews on the social networking review platforms to be shorter than blog posts, but still fairly long.[81] Reviews on booksellers' sites, which have a more limited purpose, could be the shortest. The numbers in the downloads confirm these expectations. Figure 13.2 shows the average text lengths on the distinct sites (reviews on the review platforms, blogs on the weblogs and posts on the Ezzulia forum). We see the expected trend, but we also notice that there are clear differences in text length among the book-based social networking sites. Texts on Ezzulia are of course very different, as only a small number of posts can be considered reviews; most messages represent no more than a turn in a conversation.[82]

One final thing may be worthwhile to note about online book discussion: among themselves, participants can be unashamedly bookish. The 'an'drei' account on Ezzulia uses a brief dialogue as a signature line:

> Elend: I kind of lost track of time . . .
> Breeze: For two hours?
> Elend: There were books involved.

In the Samenlezenisleuker Facebook group someone posted 'Addicted to reading? I confess, guilty'[83] – and many agree. Or, again on Samenlezenisleuker, someone quotes 'Her soul belongs to words and books.

Every time she reads, she is home.'[84] On the book discussion sites surveyed in 2016, ninety-seven persons use the word 'bookworm' in their profile. One reason why online book discussion is important, in a society where reading may be on the decline, is that it allows readers to meet others for whom reading is an essential activity.

Notes

1. The Dutch language is also used in Flanders. Some of the sites that I discuss have many visitors from Flanders, though most of the sites are based in the Netherlands. All websites were accessed in August 2018.
2. Peter Boot, 'Towards a Genre Analysis of Online Book Discussion: Socializing, Participation and Publication in the Dutch Booksphere', *Selected Papers of Internet Research*, 12:0 (2011), at <https://spir.aoir.org/ojs/index.php/spir/article/view/9076>.
3. See, for example, Elizabeth Long, *Book Clubs: Women and the Uses of Reading in Everyday Life* (Chicago: University of Chicago Press, 2003), or, for the Netherlands, Marjolein van Herten, 'Learning Communities, Informal Learning and the Humanities: An Empirical Study of Book Discussion Groups', PhD dissertation (Open University, 2015).
4. Katharina Lukoschek, '"Ich liebe den Austausch mit euch": Austausch über und anhand von Literatur in Social Reading-Communities und auf Bücherblogs', in Andrea Bartl and Markus Behmer (eds), *Die Rezension: Aktuelle Tendenzen der Literaturkritik* (Würzburg: Köningshausen und Neumann, 2017), pp. 225–52.
5. As they sometimes have. See Suzanne Van Putten-Brons and Peter Boot, 'June is Dutch Literature Month! Online Book Reviewers and Their Role in the Transmission of Dutch Literature to the English-Speaking World', in Elke Brems, Orsolya Réthelyi and Ton van Kalmthout (eds), *Doing Double Dutch: The International Circulation of Literature from the Low Countries* (Leuven: Leuven University Press, 2017), pp. 313–27.
6. Sheenagh Pugh, *The Democratic Genre: Fan Fiction in a Literary Context* (Bridgend: Seren, 2005).
7. For some large websites that have disappeared (e.g. the book discussion platform dizzie.nl) this personal archive may now be the only more or less complete representation.
8. Most of the following discussion is based on the group archive at <https://groups.google.com/forum/#!forum/nl.kunst.literatuur>.
9. Other Usenet sites where literature was being discussed in the Netherlands or in Dutch include <dds.cultuur> and <fido.belg.boeken>. The principal platform for original literature was <nl.kunst.literatuur.podium>.

10. Swane at <https://jswane.home.xs4all.nl/oud/index.html> and <http://www.janwillemswane.nl>; Valk at <http://moedwil-en-misverstand.blogspot.nl>.
11. <http://www.eco.rug.nl/~brakman/brakman> and <http://www.nescio.info/extra/insula> respectively.
12. Michel Schaeffer, *Het geheim van bol.com: Over dromen en doen, pionieren en groeien* (Amsterdam: Atlas Contact, 2017).
13. Numbers based on a download done over the last days of 2016. The download did not include all books but focused on fiction, history, psychology, spirituality and lifestyle.
14. <https://lees.bol.com/nl>.
15. <https://www.facebook.com/groups/1490058407899871>.
16. One of the reviews makes clear 'analetter' is a woman; <https://www.bol.com/nl/p/weerloos/1001004008287854>.
17. Lukoschek, '"Ich liebe den Austausch mit euch"'.
18. Especially in Germany, a large number of recent studies address that question. One example: Holger Kellermann and Gabriele Mehling, 'Laienrezensionen auf amazon.de im Spannungsfeld zwischen Alltagskommunikation und professioneller Literaturkritik', in Bartl and Behmer (eds), *Die Rezension*, pp. 173–202.
19. M. J. Daniels, '"Als ik realisme wil ga ik wel een uur uit het raam staan kijken". Een kwalitatieve en kwantitatieve analyse van Nederlandse lezersrecensies op Bol.com en Goodreads', MA thesis (Radboud Universiteit, 2016).
20. Stefan Dimitrov, Faiyaz Zamal, Andrew Piper and Derek Ruths, 'Goodreads Versus Amazon: The Effect of Decoupling Book Reviewing and Book Selling', paper presented at the Ninth International AAAI Conference on Web and Social Media, Oxford, 2015, available at <https://www.aaai.org/ocs/index.php/ICWSM/ICWSM15/paper/download/10557/10452>.
21. The analysis was performed using LIWC (Linguistic Inquiry and Word Count). See Leon Van Wissen and Peter Boot, 'An Electronic Translation of the LIWC Dictionary into Dutch', paper presented at the eLex Conference 2017, Leiden, 2017, available at <https://elex.link/elex2017/wp-content/uploads/2017/09/paper43.pdf>.
22. Jill Walker Rettberg, *Blogging* (Cambridge: Polity, 2013), p. 32.
23. Frank Meeuwsen, *Bloghelden* (Amsterdam: A. W. Bruna, 2010), p. 23.
24. Frank Meeuwsen (ibid.), the historian of the early Dutch blogosphere, doesn't even mention book bloggers.
25. <https://www.rodemuur.nl>. We encountered a few earlier articles, but these were not really book blogs. It is quite possible, however, that we missed relevant weblogs if they were not linked, directly or indirectly, from the seed set that we started with, or if our heuristics incorrectly determined that a site was irrelevant to book discussion. Also, blog owners may have removed older posts.

26. The figures do include false positives, that is, posts incorrectly classified as being about books.
27. Tobias Zeising, 'Buchblogger: Eine Analyse mit Topliste, Visualisierungen und Statistiken', at <https://www.lesestunden.de/2015/03/buchblogger-eine-analyse-mit-topliste-visualisierungen-und-statistiken>.
28. As she was a minor when posting the material discussed here, I considered withholding her name but, given the scale of her presence on the web, it would be pointless.
29. <https://www.goodreads.com/MiekeSchepens>.
30. <https://graaggelezen.blogspot.nl/2018/02/ik-las-de-schaduwbokser-geschreven-door.html>.
31. <http://marc-las.blogspot.nl/2012/03/ernst-jan-pfauth-gij-zult-bloggen-een.html>.
32. One of those articles is about book bloggers: Marc Van Oostendorp, 'Carnaval der burgerrecensenten', Neder-L, no. 0709.56 (2007), at <https://www.neerlandistiek.nl/2007/09/carnaval-der-burgerrecensenten>.
33. <http://marc-las.blogspot.nl/2012/03/ernst-jan-pfauth-gij-zult-bloggen-een.html>.
34. <http://marc-las.blogspot.nl/2011/05/joshua-foer-moonwalking-with-einstein.html>.
35. <http://marc-las.blogspot.nl/2012/07/karel-van-het-reve-met-henk-broekhuis.html>.
36. <http://bibliofem.nl/recensie-haat-mel-wallis-de-vries>.
37. In an interview with the 'Leesplein' website, the Dutch public libraries' site for reading promotion for children and teenagers, <https://www.leesplein.nl/JB_plein.php?hm=3&sm=2&id=357>.
38. <http://bibliofem.nl/gelezen-in-juli>. Translated from the Dutch by the present author.
39. <https://www.hebban.nl/spot/weloveya/nieuws/club-van-10-stopt>.
40. <http://www.ezzulia.nl>.
41. A download of the forum in September 2017, limited to the explicitly book-related forums, consists of 241,000 messages. This download is the basis for much of the following discussion.
42. <http://ezzulia.nl/forum/viewtopic.php?f=223&t=3165&start=15>.
43. <http://www.ezzulia.nl/forum/memberlist.php?search_group_id=8>.
44. <http://ezzulia.nl/forum/viewtopic.php?f=205&t=11737&start=75#p675364>.
45. <https://www.thrillzone.nl> and <https://spannings.blogspot.nl>.
46. Literature, Fantasy & SF, Thrillers, Nordic thrillers, Chicklit, Non-fiction, Graphic novels, Children's and adolescents' books. For each genre there is a forum for foreign books and for originally Dutch books.
47. <http://www.ezzulia.nl/forum/viewtopic.php?f=145&t=9576>.
48. In June 2016, around 56,000 reviews were downloaded from the site. The number of active users (who had contributed at least one review, list, response to a review or other contribution) was about 8,000.

49. This paragraph is based on a number of press releases and news items, mostly from Boekblad (<https://boekblad.nl>) and Bibliotheekblad (<https://www.bibliotheekblad.nl>).
50. <https://www.hebban.nl/artikelen/dizzienl-gooit-handdoek-in-de-ring>.
51. A. F. N. Jessen, 'Lezen als sociale activiteit: van leesgezelschap tot online lezerscommunity', MA thesis (Radboud University, 2016).
52. <https://static.hebban.nl/files/files/hebban_prijslijst_2018v20-3LR.pdf>.
53. Enno de Witt, 'Vanaf juli ook Engelstalige boeken op Hebban.nl', Boekblad, 8 June 2016 <https://boekblad.nl/Nieuws/Item/vanaf-juli-ook-engelstalige-boeken-op-hebbannl>.
54. Jessen, 'Lezen als sociale activiteit'.
55. <https://www.hebban.nl/!/mieke4a>.
56. <https://www.hebban.nl/!/Cees%20van%20Rhienen>.
57. <http://www.thrillzone.nl>.
58. <https://lees.bol.com/nl/article/cees-van-rhienen-over-red-cell-de-wereld-in-19-dagen>.
59. <https://mustreadsornot.com/2016/07/30/cees-van-rhienen-in-gesprek-met-jacob-vis-over-het-boek-merdeka>.
60. <https://www.hebban.nl/!/boekenworm20>.
61. <https://www.hebban.nl/!/claar>.
62. <https://twitter.com/MokumseHuismus>.
63. <https://twitter.com/twitcit>.
64. See, for example, Anatoliy Gruzd and DeNel Rehberg Sedo, '# 1b1t: Investigating Reading Practices at the Turn of the Twenty-First Century', *Mémoires du livre*, 3:2 (2012).
65. <https://twitter.com/NRCTwitLit>.
66. <https://twitter.com/LeesTweeps>. Its web presence is <http://twitterleesclub.nl>.
67. Joachim Vlieghe, Jaël Muls and Kris Rutten, 'Everybody Reads: Reader Engagement with Literature in Social Media Environments', *Poetics*, 54 (2016), pp. 25–37.
68. <https://www.facebook.com/groups/451488498379185>.
69. <https://samenlezenisleuker.wordpress.com/2016/10/25/interview-karin-meinen-door-sjors-bloem-van-boekenliefhebber>. Translated from the Dutch by the present author.
70. <https://www.facebook.com/groups/451488498379185/permalink/738598146334884/> and <https://www.facebook.com/groups/451488498379185/permalink/721062731421759>.
71. <https://www.goodreads.com/group/show/163712-booktubesff-awards>.
72. <https://www.goodreads.com/group/show/193735-dutch-booktube-community>.
73. <https://www.youtube.com/user/booksandquills>.
74. Sanne Vliegenthart, 'You Know More Than You Think You Do', at <https://www.caitlinmoran.co.uk/you-know-more-than-you-think-you-do-by-sanne-vliegenthart-booksandquills>.

75. <https://www.youtube.com/watch?v=cULt65xm1uU>.
76. <https://www.youtube.com/channel/UCMmznFeN3nyuVFjLP3giwTQ>.
77. Figure 13.1 shows all posts (reviews, articles, responses) from the mentioned sites. Because of lack of data, it does not include all relevant sites: for example, the short-lived Boekensalon is missing, and so are a number of smaller sites. Blogs from the early years may have disappeared, or may not have been linked to from our seed set. On the other hand, I assume that Bol and Hebban have not deleted data from the past. For Hebban, the download was in June 2016; the 2016 number should be at least twice as big.
78. Boekmeter is a kind of cross-over between a forum site like Ezullia and a review site like Hebban. Users write reviews but the reviews are parts of threads that also contain other posts. While a review is usually a monologue, with perhaps some comments and questions at the end, on Boekmeter the reviews are inherently part of a 'multilogue'. Boekmeter is a reminder that in the book discussion sphere, boundaries between site types are hard to draw.
79. Nancy K. Baym, 'The New Shape of Online Community: The Example of Swedish Independent Music Fandom', *First Monday*, 12:8 (2007), available at <https://firstmonday.org/article/view/1978/1853>.
80. Some bloggers have complained about that. See 'Krysta', 'The Unwritten Rules of the Blogosphere' <https://pagesunbound.wordpress.com/2017/02/14/the-unwritten-rules-of-the-blogosphere> and the ensuing discussion.
81. Hebban's house rules require a minimum review length of 150 words. See <https://www.hebban.nl/main/huisregels>.
82. It is difficult to distinguish those that can be considered reviews and those that cannot.
83. <https://www.facebook.com/groups/451488498379185/permalink/666856893509010>.
84. <https://www.facebook.com/groups/451488498379185/permalink/757870764407622>.

Chapter 14

Novel Ideas: The Promotion of North American Book Club Books and the Creation of Their Readers

Samantha Rideout and DeNel Rehberg Sedo

'Novel Ideas' takes its name from an electronic newsletter hyperlink tab that appears in the January 2008 edition of the Random House 'Reader's Circle'. This publication is only one of the more than 450 electronic newsletters and promotional pieces we analysed for this project. The newsletters were, and continue to be, produced and distributed to book club readers by large publishing houses' marketing departments. This unique electronic, and ephemeral, database of communiqués from 2008 until 2013 allows us to historicise the evolution of changing ways to reach readers through technological means.

In this chapter, we present a systematic analysis of these promotional pieces, which offers a rare opportunity to evaluate the books that are promoted to book club readers, and illuminates a manufactured and idealised reader that may or may not reflect how readers themselves articulate their reading identity. Concentrating on the years 2008–13, when the format of the book and promotional channels to market those books that evolved from the codex to digital iterations, our analysis provides an account of a specific period in publishing history.

During the first decade of this century, the industry and its stakeholders were grappling with a revolutionary digital transition in terms of: market consolidation; pricing concerns; book valuations; long tail sales; and implications for authors, with issues such as the pricing of their work, their relationships with readers and expected merchandising efforts.

Consolidation of book publishers, such as the Random House and Penguin merger in 2012, was compared at the time to what happened to companies like Nestlé and Johnson & Johnson.[1] During the transition of the industry to include more digital channels for purchasing and reading books, there were a host of legal actions, including the lawsuit brought against Google by publishers and authors.[2] Legal disputes concerned, among other things, pricing, as the industry responded to the market dynamics and book valuation in a new digital landscape. The US Department of Justice sued Apple and five of the nation's largest publishers alleging there was collusion to raise prices in their effort to compete with Amazon, which was described as the real industry predator.[3] Publishers expressed the fear that Amazon, with its scope of distribution, would dominate the market to the point that authors would go through Amazon to reach their readers directly and remove any need for publishers in the book market. This fear was not unwarranted, with Amazon launching a 70 per cent Kindle royalty option in 2010.[4] This type of compensation scheme changed the perception of the financial relationship between authors and publishers. The new model also created a different type of accessibility, especially for young people, who, as Marianne Martens reminds us, used to rely on teachers, parents and librarians to get books, but 'with interactive online environments, publishers create disintermediated spaces in which they can communicate directly with their target reading audience'.[5] Amazon even removed the necessity to pay for many books, including those at the top of its bestseller list, so the obstacles that once existed were significantly upset by the digital transition.[6]

Online book sales disrupted the industry in terms of new pricing models and lower distribution and production costs, as well as the opportunity for long tail sales. Trevor Fenner, Mark Levene and George Loizou, of the Department of Computer Science and Information Systems at the University London, explore patterns of exogenous and endogenous book sales, such as the long tail sales phenomenon, which allow, through digital commerce, significant profit from small sales volumes of a large number of less popular items.[7] The historic approach to supply chain management developed for the print book market and brick-and-mortar stores do not have the ability that new digital channels have to increase revenue through sales of books that would not be prudent to keep stocked, and as these long tail sales became more popular they provided a new opportunity to disrupt the conventional book marketing process. Some of the Kindle bestsellers are offered for free, and this has changed the way readers choose books and discover authors. Though social media can be a powerful tool for publishers and authors, Jamie Criswell and Nick Canty found that social media are most effective when marketing to an established community, and debut authors struggle to harness the power of social media as a marketing platform.[8] Digital technologies disrupt many aspects of the book market, but when it comes to new authors, the power of social media is limited in the same way that conventional marketing channels, like merchandising, are limited. In the world of print merchandising, readers are met with large displays and signage featuring popular authors, and book cover design includes promotions such as movie tie-ins and endorsements from other, well known authors. Meanwhile, books from small and independent publishers are difficult for readers to find because those publishers cannot compete with the in-store merchandising budget of big publishers.

The Novel Ideas database of publishers' newsletters captures large publishers' responses to the disruption of the publishing industry by new digital realities, including but not limited to e-books and their distribution. As publishers struggled with pricing in terms of the value of books and market competition, in addition to reconfiguring relationships with readers and authors, their marketing initiatives through these electronic newsletters illustrated how they responded to industry disruptions.

The major shifts in the twentieth-century book publishing industries of Canada and the United States have been well documented. Bibliographers, book historians and cultural studies scholars, including Jon Bekken, Laura Miller and André Schiffrin, critiqued the demise of small publishing houses or their amalgamations into multinational media conglomerates, and how this influenced what Danielle Fuller and DeNel Rehberg Sedo call 'the reading industry'.[9] Claire Squires and others have written about the way publishers and booksellers conducted their business internally and externally, and note that in the last decade of the twentieth century and in the early years of the twenty-first century there was a shift in how publishers conceived their markets.[10] One very specific and influential development was the recognition of, and advertising to, book club readers.[11] For example, Random House continued successful live author readings, but specifically targeted them to book club readers.

In 1995 a *Quill & Quire* article extolled the social processes of women's reading clubs and hinted at the economic implications for astute marketers,[12] but large houses with well resourced marketing departments had already identified the financial and public relations potential of the book club market segment. Over the intervening years, publishers moved the readers' guides inside the books themselves.[13] Moreover, marketing resources shifted largely to the production of online promotion through websites, social media networks and electronic newsletters and mobile texts. Our analysis of the Novel Ideas database illustrates the books that are promoted to readers, particularly book club readers; makes evident a formulaic construction of promotional language for book club books; and identifies a manufactured and idealised reader through specific discourses, categorisation of national market differences, confirmation of the Internet's role in promoting backlist books to specific niche audiences, and multiplatform engagement.

To our knowledge, there have been no sustained studies of the digital promotional pieces targeted at book club readers, which makes a study such as Novel Ideas imperative. The online ephemeral pieces contained in the dataset represent the virtual marketing efforts of mostly US and Canadian houses; it contains 457 digital newsletters or promotional emails that we received, archived and analysed using QSR Nudist as our data management system. Table 14.1 gives the name of the piece and the house or organisation that produced it. To our knowledge, the dataset contains all of the digital pieces produced for book clubs by HarperCollins (US), Random House of Canada, Penguin (Canada and US) and Simon & Schuster (US) from the years

Table 14.1 Novel Ideas dataset

Publisher/organisation	Publication	Number in set
Abbey Theatre (Ireland)	Play advertisement	1
BookBrowse	BookBrowse editor's blog	2
	BookBrowse highlights	5
BookGroupInfo (UK)	Newsletter	5
HarperCollins (Canada)	'Savvy Reader' email advertisement	69
HarperCollins (US)	Academic literature	1
	Book chatter	30
	Library news	8
	Reading group books email advertisement	1
Penguin Group (Canada)	Penguin Bookclub newsletter	2
	Penguin Books email advertisements	24
Random House of Canada	BookClubs.ca	16
	BookClubs.ca BooksBuzz	82
	BookLounge.ca	1
	BooksBuzz email advertisements	29
	Retreat by Random House	13
Random House (US)	Random House Readers' Circle newsletters	67
	Random House Readers' Circle email advertisements	4
	Random House general email advertisements	5
Simon & Schuster (US)	Book club newsletters	56
	Book club email advertisements	33
Very Short List	Book give-away email	1
Virago Press (UK)	Book club email advertisements	2

2008–13. The dataset also contains digital communiqués that were produced by organisations whose audiences were book club members and who may or may not have been supported by the publishing houses. There were also others that were produced by publishers, but targeted to general readers.

In these pieces, we can see Beth Driscoll's conceptualisation of the middlebrow in the socially inflected process of production and (by implication) in the reception of the newsletters and other items.[14] Middlebrow, as a classification for literature, has historically been (and arguably still is) 'provisional and relational, always defined by reference to its neighbours, the popular lowbrow and the elite highbrow'.[15] While the boundaries defining middlebrow are not the object of our chapter, we think the features of middlebrow that Driscoll identifies (middle-class, reverential, commercial, mediated, feminised, emotional, recreational, earnest) are obvious throughout our analysis.[16] She argues that to 'understand today's book culture, it is imperative to recognize that the most influential players – prize administrators, TV producers, educators, reviewers, and festival organizers – are descended from the middlebrow institutions of the mid twentieth century, operating in a digital environment with new global reach'.[17] In addition to considering most of the books highlighted as book club picks in the newsletters as middlebrow, the creators of these newsletters can be considered middlebrow cultural workers, and the newsletters themselves are middlebrow artefacts.

What makes a book a book club book? This question has been posed since book clubs came under scholarly scrutiny in the early 2000s. Joan Bessman Taylor argues that a book club book depends on the type of group: those clubs that are interested in science fiction will read science fiction, for example.[18] She concludes that the one overarching characteristic of a book club book is its discussability. Jenny Hartley came to the same conclusion.[19] She cautioned not to classify a book club book genre by the diversity of titles book clubs read. According to Hartley, whether literary fiction or not, a book club book must evoke empathy and engagement from the readers. This ascription can be between the reader and character, between the author and character, or 'between all the readers in the room'.[20] The book need not be written by a woman author.[21] Good book club books, according to the readers in Hartley's study, always evoke passionate discussion. While Hartley dismissed the notion that reading groups in the UK read only middlebrow fiction, arguing that the selections often reflect those chosen by the academy, these genre markers exhibit the 'feminised', 'emotional' and 'earnest' notions of middlebrow laid out by Driscoll. They also reflect the books and how they are promoted in book club newsletters.

Through electronic newsletters, publishers create a book club genre. Most of the books promoted in the electronic newsletters are explicitly categorised as 'contemporary fiction' (141 references out of 355), which is not a surprise. What is surprising is that 'mystery' (105) and 'historical fiction' (92) follow in second and third place. While 'mystery' would be considered genre fiction in most scholarly literature, and would not be classified as middlebrow, both contemporary and historical fiction might fall into that category. That publishers promote these books as book club books suggests they understand that book club readers are often avid readers, and avid readers often read across genres.[22] The publishers market to a niche audience, and yet the titles they promote include those that would not be considered 'good book club books'. That is, book club readers, according to what is promoted in these newsletters, read across genres. Important to note is that few of the titles would be considered lowbrow: there were only thirty-five references to 'romance' and two 'chick lit' references, and zero Westerns made it into the promotional pieces.

The differences between Canadian and US assumptions of what a book club book is are not as marked as is the language promoting the books, as we discuss below. The themes we identified in the books promoted in the dataset are noted in Table 14.2, and illustrate subtle thematic differences, excepting in the promotion of spiritual books in the USA. Three prominent themes in both the US and Canadian publications were family, love and war.

The construction of the book club genre illustrates the understanding publishers have of book clubs. Outside of promoting specific books to book clubs, these newsletters communicate publisher

Table 14.2 Identified themes of promoted books

Theme	US publications (n = 366)	Canadian publications (n = 139)
Bravery	8 (2%)	1 –
Death	62 (17%)	21 (15%)
Family	202 (55%)	82 (59%)
Friendship	77 (5%)	12 (9%)
Heartbreak	25 (7%)	12 (9%)
Life	41 (11%)	12 (9%)
Love	164 (45%)	53 (38%)
Self-discovery	10 (3%)	7 (5%)
Spiritual	25 (7%)	2 (1%)
War	68 (19%)	19 (14%)

perceptions of book clubs as social opportunities for women readers. The highlighting of cookbooks in conjunction with book clubs conveys and perpetuates two assumptions. First, hosting a book club is like hosting a party and requires food to be successful or complete. This perception is also highlighted in mainstream media.[23] The Simon and Schuster newsletter of 11 December 2013 featured the 'Best of the Best Book Club Picks of 2013!' The first section was 'Best books to help you cater an awesome book club party' (Plate 8), which featured several cookbooks, including one by the television personality Buddy Valastro, *Family Celebrations with the Cake Boss*. Highlighting cookbooks creates another avenue for more sales across different imprints, and part of the middlebrow culture of book clubs is the commercial aspect of reading.[24]

However, as we have noted, the middlebrow character of these newsletters is not limited to only one factor. Rather, it is illustrated in the assumed audience of women readers, what Alison Baverstock has called 'communities of interdependence'.[25] The community members do not necessarily participate in genuine dialogue with the publishers, but the copy works to create feelings of affiliation. In some instances, the newsletters go beyond assuming readers are female and instead explore the heterosexual and gendered nature of book clubs as a given parameter. For example, the Random House Reader's Circle newsletters include a 'Reading Our Readers' section that engages real readers with a monthly question and features select responses in the following newsletter. In the 22 February 2010 newsletter the question was, 'Has your book club ever had a "bring your husband to your meeting" night?' Readers responded predictably, with one reader from Fort Wayne, Indiana, discussing how husbands were assured they would not be the only male present and lured with 'lots of delicious snacks'. Susan from Owings Mills, Maryland, wrote that they have an annual 'couples' meeting, which is accompanied by a potluck dinner and a carefully curated book that they are sure both men and women will enjoy, implying that the normal book club selection is feminised. Krismar in Waverly, Iowa, said that the husband of one member of her book club was considered an honorary member because he read every book that the book club read. Krismar called him a voracious reader but added: 'I am sorry to say that he has never attended one of our meetings but his wife often shares his opinions with us!'

We know from sociologists Wendy Griswold and David Wright that reader identity is influenced by geographic, social and cultural classifications.[26] Avid readers tend to be upper-middle-class, well educated and mostly women. Book club members are not different. That book clubs are predominantly female is not new knowledge. What appears to be different is how publishers think about 'regular' avid readers, book club readers and their reading preferences.

Sales were the gauge of the popularity of books prior to the algorithmic culture of today. During the first years of the twenty-first century, the market research potential that the digital environment enabled influenced which books were acquired, published and promoted. Large publishing houses use analytical software to 'listen' to what readers talk about on social media. They 'are most likely to possess the economic and social capital to run this form of analytical marketing, and then to work the results back into [social media marketing] strategy that is part of an overarching marketing system', as Sybil Nolan and Alexandra Dane note.[27] This marketing system simultaneously deconstructs and constructs who book club readers are and what they read. As Claire Squires reminds us in her analysis of the role of editors in acquiring and promoting books, technology always has humans behind it.[28] If we consider the 'broader set of discursive practices and cultural constructs, including the centrality of human curators in selecting and promoting books, and (in commercial terms) adding value and developing brand',[29] we see that there is a human process of determining what readers are talking about and turning that discourse into promotional copy.

The marketing language and architecture of these newsletters constructs an impression of more than a white middle-class heterosexual idealised reader. There is an intimacy in the personal language and multiplatform approach of the newsletters, which is reflective of how the act of reading is at once intimate *and* social. The multiplatform design of the newsletters expects the implied reader to connect with book marketing at multiple touchpoints and integrates book marketing into the lives of the idealised reader, such as promotion of publisher social media accounts and connecting authors to book club meetings via (first) the telephone and (later) technologies such as Skype or through the publisher's website.

The elevation of authors and fostering the perception of a relationship between the implied readers and star authors are a marketing function that is consistent throughout this database. While the newsletters analysed in this chapter came at a time when independent publishers were able to compete with big publishers in unprecedented way due to the advent of digital distribution giants and the new-found access to readers, large publishers maintained a competitive advantage with the reputation of their authors. This is reflected in these newsletters, with the emphasis on increasing the fame of their most popular authors while paradoxically fostering parasocial relationships between readers and authors. Note, for example, in Plate 9, the intimacy of the copy Random House (US) uses: 'Imagine an author visiting you in your own very own living room . . .'.

John Thompson argues that:

> The larger the capital reserves of the publishers, the . . . more they are able to invest in marketing and promotion and the more they are able to spread the risks of publishing by investing in a larger number of projects in the hope that some will bear fruit.[30]

This is achieved by marketing elements such as video spotlights, where an author is both speaking in a video with some production value in a setup similar to the press junkets celebrities use to promote a film. Plate 10 illustrates how Harper Collins (CA) promoted Michael Chabon's award-winning novel *Telegraph Avenue*.

While these videos imply or represent celebrity and amplify the perceived value of the author, they also create a sense of intimacy because the author appears to be speaking directly to the implied reader viewing the video. Another marketing tactic employed by publishers to reinforce this conflicting elevated and intimate author identity are the book endorsements attributed to authors. When promoting a debut novel in the newsletter of 19 March 2010, for example, Random House enlisted the recommendations of writers Jamie Ford and Meg Waite Clayton, followed by a positive blurb from *Publishers Weekly*. These author endorsements were also tagged with one of their novels and positioned them as authorities on which books are worth reading, implying that these authors had made such valuable contributions to contemporary literature that they had earned the authority to critique the contributions of others. Their commentary positioned them as cultural authorities[31] while also speaking to the implied reader as a friend or 'trusted other'.[32] The endorsement from Jamie Ford began with 'A stellar debut novel. . .', and because it employed both informal diction and a sentence fragment, it read like a casual recommendation from a friend and suggested a parasocial relationship between the reader and Jamie Ford.

Thus these publisher newsletters focused not on sales language but on relationship building. Plate 11 illustrates the role of the newsletter editors as 'trusted others' or cultural intermediaries.[33] Randy Chen and other marketing staff members often mediated reader recommendations through personal copy to their readers, though there is no genuine conversation, only a one-sided pitch. The newsletters developed real and imagined reader community by highlighting book clubs, both actual individual book clubs and book clubs as a general concept. Where Random House Reader's Circle newsletters run a 'Reading Our Readers' column, some Penguin newsletters include a 'Book Club Classifieds' section. In this space Penguin connects with a larger community of actual Penguin book club readers, positioning Penguin as an intermediary and passive curator. The classifieds announce that 'The Blythe Book Club is looking for new members in Mississauga' or 'Kimberley has started Reflections Book Club in Thunder Bay', and includes as well individuals seeking to connect with existing book clubs ('Agatha would like to join a book club in the west end of Vancouver'). This forum develops niche regional reader communities, all linked to a specific publisher.

In a larger sense, the development of these real reader communities plays a part in constructing implied reader communities and identities. There is an intimacy in this Book Club Classifieds section, as the publisher highlights specific readers by first names (Kimberley and Agatha, and Judith) and refers to specific regions, even narrowing it down to neighbourhoods within a city (the West End of Vancouver). The intimate language tells a story that transcends geography. It acknowledges the human need to connect and socialise with others.[34] This Book Club Classifieds section suggests that reader community is a cultural necessity. Highlighting the importance other readers place on finding, forming or growing their reader community creates a cultural norm that encourages others to add more weight to their identity as book club readers or develop their own identity as a book club reader. The newsletter is reflective of middlebrow readers because the book club development outlined in the 'classifieds' is driven by geography rather than elevated literary tastes, implying social values over more intellectual values that would represent more strenuous barriers to entry, such as education level, specialised interest area or other categorisations that would identify group members as highbrow readers. Here we see nearly all of Driscoll's defining characteristics of the middlebrow reader identity, insofar as this reader community is mediated, reverential, commercial, feminised (apparently all readers have female names), recreational and earnest.

The intimacy of these marketing communications and their function to construct reader relationships is evident in the language they use. Contrary to conventional advertising practices, where 'less is more', these newsletters structure their promotional language in a 'more is more' approach. The emotional, lengthy sentences construct the idealised reader as decidedly middlebrow, someone who loves

Table 14.3 Examples of the uses of the *New York Times* bestseller list in promotional copy

Headline/copy	Publisher	Date
'... in the newest novel from beloved #1 *New York Times* bestselling Ya-Ya author Rebecca Wells'	HarperCollins	13 April 2010
'New from #1 *New York Times* Bestselling Author Mary Higgins Clark'	Simon & Schuster	13 April 2010
'... the third book in *New York Times* bestselling author Christopher Moore's wonderfully twisted vampire saga.'	HarperCollins	15 April 2010
'Jennifer Weiner's #1 *New York Times*® Bestseller is Now in Paperback'	Simon & Schuster	26 May 2010
'Funny, dark and sexy, this eighth paranormal romance from the *New York Times* and *USA Today* bestselling author is proof...'	HarperCollins	15 April 2010

reading for reading's sake. Therefore book club newsletters must be wordy and readerly, contrary to the brevity of marketing communication for other products.

One example of this formulaic promotional language is how the term 'bestseller' is leveraged. While different types of bestsellers have a distinct cultural value, such as those that appear on the *New York Times* bestseller list, all use amplifying adjectives and qualifiers in their marketing communications, as shown in Table 14.3.

Figure 14.1 compares the use of the bestseller lists published by the *New York Times* and other publications. The status achieved by

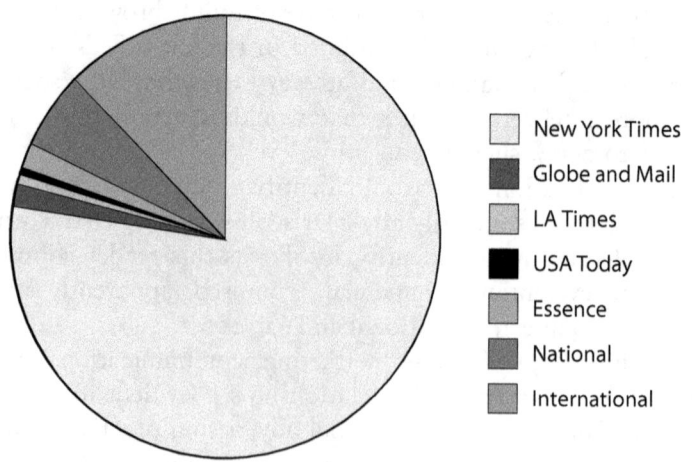

Figure 14.1 Proportional use of seven different bestseller lists in promotional material

books when they are listed on these bestseller lists have various levels of appeal to marketers because of the cultural capital and social value embedded in these publications. Figure 14.1 compares the use of bestseller lists for promotional purposes in publisher newsletters. It can be seen that while marketers do use appearances in the *Globe and Mail* and *LA Times* bestseller lists to promote their titles, the overwhelming majority of such promotion relates to the *New York Times* list. The balance of sophistication and implied intellect of the *New York Times* seems to combat the commerciality and commodification of being a bestseller, making the *New York Times* bestseller list the most commonly used by marketers.

The newsletter copy describing the books is often cumbersome, with multiple qualifiers, as indicated in Table 14.3. The 13 April 2010 example from Book Chatter, which is a HarperCollins newsletter, serves as an illustration: 'newest novel' + 'beloved' + '#1' + '*New York Times*' + 'bestselling' + 'Ya-Ya' (referring to an earlier bestselling work) + 'Rebecca Wells'. This and the other examples suggest that the standard formula for creating discourse around bestsellers is: Qualifier + amplifying adjective + rank + bestseller type + term 'bestselling' + reference to earlier bestselling work + author's name. As we can see in the illustrations, this is not the only formula, but it is an example of how the term 'bestseller' is framed. The sentences are not short and pithy, as is common in advertising, but they serve to create 'buzz' around a book.[35] Consider the third example in Table 14.3: '. . . the third book in *New York Times* bestselling author Christopher Moore's wonderfully twisted vampire saga'. This language is better read than spoken because the sheer number of words in the sentence turns it into an oratory challenge. The fifth example, which is the only occurrence of the *USA Today* bestseller list in the data, illustrates the following formula: Amplifying adjective + amplifying adjective + amplifying adjective + number in series/linkage to body of work + subgenre + genre + bestseller type + bestseller type + term 'bestselling'. This example is not a declarative sentence on its own, only the beginning of a sentence about the book. The host of amplifying adjectives and qualifiers function to frame the author's book and engage the interest of the imagined audience.

The discourse across the dataset includes the bestseller status, a qualifier such as '#1' rank, and any number of amplifying adjectives to communicate a sense of importance of the book to the imagined audience. What is significant about this finding is that when using the term 'bestseller' to market books, marketers are imagining an audience that is not trying to distinguish itself as highbrow, as Pierre

Bourdieu postulated. That is, the marketers assume that their readers will want to read what everyone else is reading. This is evident in headlines such as that from HarperCollins Canada on 28 April 2011, '100,000,000 Million Readers Can't Be Wrong' (Plate 12). However, this does not fit with what Danielle Fuller and DeNel Rehberg Sedo, and James Proctor and Bethan Benwell found in their studies of book club readers, who articulate a disdain or distrust of the 'bestseller'.[36]

According Michel Clement, Dennis Proppe and Armin Rott, when a book is framed as a bestseller, an instant brand is created in the minds of readers, one that helps consumers who are seeking signals to reduce their uncertainty in the purchase cycle.[37] This communication tactic appears in our dataset with great frequency. 'Bestseller' and 'bestselling' are often paired with other coded terms that reveal more about the publishers' imagined reader.

Here we can see the cultural value that is given to the *New York Times* bestseller list in the newsletters. It was used 137 times. 'International' was used twenty-two times and 'national' only ten. The 'template' numbers represent the consistent use of 'bestseller' or 'bestselling'. That is, month after month, the publication used the same template. The book was positioned as a bestseller or 'book club favourite/favorite' (which would seem more appropriate for this audience) only six times, and intertextual references (such as to the movies based on the book) came up only nine times. The suggestion that the book contained quality writing or award-winning content appeared twenty-eight times.

There are a few notable differences between Canadian and US marketing language. For example, as is illustrated in Table 14.4, US houses promote first-time authors more than Canadian houses do and Canadian houses ensure that readers know what authors are Canadian. Different value is given to prize-winners and bestsellers, with prize-winners trumping bestsellers in Canada. In Penguin Canada's

Table 14.4 Ways in which authors are identified in publishers' newsletters

Copy highlight	US publishing houses (n = 1,230)	Canadian publishing houses (n = 728)
American author	9	4
Canadian author	1	182
Author of another nationality	4	18
Celebrating the author	504	278
First-time author	99	32

marketing of Geraldine Brooks's *People of the Book*, the fact that Brooks won a Pulitzer Prize was most prominent in the descriptive text; that the book was a *New York Times* bestseller was featured only on the picture of the book cover and not in the short blurb beside it. This novel was also the first and most prominent book in the newsletter. Penguin Canada clearly values the status of the Pulitzer Prize and assumes the same of its imagined audience, the Canadian book club reader – even if the prize is American.

The newsletters in this database were sent to readers who had requested them. That is, the specific target audience of 'book club reader' not only identifies itself to the publishers, but also indicates individual and group identity. Unlike other publications produced by the various houses, these newsletters are not geared towards a specific genre, such as mystery, romance or contemporary literature. Most of the books promoted in the newsletters are what publishers call midlist or what we deem middlebrow. The actual readers might reject the 'middlebrow' label, but thanks to the analytical tools available and their continued targeted marketing efforts directed at this specific audience, the publishing houses might know their readers better than the readers know themselves.

Literary awards and bestseller status are both more accessible to books published by international houses versus small independent regional presses. Major publishers can leverage awards as a promotional tool, as they do bestseller status. Large houses also have the financial resources to use the Internet to move backlist books, and this database illustrates how well they do it. Understanding the patterns of book sales helps from a supply chain management perspective for both online and brick-and-mortar booksellers. Keeping low-selling books in stock is an option only for large presses because of warehousing infrastructure. The longer sales activity on the later side of the sales peak is aided by e-commerce in the form of the long tail. That is, the long tail is a 'phenomenon that allows an e-commerce business to make significant profit from small sales volumes of a large number of less popular items'.[38] This long tail sales opportunity is evident in our database.

Endorsements are a common promotional tactic in the dataset, and because endorsements frequently come from another author represented by the publisher there is a 'promotion within a promotion' in the marketing copy. This would not be possible without the opportunity presented by online stores and long tail sales. Brunonia Barry's 2012 endorsement for HarperCollins's *The Secrets of Mary Bowser* by Lois Leveen tells the imagined audience that Barry is a bestselling author, and the copy highlights the title of Barry's bestselling novel.

But instead of focusing on promoting *The Secrets of Mary Bowser*, the use of 'bestselling author' here could be a means to infuse a marketing opportunity for both books – one on the backlist and one recently published – and it could remind readers of the bestselling author to prepare for an upcoming novel.

To further illustrate the 'promotion within a promotion' concept, consider Kathryn Stockett's endorsement in Penguin's promotion on 17 February 2011 of Sarah Blake's *The Postmistress*:

> 'A beautifully written, thought-provoking novel.'
> – #1 *New York Times* bestselling author Kathryn Stockett, author of *The Help*.

In this example, which is not unlike book jacket copy, the description of the bestselling author Kathryn Stockett is longer than her endorsement of *The Postmistress*. Stockett's *The Help* was a breakaway hit for Penguin: winning awards, topping bestseller lists and becoming an Academy Award-winning movie in the summer that followed this newsletter. Information on Sarah Blake's appearance in Toronto to promote her book only appears three paragraphs down from Stockett's endorsement, suggesting that the publisher believes that '#1 *New York Times* bestselling author' Kathryn Stockett is a more powerful force for selling *The Postmistress* than the actual author. *The Help* won a number of awards of varying prestige, but those accolades are not mentioned when Stockett is identified: the blurb only highlights the fact that she scaled the *New York Times* bestseller list. Even if *The Help* is quality literary fiction, Penguin did not prioritise quality over quantity, a consistent policy among both US and Canadian publishers.

The general consistency among US and Canadian book club electronic newsletters is only one of our findings in this study. Indeed, they are more similar to one another than we originally thought they would be. Through systematic analysis, we were able to illustrate how these publishers depend on propping up books with bestseller list status, and by using marketing language that works to create 'buzz' instead of differentiating elite readers from the masses. Instead of distinguishing readers from one another, the newsletters work to create geographical communities in some instances, and imagined communities of readers as well.

Book clubs and reading groups are relevant to academic study – and to the economic realities of the book industry – because of their unique collective and social network power.[39] Novel Ideas concentrates on the digital marketing efforts of large Canadian and US publishers to reach thousands of book club readers. And while this might seem like a niche audience, publishers recognise the purchasing power these avid readers have. They promote books that are not only backlist books, but also ones that would not be considered 'book club books'. This analysis illustrates the multifunction, multipurpose nature of electronic newsletters from various publishing houses.

Notes

1. 'Random House, Penguin Agree to Merge', PublishersWeekly.com, 29 October 2012, at <https://www.publishersweekly.com/pw/by-topic/industry-news/industry-deals/article/54536-random-house-penguin-agree-to-merge.html>. The websites referred to in this chapter were accessed at the time of writing, November 2013 to November 2017.
2. Claire Cain Miller, 'Google Deal Gives Publishers a Choice: Digitize or Not', *New York Times*, 4 October 2012, available at <http://www.nytimes.com/2012/10/05/technology/google-and-publishers-settle-over-digital-books.html>.
3. Ylan Q. Mui and Hayley Tsukayama, 'Justice Department Sues Apple, Publishers Over e-Book Prices', *Washington Post*, 11 April 2012, Business section, available at <https://www.washingtonpost.com/business/technology/justice-department-files-suit-against-apple-publishers-report-says/2012/04/11/gIQAzyXSAT_story.html>.
4. Henry Blodget, 'Amazon Fires Missile at Book Industry, Launches 70% Kindle Royalty Option', Business Insider, at accessed 20 November 2017, <http://www.businessinsider.com/henry-blodget-amazon-fires-torpedo-at-book-industry-launches-70-kindle-royalty-option-2010-1>.
5. Marianne Martens, *Publishers, Readers, and Digital Engagement* (London: Palgrave Macmillan, 2016), p. 2.
6. Motoko Rich, 'With Kindle, Publishers Give Away e-Books to Spur Sales', *New York Times*, 22 January 2010, Books section <https://www.nytimes.com/2010/01/23/books/23kindle.html>.
7. Trevor Fenner, Mark Levene and George Loizou, 'Predicting the Long Tail of Book Sales: Unearthing the Power-Law Exponent', *Physica A – Statistical Mechanics and Its Applications*, 389:12 (2010), p. 2416.
8. Jamie Criswell and Nick Canty, 'Deconstructing Social Media: An Analysis of Twitter and Facebook Use in the Publishing Industry', *Publishing Research Quarterly*, 30:4 (2014), pp. 352–76.
9. Jon Bekken, 'Books and Commerce in an Age of Virtual Capital: The Changing Political Economy of Bookselling', in Roma Maria Harris and Manjunath Pendakur (eds), *Citizenship and Participation in the Information Age* (Aurora: Garamond Press, 2002), pp. 231–45; Laura Miller, 'Saving Books from the Market: Price Maintenance Policies in the United

States and Europe', in Harris and Pendakur (eds), *Citizenship and Participation*, pp. 219–30; André Schiffrin, *The Business of Books: How International Conglomerates Took Over Publishing and Changed the Way We Read* (London: Verso, 2001); Danielle Fuller and DeNel Rehberg Sedo, *Reading Beyond the Book: The Social Practices of Contemporary Literary Culture* (New York: Routledge, 2013).

10. Giles Clark and Angus Phillips, *Inside Book Publishing*, 5th edition (London: Routledge, 2014); Janet B. Friskney and Carole Gerson, 'Writers and the Market for Fiction and Literature', in Carole Gerson and Jacques Michon (eds), *History of the Book in Canada, Vol. III: 1918–1980* (Toronto: University of Toronto Press, 2007); Danielle Fuller, *Writing the Everyday: Women's Textual Communities in Atlantic Canada* (Montreal: McGill-Queen's University Press, 2004); Elizabeth Long, 'The Cultural Meaning of Concentration in Publishing', *Book Research Quarterly*, 1:4 (1985), pp. 3–27; Laura J. Miller, 'Commercial Culture and Its Discontents', in *Reluctant Capitalists: Bookselling and the Culture of Consumption* (Chicago: University of Chicago Press, 2006), pp. 1–21; Claire Squires, *Marketing Literature: The Making of Contemporary Writing in Britain* (Basingstoke: Palgrave Macmillan, 2007).

11. Danielle Fuller, DeNel Rehberg Sedo and Claire Squires, 'Marionettes and Puppeteers? The Relationship Between Book Club Readers and Publishers', in DeNel Rehberg Sedo (ed.), *Reading Communities from Salons to Cyberspace* (HoundmillsPalgrave Macmillan, 2011), pp. 181–99.

12. Linda Leith, 'Ladies of the Club: Spontaneous by Nature, Reading Groups Betray Few Common Traits, Except That They're Social, Self-Educating and Very Likely Sisterly', *Quill and Quire*, 61:5 (1995), pp. 8–9.

13. Anna S. Ivy, 'Leading Questions: Interpretative Guidelines in Contemporary Popular Reading Culture', in Rehberg Sedo (ed.), *Reading Communities*, pp. 159–80.

14. Beth Driscoll, *The New Literary Middlebrow: Tastemakers and Reading in the Twenty-First Century* (Houndmills: Palgrave Macmillan, 2014); Padmini Ray Murray and Claire Squires, 'Digital Publishing Communications Circuit', *Book 2.0*, 3:1 (2013), pp. 3–24; Simone Murray, '"Selling" Literature: The Cultivation of Book Buzz in the Digital Literary Sphere', *Logos*, 27:1 (2016), pp. 11–21.

15. Driscoll, *The New Literary Middlebrow*, p. 7.

16. Ibid., pp. 14–42.

17. Ibid., p. 4.

18. Joan Bessman Taylor, 'When Adults Talk in Circles: Book Groups and Contemporary Reading Practices', PhD dissertation (University of Illinois at Urbana-Champaign, 2007); Joan Bessman Taylor, 'Good for What? Non-Appeal, Discussibility, and Book Groups (Part 2)', *Reference and User Services Quarterly*, 47:1 (2007), pp. 26–31.

19. Jenny Hartley, *Reading Groups* (Oxford: Oxford University Press, 2001).

20. Ibid., p. 132.
21. Ibid., p. 67.
22. DeNel Rehberg Sedo, 'Badges of Wisdom, Spaces for Being: A Study of Contemporary Women's Book Clubs' (School of Communication, Simon Fraser University, 2004), available at <http://summit.sfu.ca/item/8708>.
23. See, for example, Lynn Andriani, 'Book Club Recipe Ideas', 13 August 2013, at <http://www.oprah.com/food/book-club-recipe-ideas>; Fiona Beckett, 'Wine: What to Drink with Your Book Club', *Guardian*, 9 January 2015, 'Life and style' section, available at <http://www.theguardian.com/lifeandstyle/2015/jan/09/wine-to-drink-book-club>; and Lisa Cohen Lee and Courtney Hargrave, 'WD Giveaways', *Woman's Day*, 69:11 (20 June 2006), pp. 28–8.
24. Driscoll, *New Literary Middlebrow*, 23–25.
25. Alison Baverstock, 'Online Marketing', in *How to Market Books*, 5th edition (Abingdon: Routledge, 2015), pp. 399–477.
26. Wendy Griswold, *Regionalism and the Reading Class* (Chicago: University of Chicago Press, 2008); David Wright, 'Watching the Big Read with Pierre Bourdieu: Forms of Heteronomy in the Contemporary Literary Field', CRESC Working Paper No. 45 (Manchester: Centre for Research on Socio-Cultural Change: December 2007), available at <http://www.cresc.ac.uk/publications/documents/wp45.pdf>.
27. Sybil Nolan and Alexandra Dane, 'A Sharper Conversation: Book Publishers' Use of Social Media Marketing in the Age of the Algorithm', *Media International Australia*, 168:1 (2018), pp. 153–6, available at <https://doi.org/10.1177/1329878X18783008>.
28. Claire Squires, 'Taste and/or Big Data? Post-Digital Editorial Selection', *Critical Quarterly*, 59:3 (2017), pp. 24–38.
29. Ibid., p. 36.
30. John B. Thompson, *Merchants of Culture: The Publishing Business in the Twenty-First Century*, 2nd edition (Oxford: Wiley, 2013), p. 6.
31. Pierre Bourdieu, *Distinction: A Social Critique of the Judgement of Taste* (Cambridge, MA: Harvard University Press, 1984); Pierre Bourdieu, *The Field of Cultural Production* (New York: Polity Press, 1993).
32. Rehberg Sedo, 'Badges of Wisdom', p. 140.
33. Bourdieu, *Distinction*, pp. 365–71.
34. Benedict Anderson, *Imagined Communities: Reflections on the Origin and Spread of Nationalism* (London: Verso, 1991).
35. Renee Dye, 'The Buzz on Buzz', *Sydney Review of Books*, 78:6 (December 2000), pp. 139–46.
36. Danielle Fuller and DeNel Rehberg Sedo, 'Suspicious Minds: Richard & Judy's Book Club and Its Resistant Readers', in *The Richard & Judy Book Club Reader: Popular Texts and the Practices of Reading* (Farnham: Ashgate, 2011), pp. 21–42; James Proctor and Bethan Benwell, *Reading Across Worlds: Transnational Book Groups and the Reception of Difference* (Houndmills: Palgrave Macmillan, 2015).

37. Michel Clement, Dennis Proppe and Armin Rott, 'Do Critics Make Bestsellers? Opinion Leaders and the Success of Books', *Journal of Media Economics*, 20:2 (30 May 2007), p. 77.
38. Fenner et al., 'Predicting the Long Tail of Book Sales', p. 2416.
39. Fuller et al., 'Marionettes and Puppeteers?', pp. 181–99.

Chapter 15

Making the Story Real: Readers, Fans and the Novels of John Green

Jennifer Burek Pierce

A brief history of John Green's rise as a contemporary novelist and media figure, a favourite of readers and viewers alike, parallels and plays a role in the changing dynamics of contemporary reading. That story could begin in 2006, when Green's first novel, *Looking for Alaska*, won the American Library Association's seventh Printz Award for young adult literature.[1] Numerous publications praised the novel, and reviewers compared it to classics like *The Catcher in the Rye*.[2] It was a contender for the annual *Los Angeles Times* book prize, as well as making other lists of noted titles and, in years to come, lists of commonly challenged or banned ones.[3] *Looking for Alaska* was also Green's only pre-YouTube novel, and thus one where awards and critical notices rather than informal reactions most readily documented its initial reception. The shifts that followed during the next decade and a half, as Green's reputation grew and social media became an endemic cultural force, generated new, digital experiences of reading. Readers, in sharing their responses, form a community oriented to books and narratives. These changes ask us, as readers and scholars, to think about the interactions between authors, texts and readers in new ways, or even to reconceptualise these elements of our enduring scholarly interest.[4] In 2009, Robert Darnton observed that 'the study of books need not be limited to a particular technology', a truism that seems ever more apt.[5]

After Green and his brother Hank Green began videoblogging in 2007, the process of writing his next novel was recounted in their Vlogbrothers videos, sometimes in the company of other notable names in young adult literature, prior to its publication and acclaim.[6] Jubilant word that that novel, *An Abundance of Katherines*, had won an accolade from the American Library Association (ALA) in 2007 was shared via Vlogbrothers before some traditional media outlets carried news of that year's ALA Youth Media Awards, where reporting on the winners of those Awards tends to focus on the Caldecott and the Newbery Medals.[7] Vlogbrothers viewers witnessed Green reacting to news of his winning a Michael L. Printz Honor during the customary phone call from the award committee, but the *New York Times*, which still collapsed young adult titles into its children's books pages, made no mention of the young adult prize in its coverage of the awards, which soon turned to the controversy over children finding the word *scrotum* on the first page of that year's Newbery medallist.[8] In retrospect, this episode seems like a pivotal moment, one that highlighted Green's ability to celebrate and connect with readers at important moments. In the years since, Green has become increasingly consequential, recognised for writing that resonates with adult critics and young readers alike, as well as being associated with extensive and innovative engagement with new media.[9] All this suggests that his use of social media, a practice likewise adopted by untold numbers of his readers, factors significantly in the ways people read and make meaning of stories in the early twenty-first century.

John Green's readers leave commentaries scattered across a digital landscape, and we must identify those testimonials and draw the lines between these points while it is still possible to do so. Scholars from multiple disciplines illuminate this process of discovery, which depends on online and real-world searches alike. The signs created by readers, however, foreground and modify the processes of locating and interpreting these twenty-first-century testimonials to feelings for books. Studies by Paul Gutjahr and Christine Pawley, for example, direct our attention to means of studying actual readers, particularly communities of readers connected by either common reading or geographical place.[10] Tempered by concerns that emerge in the study of fandom and the ethics of Internet researchers, though, I make no effort to position these readers beyond their interest in a particular author and his work.[11] If, as Leah Price has argued, 'the history of books is centrally about ourselves' and is invested in 'conditions of possibility for our own reading', then it is essential to acknowledge myself as a reader, a traveller and a researcher in relation to this story.[12] The materials gathered, whether through my own efforts to locate a site along one of Amsterdam's waterways or via iterative searches of social media platforms, represent the available traces of readers' responses to the story Green created as a tribute to his friendship with Esther Earl, who died of cancer in her teens.

This chapter is anchored, as is my previous work, by Roger Chartier's sense of historical research as a process where, 'by their choices and comparisons, historians assign new meaning to speech pulled out of the silence of the archive'.[13] Speech, in this case, is composed of the words and images that document fans' experiences of Green's *The Fault in Our Stars* (2012). One must learn the language of that media, its terms, from authors and readers.[14] While researchers theorise computer-mediated communication as cultural study, the role of real-world places, particularly the Amsterdam bench where the two central characters, Hazel and Gus, sit during a crucial conversation, invokes attention to material culture as well.[15] The result, to invoke the words of José van Dijck, is that the online 'culture of connectivity' is also the culture of reading, of the way it is represented in the here and now.[16] The amalgam of these critical and scholarly interests grounds this historical chapter that documents twenty-first-century readers' responses to a story that plays out across continents.

A significant chapter in that history, then, begins with Green's fifth novel, *The Fault in Our Stars*, about two teens whose cancer confounds their love story, but not before a fateful trip from Indiana to Amsterdam. When Green offered, via social media, to sign every copy of the first edition, eager readers leaped at the chance.[17] They propelled his book to 141 weeks on the *New York Times* bestseller list and into an internationally successful movie in 2014.[18] Vlogbrothers, too, won new viewers as a result.[19] While Green's prominence led glib detractors to complain that his success resulted from systemic advantages, readers' devotion defies this petty, and caustic, commentary.[20] Green has attributed the popularity of his work, variously, to long-time YouTube viewers, to editors and an agent who supported his literary development, and to the librarians and booksellers who have endorsed and recommended his work to readers.[21] Importantly, he gives enormous credence to those readers.

The Fault in Our Stars (or *TFiOS*, as it is known among fans, following a video in which Green reduced the title's Shakespearean allusion to an acronym) is an undeniably popular and critically acclaimed book. In addition to its status as a *New York Times* bestseller, the book has earned numerous awards, among them the *Booklist* Editors' Choice: Books for Youth, a Goodreads Choice Award and the 2013 Odyssey Award for Excellence in Audiobook Production. The movie version of this story also accumulated numerous award nominations and wins, including the MTV Movie Awards for Movie of the Year and Best Kiss.[22] The 2017 Nerdfighteria census (a survey of the community that has developed around the brothers' YouTube videos) found that upwards of 90 per cent of more than 50,000 respondents had read the book, five years after its initial publication. Although this proportion of readers represents a decline from the

2014 and 2015 censuses of Nerdfighteria, when approximately 95 per cent of survey-takers affirmed their reading of *TFiOS*, the 2017 *TFiOS* readership remains the highest of all Green's books.[23] During a spring 2018 episode of the podcast *Dear Hank and John*, Green estimated that *TFiOS* had been translated into approximately fifty languages, a further indicator of its appeal.[24] His count represents a reasonable gloss of numbers found in other sources.[25] These figures and awards demonstrate multiple facets of the book's readership, notably an impressive global reach, further documented by fans themselves.

Readers share their feelings for *TFiOS* in varied media. These testimonials signal both the importance of this book to its readers and the ways contemporary reading extends beyond the codex. Matt Kirschenbaum and Sarah Werner observe that 'even a mainstream piece of literary fiction ... is released into the kind of networked media environment that characterises our most mundane daily interactions', and thus 'books become transmedia properties, franchises spanning multiple formats, media channels and distribution networks'.[26] This description is akin to Ted Striphas's three-part characterisation of intermediation, which observes that 'relationships among media are socially produced and historically contingent' and 'media rarely if ever share one-dimensional, causal relationships'.[27] Given Green's YouTube productions and rich use of other social media platforms, from Reddit to Tumblr and Twitter, his novels exemplify this sort of contemporary enterprise. Readers' participation in this media environment creates access to their responses to the novel, whether in cyberspace or on a city bench in Amsterdam.

What neither Kirschenbaum and Werner nor Striphas pursue is the way that the dynamic, digital environment in which people read fosters the formation of community around narratives. Common ideas and values, particularly consensus about where poignant meaning lies within the narrative, result from readers' intangible, international convictions. *TFiOS* readers share a sense of connection and togetherness because of their ties to the story, and those bonds are demonstrated through intersections between text and wide-ranging paratexts, including social media commentaries, which enlarge the book's epitext, as conceived by Gérard Genette.[28] Perhaps fostered by Green's openness to readers' own concepts of meaning and the affordances of untold social media platforms, readers espouse connection with story, place and each other as aspects of reading *TFiOS*.

How do we understand the *TFiOS* readership? One source of information is the Nerdfighteria census, conducted by Hank Green since 2013, in which respondents repeatedly testify to their passion for his brother's books. Is it possible, though, to say whether those whose expressions we can trace through public places and online commentaries are viewers or readers, or readers and viewers, much less whether they found *TFiOS* online or at their local bookstores? The entwining strands of the Green brothers' productions – the references to novels and movies in Vlogbrothers videos, the promotion of books via Twitter and Facebook, the discussion of novels on Reddit, and the book-signings and gatherings like NerdCon – complicate such origin stories, perhaps rendering them irrelevant. What we can see, when readers' engagement is social and public, is that books and stories with genuine feeling for young people's lives resonate with readers in an era when surveys point to a decline in leisure reading.[29] It is also worth noting, in this context, that *TFiOS* readers are not all young adults. Green posits that '[m]ost of *TFiOS*'s readers are adults', a contention congruent with industry data indicating that adults purchase 65 per cent of titles marketed to a young adult audience.[30] These demographic details remind us that tributes to *TFiOS* and its representations of love and connection are not always created by adolescents.

Readers follow multiple pathways to this story, and make their own in sharing their reactions to it, and the ways those journeys intersect are many and varied. While some readers seek out every path that affords an encounter with the story, others, because of a lack of time, inclination or other resources, will be more selective. Evidence of readers' strong feelings for *TFiOS* also highlights their inclination to value connection and continuity, to embrace this narrative and make it part of their own stories. In this, their responses are transformational, not passive. If we accept Striphas's construction of contemporary reading as 'a range of techniques and activities whereby individuals and groups interact with the manifest content of books', then the readers of *TFiOS* offer us an encompassing sense of what reading may entail.[31] Particularly when researchers find strong similarities in the brain's processing of audiobook and print versions of a story, the range of ways readers respond to a title like *TFiOS* becomes increasingly salient.[32] Green's readers engage his stories and the elements of their creation in myriad places, and it is no small thing that those elements of creation include readers themselves.

When readers respond to *TFiOS*

Green has declared that his books depend on readers for meaning, writing that 'a book is, more than any new media, a cocreation of reader and writer'.[33] In commenting on *TFiOS*, he has urged readers to be self-reliant in their interpretations. Green argues that his own intentions are less important than readers' sense of what they have read:

> Whether the author intended a symbol or a theme or whatever is irrelevant; if you find that it aids you in your observation and interrogation of the universe, then it succeeds regardless of authorial intent.[34]

This guidance to readers, his insistence that they make their own meaning of the story and of 'the universe', is doubly significant in the case of *TFiOS*, where readers have been inspired to translate their interest in the story to places in the world.

In giving authority and autonomy to readers, Green echoes strands of reader response theory. His 2010 statement reads like a cogent modernisation of Wolfgang Iser's contention that 'the convergence of text and reader brings a literary work into existence'.[35] Although many theorists' work might be brought to bear on Green's characterisation of reading, the ideas of Iser and Georges Poulet seem most apt. For Poulet, a book possesses an animating force that engages a reader, resulting in 'transformation'. In reading, Poulet finds a 'consciousness [that] is open to me, welcomes me, lets me look deep inside itself, and even allows me, with unheard-of license, to think what it thinks and feel what it feels'.[36] Certainly, Green's emphasis on the role of the reader, in tandem with readers' commitment to *TFiOS*, evokes Poulet's vision of reading. While Iser's reflections on reader response are less intensely personified, less feeling, they are nonetheless reliant on the reader's mind and engagement with a text. Like Green, Iser has argued the reader's role has an 'equal measure' in literature's significance, that 'the "stars" in a literary text are fixed; the lines that join them are variable'. Readers construct those joining lines, as Iser explained, by 'filling the gaps left by the text itself'.[37] Iser's contention that there is always something left to the imagination, that no story can, of itself, be complete, parallels both Green's concept of reading and what Green's readers seem to do.

Readers' pursuit of those Iserian gaps, filled with an abiding affection for *TFiOS*, sometimes extends beyond the imaginings that Poulet and Iser envisioned. Contemporary reading practices, and the reading of this title in particular, are not confined to the page or even conversations among friends. Green has argued that 'the reader . . . alone, can make a story real', and the popularity of *TFiOS* has seen attention fixed on sites in the real world as a way of reading the novel.[38] Among the ways readers have engaged with this book, some graft the story of Hazel and Gus onto the real world and into their own lives.

Those traces of readers' commitment to Green's story, their demonstrations of having read, can be found across social media platforms, from YouTube to Goodreads to Pinterest and personal blogs.

My interest is in the way readers use various platforms to document their connections to real-world places found in the story, since the setting for *TFiOS* includes distinctive venues on two continents. Over the course of the story, readers and viewers follow characters to the *Funky Bones* outdoor sculpture at Newfields in Indianapolis and the historic Anne Frank House in Amsterdam.[39] Both book and movie also refer to seemingly ordinary places, like the intersection of 86th Street and Ditch Road in Indianapolis, which would also feature in Green's next novel, *Turtles All the Way Down*; characters' homes; a church where a support group meets; and a canal-side bench in Amsterdam. The site of a pivotal conversation in which Gus explains his recent diagnosis with an aggressively metastatic cancer, the bench where that exchange was filmed for the movie is sought out by readers.[40] It is laden with the *soi-disant* love locks found on Parisian bridges, and its worn surface has been written over with dialogue from *TFiOS*.

More than any other place, that canal-side bench anchors the *TFiOS* fandom. Located along the second canal ring where the Leidengracht and Herengracht canals intersect, the bench, referred to as the *TFiOS* bench by fans, is simultaneously ordinary and extraordinary.[41] The movie's DVD release features the bench on its cover, but those who look for it observe that its out-of-the-way location and undistinguished appearance make it inconspicuous, and for those who live in Amsterdam it is simply another city bench.[42] It has been graffiti'd and even stolen (but then replaced). It generates discussion on sites like TripAdvisor and Foursquare, and readers leave traces of their visits at the real-world site and in cyberspace. In 2014, someone created a Twitter account for the bench, @TFIOSBench, collecting and retweeting visitor photos and commentaries. Collectively, online outlets offer a montage of reader reactions to *TFiOS* that reflect the intersection of a fictional story and real lives. This activity also reflects the formation of a community of readers, a group of individuals who do not know one another but who nonetheless know of this place and of the importance now attached to it. Less the novel and interactions with its readers, there would be few signals that suggested the merits of this bench.

We are accustomed to marginalia as a proxy for readers' passionate reactions to texts.[43] While myriad readers certainly annotate their copies of *TFiOS*, some also leave comments on the bench, so that, in the *TFiOS* bench, we have a public kind of marginalia that reveals readers' responses to the story of Hazel and Gus. Visitor reviews and photos, particularly those shared via blogs and major social media platforms, document the words, images and artefacts that readers leave to articulate their feelings for this book. The succession of photos posted online invites the inference that the bench is periodically repainted, as words and images displayed in one photo are not always evident in another picture.[44] Images of the bench, rather than the bench itself, then, best document the phenomenon of public, performative marginalia.[45] Readers' words on the *TFiOS* bench evince several patterns, which I want to recognise with five categories of intersecting commentaries. While each piece of marginalia is no doubt sincere and heartfelt, the work of an individual reader or viewer, there is nonetheless considerable duplication, and thus common themes link or cluster them. Each cluster, in some way, resonates with the ways fictional and historical figures are remembered at other sites, too.

First, there are instances of this public marginalia that echo the narrative. Fans quote memorable, meaningful lines from the book and the movie. Hazel and Gus's '"Okay?" "Okay"' exchange, usually less the accompanying dialogue that equates these seemingly innocuous words with another couple's promises to love one another always, frequently appears on the bench.[46] Possessing the dual virtues of brevity and significance, the exchange has been a favourite emblem in multiple media, including parodies. Almost any photo of graffiti on the bench, if scrutinised, yields an iteration of these words. That Hazel's words are quoted is logical, given her role as the book's first-person narrator. She is echoed primarily through two phrases. The first is Hazel's invocation of René Magritte's *Ceci n'est pas une pipe*, reflecting her emulation of a character's use of that trope in a fictional book, *An Imperial Affliction*, that is the catalyst for the Amsterdam trip in *TFiOS*, and the second is her private eulogy for Gus, in which she painfully yet pragmatically observes, 'Some infinities are bigger than other infinities'.[47] Gus's commentaries on metaphor appear, too, as well as his insistence that 'It would be a pleasure to have my heart broken by you'.[48] The iconic status of these phrases is suggested, in part, by their presence on *TFiOS* merchandise as well as being rendered as graffiti.[49] That quotations on the bench, representative of the narrative or of an individual character's perspective, are ones that resonate with readers must be inferred from the effort it takes to leave such traces. One commentator has reported that during his observation of the bench, he and his family 'met people from Chile, Denmark, Hungary, Mexico, the UK and the US – all of whom had come to the city specifically to see this bench'.[50] These echoes of the book, left at a site of a pivotal scene, suggest readers' desire to commune with a facet of a compelling story. They repeat some small part of the narrative, and that quotation, no matter how brief, serves as synecdoche for their attachment to the story and its characters.

Also in evidence are words of appreciation, a category of remarks acknowledging author and actors alike. Fans leave comments like 'thank you, John' and even 'John Green ruined my life, slowly at first, then all at once', playing on Hazel's description of how she fell in love. They write, 'I love u Ansel' (Ansel Elgort played Gus) and praise Shailene Woodley's performance as Hazel. One comment on a photo uploaded to Foursquare declared *TFiOS* to be the 'best film ever'. Such remarks indicate intent and reveal their writers' feelings for the story as motivation for their visits. In other words, these acts are not random; they are linked directly to reading *TFiOS*.

Another category of bench notes reflects readers' augmentation of the story. Like women leave 'I voted' stickers at Susan B. Anthony's grave and *Harry Potter* readers pose at the imaginary Platform 9¾ at King's Cross Station in London, readers and viewers visit the bench to continue the story by entwining it with their own.[51] A notable sign of this is the multitude of padlocks emblazoned with hearts and initials. Some visitors add their initials, rather than locks, to the bench. In a sense, many seem to be telling their own love stories, articulating the fact that they have the good fortune of one of the 'bigger infinities' together. These augmenting notes are about what the story makes possible, the possibilities others realise as a result of its words.

A fourth and rather smaller category of public marginalia is more discursive, representing the writer's own story and its connection with *TFiOS*. These words are more varied, and seeing them as a response depends on familiarity with the story's content and themes. For example, one set of published 2015 photos of the bench alludes to characters' cancer diagnoses when it includes the legend 'Way to kick cancer's ass/We <3 Maddie'.[52] There are also multiple indicators that, in that same year, people affixed small plaques to the back of the bench with messages promoting websites for various purposes. One that asked visitors to 'Join the fight against cancer' depicted three people sitting on a bench like the one to which it was affixed, a graphic representation of the idea that by participating in the creator's initiative, the viewer joined Gus and Hazel where they sat. *TFiOS* and the *TFiOS* bench, then, represent points of departure for readers who see the story as a foundation for their own narratives.

In *Ex Libris*, Anne Fadiman recounted her own impassioned efforts to read books that shaped her life at the sites where they were set or written; she closes with her young daughter's first 'you are there' moment.⁵³ A final category of public marginalia at the *TFiOS* bench and accompanying social media posts documents readers' 'you are there' experiences. These experiences differ from literary tourism in that there is no official entity legitimising the site and no effort by visitors to claim that stopping by the bench endows their trips with a particular cultural valence.⁵⁴ Some messages are simply a reader's name or initials, sometimes accompanied by the date; some signers also identify the places they came from to find the bench, whether Corsica or the United States. The premise is simple, yet profound: readers have found a place where fiction and real worlds intersect, and they have been there and testified to that connection. Something meaningful happened in a story, a tale so vivid and significant that it inspired them to come to the place where it happened.

This theme is also embodied in reader photos, which range in content and tenor, at the bench. Even years after the release of both book and movie, the bench brings fans to Amsterdam. One blogger reports lines of people waiting to sit on the bench and take photos on a fine spring day in 2016, while other commentators mention being able to linger there.⁵⁵ It is worth noting that although some sources suggest that Green's fans, those most moved by the story, are predominantly adolescent young women, online photographs documenting visits the *TFiOS* bench are shared by people of colour, young men and families. There is also some diversity in the composition of those images. There are, indeed, any number of photos in which friends and lovers recreate the famed Gus and Hazel pose. There are also photos of individuals with their copies of *TFiOS*, some taken from behind the bench or across the canal, and some shots of the bench itself. Selfies, too, feature in the mix. Collectively, these images document readers' experiences of place and draw them into more direct contact with some part of the narrative.

Photos of the bench posted on platforms, whether via personal blogs or Facebook, express connection between the person, the place and the story it represents. John Berger, in *Ways of Seeing*, expounds on the relationship constructed by physical connection to things one might view from a distance, writing 'To touch something is to situate oneself in relation to it'. Many fan photos evince this notion, constructing a relationship between self and site. Coincidentally, Berger's discussion of the role of photographs, his articulation of the idea that personally generated images are no mere 'mechanical record', relies on a key word used in *TFiOS* and inscribed on the bench by readers: 'we are aware, however slightly, of the photographer selecting that sight from an *infinity* of other possible sights'. He continues, 'our perception and our appreciation of an image also depends on our own way of seeing'.[56] To those not invested in this particular story or community, bench images may seem insignificant, but the seemingly ordinary canal-side photos resonate with *TFiOS* readers. By posting or sharing their ability to reduce the distance between themselves and the site of the narrative online, readers and visitors transmit their experience to others, signalling their affiliations. It is a public communication of one's relationships to the community and its canon.

Reviews on Yelp! and other tourism-oriented sites testify to the meanings readers associate with this otherwise nondescript bench. Well into April 2017, the bench was labelled the Fault in Our Stars Bench on Google Maps and had accrued at least seventy-five reviews. Those commentaries marked the contours of the readerly community. As one Google Maps reviewer proclaimed, 'If you know what this is, you don't need any other information'.[57] Like him, another visitor described meeting people and making friends at the *TFiOS* bench. Google Maps once contained these and other more extensive commentaries. The record of those visits have since been eradicated by Google's changing technologies; as one 2018 reviewer observed, 'Disappointed they remarked it since Hank's video'.[58] At this juncture, the narrative and screen shots included in Hank Green's Vlogbrothers post-VidCon EU 2017 video offer the only documentable access to the older commentaries.[59]

Hank's video, likely for humorous effect or even simple contrast, includes screen shots of visitors who arrived at this pinned site identified as a 'tourist attraction', and found, simply, a bench. Those kinds of comments continue to accumulate in reviews on Google Maps. Their mystified, sometimes disgruntled, remarks contrast with those of readers. As one more recent visitor warned the uninitiated:

> A friend & I sat on said bench unaware there was anything special about it besides some silly locks attached. Had numerous teenage girls hovering around us until they finally asked us to move so they could take photos & giggle. Would recommend the bench beside it if you've never seen the movie & don't want to be stared at.[60]

Other voices explain what the teens hovering around the bench saw in this venue: 'It may not be the most comfortable or most traditionally beautiful, but it shows relationships, lives, and how each of us, indivisually [sic], have a story that all of us are in, playing a part'.[61] While this writer doubtlessly meant to use the established adjectival form for individuals' own stories, her neologism is a lovely reminder that visitors create images of this place, visualising their time at the bench, and of the word *indivisible*, calling attention to the unity of community. Her statement, like Hank's YouTube review, puts into words the core reason readers come here. He told viewers that the bench is special 'because of what people bring to it', characterising it as 'a physical space that was important to them or their relationships'. He observed, 'Each person brings to this thing their own stories and their own connections'. I would add, also, that in doing so, they connect with one another and this narrative in new ways.

Commentaries on personal visits to the bench appear on multiple platforms. Some may seem minimalist, like the string of five-star ratings on Google Maps and Facebook. Of the 1,500 Facebook check-ins recorded through to the spring of 2018, few offered public commentary, and all who rated their encounters gave the bench five stars. While the flawless rating might be regarded as uncritical endorsement of a site whose graffiti, in other contexts, would be regarded as vandalism or blight, the conventions of the community's communications across platforms instead render it analogous to the upvoting with + signs in Vlogbrothers' YouTube comments and a similar feature on Reddit. Given the Google Map reviewer's observation that additional information about the bench is superfluous for those to whom it appeals, these ratings are an effective, efficient means of communicating within the community. The quick mechanism of endorsing high-quality online commentary, transferred to this site, tells other members of the community that it represents an authentic experience and also signals belonging.

Thus, the bench itself and multimedia representations of it testify to the place of the book in readers' lives and hearts. Berger offers a perceptive way of understanding readers' decisions to view the bench. He has written that 'seeing . . . establishes our place in the surrounding world', and this statement does much to contextualise and interpret readers' decisions to seek out and document their visits to Amsterdam.[62] While such actions and the resulting social media posts have been dismissed as 'selfie tourism', and some readers themselves express dismay over re-creations of the bench-based movie scene, Berger's commentary aligns readers' interests in this place with their lived experiences.[63] By sharing their viewing of the bench, their visits to this site, they express a belief that the story is something more than a book they've read or a movie they've seen. They have paused and spent some small part of their lives, their time, in an iconic place. The bench is no longer a distant site, but one where they have, for at least a short time, been. To borrow Berger's expression, it has become part of their 'surrounding world'.

Readers have chosen the canal-side bench as a place to make the story real. Readers use this place to craft stories where young love, rather than being cruelly cut short, endures. By siting their own happiness and testimonials of affection at a place where Green's characters acknowledge their own mortality and foreshortened lives, they entwine their own stories and those of his characters. Combined with questions and comments that readers send to Green on social media, attention to this canal-side bench in Amsterdam evokes new, happier endings for a story whose characters' ends are both deeply felt and unsettling. Esther Earl's sister has described *TFiOS* as something like 'a sequel' for her sister, whose life and friendship inspired the novel. Of the narrative's central love story, Evangeline Earl has written, 'My sister never got to have a relationship like that', and she finds herself both 'unbearably sad and yet, oddly, uplifted' by the depiction of it.[64] Some readers, too, seem taken with the idea that there could be more of Hazel's life than they have seen on page or screen. Questions to Green, like 'What happens to Hazel?' and 'Deep down, do you have a sense of when Hazel dies?', suggest that readers believe there should be more to her story.[65] Readers participate in creating that continuation. When they seek out the places where her story has unfolded, they enact a bit of that story and carry it into their world. By giving a fictional character a new and perhaps different life than she could have had in the originating narrative, these readers, at least briefly, extend and even rewrite the arc of Hazel's story.

Conclusion

The Fault in Our Stars is a narrative, manifest as a novel, a movie and more. Readers encountered this story through the author's discussion of it in Vlogbrothers videos before it was published as a book, when it became possible for readers to spend time with a print or digital text, in English as well as other languages, Braille among them, or an award-winning audiobook read aloud by Kate Rudd.[66] The story exists, at least in part, as video performances by the author, and its big-screen iteration might appear in one's cable television listings.[67] As Kirschenbaum has noted, 'Today you cannot write seriously about contemporary literature without taking into account myriad channels and venues for online exchange'.[68] Readers' public mentions of *TFiOS* often refer to title rather than medium, and the fact that there are so many iterations of this story, so many ways to grapple with Hazel's love and loss, means we must prioritise the story over the medium that conveys it. A community of readers and their decisions, in public discourse and images, require that reconceptualisation.

It is fundamental to understanding why a reader seeks out a seemingly ordinary bench off the beaten path in a city with a thriving art scene, internationally renowned museums, boat tours and proximity to UNESCO World Heritage cultural sites. Because of the deep feelings *TFiOS* inspires, including the bonds of a community, this ordinary place is sought out by readers. The story of young love, fully realised yet tragically foreshortened, touches readers, and readers in turn want to touch some tangible element of this story. They make, year after year, the choice of spending a short though far from inconsequential amount of time at the *TFiOS* bench. The gesture, however personal, is not a purely private one; for many, these images are shared via social media, serving as one element shaping the contours of the community of readers.

This, too, is significant: *TFiOS* readers write back. They write to the author, to themselves, to each other and to the world at large. Along with the author, who has provided them with compelling stories, they have shared their own voices and images. While their interests are shared ones, their commentaries are not collected in any centralised outlet, and locating them is an iterative search process whose results shift daily. I believe that for every *TFiOS* tribute we can see online, others have doubtlessly vanished, and still more are available only to individuals and their selected connections.

Documenting the digital traces of readerly engagement with *TFiOS* uncovers immersive, multimedia reading, whether feelings for one's own paperback edition or a determined series of encounters with the story in multiple media and formats. For all this, reading remains ephemeral. The traces of readers' travels and of their testimonials to what *The Fault in Our Stars* has meant to them, left in various digital realms, are all too likely to disappear. They constitute what Kirschenbaum has called 'a new kind of archive taking shape', but that unbounded archive is fundamentally unstable.[69] Platform changes and users' decisions about their accounts signal the potential for these glimpses into readers' minds and hearts to vanish. Google's decision to re-mark its maps, Facebook users' decisions to delete their accounts in the wake of the Cambridge Analytica scandal, and the established challenge of preserving YouTube video all signal the ways that the history of this community's reading could vanish.[70] A history of contemporary reading practices, then, must pursue a documentarian role and support efforts to preserve readers' testimonies to the stories that matter to them. In this context, the fault is in our systems and our policies for preservation. Without strategies for collecting evidence of contemporary communities of readers, only chance allows these scattered voices to endure.

Notes

1. John Green recounts his creation of the award-winning title in 'Becoming a YA Writer', *Booklist*, 102:13 (1 March 2006), pp. 84–5.
2. Select reviews are available at 'Looking for Alaska', <http://www.john-greenbooks.com/looking-for-alaska> (last accessed 17 May 2018).
3. Office of Intellectual Freedom, American Library Association, 'Top Ten Challenged Books of 2016', at <https://www.oif.ala.org/oif/?p=9226> (last accessed 12 Aug. 2018); John Green, 'I Am Not a Pornographer', Vlogbrothers, 30 January 2008, at <https://www.youtube.com/watch?v=fHMPtYvZ8tM> (last accessed 17 May 2018).
4. These elements represent selected nodes in Robert Darnton's communications circuit and subsequent scholarly arguments for its modification; see Robert Darnton, 'What Is the History of Books?', *Daedalus*, 111:3 (1982), pp. 65–83; Robert Darnton, '"What Is the History of Books?" Revisited', *Modern Intellectual History*, 4:3 (2007), pp. 495–508.
5. Robert Darnton, *The Case for Books: Past, Present, and Future* (New York: Public Affairs, 2009), p. xiii.
6. Vlogbrothers, Brotherhood 2.0, 16 January 2007, at <https://nerdfighteria.info/v/qIx3h0dI4PA> (last accessed 17 May 2018).
7. Brotherhood 2.0, 22 January 2007, at <https://www.youtube.com/watch?v=Ck-dW8YGyes> (last accessed 1 May 2018).
8. Lawrence van Gelder, 'Arts, Briefly: Children's Book Award Winners', *New York Times*, 23 January 2007, available at <https://www.nytimes.com/2007/01/23/arts/23arts.html> (last accessed 17 May 2018).
9. Shailene Woodley, 'John Green: Author and Teen Whisperer', 'The 100 Most Influential People', *Time*, 23 April 2014, available at <http://time.com/collection/2014-time-100> (last accessed 17 May 2018).
10. Paul Gutjahr, 'No Longer Left Behind: Amazon.com, Reader Response, and the Changing Fortunes of the Christian Novel in America', *Book History*, 5 (2002), pp. 209–36; Christine Pawley, 'Seeking "Significance": Actual Readers, Specific Reading Communities', *Book History*, 5 (2002), pp. 143–60. Other approaches to studying present-day readers may be found in section of A. Lang (ed.), *From Codex to Hypertext: Reading at the Turn of the Twenty-first Century* (Amherst: Amherst: University of Massachusetts Press, 2012), part II: methods.
11. A. Markham and E. Buchanan, 'Ethical Decision-Making and Internet

Research: Recommendations from the AoIR Working Committee 2.0' (2012), at <https://aoir.org/ethics> (last accessed 13 August 2018).
12. Leah Price, 'Reading: State of the Discipline', *Book History*, 7 (2004), p. 318.
13. Roger Chartier, quoted in Jennifer Burek Pierce, *What Adolescents Ought to Know: Sexual Health Texts in the Early Twentieth Century* (Amherst: University of Massachusetts Press, 2011), p. 12.
14. Burek Pierce, *What Adolescents Ought to Know*, pp. 6–14.
15. Potential methodological models for online cultural studies include Danah Boyd, *It's Complicated: The Social Lives of Networked Teens* (New Haven: Yale University Press, 2014); André Brock, 'Critical Technocultural Discourse Analysis', *New Media and Society*, 20:3 (2018), pp. 1012–30; Susan Herring and Jannis Androutsopoulos, 'Computer-Mediated Discourse 2.0', in D. Tannen, H. E. Hamilton and D. Schiffrin (eds), *The Handbook of Discourse Analysis*, 2nd edition (Oxford: Wiley, 2018), pp. 127–51.
16. José van Dijck, *The Culture of Connectivity: A Critical History of Social Media* (New York: Oxford University Press, 2013).
17. Clair Kirch, 'YA Author John Green to Sign All First Editions of Next Novel', *Publishers Weekly*, 29 June 2011, available at <https://www.publishersweekly.com/pw/by-topic/childrens/childrens-authors/article/47821-ya-author-john-green-to-sign-all-first-editions-of-next-novel.html> (last accessed 13 August 2018).
18. See Young Adult Best Sellers, *New York Times*, at <https://www.nytimes.com/books/best-sellers/young-adult> (last accessed 13 May 2018) and Natalie Robehmed, '"Insurgent" and Why Young Adult Novels Make Box Office Hits', Forbes, 25 March 2015, at <https://www.forbes.com/sites/natalierobehmed/2015/03/25/insurgent-and-why-young-adult-novels-make-box-office-hits/#473e423e4bf1> (last accessed 13 May 2018).
19. Hank Green alludes to the 'TFiOS effect' in more than one Nerdfighteria census analysis video; see, for example, hankschannel, '2016 Nerdfighteria Census Analysis', YouTube, 11 October 2016, at <https://www.youtube.com/watch?v=MGacCLOLUao> (last accessed 13 August 2018).
20. Aja Romano observes that most social media commentaries antagonistic to Green's success were removed following the attention that they generated. Aja Romano, 'Young Adult Publishing and the John Green Effect', Daily Dot, 20 February 2014, at <https://www.dailydot.com/parsec/fandom/john-green-young-adult-publishing-overshadows-women-criticism> (last accessed 18 May 2018).
21. 'Conversations with Keynoters: On We Go, with John Green', *Publisher's Weekly*, 2 February 2015, p. 4; John Green, 'Accio Decade Hallows', Vlogbrothers, 17 July 2017, at <https://www.youtube.com/watch?v=T90l1QoPcuI> (last accessed 18 May 2018).
22. See the Internet Movie Database (IMDb) entry for *The Fault in Our Stars*

for a full list of nominations and awards, at <https://www.imdb.com/title/tt2582846/awards> (last accessed 18 May 2018).
23. hankschannel, '2017 Nerdfighteria Census Analysis', YouTube, 18 January 2018, at <https://www.youtube.com/watch?v=b9fS7vUP-yw> (last accessed 14 August 2018.
24. *Dear Hank and John*, Episode 132, 19 March 2018, at <https://soundcloud.com/dearhankandjohn> (last accessed 14 August 2018).
25. While WorldCat records list approximately thirty-three languages and some fifty nations where the book has been published, other sources present similar numbers to Green: Nicola Christie, 'How Did *The Fault in Our Stars* Become a Bestseller and Hollywood Hit Movie?', *Independent*, 11 June 2014, available at <https://www.independent.co.uk/arts-entertainment/books/features/how-did-the-fault-in-our-stars-a-tough-talking-book-about-two-teenagers-dying-of-cancer-become-a-9530575.html> (last accessed 7 June 2018).
26. Matthew Kirschenbaum and Sarah Werner, 'The State of the Discipline: Digital Scholarship and Digital Studies', *Book History*, 17 (2014), pp. 425, 452.
27. Ted Striphas, *The Late Age of Print: Everyday Book Culture from Consumerism to Control* (New York: Columbia University Press, 2011), pp. 15–16.
28. Gérard Genette, *Paratexts: Thresholds of Interpretation*, trans. Jane E. Lewin (New York: Cambridge University Press, 1997).
29. National Endowment for the Arts, 'To Read or Not to Read: A Question of National Consequence', March 2008, at <https://www.arts.gov/publications/read-or-not-read-question-national-consequence-0> (last accessed 18 May 2018).
30. John Green, Reddit AMA, responding to a question that begins 'Do you think you would still consider writing something outside the YA bracket?', 12 October 2017, at <https://www.reddit.com/r/tatwdspoilers> (last accessed 14 August 2018); Jonathan Alexander, 'Pedagogic, Not Didactic: Michael Cart on Young Adult Novels', *Los Angeles Review of Books*, 8 April 2018, available at <https://lareviewofbooks.org/article/pedagogic-not-didactic-michael-cart-on-young-adult-fiction> (last accessed 18 May 2018).
31. Striphas, *The Late Age of Print*, p. 12.
32. Daniel Willingham, 'Is Listening to an Audio Book Cheating?', Science and Education blog, 24 July 2016, at <http://www.danielwillingham.com/daniel-willingham-science-and-education-blog/is-listening-to-an-audio-book-cheating> (last accessed 18 May 2018).
33. John Green, 'The Future of Reading', *School Library Journal*, 56:1 (January 2010), pp. 24–8.
34. John Green, 'The Fault in Our Stars – FAQ', at <http://www.johngreenbooks.com/the-fault-in-our-stars-faq/?offset=1469564348263> (last accessed 18 May 2018).

35. Wolfgang Iser, 'The Reading Process: A Phenomenological Approach', in J. P. Tompkins (ed.), *Reader-Response Criticism from Formalism to Post-Structuralism* (Baltimore: Johns Hopkins University Press, 1980), p. 50.
36. Georges Poulet, 'Criticism and the Experience of Interiority', in Tompkins (ed.), *Reader-Response Criticism*, pp. 43, 42.
37. Iser, 'The Reading Process', pp. 57, 55.
38. Green, 'The Future of Reading'.
39. *Funky Bones* was created by Atleier Van Lieshout in 2008 and accessioned by the Indianapolis Museum of Art in 2010, as described at <http://collection.imamuseum.org/artwork/26639> (last accessed 14 August 2018). The role of Sarah Urist Green, John Green's wife, in creating the Virginia B. Fairbanks Art and Nature Park, which is now home to *Funky Bones*, is noted in her short biography for NerdCon: Nerdfighteria 2017, at <https://nerdconnerdfighteria2017.sched.com/speaker/sarahuristgreen> (last accessed 18 May 2018).
40. It should be acknowledged that, in the novel, Hazel and Gus leave the Vondelpark, where Hazel focuses on 'the creek carving a path around the huge tree, a heron standing at the water's edge, searching for breakfast amid the millions of elm petals floating in the water' (*TFiOS*, pp. 209–11).
41. A replica was created for Fox Studios, according to Kat Rosenfield, 'Hazel and Gus Are Together Again on Their Amsterdam Bench', MTV News, 21 November 2014, at <http://www.mtv.com/news/2005079/hazel-and-gus-TFiOS-bench> (last accessed 18 May 2018).
42. Posted reviews on Facebook's The Bench TFiOS Leidesegracht 4, Amsterdam, the Netherlands (Unofficial Page) (last accessed 28 April 2018) included one that noted 'it took ages to find' the bench because nothing distinguished it for those who live and work in the city.
43. H. J. Jackson, *Marginalia: Readers Writing in Books* (New Haven: Yale University Press, 2002).
44. My contention is that repainting is routine maintenance, rather than an effort to remove graffiti; see, for example, Russell Shorto's discussion of *gedogen*, or the Dutch tolerance for illegal but harmless behaviours, in *Amsterdam: A History of the World's Most Liberal City* (New York: Doubleday, 2013), p. 15.
45. I am indebted to Colleen Theisen for the linkage of fandom and performance in the context of reading *TFiOS*; personal communication, 1 April 2018.
46. Green, *TFiOS*, pp. 72–3. One set of bench pictures is available at Mak Sin Wee, 'The Fault in Our Stars Amsterdam Tour – Netherlands', Wanderlust blog, at <http://www.maksinwee.com/2015/01/the-fault-in-our-stars-amsterdam-tour.html> (last accessed 18 May 2018); another is in the present author's possession, and more can be seen by doing Google searches on 'TFiOS bench Amsterdam' or 'TFiOS bench nerdfighter' and filtering the results for images.

47. Green, *TFiOS*, p. 260. Bench images from Elise, 'Amsterdam', Wait, What? blog, 18 October 2014, at <https://elisetoday.wordpress.com/2014/10/18/amsterdam/> (last accessed 18 May 2018) include multiple quotes, adaptations and even a few graphic representations like the pipe and Gus's cigarette.
48. Photograph, May 2017, in the author's possession.
49. For instance on the *Fault in Our Stars* collage poster, available at <https://store.dftba.com/products/the-fault-in-our-stars-collage-poster-1> (last accessed 18 August 2018).
50. Roger Tagholm, 'In Amsterdam, a Bench Has Created a YA Pilgrimage', Publishing Perspectives, 21 July 2015, at <https://publishingperspectives.com/2015/07/in-amsterdam-a-bench-has-created-a-ya-pilgrimage> (last accessed 18 May 2018).
51. A brief if somewhat apocryphal history of love locks is at 'Love Locks', Wikipedia, at <https://en.wikipedia.org/wiki/Love_lock> (last accessed 18 May 2018); the *TFiOS* bench is not listed either on Wikipedia or on Amsterdam sites that discuss the locks as a local phenomenon, for example at <https://www.jlgrealestate.com/2016/04/15/amsterdams-very-own-bridge-of-love/?lang=en> (last accessed 18 May 2018). This absence suggests fans' independence in their story-telling at the bench.
52. Tagholm, 'In Amsterdam'.
53. Anne Fadiman, 'You Are There', in *Ex Libris: Confessions of a Common Reader* (New York: Farrar, Straus and Giroux, 1998).
54. For a discussion of cultural tourism and its high culture valence, see Benjamin Earl, 'Literary Tourism: Constructions of Value, Celebrity and Distinction', *International Journal of Cultural Studies*, 11:4 (2008), pp. 401–17. In this context, it should be noted that *TFiOS* is not mentioned on the City of Amsterdam tourism information site.
55. Ameesha Patel, 'Amsterdam in Five Days', Bold in Origin blog, 8 April 2017, at <https://www.boldinorigin.co.uk/2017/04/amsterdam-in-5-days_8.html> (last accessed 1 May 2018); Ameesha Patel, personal communication, 5 June 2018.
56. John Berger, *Ways of Seeing* (Penguin: New York, 1990), pp. 8, 10, emphasis added.
57. Hank Green, 'Review: the TFiOS Bench – Amsterdam', Vlogbrothers, 14 April 2017, at <https://www.youtube.com/watch?v=3_4d9xULKLU> (last accessed 18 May 2018).
58. This remark was located via the extant Google Maps site giving the pinned location of the 'TFIOS Bench'; changes to Google Maps are so routine that a Google search for 'google maps change' autocompletes as 'google maps changed again'.
59. Green, 'Review: the TFiOS Bench – Amsterdam'.
60. This remark, attributed to Andrew Peterson, is one of several available via the TFIOS Bench pin, which marks a 'reenactment site' on Google Maps, at <https://www.google.com/maps/place/TFIOS+Bench/@52.3674999,

4.8862529,15z/data=!4m5!3m4!1s0x0:0xd557ccff55cd854a!8m2!3d52.3674999!4d4.8862529> (last accessed 14 August 2018).
61. Google Maps, ibid.
62. Berger, *Ways of Seeing*, p. 7.
63. For the phrase *selfie tourism*, see Scott Reyburn, 'What the Mona Lisa Tells Us About Art in the Instagram Era', *New York Times*, 27 April 2018, available at <https://www.nytimes.com/2018/04/27/arts/design/mona-lisa-instagram-art.html> (last accessed 14 August 2018).
64. Evangeline Earl, 'My Sister Esther Inspired "The Fault in Our Stars." The Movie Is Her Sequel', *Washington Post*, 12 June 2014, available at <https://www.washingtonpost.com/opinions/my-sister-esther-inspired-the-fault-in-our-stars-the-movie-is-her-sequel/2014/06/12/504c2ca4-efef-11e3-914c-1fbd0614e2d4_story.html?utm_term=.91f628d44ccb> (last accessed 18 May 2018).
65. Green, 'The Fault in Our Stars – FAQ'.
66. American Library Association, 'Amazing Audiobooks for Young Adults' (2013), available at <//www.ala.org/awardsgrants/fault-our-stars-0> (last accessed 18 May 2018).
67. *The Fault in Our Stars*, DVD, Josh Boone, 20th Century Fox, 2014; John Green, Twitter, 1 May 2018 (last accessed 1 May 2018).
68. Matthew Kirschenbaum, 'What Is an @uthor?', *Los Angeles Review of Books*, 6 February 2015, available at <https://lareviewofbooks.org/article/uthor/#!> (last accessed 18 May 2018).
69. Ibid.
70. Nicholas Confessore, 'Cambridge Analytica and Facebook: The Scandal and the Fallout So Far', *New York Times*, 8 April 2018, available at <https://www.nytimes.com/2018/04/04/us/politics/cambridge-analytica-scandal-fallout.html> (last accessed 18 May 2018); Lindsay Mattock, Colleen Theisen and Jennifer Burek Pierce, 'A Case for Digital Squirrels: Using and Preserving YouTube for Popular Culture Research', *First Monday*, 23:1 (1 January 2018), available at <https://firstmonday.org/ojs/index.php/fm/article/view/8163/6625> (last accessed 13 August 2018).

Select Bibliography

The bibliography lists mostly print publications cited in the text as well as suggested further reading.

A New Commonplace Book; Being an Improvement on That Recommended by Mr. Locke (London: printed for J. Walker, 1799).
Adam-Smith, Patsy, *Hear the Train Blow: An Australian Childhood* (Sydney: Ure Smith, 1964).
Adam-Smith, Patsy, *Outback Heroes* (Sydney: Lansdowne Press, 1981).
Alexander, Jonathan, 'Pedagogic, Not Didactic: Michael Cart on Young Adult Novels', *Los Angeles Review of Books*, 8 April 2018, available at <https://lareviewofbooks.org/article/pedagogic-not-didactic-michael-cart-on-young-adult-fiction> (last accessed 18 May 2018).
Allan, David, *A Nation of Readers: The Lending Library in Georgian England* (London: British Library, 2008).
Allan, David, *Commonplace Books and Reading in Georgian England* (Cambridge: Cambridge University Press, 2010).
Altick, Richard D., *The English Common Reader: A Social History of the Mass Reading Public, 1800–1900*, 2nd edition (Columbus: Ohio State University Press, 1998).
Ambady, Nalini, and Robert Rosenthal, 'Half a Minute: Predicting Teacher Evaluations from Thin Slices of Nonverbal Behavior and Physical Attractiveness', *Journal of Personality and Social Psychology*, 64:3 (1993), pp. 431–41.
Ambjörnsson, Ronny, *Den skötsamme arbetaren: Idéer och ideal i ett norrländskt sågverkssamhälle 1880–1930* (Stockholm: Carlsson, 1988).
American Library Association, 'Amazing Audiobooks for Young Adults' (2013), available at <//www.ala.org/awardsgrants/fault-our-stars-0> (last accessed 18 May 2018).
Anderson, Benedict, *Imagined Communities: Reflections on the Origin and Spread of Nationalism* (London: Verso, 1991).
Anderson, R. D., *Scottish Education Since the Reformation* (Dundee: Economic and Social History Society of Scotland, 1997).
Andrews, James T., *Science for the Masses: The Bolshevik State, Public*

Science and the Popular Imagination in Soviet Russia, 1917–1934 (College Station: Texas A&M University Press, 2003).

Atwood, Roy Alden, 'The Handwritten Newspapers Project: An Annotated Bibliography and Historical Research Guide to Handwritten Newspapers from Around the World' <https://handwrittennews.com> (accessed 17 November 2017).

Auden, Wystan Hugh, *A Certain World: A Commonplace Book* (London: Faber & Faber, 1982).

Banham, Joanna, Sally MacDonald and Julia Porter, *Victorian Interior Style* (London: Studio Editions, 1995).

Barykin, V. E., 'F. F. Pavlenkov and D. I. Pisarev', *Zhurnalistika i literatura* (Moscow, 1972), p. 222.

Barykin, V. E., and V. A. Fokeev, 'F. F. Pavlenkov', in *Bibliotechnaia entsiklopediia* (Moscow: Pashkov dom, 2007), p. 778.

Baverstock, Alison, 'Online Marketing', in *How to Market Books*, 5th edition (Abingdon: Routledge, 2015), pp. 399–477.

Baxter, Lucy, *The Life of William Barnes, Poet and Philologist* (London: Macmillan, 1887).

Baym, Nancy K., 'The New Shape of Online Community: The Example of Swedish Independent Music Fandom', *First Monday*, 12:8 (2007), available at <https://firstmonday.org/article/view/1978/1853>.

Beddoe, Joe, 'Mechanics' Institutes and Schools of Arts in Australia', *Australasian Public Libraries and Information Services*, 16:3 (2003), pp. 123–4.

Bekken, Jon, 'Books and Commerce in an Age of Virtual Capital: The Changing Political Economy of Bookselling', in Roma Maria Harris and Manjunath Pendakur (eds), *Citizenship and Participation in the Information Age* (Aurora: Garamond Press, 2002), pp. 231–45.

Belanger, Terry, *Lunacy and the Arrangement of Books* (New Castle: Oak Knoll, 1982).

Bell, John, *Bell's Common-Place Book for the Pocket; Form'd Generally upon the Principles Recommended and Practised by Mr. Locke* (London: printed for John Bell, 1770).

Bell, Robert (ed.), *The Story-Teller; or, Table-Book of Popular Literature. A Collection of Romances, Short Standard Tales, Traditions, and Poetical Legends of All Nations* (London: Cunningham and Mortimer, May 1843).

Berger, John, *Ways of Seeing* (Penguin: New York, 1990).

Bergman-Carton, Janis, *The Woman of Ideas in French Art, 1830–1848* (New Haven: Yale University Press, 1995).

Berrenberg, Christian, *'Es ist deine Pflicht zu benutzen, was du weisst!' Literatur und literarische Praktiken in der norwegischen Arbeiterbewegung 1900–1931* (Würzburg: Ergon Verlag, 2014).

Bessant, Judith, '"Ferrets to Look After and Rabbits to Chase": The Rural Myth and Experiences of Young Country Australians', in R. C. Petersen and G. W. Rodwell (eds), *Essays in the History of Rural Education in Australia and New Zealand* (Casuarina: William Michael Press, 1993), p. 119.

Bibliotechnaia entsiklodepiia (Moscow: Izdatel'stvo 'Pashkov dom, 2007).

Black, Alistair, 'The Past Public Library Observed: User Perceptions and Recollections of the Twentieth-Century British Public Library Recorded in the Mass-Observation Archive', *Library Quarterly*, 76:4 (2006), pp. 450–1.

Blium, A. V., *Ocharovannye kingi: sbornik khudozhennykh proizvedenii (rasskazov, ocherkov, esse), posviashchennykh knige, chteniiu, bibliofilam* (Moscow, 1982).

Blium, A. V., *Pavlenkov v Viatke* (Kirov: Volgo-Viat. kn. izd-vo, Kirov. otd-nie, 1976).

Bogdanov, I. M., *Gramotnost' i obrazovanie v dorevoliutsionnoi Rossii i v SSSR* (Moscow, 1964).

Bogel, Ann, 'Other People's Bookshelves', 6 November 2013, at <https://www.modernmrsdarcy.com/other-peoples-bookshelves> (last accessed October 2019).

Boot, Peter, 'Towards a Genre Analysis of Online Book Discussion: Socializing, Participation and Publication in the Dutch Booksphere', *Selected Papers of Internet Research*, 12:0 (2011), at <https://spir.aoir.org/ojs/index.php/spir/article/view/9076> (last accessed August 2018).

Bourdieu, Pierre, *Distinction: A Social Critique of the Judgement of Taste* (Cambridge, MA: Harvard University Press, 1984).

Bourdieu, Pierre, *The Field of Cultural Production* (New York: Polity Press, 1993).

Boyd, Danah, *It's Complicated: The Social Lives of Networked Teens* (New Haven: Yale University Press, 2014).

Bristol, Michael D., and Arthur F. Marotti, *Print, Manuscript, and Performance: The Changing Relations of the Media in Early Modern England* (Columbus: Ohio State University Press).

Bristow, Joseph, 'Coventry Patmore and the Womanly Mission of the Mid-Victorian Poet', in Andrew H. Miller and James Eli Adams (eds), *Sexualities in Victorian Britain* (Bloomington: Indiana University Press, 1996), pp. 118–39.

Brock, André, 'Critical Technocultural Discourse Analysis', *New Media and Society*, 20:3 (2018), pp. 1012–30.

Brokaw, Cynthia, *Commerce in Culture: The Sibao Book Trade in the Qing and Republican Periods* (Cambridge, MA: Harvard University Asia Center, 2007).

Brooks, Jeffrey, 'How a Soldier Saved Peter I: A Kudzu Vine of Russia's Popular Fiction', *Russian History/Histoire Russe*, 35:2 (summer 2008), pp. 1–19.

Brooks, Jeffrey, 'How Tolstoevskii Pleased Readers and Rewrote a Russian Myth', *Slavic Review*, 64:3 (2005), pp. 538–59.

Brooks, Jeffrey, 'Laughing with the Count: Humor in *War and Peace* and Beyond', in Inessa Mezdzhibovskaya (ed.), *Tolstoy and His Problems: Views from the Twenty-First Century* (Evanston: Northwestern University Press, 2018), pp. 224–49.

Brooks, Jeffrey, 'Literacy and the Print Media in Russia, 1861–1928', *Communication*, 11 (1988), pp. 47–61.

Brooks, Jeffrey, 'Popular Philistinism and the Course of Russian Modernism', in Gary Saul Morson (ed.), *Literature and History: Theoretical Problems and Russian Case Studies* (Stanford: Stanford University Press, 1986), pp. 90–110.

Brooks, Jeffrey, 'Public and Private Values in the Soviet Press, 1921–1928', *Slavic Review*, 48:1 (spring 1989), pp. 16–35.

Brooks, Jeffrey, 'Revolutionary Lives: Public Identities in *Pravda* during the 1920s', in Stephen White (ed.), *New Directions in History* (Cambridge: Cambridge University Press, 1991), pp. 27–40.

Brooks, Jeffrey, 'Russian Nationalism and Russian Literature', in Ivo Banac et al. (eds), *Nation and Ideology: Essays in Honor of Wayne S. Vucinich* (Boulder: East European Monographs, 1981), pp. 315–34.

Brooks, Jeffrey, 'Socialist Realism in *Pravda*: Read All About It', *Slavic Review*, 53:4 (winter 1994), pp. 973–91.

Brooks, Jeffrey, 'Studies of the Reader in the 1920s', *Russian History/Histoire Russe*, 9:2–3 (1982), pp. 187–202.

Brooks, Jeffrey, *Thank You, Comrade Stalin: Soviet Culture from Revolution to Cold War* (Princeton: Princeton University Press, 2000).

Brooks, Jeffrey, 'The Breakdown in the Production and Distribution of Printed Material, 1917–1927', in Abbott Gleason, Peter Kenez and Richard Stites (eds), *Bolshevik Culture: Experiment and Order in the Russian Revolution* (Bloomington: Indiana University Press, 1985), pp. 151–74.

Brooks, Jeffrey, *The Firebird and the Fox: Russian Culture Under Tsars and Bolsheviks* (Cambridge: Cambridge University Press, 2019).

Brooks, Jeffrey, 'The Russian Nation Imagined: The Peoples of Russia as Seen in Popular Imagery, 1860s–1890s', *Journal of Social History*, 43 (2010), pp. 535–57.

Brooks, Jeffrey, 'The Young Chekhov: Reader and Writer of Popular Realism', in Damiano Rebecchin and Raffaella Vassena (eds), *Reading in Russia: Practices of Reading and Literary Communication, 1760–1930* (Milan: Ledizioni, 2014), pp. 201–18.

Brooks, Jeffrey, 'The Zemstvos and the Education of the People', in T. Emmons et al. (eds), *The Russian Zemstvo* (Cambridge: Cambridge University Press, 1982), pp. 243–78.

Brooks, Jeffrey, *When Russia Learned to Read: Literacy and Popular Literature, 1861–1917* (Princeton: Princeton University Press, 1985).

Brown, Hubert O., 'American Progressivism in Chinese Education: The Case of Tao Xingzhi', in Ruth Hayhoe and Marianne Bastid (eds), *China's*

Education and the Industrialized World (Armonk: M. E. Sharpe, 1987), pp. 120–38.

Brown, Kathryn, *Women Readers in French Painting 1870–1890: A Space of the Imagination* (Farnham: Ashgate, 2012).

Burns, Robert, *Robert Burns' Common Place Book* (Edinburgh: privately printed, 1872).

Campbell, Craig, and Helen Proctor, *A History of Australian Schooling* (Crows Nest: Allen and Unwin, 2014).

Caracciolo, Peter L. (ed.), *The Arabian Nights in English Literature: Studies in the Reception of the Thousand and One Nights into British Culture* (Basingstoke: Macmillan, 1988).

Carswell, Beth, 'Undercover: Judging People By Their Books' See <https://www.abebooks.com/books/shelves-shelf-physical-paper-snoop/judge-people-cover.shtml> (last accessed October 2019).

Casteras, Susan, *Images of Victorian Womanhood in English Art* (Madison: Fairleigh Dickinson University Press, 1987).

Catalogue of the . . . Central Lending Library. (Leeds: Goodall and Suddick, 1884).

Catalogue of the Miners' Library (Paisley: Paisley College of Technology, 1979).

Catalogue of the Principal Books in Circulation at Mudie's Select Library, January, 1865 (London: Mudie's Select Library, 1865).

Chartier, Roger, 'Texts, Printing, Readings', in Lynn Hunt (ed.), *The New Cultural History* (Berkeley: University of California Press, 1989), pp. 154–75.

Chartier, Roger, *The Order of Books: Readers, Authors, and Libraries in Europe Between the Fourteenth and Eighteenth Centuries* (Palo Alto: Stanford University Press, 1994).

Chauncey, Helen R., *Locality and State During the Chinese Republic* (Honolulu: University of Hawai'i Press, 1992).

Chen Kangqi 陳康祺 (1840–90), *Langqian jiwen* 郎潛紀聞 [*Chronicles of an Unpromoted Official*] (Beijing: Zhonghua shuju, 1984).

Cheng Benhai, *Zai Xiaozhuang* [*At Xiaozhuang*] (Shanghai: Shanghai zhonghua shuju, 1930).

Christie, Nicola, 'How Did *The Fault in Our Stars* Become a Bestseller and Hollywood Hit Movie?', *Independent*, 11 June 2014, available at <https://www.independent.co.uk/arts-entertainment/books/features/how-did-the-fault-in-our-stars-a-tough-talking-book-about-two-teenagers-dying-of-cancer-become-a-9530575.html> (last accessed 7 June 2018).

Christopher, Andrew, and Barry Schlenker, 'The Impact of Perceived Material Wealth and Perceiver Personality on First Impressions', *Journal of Economic Psychology*, 21:1 (2000), pp. 1–19.

Clark, Charles E., *Uprooting Otherness: The Literacy Campaign in NEP-Era Russia* (Selinsgrove: Associated University Presses, 2000).

Clark, Giles, and Angus Phillips, *Inside Book Publishing*, 5th edition (London: Routledge, 2014).
Clement, Michel, Dennis Proppe and Armin Rott, 'Do Critics Make Bestsellers? Opinion Leaders and the Success of Books', *Journal of Media Economics*, 20:2 (30 May 2007), p. 77.
Colclough, Stephen, 'Recovering the Reader: Commonplace Books and Diaries as Sources of Reading Experience', *Publishing History*, 44 (January 1998), pp. 5–37.
Collins, Charles Allston, 'Our Audience', *Macmillan's Magazine*, 8 (May–October 1863), p. 164.
'Commonplace Books', *Chambers's Journal*, 3 January 1880, p. 217.
Confessore, Nicholas, 'Cambridge Analytica and Facebook: The Scandal and the Fallout So Far', *New York Times*, 8 April 2018, available at <https://www.nytimes.com/2018/04/04/us/politics/cambridge-analytica-scandal-fallout.html> (last accessed 18 May 2018).
'Conversations with Keynoters: On We Go, with John Green', *Publisher's Weekly*, 2 February 2015, p. 4.
Cooper, Thomas, *Life of Thomas Cooper* (London: Hodder and Stoughton, 1872).
Corbett, Barbara, *A Fistful of Buttercups: Glimpses into a Country Childhood of the 1920s* (Kenthurst: Kangaroo Press, 1983).
Cornaby, William Arthur, *China Under the Search-Light* (London: T. Fisher Unwin, 1901).
Crawford, John C., 'Leadhills Library and a Wider World', *Library Review*, 46 (1997), pp. 539–53.
Crawford, John C., 'Reading and Book Use in Eighteenth-Century Scotland', *Bibliotheck*, 19 (1994), pp. 24–5.
Criswell, Jamie, and Nick Canty, 'Deconstructing Social Media: An Analysis of Twitter and Facebook Use in the Publishing Industry', *Publishing Research Quarterly*, 30:4 (2014), pp. 352–76.
Cryle, Denis, and Betty Cosgrove, 'The Rural Reader: An Australian Survey (1930–1970)', *Australian Library Journal*, 48:2 (1999), pp. 128–36.
Cuddy-Keane, Melba, *Virginia Woolf: The Intellectual and the Public Sphere* (Cambridge: Cambridge University Press, 2003).
Culp, Robert, *Articulating Citizenship: Civic Education and Student Politics in Southeastern China, 1912–1940* (Cambridge, MA: Harvard University Press, 2007).
Culp, Robert, 'Teaching Baihua: Textbook Publishing and the Production of Vernacular Language and a New Literary Canon in Early Twentieth-Century China', *Twentieth-Century China*, 34:1 (2009), pp. 4–41.
Daniels, M. J., '"Als ik realisme wil ga ik wel een uur uit het raam staan kijken". Een kwalitatieve en kwantitatieve analyse van Nederlandse lezersrecensies op Bol.com en Goodreads', MA thesis (Radboud Universiteit, 2016).

Darnton, Robert, *The Case for Books: Past, Present, and Future* (New York: Public Affairs, 2009).
Darnton, Robert, 'What Is the History of Books?', *Daedalus*, 111:3 (1982), pp. 65–83.
Darnton, Robert, '"What Is the History of Books?" Revisited', *Modern Intellectual History*, 4:3 (2007), pp. 495–508.
Davison, Graeme, and Marc Brodie, *Struggle Country: The Rural Ideal in Twentieth Century Australia* (Clayton: Monash University ePress, 2005).
DeFrancis, John, *Nationalism and Language Reform in China* (Princeton: Princeton University Press, 1950).
Desiaterik, V., *Pavlenkov* (Moscow: Molodaia gvardiia, 2006).
Devine, T. M., *The Scottish Nation 1700–2007* (London: Penguin, 2006).
Dianina, Katia, *When Art Makes News: Writing Culture and Identity in Imperial Russia* (DeKalb: Northern Illinois University Press, 2013).
Dimitrov, Stefan, Faiyaz Zamal, Andrew Piper and Derek Ruths, 'Goodreads Versus Amazon: The Effect of Decoupling Book Reviewing and Book Selling', paper presented at the Ninth International AAAI Conference on Web and Social Media, Oxford, 2015, available at <https://www.aaai.org/ocs/index.php/ICWSM/ICWSM15/paper/download/10557/10452>.
Dinershtein, E. A., *I. D. Sytin* (Moscow: Kniga, 1983).
Dobrenko, Evgeny, *The Making of the State Reader: Social and Aesthetic Contexts of the Reception of Soviet Literature*, trans. Jesse M. Savage (Stanford: Stanford University Press, 1997).
Dong Baoliang (ed.), *Tao Xingzhi jiaoyu xueshuo* [*The Educational Theory of Tao Xingzhi*] (Wuhan: Hubei jiaoyu chubanshe, 1993).
Dong Yuanqian and Shi Yuying (eds), *Yu Ziyi: jiaoyu lunzhu xuan* [*Yu Ziyi: A Selection of Education Treatises*] (Beijing: Renmin jiaoyu chubanshe, 1991).
Doronina, N. D., 'Brat'ia Vasnetsovy: stanovlenie', in Iu. A. Gorbunov (ed.), *Knizhnaia provintsiia: sbornik statei* (Kirov: Izdatel'skii dom Gertsenka, 2017), p. 14.
Doust, Janet, 'British Literature and Australian Identity', in Kate Darian-Smith et al. (eds), *Exploring the British World: Identity, Cultural Production, Institutions* (Melbourne: RMIT Publishing, 2004), p. 506.
Dralyuk, Boris, *Western Crime Fiction Goes East: The Russian Pinkerton Craze 1907–1934* (Leiden: Brill, 2012).
Driscoll, Beth, *The New Literary Middlebrow: Tastemakers and Reading in the Twenty-First Century* (Houndmills: Palgrave Macmillan, 2014).
Driscoll, Catherine, *The Australian Country Girl: History, Image, Experience* (Farnham: Ashgate, 2014).
Drury, Annmarie, *Translation as Transformation in Victorian Poetry* (Cambridge: Cambridge University Press, 2015).
Dryasdust (Walter Scott), *The Common-Place Book of Literary Curiosities, Remarkable Customs, Historical and Domestic Anecdotes, and Etymological Scraps* . . . (London: John Bumpus, 1825).

Dye, Jill, 'Books and Their Borrowers from the Library of Innerpeffray 1680–1850', PhD thesis (University of Stirling: 2018), available at <https://dspace.stir.ac.uk/handle/1893/28881#.XcVzTFX7SHs> (last accessed November 2019).

Dye, Renee, 'The Buzz on Buzz', *Sydney Review of Books*, 78:6 (December 2000), pp. 139–46.

Earl, Benjamin, 'Literary Tourism: Constructions of Value, Celebrity and Distinction', *International Journal of Cultural Studies*, 11:4 (2008), pp. 401–17.

Earl, Evangeline, 'My Sister Esther Inspired "The Fault in Our Stars." The Movie Is Her Sequel', *Washington Post*, 12 June 2014, available at <https://www.washingtonpost.com/opinions/my-sister-esther-inspired-the-fault-in-our-stars-the-movie-is-her-sequel/2014/06/12/504c2ca4-efef-11e3-914c-1fbd0614e2d4_story.html?utm_term=.91f628d44ccb> (last accessed 18 May 2018).

Ebbatson, Roger, 'Knowing the Orient: The Young Tennyson', *Nineteenth-Century Contexts*, 36:2 (2014), pp. 125–34.

Edinburgh (Scotland) Public Library, *Catalogue of Books in the Lending Library* (Edinburgh: Edinburgh Public Library Committee at the Darien Press, 1890).

Edmond, Lauris, *Hot October: An Autobiographical Story* (Wellington: Allen and Unwin, 1989).

Edwards, Louise, *Gender, Politics, and Democracy: Women's Suffrage in China* (Stanford: Stanford University Press, 2008).

Eklof, Ben, 'Russian Literacy Campaigns 1861–1939', in R. F. Arnove et al. (eds), *National Literacy Campaigns* (New York: Springer, 1987), p. 126.

Eklof, Ben, 'Schooling and Literacy in Late Imperial Russia', in Daniel P. Resnick (ed.), *Literacy in Historical Perspective* (Washington, DC: Library of Congress, 1983), pp. 105–6.

Engelsing, Rolf, *Zur Sozialgeschichte deutscher Mittel- und Unterschichten* (Göttingen: Vandenhoeck and Ruprecht, 1978).

Fadiman, Anne, 'You Are There', in *Ex Libris: Confessions of a Common Reader* (New York: Farrar, Straus and Giroux, 1998).

Fang Yuyan, *Fang Yuyan jiaoyu wenji: Tao Xingzhi ji qi shenghuo jiaoyu* [Collected Education Works of Fang Yuyan: Tao Zingzhi and His Life Education] (Chengdu: Sichuan jiaoyu chubanshe, 1995).

Fenner, Trevor, Mark Levene and George Loizou, 'Predicting the Long Tail of Book Sales: Unearthing the Power-Law Exponent', *Physica A – Statistical Mechanics and Its Applications*, 389:12 (2010), p. 2416.

Flint, Kate, *The Woman Reader 1837–1914* (Oxford: Oxford University Press, 1994).

Foote, I. P., 'Counter-Censorship: Authors v. Censors in Nineteenth-Century Russia', *Oxford Slavonic Papers*, 27 (1994), pp. 62–105.

Forster, E. M., *Commonplace Book* (Palo Alto: Stanford University Press, 1987).

France, Peter (ed.), *The Oxford Guide to Literature in English Translation* (Oxford: Oxford University Press, 2000).
Franklin, Michael J., *Orientalist Jones: Sir William Jones, Poet, Lawyer, and Linguist, 1746–1794* (Oxford: Oxford University Press, 2011).
Fraser, Hilary, *Beauty and Belief: Aesthetics and Religion in Victorian Literature* (Cambridge: Cambridge University Press, 1986).
Free Public Library and Museum, *Catalogue of the Lending Library* (Derbyshire: Wilkins and Ellis, 1879).
Freud, Sigmund, 'Creative Writers and Daydreaming', in *The Standard Edition of the Complete Psychological Works of Sigmund Freud*, trans. and ed. James Strachey et al. (London: Hogarth Press, 1959), vol. IX, pp. 141–54.
Friskney, Janet B., and Carole Gerson, 'Writers and the Market for Fiction and Literature', in Carole Gerson and Jacques Michon (eds), *History of the Book in Canada, Vol. III: 1918–1980* (Toronto: University of Toronto Press, 2007).
Frolova, I. I. (ed.), *Kniga v Rossii 1861–1881* (Moscow: Kniga, 1988).
Frolova, I. I. (ed.), *Kniga v rossii, 1881–1895* (St Petersburg, 1997).
Fuller, Danielle, *Writing the Everyday: Women's Textual Communities in Atlantic Canada* (Montreal: McGill-Queen's University Press, 2004).
Fuller, Danielle, and DeNel Rehberg Sedo, *Reading Beyond the Book: The Social Practices of Contemporary Literary Culture* (New York: Routledge, 2013).
Fuller, Danielle, and DeNel Rehberg Sedo, 'Suspicious Minds: Richard & Judy's Book Club and Its Resistant Readers', in *The Richard & Judy Book Club Reader: Popular Texts and the Practices of Reading* (Farnham: Ashgate, 2011), pp. 21–42.
Fuller, Danielle, DeNel Rehberg Sedo and Claire Squires, 'Marionettes and Puppeteers? The Relationship Between Book Club Readers and Publishers', in DeNel Rehberg Sedo (ed.), *Reading Communities from Salons to Cyberspace* (HoundmillsPalgrave Macmillan, 2011), pp. 181–99.
Gan Yuyuan (ed.), *Xin Zhonghua minzhong jiaoyu* [*New China Mass Education*] (Shanghai: Zhonghua shuju, 1932).
Garber, Marjorie, *Profiling Shakespeare* (New York: Routledge, 2008).
Garvey, Ellen Gruber, *Writing with Scissors: American Scrapbooks from the Civil War to the Harlem Renaissance* (New York: Oxford University Press, 2012).
Genette, Gérard, *Paratexts: Thresholds of Interpretation*, trans. Jane E. Lewin (New York: Cambridge University Press, 1997).
Girardot, Norman J., *The Victorian Translation of China: James Legge's Oriental Pilgrimage* (Berkeley: University of California Press, 2002).
Gladstone, W. E., *On Books and the Housing of Them* (New York: Dodd Mead, 1891).
Goffman, Erving, *The Presentation of Self in Everyday Life* (New York: Anchor, 1956).

Gorbunov, Iu. (ed.), *Florenty Pavlenkov. Ego zhizn' i izdatel'skaia deiatel'nost'* (Cheliabinsk: Ural Ltd, 1999).

Gosling, Sam, *Snoop: What Your Stuff Says About You* (New York: Basic Books, 2008).

Graham, Jeanine, *'My Brother and I . . .': Glimpses of Childhood in Our Colonial Past* (Dunedin: Hocken Library, University of Otago, 1992).

Grant, James, *History of the Burgh and Parish Schools* (Glasgow: William Collins, Sons and Co., 1876).

Green, John, 'Accio Decade Hallows', Vlogbrothers, 17 July 2017, at <https://www.youtube.com/watch?v=T90l1QoPcuI> (last accessed 18 May 2018).

Green, John, 'Becoming a YA Writer', *Booklist*, 102:13 (1 March 2006), pp. 84–5.

Green, John, 'I Am Not a Pornographer', Vlogbrothers, 30 January 2008, at <https://www.youtube.com/watch?v=fHMPtYvZ8tM> (last accessed 17 May 2018).

Green, John, 'The Fault in Our Stars – FAQ', at <http://www.johngreenbooks.com/the-fault-in-our-stars-faq/?offset=1469564348263> (last accessed 18 May 2018).

Green, John, 'The Future of Reading', *School Library Journal*, 56:1 (January 2010), pp. 24–8.

Grenby, Matthew, *The Child Reader, 1700–1840* (Cambridge: Cambridge University Press, 2012).

Griswold, Wendy, *Regionalism and the Reading Class* (Chicago: University of Chicago Press, 2008).

Gruzd, Anatoliy, and DeNel Rehberg Sedo, '# 1b1t: Investigating Reading Practices at the Turn of the Twenty-First Century', *Mémoires du livre*, 3:2 (2012).

Gutjahr, Paul, 'No Longer Left Behind: Amazon.com, Reader Response, and the Changing Fortunes of the Christian Novel in America', *Book History*, 5 (2002), pp. 209–36.

Hadju, David, *The Ten Cent Plague: The Great Comic-Book Scare and How It Changed America* (New York: Farrar, Straus and Giroux, 2008).

Hammond, Mary, 'Reading While Travelling in the Long Nineteenth Century', in Mary Hammond (ed.), *The Edinburgh History of Reading: Modern Readers* (Edinburgh: Edinburgh University Press, 2020), pp. 104–23.

Harrison, Henrietta, *The Making of the Republican Citizen: Political Ceremonies and Symbols in China, 1911–1929* (New York: Oxford University Press, 2000).

Hartley, Jenny, *Reading Groups* (Oxford: Oxford University Press, 2001).

Hayford, Charles, *To the People: James Yen and Village China* (New York: Columbia University Press, 1990).

He Chunshan 賀春珊 (ed.), *Fenlei chidu guanhai* 分類尺牘觀海 [*Vast Manual of Classified Correspondence*] (Shanghai: Guangyi shuju, 1921).

Heimo, Anne, 'Socialist Endeavors, Fist Presses and Pen Wars: Literary Practices of Early Finnish Migrants in Australia', in Ann-Caterine Edlund, T. G. Ashplant and Anne Kuismin (eds), *Reading and Writing from Below: Exploring the Margins of Modernity* (Umeå: Umeå University, 2016), pp. 97–114).

Hellman, Ben, *Fairy Tales and True Stories: The History of Russian Literature for Children and Young People, 1574–2010* (Leiden: Brill, 2013).

Helsinger, Elizabeth, 'Authority, Desire, and the Pleasures of Reading', in Deborah Epstein Nord (ed.), *Sesame and Lilies* (New Haven: Yale University Press, 2002), pp. 113–41.

Hennelly, Jr, Mark M., 'Jane Eyre's Reading Lesson', *ELH*, 51:4 (winter 1984), pp. 693–717.

Herring, Susan, and Jannis Androutsopoulos, 'Computer-Mediated Discourse 2.0', in D. Tannen, H. E. Hamilton and D. Schiffrin (eds), *The Handbook of Discourse Analysis*, 2nd edition (Oxford: Wiley, 2018), pp. 127–51.

Hill, Lewin, *Verse, Prose, and Epitaphs from the Commonplace Book of Lewin Hill, C.B.: 1848–1908* (London: Brown Langham, 1920).

Horn, Pamela, *Pleasures and Pastimes in Victorian Britain* (Stroud: Sutton Publishing, 1999).

Horta, Paulo Lemos, *Marvellous Thieves: Secret Authors of the Arabian Nights* (Cambridge, MA: Harvard University Press, 2017).

Houston, R. A., *Scottish Literacy and the Scottish Identity* (Cambridge: Cambridge University Press, 1985).

Huang Jinlin, *Lishi, shenti, guojia: jindai zhongguo de shenti xingcheng, 1895–1937* [*History, Body, Nation-State: The Formation of the Modern Chinese Body, 1895–1937*] (Taibei: Lianjing chuban shiye gongse, 2000).

Hunter, Kathryn, and Pamela Riney-Kehrberg, 'Rural Daughters in Australia, New Zealand, and the United States: An Historical Perspective', in Ruth Panelli et al. (eds), *Global Perspectives on Rural Childhood and Youth: Young Rural Lives* (New York: Routledge, 2007).

Hutton, Mary, 'From Millions of Cats to Te Kuia me te Pungawerewere: Children's Reading in New Zealand 1940–1990', in *Fabulous and Familiar: Children's Reading in New Zealand, Past and Present* (Wellington: National Library of New Zealand, 1991), p. 21.

Iakovenko, V. I., 'At the Market Fairs with Books: A Letter from Poltava Guberniia' (*S knigami po iarmarkam: pis'mo iz poltavskoi gubernii*), *Vestnik Evropy*, 9 (September 1894), pp. 401–19.

Iakovenko, V. I., 'O pavlenkovskikh bibliotekakh, Dolkad prochitan na 2-m publichnom sobranii 7 June 1911', in Vserossiiskii s"ezd po bibliotechnomu delu, *Trudy pervogo vserossiiskago s"ezda po bibliotechnomu delu, sostoaivshagosia v S-Peterburge s 1 po 7 iunia 1911 g. v 2-chastiakh* (Saint Petersburg, 1912), p. 25.

Iser, Wolfgang, 'The Reading Process: A Phenomenological Approach', in Jane P. Tompkins (ed.), *Reader-Response Criticism from Formalism to*

Post-Structuralism (Baltimore: Johns Hopkins University Press, 1980), p. 50.

Ivy, Anna S., 'Leading Questions: Interpretative Guidelines in Contemporary Popular Reading Culture', in DeNel Rehberg Sedo (ed.), *Reading Communities from Salons to Cyberspace* (Houndmills: Palgrave Macmillan, 2011), pp. 159–80.

Jackaman, Peter, 'The Company, the Common Man and the Library: Leadhills and Wanlockhead', *Library Review*, 29 (1980), pp. 27–32.

Jackson, H. J., *Marginalia: Readers Writing in Books* (New Haven: Yale University Press, 2002).

Jameson, Anna, *A Commonplace Book of Thoughts, Memories, and Fancies: Original and Selected* (London: Longman, 1854).

Jarrett, Christian, 'The Psychology of Stuff and Things', *Psychologist*, 26:8 (August 2013), pp. 560–5.

Javadi, Hasan, *Persian Literary Influence on English Literature* (1987; Costa Mesa: Mazda, 2005).

Jessen, A. F. N., 'Lezen als sociale activiteit: van leesgezelschap tot online lezerscommunity', MA thesis (Radboud University, 2016).

Joachim, Margaret J., 'Reading in God's Treasure House: The Societies for Purchasing Books at Leadhills and Wanlockhead, 1741–1820', unpublished MA dissertation (Institute of English Studies, School of Advanced Study, University of London, 2016).

Joachim, Margaret J., 'The Cyclopaedia Saga: Pitfalls of a Serial Publication Purchase in the Early Nineteenth Century', *Journal of the Edinburgh Bibliographical Society*, 13 (2018), pp. 81–103.

Jones, David J., 'William Herbert Ifould and the Development of Library Services in New South Wales, 1912–1942', PhD dissertation (University of New South Wales, 1993).

Judge, Joan, *Republican Lens: Gender, Visuality, and Experience in the Early Chinese Periodical Press* (Berkeley: University of California Press, 2015).

Judge, Joan, 'Science for the Chinese Common Reader? Myriad Treasures and New Knowledge at the Turn of the Twentieth Century', *Science in Context*, 30:4 (winter 2017), pp. 362–3.

Kaidanova, Olga, *Ocherki po istorii narodnogo obrazovaniia v Rossii i v SSSR* (Brussels: Imp. E. Gelezniakoff, 1939).

Kaske, Elisabeth, *The Politics of Language in Chinese Education, 1895–1919* (Leiden: Brill, 2008).

Keenan, Barry, *The Dewey Experiment in China: Educational Reform and Political Power in the Early Republic* (Cambridge, MA: Harvard University Press, 1977).

Kenecz, Peter, 'Liquidating Illiteracy in Revolutionary Russia', *Russian History*, 9:2–3 (1982), pp. 173–86.

Keys, Molly, *Bellbirds and Blowflies: A Bush Girl's Diary 1942–46* (Armidale: M. Keys, 1990).

Khapaeva, Dina, *Nightmare: From Literary Experiments to Cultural Project* (Leiden: Brill, 2012).

King, Carole, 'The Rise and Decline of Village Reading Rooms', *Rural History*, 20:2 (October 2009), pp. 163–86.

King, Peter, *The Life of John Locke: With Extracts from His Correspondence, Journals, and Common-Place Books* (London: Henry G. Bohn, 1858).

Kirschenbaum, Matthew, 'What Is an @uthor?', *Los Angeles Review of Books*, 6 February 2015, available at <https://lareviewofbooks.org/article/uthor/#!> (last accessed 18 May 2018).

Kirschenbaum, Matthew, and Sarah Werner, 'The State of the Discipline: Digital Scholarship and Digital Studies', *Book History*, 17 (2014), pp. 425–52.

'Krysta', 'The Unwritten Rules of the Blogosphere' <https://pagesunbound.wordpress.com/2017/02/14/the-unwritten-rules-of-the-blogosphere> (last accessed August 2018).

Kuhn, Philip A., 'T'ao Hsing-chih, 1891–1946, An Educational Reformer', *Harvard Papers on China*, 13 (1959), pp. 163–95.

Lang, A. (ed.), *From Codex to Hypertext: Reading at the Turn of the Twenty-first Century* (Amherst: University of Massachusetts Press, 2012).

Lederle, M. M., *Mneniia russkikh liudei o luchshikh knigakh dlia chteniia* (St Petersburg: M. M. Lederle, 1895).

Leith, Linda, 'Ladies of the Club: Spontaneous by Nature, Reading Groups Betray Few Common Traits, Except That They're Social, Self-Educating and Very Likely Sisterly', *Quill and Quire*, 61:5 (1995), pp. 8–9.

Leonard, Suzanne, '"I really must be an Emma Bovary": Female Literacy and Adultery in Feminist Fiction', *Genders*, 51 (2010).

Li Buqing 李步青 and Lian Fang 廉方, 'Xie zai Xiangguosi minzhong duwu diaocha junshou' 写在相国寺民众读物调查卷首 ('Introduction to the Investigation of Mass Reading Materials at the Xiangguo Temple), reprinted in Li Wenhai 李文海 (ed.), *Minguo shiqi shehui diaocha congbian: wenjiao shiyejuan* 民国时期社会调查丛编：文教事业卷 [*Compendium of Republican-Era Surveys: Volume on Cultural and Educational Institutions*] (Fuzhou: Fujian jiaoyu chubanshe, 2004).

Li Jinxi, *Guoyu yudong shigang* [*A Survey of the National Language Movement*] (Shanghai: Shanghai shudian, 1990).

Lianbin, Dai, 'Books, Reading, and Knowledge in Ming China', PhD dissertation (University of Oxford, 2012).

'Librarians of Reddit, do you judge people based on their books?', at <https://www.reddit.com/r/AskReddit/comments/19o4ne/librarians_of_reddit_do_you_judge_people_based_on/> (last accessed October 2019).

Long, Elizabeth, *Book Clubs: Women and the Uses of Reading in Everyday Life* (Chicago: University of Chicago Press, 2003).

Long, Elizabeth, 'The Cultural Meaning of Concentration in Publishing', *Book Research Quarterly*, 1:4 (1985), pp. 3–27.

Love, Harold, *Scribal Publication in Seventeenth-Century England* (Oxford: Clarendon, 1993).

Lovell, Stephen, *The Russian Reading Revolution: Print Culture in the Soviet and Post-Soviet Era* (London: Palgrave Macmillan, 2000).

Lukoschek, Katharina, '"Ich liebe den Austausch mit euch": Austausch über und anhand von Literatur in Social Reading-Communities und auf Bücherblogs', in Andrea Bartl and Markus Behmer (eds), *Die Rezension: Aktuelle Tendenzen der Literaturkritik* (Würzburg: Köningshausen und Neumann, 2017), pp. 225–52.

Lyons, Martyn, 'Case-Study: The Bush Book Club of New South Wales', in Martyn Lyons and John Arnold (eds), *A History of the Book in Australia 1891–1945: A National Culture in a Colonised Market* (St Lucia: University of Queensland Press, 2001), p. 204.

Lyons, Martyn, 'Reading Practices in Australia', in Martyn Lyons and John Arnold (eds), *A History of the Book in Australia 1891–1945: A National Culture in a Colonised Market* (St Lucia: University of Queensland Press, 2001), p. 349.

Lyons, Martyn, and Lucy Taksa, *Australian Readers Remember: An Oral History of Reading 1890–1930* (Melbourne: Oxford University Press, 1992).

Mackness, Constance, *Gem of the Flat* (Sydney: Angus and Robertson, 1914).

Malmstad, John E., and Nikolay Bogomolov, *Mikhail Kuzmin: A Life in Art* (Cambridge, MA: Harvard University Press, 1999).

Mandel, B. P., *Knizhnoe delo i istoriia knigi* (Moscow: Direct Media, 2014).

Manley, Keith A., *Books, Borrowers and Shareholders: Scottish Subscription and Circulating Libraries Before 1825* (Edinburgh: Edinburgh Bibliographical Society, 2012).

Markham, A., and E. Buchanan, 'Ethical Decision-Making and Internet Research: Recommendations from the AoIR Working Committee 2.0' (2012), at <https://aoir.org/ethics> (last accessed 13 August 2018).

Martens, Marianne, *Publishers, Readers, and Digital Engagement* (London: Palgrave Macmillan, 2016).

Mattock, Lindsay, Colleen Theisen and Jennifer Burek Pierce, 'A Case for Digital Squirrels: Using and Preserving YouTube for Popular Culture Research', *First Monday*, 23:1 (1 January 2018), available at <https://firstmonday.org/ojs/index.php/fm/article/view/8163/6625> (last accessed 13 August 2018).

McAleer, Joseph, *Popular Reading and Publishing in Britain 1914–1950* (Oxford: Clarendon Press, 1992).

McDowell, Kathleen, 'Toward a History of Children as Readers, 1890–1930', *Book History*, 12 (2009), p. 261.

McKitterick, David, *Print, Manuscript and the Search for Order, 1450–1830* (Cambridge: Cambridge University Press, 2003).

McRae, J., 'Urgent Reforms in Victorian education', *Teachers Journal*, 13:10 (1930), p. 368.

McReynolds, Louise, *The News Under Russia's Old Regime: The Development of a Mass Circulation Press* (Princeton: Princeton University Press, 1991).
Meeuwsen, Frank, *Bloghelden* (Amsterdam: A. W. Bruna, 2010).
Merkel-Hess, Kate, *The Rural Modern: Reconstructing the Self and the State in Republican China* (Chicago: University of Chicago Press, 2016).
Miao Feng, 'The Politics of Education: Popular Education, Quotidian Experience, and Contention over the Masses in China, 1927–1937', PhD dissertation (New York University, 2013).
Miller, Claire Cain, 'Google Deal Gives Publishers a Choice: Digitize or Not', *New York Times*, 4 October 2012, available at <http://www.nytimes.com/2012/10/05/technology/google-and-publishers-settle-over-digital-books.html> (last accessed November 2017).
Miller, Laura, *Reluctant Capitalists: Bookselling and the Culture of Consumption* (Chicago: University of Chicago Press, 2006).
Miller, Laura, 'Saving Books from the Market: Price Maintenance Policies in the United States and Europe', Roma Maria Harris and Manjunath Pendakur (eds), *Citizenship and Participation in the Information Age* (Aurora: Garamond Press, 2002), pp. 219–30.
Milton, John, *A Common-Place Book of John Milton*, ed. Alfred J. Horwood (Westminster: printed for the Camden Society, 1876).
Ming Xie, *Ezra Pound and the Appropriation of Chinese Poetry: Cathay, Translation and Imagism* (1999; New York: Routledge, 2015).
Mironov, Boris N., 'The Development of Literacy in Russia and the USSR from the Tenth to the Twentieth Centuries', *History of Education Quarterly*, 31:2 (summer 1991), p. 251.
Moore, Lindy, 'Urban Schooling in 17th- and 18th-Century Scotland', in Robert Anderson, Mark Freeman and Lindsay Paterson (eds), *The Edinburgh History of Education in Scotland* (Edinburgh: Edinburgh University Press, 2015), p. 80.
Moss, Ann, *Printed Commonplace-Books and the Structuring of Renaissance Thought* (Oxford: Clarendon Press, 1996).
Murphy, Nora A., 'Appearing Smart: The Impression Management of Intelligence, Person Perception Accuracy, and Behavior Social Interaction', *Personality and Social Psychology Bulletin*, 33:3 (2007), pp. 325–39.
Murray, Heather, *Come, Bright Improvement! The Literary Societies of Nineteenth-Century Ontario* (Toronto: University of Toronto Press, 2002).
Murray, Padmini Ray, and Claire Squires, 'Digital Publishing Communications Circuit', *Book 2.0*, 3:1 (2013), pp. 3–24.
Murray, Simone, '"Selling" Literature: The Cultivation of Book Buzz in the Digital Literary Sphere', *Logos*, 27:1 (2016), pp. 11–21.
National Endowment for the Arts, 'To Read or Not to Read: A Question of National Consequence', March 2008, at <https://www.arts.gov/publications/read-or-not-read-question-national-consequence-0> (last accessed 18 May 2018).

Nead, Lynda, *Myths of Sexuality: Representations of Women in Victorian Britain* (Oxford: Basil Blackwell, 1988).

Niall, Brenda, *Australia Through the Looking-Glass: Children's Fiction 1830–1980* (Carlton: Melbourne University Press, 1984).

Niranjana, Tejaswini, *Siting Translation: History, Post-Structuralism and the Colonial Context* (Berkeley: University of California Press, 1992).

Nolan, Sybil, and Alexandra Dane, 'A Sharper Conversation: Book Publishers' Use of Social Media Marketing in the Age of the Algorithm', *Media International Australia*, 168:1 (2018), pp. 153–6, available at <https://doi.org/10.1177/1329878X18783008>.

Office of Intellectual Freedom, American Library Association, 'Top Ten Challenged Books of 2016', at <https://www.oif.ala.org/oif/?p=9226> (last accessed 12 August 2018).

Okker, Patricia, *Our Sister Editors: Sarah J. Hale and the Tradition of Nineteenth-Century American Women Editors* (Athens: University of Georgia Press, 1995).

Pawley, Christine, 'Seeking "Significance": Actual Readers, Specific Reading Communities', *Book History*, 5 (2002), pp. 143–60.

Pawley, Christine, 'What to Read and How to Read: The Social Infrastructure of Young People's Reading, Osage, Iowa, 1870–1900', *Library Quarterly*, 68:3 (1998), pp. 276–97.

Pearce, Lynne, *Feminism and the Politics of Reading* (London: Arnold, 1997).

Pepper, Suzanne, *Radicalism and Education Reform in 20th-Century China: The Search for an Ideal Development Model* (New York: Cambridge University Press, 1996).

Peterson, Glen, *The Power of Words: Literacy and Revolution in South China, 1949–95* (Vancouver: University of British Columbia Press, 1997).

Pierce, Jennifer Burek, *What Adolescents Ought to Know: Sexual Health Texts in the Early Twentieth Century* (Amherst: University of Massachusetts Press, 2011).

Pomelov, V. B., 'Prosvetitel' i metodist nachal'noi shkoly F.F. Pavlenkov. K 175-letiu izdatelia, prosvetitelia i pedagoga-metodista', *Nachal'naia shkola*, 10 (2014), pp. 6–7.

Pomelov, V. B., 'Vklad F. F. Pavlenkova v rasvitie prosveshcheniia v Viatskoi gubernii', *Vestnik Viatskogo gosudarstvennogo universiteta* (2015), p. 125, at <https://cyberleninka.ru/article/n/pavlenkova-v-razvitie-prosvescheniya-v-vyatskoy-gubernii> (last accessed on 11 April 2018).

Porter, Dahlia, 'Poetics of the Commonplace: Composing Robert Southey', *Wordsworth Circle*, 42:1 (2011), pp. 27–33.

Posefsky, Peter C., *The Nihilist Imagination: Dmitrii Pisarev and the Cultural Origins of Russian Radicalism (1860–1868)* (New York: Peter Lang, 2003).

Potter, Ambrose George, *A Bibliography of the Rubáiyát of Omar Khayyám* (1929; Hildesheim: Georg Olms, 1994).

Potter, Jane, 'For Country, Conscience and Commerce: Publishers and

Publishing, 1914–18', in Mary Hammond and Shafquat Towheed (eds), *Publishing in the First World War: Essays in Book History* (Basingstoke: Palgrave Macmillan, 2007), p. 12.

Poulet, Georges, 'Criticism and the Experience of Interiority', in Jane P. Tompkins (ed.), *Reader-Response Criticism from Formalism to Post-Structuralism* (Baltimore: Johns Hopkins University Press, 1980), p. 42.

Pownall, Eve, 'Books and the Open Road', *Australasian Book News and Library Journal*, 1:9 (1947), p. 407.

Price, Leah, *How to Do Things with Books in Victorian Britain* (Princeton: Princeton University Press, 2012).

Price, Leah, 'Reading: State of the Discipline', *Book History*, 7 (2004), p. 318.

Price, Leah, *The Anthology and the Rise of the Novel: From Richardson to George Eliot* (Cambridge: Cambridge University Press, 2003).

Proctor, James, and Bethan Benwell, *Reading Across Worlds: Transnational Book Groups and the Reception of Difference* (Houndmills: Palgrave Macmillan, 2015).

Pugh, Sheenagh, *The Democratic Genre: Fan Fiction in a Literary Context* (Bridgend: Seren, 2005).

Qu Xingui and Tang Liangyan (eds), *Zhongguo jindai jiaoyu shi ciliao huibian: xuezhi yanbian* [*A Collection of Modern Chinese Education History Materials: The Evolution of the Education System*] (Shanghai: Shanghai Jiaoyu chubanshe, 2007).

Rackham, Rachel, 'Like a "Caged Bird": Jane Eyre's Flight to Freedom Through Imagery in *Jane Eyre*', *Criterion: A Journal of Literary Criticism*, 10:2 (2017), pp. 85–92.

Rassudovskaia, N., *Izdatel' F. F. Pavlenkov (1839–1900). Ocherk zhizni i deiatel'nosti* (Moscow: Izd. Vsesoiuznoi knizhnoi palaty, 1960).

Raty, Hannu, and Leila Snellman, 'Children's Images of an Intelligent Person', *Journal of Social Behavior and Personality*, 12 (1997), pp. 773–84.

Rawski, Evelyn, *Education and Popular Literacy in Late Qing China* (Ann Arbor: University of Michigan Press, 1979).

Raymond, Boris, 'Libraries and Adult Education: The Russian Experience', *Journal of Library History*, 16 (spring 1981), pp. 396–7.

Rayner, S. A., *Correspondence Education in Australia and New Zealand* (Melbourne: Melbourne University Press, 1949).

Reed, Christopher A., *Gutenberg in Shanghai: Chinese Print Capitalism, 1876–1937* (Honolulu: University of Hawai'i Press, 2004).

Rehberg Sedo, DeNel, 'Badges of Wisdom, Spaces for Being: A Study of Contemporary Women's Book Clubs' (School of Communication, Simon Fraser University, 2004), available at <http://summit.sfu.ca/item/8708> (last accessed November 2017).

Rich, Motoko, 'With Kindle, Publishers Give Away e-Books to Spur Sales', *New York Times*, 22 January 2010, Books section, available at <https://www.nytimes.com/2010/01/23/books/23kindle.html> (last accessed November 2017).

Richter, Virginia, and Ursula Kluwick, "'Twixt Land and Sea: Approaches to Littoral Studies', in Virginia Richter and Ursula Kluwick (eds), *The Beach in Anglophone Literatures and Cultures: Reading Littoral Space* (Farnham: Ashgate, 2015), pp. 1–20.

Robehmed, Natalie, '"Insurgent" and Why Young Adult Novels Make Box Office Hits', Forbes, 25 March 2015, at <https://www.forbes.com/sites/natalierobehmed/2015/03/25/insurgent-and-why-young-adult-novels-make-box-office-hits/#473e423e4bf1> (last accessed 13 May 2018).

Roe, Nicholas, *Fiery Heart: The First Life of Leigh Hunt* (New York: Random House, 2010).

Romano, Aja, 'Young Adult Publishing and the John Green Effect', Daily Dot, 20 February 2014, at <https://www.dailydot.com/parsec/fandom/john-green-young-adult-publishing-overshadows-women-criticism> (last accessed 18 May 2018).

Rose, Jonathan, 'Rereading the English Common Reader: A Preface to a History of Audiences', *Journal of the History of Ideas*, 53:1 (January–March 1992), p. 52.

Rose, Jonathan, *The Intellectual Life of the British Working Classes*, 2nd edition (New Haven: Yale University, 2010).

Rubakin, N. A., 'Zhurnal i chitateli', *Novyi zhurnal dlia vsekh*, no. 37 (1911), p. 120.

Sakakida Rawski, Evelyn, *Education and Popular Literacy in Ch'ing China* (Ann Arbor: Michigan University Press, 1979).

Salmi-Niklander, Kirsti, 'Crooks and Heroes, Priests and Preachers: Religion and Socialism in the Oral-Literary Tradition of a Finnish-Canadian Mining Community', in Tiiu Jaago (ed.), *Lives, Histories and Identities* (Tartu: University of Tartu, 2002), vol. I, pp. 131–58.

Salmi-Niklander, Kirsti, 'Manuscripts and Broadsheets: Narrative Genres and the Communication Circuit Among Working-Class Youth in Early 20th-Century Finland', *Folklore*, 33 (2006), pp. 109–26.

Sarbei, V. V., 'Populizator Shevchenka V. I. Iakovenko', in *Zbirnyk prats' chotyrnadtsiatoï naukovoï shevchenkivs'koï konferentsiï* (9–10 bereznia 1965 v. Poltavi) (AN URSR. In-t lit. im. T. H. Shevchenka, Kyïv, 1966), p. 221.

Schaeffer, Michel, *Het geheim van bol.com: Over dromen en doen, pionieren en groeien* (Amsterdam: Atlas Contact, 2017).

Schiffrin, André, *The Business of Books: How International Conglomerates Took Over Publishing and Changed the Way We Read* (Londo: Verso, 2001).

Scott, W. J., *Reading, Film and Radio Tastes of High School Boys and Girls* (Wellington: New Zealand Council for Educational Research, 1947).

Shirinovskaia, L. A., 'F. F. Pavlenkov i Pavlenkovskie biblioteki', *Chtenie v bibliotekakh Rossii vyp 4* (St Petersburgh: Rossiĭskaia natsional'naia biblioteka, 2004), p. 122.

Simon, Josep, *Communicating Physics: The Production, Circulation, and*

Appropriation of Ganot's Textbooks in France and England, 1851–1887 (Pittsburgh: University of Pittsburgh Press, 2011).

Slukhovskii, M. I., *Kniga i derevnia* (Moscow, 1928).

Smith, Michelle, 'Transforming Narratives of Colonial Danger: Imagining the Environments of New Zealand and Australia in Children's Literature', in Shirleene Robinson and Simon Sleight (eds), *Children, Childhood and Youth in the British World* (Houndmills: Palgrave Macmillan, 2016), p. 197.

Sokolov, V. Iu., 'Otkrytie i organizatsia deiatel'nosti pavlenkovskikh bibliotek Kievskim obshchestvom gramotnosti v 1900–1907 gg.', in Iu. A. Gorbunov (ed.), *Knizhnaia provintsiia: sbornik statei* (Kirov: Izdatel'skii dom Gertsenka, 2017), p. 104.

Southey, Robert, *Southey's Common-Place Book*, ed. John Warter Wood (London: Longman, Brown, Green and Longmans, 1850–1).

Spence, Eleanor, 'A Special Sort of Dreaming', in Michael Dugan (ed.), *The Early Dreaming: Australian Children's Authors on Childhood* (Milton: Jacaranda Press, 1980), p. 98.

Squires, Claire, *Marketing Literature: The Making of Contemporary Writing in Britain* (Basingstoke: Palgrave Macmillan, 2007).

Squires, Claire, 'Taste and/or Big Data? Post-Digital Editorial Selection', *Critical Quarterly*, 59:3 (2017), pp. 24–38.

St Clair, William, *The Reading Nation in the Romantic Period* (Cambridge: Cambridge University Press, 2004).

Stacey, Elizabeth, and Lya Visser, 'The History of Distance Education in Australia', *Quarterly Review of Distance Education*, 6:3 (2005), p. 254.

Strand, David, *An Unfinished Republic: Leading by Word and Deed in Modern China* (Berkeley: University of California Press, 2011).

Striphas, Ted, *The Late Age of Print: Everyday Book Culture from Consumerism to Control* (New York: Columbia University Press, 2011).

Tagholm, Roger, 'In Amsterdam, a Bench Has Created a YA Pilgrimage', Publishing Perspectives, 21 July 2015, at <https://publishingperspectives.com/2015/07/in-amsterdam-a-bench-has-created-a-ya-pilgrimage> (last accessed 18 May 2018).

Taylor, Joan Bessman, 'Good for What? Non-Appeal, Discussibility, and Book Groups (Part 2)', *Reference and User Services Quarterly*, 47:1 (2007), pp. 26–31.

Taylor, Joan Bessman, 'When Adults Talk in Circles: Book Groups and Contemporary Reading Practices', PhD dissertation (University of Illinois at Urbana-Champaign, 2007).

Taylor, Susan B., 'Image and Text in *Jane Eyre*'s Avian Vignettes and Bewick's *History of British Birds*', *Victorian Newsletter*, 101 (2002), pp. 5–12.

The Statistical Accounts of Scotland 1791–1845 at <https://stataccscot.edina.ac.uk/static/statacc/dist/home> (last accessed October 2019).

Thompson, John B., *Merchants of Culture: The Publishing Business in the Twenty-First Century*, 2nd edition (Oxford: Wiley, 2013).

Tinsley, Katherine, and Carl F. Kaestle, 'Autobiographies and the History of Reading: The Meaning of Literacy in Individual Lives', in Carl F. Kaestle et al. (eds), *Literacy in the United States: Readers and Reading Since 1880* (New Haven: Yale University Press, 1991), p. 226.

Todd, William Mills, 'Tolstoy and Dostoevsky: The Professionalization of Literature and Serialized Fiction', *Dostoevsky Studies*, 15 (2011), pp. 29–36.

Towsey, Mark R. M., *Reading the Scottish Enlightenment: Books and Their Readers in Provincial Scotland, 1750–1820* (Leiden: Brill, 2010).

Toynbee, Claire, *Her Work and His: Family, Kin and Community in New Zealand 1900–1930* (Wellington: Victoria University Press, 1995).

Trewby, Mary, *The Best Years of Your Life: A History of New Zealand Childhood* (Auckland: Viking, 1995).

Trigos, Ludmilla A., and Carol Ueland, 'Creating a National Biography Tradition: F. F. Pavlenkov's *Life of Remarkable People 1890–1924*', *Slavonic and East European Review*, 96:1 (2018), pp. 41–66.

Turner Shaw, Mary, 'Education of a Squatter's Daughter', in Patricia Grimshaw and Lynne Strahan (eds), *The Half-Open Door: Sixteen Modern Australian Women Look at Professional Life and Achievement* (Sydney: Hale and Iremonger, 1982), p. 291.

Turunen, Risto, 'From the Object of History to the Subject of History: The Writing Factory Workers in Finland in the Early 20th Century', in Heiko Droste and Kirsti Salmi-Niklander (eds), *Handwritten Newspapers as an Alternative Medium During the Early Modern and Modern Periods* (forthcoming).

Ushakova, I. A., 'Svetitskaia sel'saia biblioteka im. F. F. Pavlenkova – filial MKUK "Falenskaia TsB"', in *Vestnik Kirovskogo filiala Kluba IuNESKO Sodruzhestvo pavlenkovskikh bibliotek* (Kirov: Gertsenka, 2014), pp. 48–50.

van Dijck, José, *The Culture of Connectivity: A Critical History of Social Media* (New York: Oxford University Press, 2013).

van Herten, Marjolein, 'Learning Communities, Informal Learning and the Humanities: An Empirical Study of Book Discussion Groups', PhD dissertation (Open University, 2015).

Van Oostendorp, Marc, 'Carnaval der burgerrecensenten', Neder-L, no. 0709.56 (2007), at <https://www.neerlandistiek.nl/2007/09/carnaval-der-burgerrecensenten/>.

Van Putten-Brons, Suzanne, and Peter Boot, 'June is Dutch Literature Month! Online Book Reviewers and Their Role in the Transmission of Dutch Literature to the English-Speaking World', in Elke Brems, Orsolya Réthelyi and Ton van Kalmthout (eds), *Doing Double Dutch: The International Circulation of Literature from the Low Countries* (Leuven: Leuven University Press, 2017), pp. 313–27.

Van Wissen, Leon, and Peter Boot, 'An Electronic Translation of the LIWC Dictionary into Dutch', paper presented at the eLex Conference 2017,

Leiden, 2017, available at <https://elex.link/elex2017/wp-content/uploads/2017/09/paper43.pdf>.

VanderVen, Elizabeth, 'It's Time for School: The Introduction of the New Calendar in Haicheng County Primary Schools, Northeast China, 1905–1919', *Twentieth-Century China*, 32:2 (April 2007), pp. 60–83.

Vincent, David, *Bread, Knowledge and Freedom: A Study of Nineteenth-Century Working Class Autobiography* (London: Europa, 1981).

Vincent, David, *The Rise of Mass Literacy: Reading and Writing in Modern Europe* (Cambridge: Polity Press, 2000).

Vishnevskii, S. S., 'The Most Well-Read Country in the World' (1986), in Adele Barker and Bruce Grant (eds), *The Russia Reader: History, Politics, Culture* (Durham: Duke University Press, 2010), p. 627.

Vlieghe, Joachim, Jaël Muls and Kris Rutten, 'Everybody Reads: Reader Engagement with Literature in Social Media Environments', *Poetics*, 54 (2016), pp. 25–37.

Vlogbrothers, Brotherhood 2.0, 16 January 2007, at <https://nerdfighteria.info/v/qIx3h0dI4PA> (last accessed 17 May 2018).

von Geldern, James, and Louise McReynolds (eds), *Entertaining Tsarist Russia* (Bloomington: Indiana University Press, 1998).

Wagner, Robin, '"A Little Bit of Love for Me and a Murder for My Old Man": The Queensland Bush Book Club', in B. J. McMullin (ed.), *Collections, Characters and Communities: The Shaping of Libraries in Australia and New Zealand* (Melbourne: Australian Scholarly Publishing, 2010), p. 123.

Walker, Martyn, *The Development of the Mechanics' Institute Movement in Britain and Beyond* (Abingdon: Routledge, 2017).

Walker Rettberg, Jill, *Blogging* (Cambridge: Polity, 2013).

Waller, Philip, *Writers, Readers, and Reputations: Literary Life in Britain, 1870–1918* (Oxford: Oxford University Press, 2006).

Wang Cheng-hua 王正華, 'Shenghuo, zhishi, yu wenhua shangpin: wan Ming Fujian ban "Riyong leishu" yu qi shuhua men' 生活知識與文化商品： 晚明福建版'日用類書'與其書畫門 ['Daily Life, Commercialized Knowledge, and Cultural Consumption: Late Ming Fujian Household Encyclopedias on Calligraphy and Painting'], *Zhongyang yanjiuyuan jindaishi yanjiusuo jikan* 中央研究院近代史研究所集刊 41 (September 2003), pp. 1–85.

Warner, Marina, *Stranger Magic: Charmed States and the Arabian Nights* (London: Vintage, 2012).

Webby, Elizabeth, 'Not Reading the Nation: Australian Readers of the 1890s', *Australian Literary Studies*, 22 (May 2006), pp. 308–18.

Webby, Elizabeth, 'The Beginnings of Literature in Colonial Australia', in Peter Pierce (ed.), *The Cambridge History of Australian Literature* (Cambridge: Cambridge University Press, 2009), pp. 34–51.

Weiss, Lauren, 'The Literary Clubs and Societies of Glasgow During the Long Nineteenth Century: A City's History of Reading Through Its Communal Reading Practices and Productions', PhD dissertation (University of Stirling, 2017).

Weiss, Lauren, 'The Manuscript Magazines of the Wellpark Free Church Young Men's Literary Society', in Paul Raphael Rooney and Anna Gasperini (eds), *Media and Print Culture Consumption in Nineteenth-Century Britain: The Victorian Reading Experience* (Basingstoke: Palgrave Macmillan, 2016), pp. 53–73.

Williams, James, 'A Leadhills Diary for 1745, Transcribed by Miss E. M. Brown', *Transactions of the Dumfries and Galloway Natural History and Antiquarian Society*, 3rd series, 54 (1979), pp. 105–31.

Willingham, Daniel, 'Is Listening to an Audio Book Cheating?', Science and Education blog, 24 July 2016, at <http://www.danielwillingham.com/daniel-willingham-science-and-education-blog/is-listening-to-an-audio-book-cheating> (last accessed 18 May 2018).

Wilson, D. L., *Jefferson's Literary Commonplace Book* (Princeton: Princeton University Press, 2014).

Withrington, Donald J., *Going to School* (Edinburgh: National Museums Scotland, 1997).

Woodley, Shailene, 'John Green: Author and Teen Whisperer', 'The 100 Most Influential People', *Time*, 23 April 2014, available at <http://time.com/collection/2014-time-100> (last accessed 17 May 2018).

Woodside, Alexander, 'Real and Imagined Communities in the Chinese Struggle for Literacy', in Ruth Hayhoe (ed.), *Education and Modernization: The Chinese Experience* (Oxford: Pergamon Press, 1992), pp. 23–45.

Woof, Pamela, 'The Uses of Notebooks', *Coleridge Bulletin*, New Series 31 (summer 2008), 15.

Wright, David, 'Watching the Big Read with Pierre Bourdieu: Forms of Heteronomy in the Contemporary Literary Field', CRESC Working Paper No. 45 (Manchester: Centre for Research on Socio-Cultural Change: December 2007), available at <http://www.cresc.ac.uk/publications/documents/wp45.pdf>.

Wright, Judith, 'Seven Years of Correspondence School', in Geoffrey Dutton (ed.), *Snow on the Saltbush: The Australian Literary Experience* (Ringwood: Viking Press, 1984), p. 77.

Wu Huifang 吳蕙芳, *Wanbao quanshu: Ming Qing shiqi de minjian shenghuo shilu* 萬寶全書：明清時期的民間生活實錄 [*Comprehensive Compendia of Countless Treasures: [A Veritable Record] of Popular Life in the Ming and Qing Periods*] (Taipei: Hua Mulan wenhua gongzuo fang, 2005).

Wu Jen-shu and Ling-ling Lien, 'From Viewing to Reading: The Evolution of Visual Advertising in Late Imperial China', in Christian Henriot and Wen-shin Yeh (eds), *Visualizing China, 1845–1965: Moving and Still Images in Historical Narratives* (Leiden: Brill, 2013), p. 252.

Yen, James, *China's New Scholar-Farmers* (Beijing: Chinese National Association for the Mass Education Movement, 1929).

Yeo, Richard, *Notebooks, English Virtuosi, and Early Modern Science* (Chicago: University of Chicago Press, 2014).

Yohannan, John D., *Persian Poetry in England and America: A 200 Year History* (Delmar: Caravan Books, 1977).

Youngblood, Denise, *Movies for the Masses: Popular Cinema and Soviet Society in the 1920s* (Cambridge: Cambridge University Press, 1992).

Yusheng Yao, 'Rediscovering Tao Xingzhi as an Educational and Social Revolutionary', *Twentieth-Century China*, 27:2 (April 2002), pp. 88–91.

Zeising, Tobias, 'Buchblogger: Eine Analyse mit Topliste, Visualisierungen und Statistiken', at <https://www.lesestunden.de/2015/03/buchblogger-eine-analyse-mit-topliste-visualisierungen-und-statistiken>.

Zhang Kaiyuan and Tang Wenquan, *Pingfan de shensheng – Tao Xingzhi* [*Tao Xingzhi: A Confucius After Confucius*] (Wuhan: Hubei jiaoyu chubanshe, 1992).

Zhaoming Qian (ed.), *Ezra Pound and China* (Ann Arbor: University of Michigan Press, 2003).

Zhaoming Qian, *Orientalism and Modernism: The Legacy of China in Pound and Williams* (Durham: Duke University Press, 1995).

Zhou Zhenhe 周振鶴 (ed.), *Wan Qing yingye shumu* 晚清營業書目 [*Late Qing Trade Catalogues*] (Shanghai: Shanghai shudian chubanshe. 2005).

Index of Methods and Sources

America: Rehberg Sedo and Rideout (Ch. 14)
Australia: Lowe (Ch. 9)
Britain: Hess (Ch. 1), Weiss (Ch. 4), Yeates (Ch. 5), Bubb (Ch. 6)
Canada: Rehberg Sedo and Rideout (Ch. 14)
Children: Branagh-Miscampbell (Ch. 3), Lowe (Ch. 9)
China: Bubb (Ch. 5), Judge (Ch. 11), Smith (Ch. 12)
Collections: Lowe (Ch. 9), Gonzalez and Weir-Williams (Ch. 10)
Commonplace books: Hess (Ch. 1)
Iconography: Yeates (Ch. 5)
India: Bubb (Ch. 5)
Iran: Bubb (Ch. 6)
Libraries: Joachim (Ch. 2), Ueland and Trigos (Ch. 8)
Literary societies: Weiss (Ch. 4)
Middle East: Bubb (Ch. 6)
Netherlands: Boot (Ch. 13)
New Zealand: Lowe (Ch. 9)
Online book groups: Boot (Ch. 13), Rehberg Sedo and Rideout (Ch. 14), Burek Pierce (Ch. 15)
Russia: Brooks (Ch. 7), Ueland and Trigos (Ch. 8)
Scotland: Joachim (Ch. 2), Branagh-Miscampbell (Ch. 3)
Women: Yeates (Ch. 5)
Working classes: Joachim (Ch. 2,) Brooks (Ch. 7), Ueland and Trigos (Ch. 8), Judge (Ch. 11), Smith (Ch. 12)

General Index

Page numbers in italics denote display material in tables and figures. Numbers preceded by p refer to plates. Those followed by 'n' refer to notes. Chinese names are presented in uninverted form. Abbreviation 'trans.' has been used for 'translator'.

#shelfie, 215
@TFIOSBench, 305

Act for Settling of Schools (Scotland, 1696), 57–8
Adam-Smith, Patsy, 185
ALA medals *see* American Library Association (ALA) medals
Alchevskaia, Kh. D., 165
Allan, David, 2, 12, 56
Alleine, Joseph, 46
  Works, 46, 46
Allingham, Helen, *Alfred Lord Tennyson*, 107
Alsemgeest, Britt, 271
Alston, Robin, 56, 59, 60, 65
Altick, Richard D., 1, 11, 75, 162, 163
Amazon, 120, 206, 258, 260, 261, 262, 281
Ambrose, Isaac, *Prima, Media and Ultima*, 34
American Library Association (ALA) medals, 299–300
Amhurst Tyssen-Amherst, Lord William, 120
Analects of Confucius, 117, 122, 133, 243
Anderson, R. D., 57
Annemieke, 269, 270

Apple Inc., 281
Arabian Nights, 46, 117, 118, 122, 125, 130, 132
Aristotle, 12
Arnold, Edwin, 125
  Indian Song of Songs, 128
Arnold, Matthew, 20, 24
Arscott, Caroline, 110, 111
Asian classic literature, 132–3
  availability in Victorian England, 118–21
  Lubbock's list, 116–18, 124, 125, 132, 133
  readerly traces, 126–32
  scholarly vs. popular translations, 4, 121–6
Atwood, Roy Alden, 76
Austen, Jane, *Pride and Prejudice*, 8, 9–10, 25
Australia (child readers)
  agency, 180, 181
  bush book clubs, 181, 189, 190–1, 193
  class and background, 182–3
  education and schooling, 180–1, 182, 184, 185
  Gem of the Flat (Mackness), 180
  idealisation of rural life, 180, 183–4

informal networks of literature provision, 181, 191, 192
libraries, 181, 187–8, 192
parental influence on child readers, 185–6, 187
white Australia, 189
authors
book club newsletters, promotion of, 287–8, 293
digital revolution and publisher relationship, 281
Ezzulia, 265
intention and co-created meaning, 303–4
legal disputes, 281
using social media, 8, 281–2, 299–300, 301, 303, 309, 310, 311
awards, 292–3, 299–300, 301

Babel, Isaac, 151
backlist books, 8, 283, 293–4, 295
Barnard, P. M., 121
Barnes, William, 119
Barry, Brunonia, 293–4
'Basically Britt' Book Tube channel, 271
Baym, Nancy, 273
beaches, reading at, 3, 96, 109–11, 112
belles-lettres
Horace Shipp, 87
orthodox literature in China, 222
post-revolutionary Russia, 4, 147, 151
Bennet, Mary (*Pride and Prejudice*, character), 9–10, 25
Berger, John, 308, 310, 311
Bergman-Carton, Janis, 96
Bernard Quaritch Ltd, 121
Bessant, Judith, 183, 184
bestseller status, 290–3, 294
Bethnal Green Literary Society/ Friends' Hall Literary Society, 77, 84–8

Bible, The, 34, 67, 68, 79, 116, 117, 127, 203
'Billabong' novels (Bruce), 182–3
'Billy' bookcase, 213–14
Bitner, V. V., 145
Black, Alexander, 121
Blake, Sarah, *The Postmistress*, 294
Blinov, Nikolai Nikolaevich, 164, 165–6
Blium, A. V., 140
Blok, Alexander, 144
Boekensalon, 267, 279n
Boekmeter, 272, 272
Bohn, Henry G., 121, 124
bol.com, 258, 260–2, 263, 267, 272, 272, 273, 274
book blogs, Netherlands, 258, 262–5, 267, 268, 269–70, 272, 272, 273, 274
'Book Club Classifieds' (Penguin book club newsletter), 289
book club newsletters, 7–8, 280, 294–5
backlist book promotion, 8, 283, 293–4, 295
bestseller status, 290–3
book clubs as social events, 285–6
digital environment, 280–2
gendered readers, 286–7
language, 283, 287, 288, 289–93, 294
long tail sales, 280, 281, 293
manufactured and idealised reader, 7–8, 280, 283, 287, 292, 293
Novel Ideas dataset contents of, 280, 283–4
promoting authors, 287–8
promotional emails, 283
reader communities, 7, 288–9, 294
book clubs
bush book clubs, 5, 181, 183, 189–91, 192, 193
defined, 284

genre, 285
middlebrow readers, 200, 284–5, 286, 289, 291–2, 293
social networking sites, 267, 270
see also book club newsletters
book collections
 aesthetics, 199, 210–12
 and designations of high-to-lowbrow, 198–200
 impression formation, 199, 208–10
 Pepys, 6, 201
 private versus public display, 5, 198, 205–10, 214–15
 utility, 199, 212–14
 and the working class reader, 202–3, 204
 see also libraries
book discussion forums, 258, 265–6, 272, *272*, 274, *274*, 275
'booksandquills' Book Tube channel, 270–1
booksellers
 Amazon, 120, 206, 258, 260, 261, 262, 281
 Asian classic literature, 119, 120, 121, 124
 Chinese bookstalls, 222, 223, 228–32
 F. F. Pavlenkov, 160
 independent, 214
 long tail sales, 280, 281, 293
 miners' Societies for Purchasing Books, 30, 40–2, *41*, 43, 44–5, 51
 and the private library, 201–2, 210
 Russia's literacy transition, 140
 websites (book reviews), 258, 260–2, 263, 267, 272, *272*, 273, 274, *274*
BookTube, 270–1
book wheels, 12
Bright, John, 120
Brinsmead, Hesba, 187
Bristol, Micheal, 89

Brontë, Charlotte, *Jane Eyre*, 103, 104–5
Brooks, Geraldine, *People of the Book*, 293
Brooks, Jeffrey, 157–8
Brown, Kathryn, 104, 111
Bruce, Mary Grant, 182–3, 187
Brunton, Mary, *Discipline*, 41
Bukharin, Nikolai, 147, 151
bulletin-board-style forums, 258, 265–6, 272, *272*, 274, *274*, 275
burgh schools, 2, 57, 58, 60
Burns, Robert, 18–19, 47
Burton, Richard
 Arabian Nights translation (*The Book of the Thousand Nights and a Night*), 125
 Vikram and the Vampire, 124
bush book clubs, 5, 181, 183, 189–91, 192, 193
Byron, George Gordon (Lord Byron), 26n, 118, 123
 'The Destruction of Sennacherib', 126
 The Giaour, 129

Canada, 282, *283*, 292–3
Carpaccio, Vittore, *The Dream of St Ursula*, 101–2
Carswell, Beth, 210
Casteras, Susan, 98, 99
CCP *see* Chinese Communist Party (CCP)
censorship
 anthologies and literary annuals, 11
 by parents, 186–7, 192
 Lady Chatterley's Lover, 204
 libraries and bush book clubs (rural Australia and New Zealand), 181, 188, 191, 192, 193–4
 Russia, 4, 138, 146, 149, 150, 152, 161, 164, 165, 166–7

Chabon, Michael, *Telegraph Avenue*, 288
Champion, Joseph, *Shahnameh* (trans.), 121
charity schools, 2, 58, 61, 64, 67, 70, 71
Chartier, Roger, 11–12, 300–1
Chaucer, Geoffrey, 'The Miller's Tale', 201
Chekhov, Anton, 4, 143, 144, 145, 146, 171
Chen Haozi, *Huajing (Mirror of Flowers)*, 226
Cheng Benhai, 245
Cherkasov, V. D., *159*, 164, *165*, 170
child readers
  Asian classic literature, 122, 125
  comics, 186–7, 203–4
  education reforms in Tsarist Russia, 138–9
  illustrated serial books in China, 231
  literacy in eighteenth century Scotland, 35
  in rural Australia and New Zealand, 180–94
  schoolboy magazines, 84
  see also mothers; school libraries
China
  Chinese literature and the English general reader (1845–1915), 117, 122, 123, 125, 129, 132, 133
  common readers, defined, 219
  literacy rates, 221–2
  literacy and the Rural Reconstruction Movement, 6, 238–50
  model readers, 218, 219, 223
  Qing period, 241
  reading primers, 222, 231, 239, 244, 248
  reading spaces, 219, 228–32
  Tianjin Binhai Library 211, p7
  wanbao quanshu (comprehensive compendia of myriad treasures) books, 6, 219–27, 231, 232
Chinese Communist Party (CCP), 249, 250
Christopher, Andrew, 208
Chukovsky, Kornei, 144, 149–50
Cicero, 12, 13, 200–1
citizenship (China), 6, 218, 240–1, 242–3, 246, 247, 248, 249, 250
City Temple Literary Society, 85
close reading, 23, 24
Clouston, W. A., *Arabian Poetry for English Readers*, 124
coastal resorts, reading at, 3, 96, 109–11, 112
Colclough, Stephen, 126–7
Coleman, Lauren, 211
Collins, Suzanne, *The Hunger Games*, 5, 198
comics, 186–7, 203–4
commonplace books, 1–2
  and classic rhetoric, 12
  compilation by poets, 10, 12
  and knowledge, 9–10, 11, 12, 13, 14, 16–17, 20–5
  Locke's method, 11, 14–16, 18, 24
  marketing of, 11, 16–20
  readerly traces of Asian Classic literature, 4, 126–30, 132
Communist Party (Chinese, CCP), 249, 250
Confucius
  Chinese literary canon, 219, 238, 241, 242, 243, 244, 250
  and the English general reader (1845–1915), 117, 122, 125, 129, 133
cookbooks, 5, 286
Cooper, Thomas, 122
Cope, Charles W., *Life Well Spent* (Cope), 98, 99, 100
Corbett, Barbara, 185–6

correspondence schooling (Australia and New Zealand), 180–1, 182, 184, 185
Costello, Louisa, *The Rose Garden of Persia*, 3, 123–4, 125
Cottage, Samuel, 87
Crawford, Katherine, 42, 43
Crimezone, 265, 266–7
criticism *see* literary criticism

daily-use literature *see wanbao quanshu* (*comprehensive compendia of myriad treasures*)
Dalziel, Andrew, 33, 34
Dalziel family, 33
Dalziel, John, 33, 34
Darmesteter, James, *Zend-Avesta* (ed. and trans.), 127
detective fiction, 145, 146, 147, 151
Devine, Tom, 58
Dewey, John, 239, 243, 244
Dickens, Charles
　book display of, 211–12
　in George Heriot's Hospital School library, 61
　portrait of, 107
　publication in Russia, 169
Dickinson, William, 41, 42
didactic texts *see* literary guidebooks; Lubbock's list
digital revolution, 281, 287; *see also* book club newsletters; online book discussion (Netherlands)
discussion forums, 258, 265–6, 272, 272, 274, 274, 275
Disraeli, Benjamin, 130
Disraeli, Isaac, 13–14
dizzie, 266, 272
Dobrenko, Evgeny, 157
Donaldson, James, 62–3
Donaldson's Hospital School library, 58, 62–3, 67–8
Dostoevsky, Fyodor, 140, 142, 143, 144, 146

Dow, Alexander, *Bahar-i-Danish* (trans.), 123
Driscoll, Beth, 284–5, 289
Dryasdust, Jonas (character created by Sir Walter Scott), 13, 16
Du Fu, 122
Dumfries, Margaret, Countess of, 42, 43
'Dutch Studies' weblog ('Neerlandistiek', Van Oostendorp), 264
Dutton, Edmund, 87

Earl, Esther, 300, 311
Earl, Evangeline, 311
Easley, Alexis, 75, 88
Eastern literature *see* Asian classic literature
Eastwick, Edward, 120
e-books, 205, 206, 210, 214–15, 281, 282
e-commerce, 260, 281, 293
Edis, Robert, *Decoration and Furniture of Town Houses*, 106
Edmond, Lauris, 183, 186–7
education
　Chinese bookstalls, 228–9, 230, 231
　civil service examination system (China), 219, 222, 241
　commonplace books, 9–10, 11, 12, 13, 14, 16–17, 18, 20–5
　correspondence schooling (Australia and New Zealand), 180–1, 182, 184, 185
　Elementary Education Act (England and Wales, 1870), 116
　London literary societies, 3, 75, 79, 84–5, 88
　Lubbock's list, 116–17, 118
　mutual improvement and the reading societies of Scottish lead miners, 31, 44, 48–9, 51
　post-revolutionary Russia, 4, 157

Russia's pre-revolutionary period, 138–9, 143–5, 162–3
Scotland, 35, 57–9
see also literacy; schools
Education Act (Scotland, 1872), 57
Egg, Augustus, *Past and Present*, 98, 99, 102
Eklof, Ben, 162–3
Elementary Education Act (England and Wales, 1870), 116
Elgort, Ansel, 307
elite readers *see* highbrow literature
Ellis, Sarah, 100
Elzevier, Louis, 201
England *see* London literary societies
eroticism, visual depictions of women readers 104, 107, 108, 110, 111, p4
Erskine, Mary, 63
Ethiopia, 137
Everyman's Library, 5, 202–3, 204
Eyre, Jane (*Jane Eyre*, character), 3, 103, 104–5
Ezzulia, 265–6, 272, 272, 274, 274

Facebook
    Cambridge Analytics scandal, 312
    The Fault in Our Stars bench, 308, 310, 312
    online book discussion (Netherlands), 261, 266, 267, 268–9, 270, 272, 273–4
Fadiman, Anne, 307–8
Fang Yuyan, 249
Fatchen, Max, 187
faux books, 211–12
Febvre, Lucien, 1
Fielding, Henry, 48
    Tom Jones, 38, 203
Field, The (*Niva*) magazine, 142, 143
Firdausi, 129, 130
    Shahnameh (*Epic of Kings*,), 117, 118, 121, 124
FitzGerald, Edward, 3, 120, 131

FitzGerald, R., 129, 130
Flint, Kate, 96, 97, 108
folk tales, 91, 140, 141
Ford, Jamie, 288
Freud, Sigmund, 207
Friends' Hall Literary Society/ Bethnal Green Literary Society, 77, 84–8
Frith, William Powell
    Charles Dickens, 107
    Derby Day, 111
    The Railway Station, 111
    Ramsgate Sands 110-111, p4
Furness, H. H., 131

Galland, Antoine, 122
Gall, Franz Joseph, 199
Ganot, Adolphe, physics textbooks, 158–60
gentlemen's libraries, 48, 106, 120, 201–2; *see also* household libraries
George Heriot's Hospital School library, 57, 58, 61–2, 64, 70
Gibb, E. J. W., 125
Gibbon, Edward, *Decline and Fall of the Roman Empire*, 129
Gladstone, William, 212–13, 214
Gladwin, Francis, 121
Globe and Mail bestseller lists, 290, 291
Goeken, Paul (Suzanne Vermeer), 265
Goffman, Erving, 210
Gogol, Nikolai, 143, 144, 169
Goldsmith, Oliver, *The Vicar of Wakefield*, 38, 47
Goodreads, 258, 261, 262, 263, 266, 267, 269–70
Google
    book industry consolidation, 281
    Fault in Our Stars bench (Google Maps), 309, 310, 312
    online book discussion, 259, 263
Gorbunov, Iunii, 172

Gorky, Maxim, 139, 144, 170
Gosling, Sam, 209
Gracie, John, 41, *43*
Graham, Jeanine, 182
grammar school libraries, 2, 58–60, 62, 66, 68–70, 71
Grant, James, 58
Green, Hank (Vlogbrothers), 8, 299–300, 301, 302, 303, 309, 310, 311
Green, John
   An Abundance of Katherines, 299
   Looking for Alaska, 299
   The Fault in Our Stars (Green), 301–313
   videoblogging, 8, 299–300, 301, 303, 309, 310, 311
Greg, W. R., 104
Griendt, Femke van der, 263, 264–5
Griffith-Jones, Mervyn, 203, 204
Griffiths, Morwena, 105
Griffiths, R. T. H., *Rámáyan of Válmíki*, 118
Grunberg, Arnon, *Tirza*, 266

Hackett, J. T., 126
Hadley, Arthur, 84–5, 87, 88
Hafez (Hafiz), 121, 122, 123, 128
Handwritten Newspaper Project, 76
Harbour, Robin, 31
HarperCollins 283, *283*, 288, *290*, 291, 292, 293, p10, p12
Hartley, Jenny, 284
Hartman, Corine, 265
Hart, Mrs (of Castlemilk), 65
Hazlitt, William, 10
Hebban, 265, 266, 267–8, 272, *272*, 273
Heijne, Bas, 268
Heinemann, 132
Hemans, Felicia, 'Last Constantine, The', 129
Henderson, John, 37, 39, 40, *42*, 44

Henshall, J. H., *Thoughts*, 107
Herald of Learning (*Vestnik znaniia*), 143–144, 145
Herbert, A. P., 199
Herni, Eric, 265
Hichens, Robert, *The Garden of Allah*, 132
highbrow literature
   Battle of the Brows, 200
   bestseller status, 291
   book club aspirations, 291–2
   bookshelf display and impression management, 198, 205–6, 208–9, 210, 211, 214
   China, 218, 219, 223, 238, 241, 242, 250
   defining middlebrow, 199, 284
   etymology, 198, 199
   intelligence, 198, 199, 214
   Russia's literacy transition, 142, 143, 144, 163
Hill, Lewin, 128, 129
Hill, Peter, 40–1, *41*, 42, 44–5
Hindu epics, 118
Hollander, Loes den, 265
Horncastle, F., 121
Horsley, John Callcott, *A Pleasant Corner*, 103
hospital school libraries, 2, 57, 58, 61–4, 67–8, 70
Hou Guangdi, 227
household libraries, 48, 96, 103, 105, 106–9, 201–2
Houston, R. A., 57
Huang Yanpei, 243, 244
Hunt, Leigh, 17, 23–4, 123
   The Town (Hunt), 17
Hunt, William Holman, *The Awakening Conscience*, 100
Hu Shi, 243

Iakovenko, V. I., 170, 171, 172
Iakovlevich, Fedor, 158
Idioot, De ('The idiot') Book Tube channel, 271

Iedereenleest (Everybody reads) Facebook group, 268
Ifould, William Herbert, 188
IKEA 'Billy' bookcase, 213–14
Ilf, Ilya, 151
indexes, commonplace books, 12, 15–16, *15*, 18
Instagram, 264–5, 268
intelligence
  bookshelf display and impression management, 5, 198, 200, 205–6, 208–9, 210, 211, 214
  child readers (rural Australia), 180, 186
  high and lowbrow designation, 198, 199, 214
  see also education
interior spaces (Victorian women readers), 96, 97, 111
  disordered households, 100–2
  household libraries, 96, 103, 105, 106–9
  motherhood and domesticity, 98–101, 102
  solitary reading, 102–6, 107
internet *see* book club newsletters; online book discussion (Netherlands); social media
Iser, Wolfgang, 304
Islington Presbyterian Church Young Men's Association, 76–7, 78, 80–2

Jameson, Anna, 20, 21, 22–3, 24
Jamestown (later Westerkirk) library, 30–1, 44–5, *45*
Jami, *Haft Awrang (Seven Thrones)*, 120
Jane Eyre (Brontë), 3, 103, 104–5
Japanese literature, 4, 122, 124, 131
Jarrett, Christian, 209
Johnson, Samuel, 1
  dictionary of, 12
Johnston, Bryce, *Commentary on the Revelation of St John*, 47, *47*

Jones, William, 119, 121, 123, 129
journals *see* periodicals
Jude, D. H., 130
Julien, Stanislas, *The Chalk Circle* (trans.), 121
juvenile libraries, 55, 60, 66, 69

Kabir, 4, 131
Kaestle, Carl F., 183
Kaifeng bookstall survey (1934), 228–9, 231
Kalidasa, *Sakuntala*, 117, 118, 121, 125
Kashefi, *Anvār-i Suhaylī (Lights of Canopus)*, 120, 128
Keats, John, 10
  'Eve of St Agnes, The', 23–4
Kerr, Robert, 106
Keys, Molly, 183–4
Khayyam, Omar, *Rubáiyát of Omar Khayyám*, 3, 120, 130–2
Kindle books, 206, 281
King, Andrew, 75, 88
King, Peter, 18, 20
Kirschenbaum, Matthew, 302, 311, 312
Kittredge, George Lyman, 127
Kluwick, Ursula, 111
Koran (Qur'an), 117, 118, 125, 128
Krupskaia, N. K., 157

LA Times bestseller lists, 290, 291
Laing, Gilbert, *43*, 50
Laing, Samuel, *43*, 44
language
  book club newsletters (North America and Canada), 283, 287, 288, 289–93, 294
  Chinese vernacular, 223, 241–2, 243, 244, 250
  for commonplace books, 13, 16, 18
  creative writing as play, 207
  Dutch weblogs, 269–70
  Ethiopia, 137

London literary society
  magazines, 79, 81
  poetic, 24
  Russia's literacy transition, 138, 141, 147, 148, 152
  school library purchases (Scotland), 59, 60, 68, 69
  Scottish education system, 35, 58, 60
Latin
  commonplace books, 13, 16, 18
  school library purchases (Scotland), 60, 68, 69
  Scottish education system, 35, 58, 60
Laurie, John, 38
Lavrov, Petr, 160, 170
Lawrence, D. H., *Lady Chatterley's Lover* 204, p6
lead miners (Scotland)
  terms of employment, 33–4
  see also Society for Purchasing books in Leadhills; Society for Purchasing books in Wanlockhead
Leadhills Miners' Library *see* Society for Purchasing books in Leadhills
Lederle, M. M., 139–40
Leestweeps ('Reading tweeps'), 268
Legge, James, 119, 122
Lenin, Vladimir, 146, 147, 148, 157
Leonard, Suzanne, 105
Leslie, C. R., *The Library at Holland House*, 107
Leveen, Lois, *The Secrets of Mary Bowser*, 293–4
Li Po, 122
libraries
  Asian literature, 120, 122, 132, 133
  commonplace book availability, 20, 23
  in France, 160
  household, 48, 96, 103, 105, 106–9, 201–2

Leighton (Dunblane), 60
miners' *see* Society for Purchasing books in Leadhills; Society for Purchasing books in Wanlockhead; Westerkirk Parish Library
Nolinsk Library, memorial exhibition dedicated to F. F. Pavlenkov 173, p5
Pavlenko's reading rooms, 5, 170–1, 172–3
  and reading rooms in China, 228, 230–1
  rural Australia and New Zealand, 5, 181, 187–9, 192
  Soviet policy enforcement, 150–1
  Westerkirk Parish library, 30–1, 44–5, 45
  see also book collections; school libraries
literacy
  and the Chinese Rural Reconstruction Movement, 6, 238–50
  defining China's common reader, 219
  Ethiopia, 137
  non-Western nations, 6
  Pavlenkov's literacy project, 5, 158, 160, 163, 164–73
  primers, 164–7, 168, 222, 231, 239, 244, 248
  rural Australia and New Zealand, 182, 185
  Scotland, 35, 49, 57
  in the Soviet Union, 4, 138, 147, 157
  Tsarist Russia, 4, 5, 138, 139, 143, 157–8, 162–3, 168, 170, 171
  Xu Xu's Shanghai survey (1933), 221–2
  see also education
literary annuals, 11, 78
literary awards, 292–3, 299–300, 301

literary criticism
  commonplace books, 10, 22–4
  London literary society magazines, 79, 81, 82, 86, 87
  online discussion of books, 7, 259, 264
literary guidebooks, 3, 96, 97, 98, 102–3, 105–6; *see also* Lubbock's list
literary societies, 77; *see also* London literary societies
literary theory, 304
Littlejohn, Linda, 186
'Lives of Remarkable People' series (Pavlenkov), 5, 160, 169–70, 172
Lobley, James, *The Demurer*, 105
Locke, John, 11, 14–16, 19, 20, 24, 25, 79, 129
Locker-Lampson, Frederick, *Patchwork*, 2, 12
London literary societies, 3, 75–8, 88–9
  Friends' Hall Literary Society/Bethnal Green Literary Society, 77, 84–8
  Islington Presbyterian Church Young Men's Association, 76–7, 78, 80–2
  Park Church Literary Society, 76, 77–80
  St Martin's Literary Society, 77, 83–4
London Presbyterian Literary Societies Union, 78
long tail sales, 280, 281, 293
Longman & Co., 40, 124
Loudon, Flora Campbell, Countess of, 42, 43
Lovell, Stephen, 157
lowbrow literature
  in the Battle of the Brows, 200
  book club selections, 285
  comics, 203–4
  defining middlebrow, 199, 284
  display/hiding, 205, 206, 208, 211
  ebooks, 207, 214–15
  etymology, 198, 199
  novels, 4, 97, 145–6, 151, 203, 205, 214–15
Lubbock's list, 116–18, 124, 125, 132, 133
lubki, 140, 141, 158
'lucid reading', 205
Lufei Kui, 242
Lukoschek, Katharina, 259
Lunacharsky, Anatoly Vasilyevich, 149, 150
Lunkevich, V. V., 167–8
Lyons, Martyn, 181, 182–3, 186

Macé, Jean-François, 160, 171
Mackness, Constance, *Gem of the Flat*, 180
magazines
  bush book clubs, 189, 191
  for children (rural Australia and New Zealand), 186–7, 189
  Lees Magazine, 261, 267
  Pavlenkov's contributions to, 158
  see also manuscript magazines; periodicals
Mahabharata, 117, 118, 119
Main, Barbara York, 184
male readers (artistic depiction), 16, 104, 105
Mandelstam, Osip, 151
manuscript magazines, 3, 75–8
  Friends' Hall Literary Society/Bethnal Green Literary Society, 77, 85–8
  Friends' Hall Literary Society MSS Magazine, 77, 84, 85–8
  Islington Presbyterian Church Young Men's Association, 80–2
  Park Church Literary Society, 78–80
  and print culture, 76, 88–9

St Martin's Review (St Martin's Literary Society), 77, 83–4
Mao Dun, 229, 231
marginalia
  English responses to Asian literature, 4, 126, 131
  TFiOS bench, 305–8
Marks, A. F., 143, 168
Marotti, Arthur, 89
Martin, Henri Jean, 1
Martineau, Harriet, *Eastern Life*, 128
Martineau, R. B., *The Last Chapter*, 102, 103
McCall, George, 33
McKitterick, David, 89
McRae, J., 186
Meason, Gilbert, 42, 43, 44
Mechanics Institutes, 188; *see also* Working Men's College (Great Ormond Street)
Meinen-Benjamins, Karin, 268–9
Merezhkovsky, Dmitry, 143, 144
Mess Mend series, 151–2
Miao Feng, 249
middlebrow literature
  book clubs, 200, 284–5, 286, 289, 291–2, 293
  Chinese *wanbao quanshu*, 6, 219–27, 231, 232
  defined, 199–200, 284
  Pavlenkov's literacy project, 167–70
  Priestley and the Battle of the Brows, 200, 202
Mill, John Stuart, 160
'Miller's Tale, The' (Chaucer), 201
Milton, John, 9, 19
miners' libraries (Scotland) *see* Society for Purchasing books in Leadhills; Society for Purchasing books in Wanlockhead; Westerkirk Parish Library
Mitford, A. B., *Tales of Old Japan*, 124

modernism, Russian, 144, 145, 146, 154
Monier-Williams, Monier, 125
Moore, Lindy, 58
Moore, Thomas, 123
  Lalla Rookh, 123, 126
Morgan, Jane Norton, 131–2
Morrow, Albert (poster for *The New Woman*), 102
Morton, John, 75, 88
mothers
  and children's reading, 99–100, 186–7, 191, 193
  visual depictions of 98-101, 99, 102, p1
Mozoomdar, Protap Chunder, 131
Mudie's Select Library, 20, 28n
Muir, John, 59
Munro, D., 60
Murphy, Nora, 208–9
Murray, Heather, 76
Murray, John, 125
mutual improvement societies *see* London literary societies; Society for Purchasing books in Leadhills; Society for Purchasing books in Wanlockhead; Westerkirk Parish library

Naidu, Sarojini, 128
National Association for the Promotion of Commoners' Education (China), 239, 244
NDC/VBK, 267
'Neerlandistiek' weblog ('Dutch Studies', Van Oostendorp), 264
Nell, Victor, 205
Nerdfighteria censuses, 301–2
Netherlands
  The Fault in Our Stars bench, 301, 305–11, 312
  see also online book discussion (Netherlands)
New Journal for All (*Novyi zhurnal dlia vsekh*), 143–144

Newman, Jeremiah, *The Lounger's Common-Place Book*, 16–17, 20
Newman, John Henry, 20, 129
New South Wales Bush Book Club, 189, 190, 191
New York Times
  bestseller list, 290, *290*, 291, 292, 294, 301
  book categorisation, 300
New Zealand (child readers)
  agency, 181
  bush book clubs, 181, 190
  class, 182
  education and schooling, 180–1, 182, 184
  idealisation of rural life, 180, 183, 184
  informal networks of literature provision, 181
  libraries, 181, 188, 190, 192
  parental influence, 185, 186–7
newsletters *see* book club newsletters
Nicholls, C. W.
  A Seaside Romance, 109
  Courtship on the Beach, 109
Nicolson, Harold, 200
Nicol, William, *Quiet* 98, 100, p1
Nieuwenhuis, Corina, 268–9
Nimmo, Hay and Mitchell, 130
nl.kunst.literatuur, 258, 259–60
Nolinsk Library, memorial exhibition dedicated to F. F. Pavlenkov 173, p5
North America
  Comics Code, 203–4
  see also book club newsletters
Novel Ideas study *see* book club newsletters
novels
  book collection presentation, 198, 205, 207–8, 215
  child readers in rural Australia and New Zealand, 180, 185–6, 188, 189, 192

depictions of rural Australia and New Zealand, 182–3
Freud on, 207
Lady Chatterley's Lover (Lawrence) 204, p6
in Leadhills Society for Purchasing books, 37, 38, *38*, 39, *39*, 48
Pride and Prejudice (Austen), 8, 9–10, 25
Protestant objections to, 203–4
in Russia, 140–3, 144, 145–6, 147, 151–2, 169
in school libraries (Scotland), 61, 62, 68–9
The Fault in Our Stars, 301–313
Victorian women readers, 3, 97, 100, 101, 108, 109
in Wanlockhead Society for Purchasing books, 38, *38*, 39, *39*, 40, 41, *43*, 44, 48, 51
in Westerkirk Parish library, 45
women's reading's depicted in *Jane Eyre*, 3, 103, 104–5
see also book club newsletters; online book discussion (Netherlands)

Okker, Patricia, 97–8, 106
Ong, Walter J., 89
online book discussion (Netherlands)
  book-based social networking sites, 258, 265, 266–8, 272, *272*, 273
  book weblogs, 258, 262–5, 267, 268, 269–70, 272, *272*, 273, 274
  booksellers' websites (bol.com), 258, 260–2, 263, 267, 272, *272*, 273, 274, *274*
  bulletin-board-style forums, 258, 265–6, 272, *272*, 274, *274*, 275
  general-purpose social media, 258, 264–5, 266, 268–9, 270, 272, 273–4

Goodreads, 258, 261, 262, 263, 266, 267, 269–70
Netherlands, book-based social networking sites, 258, 265, 266–8, 272, 272, 273
Usenet groups (nl.kunst.literatuur), 258, 259–60
videoblogging, 270–1
Opdop, Martin *see* van Oostendorp, Marc
oriental literature *see* Asian classic literature
Orsel, Victor, *Le Bien et le Mal*, 102
Osborn, Emily, *The Governess*, 102
Otto family, 35, 44, 45, 45

Page, Doris, 193
Palmer, E. H., 125, 128
Palmer, Thomas Ambrose, 3–4, 130–1, 132
parish schools, 2, 55, 57–8, 62, 64, 64–5, 70
Park Church Literary Society, 76, 77–80
Pastukhov, N. I., 145
pauper (charity) school libraries, 2, 58, 61, 64, 67, 70, 71
Pavlenkov, Florenty Fedorovich
  early career, 158–60
  Encyclopedic Dictionary (ed. Lavrov), 160, 170
  exile in Viatka, 162, 163–4, 167
  and Pisarev, 159, 160–2, 167
  reading room legacy, 5, 170–1, 172–3
  scholarly interest (during the Soviet and post-Soviet era), 171–2
  serial publications, 5, 160, 169–70, 172
  teach-yourself-to-read primers, 164–7, 168
  textbooks, 158–60, 167–8
Pawley, Christine, 192, 300

Payne, Christiniana, 111
Peasant Newspaper (*Krest'anskaia gazeta*), 147, 149, 150
Penguin Books
  bookclub newsletter, 283, *283*, 289, 292–3, 294
  Lady Chatterley's Lover (Lawrence) 204, p6
  Random House merger (2012), 280
  Regina v. Penguin Books Ltd, 203, 204
'People's Popular Science Library' (Pavlenkov), 5, 167–8
Pepys, Samuel, 6, 200, 201–2, 214
periodicals
  and book choices of the Leadhills and Wanlockhead reading societies, 35–6
  educational reform in China, 239, 243, 246, 247, 249
  Once a Week, 110
  publication of Lubbock's list, 117
  Russia's literacy transition, 142, 143–4, 145, 146
  school libraries (Scotland), 61, 62, 68
  Sydney Stock and Station Journal, 189
  see also magazines
Persian literature, 117, 118, 120, 121, 122, 123–4, 125, 128, 130, 132
Petit de Billier, Amélina, 128
Petrov, Evgeny, 151
phrenology, 199
Pisarev, Dmitri, 159, 160–2, 167
poetry
  availability of Eastern poetry in nineteenth century England, 119, 120, 121
  child readers, 69, 70, 186
  Eastern poetry on Lubbock's list, 117, 118, 132
  'Experientia Doucet' (Cecil Winton Brett), 110

London literary society
  magazines, 79, 80, 83, 84, 86–7
  in the miners' Societies for Purchasing Books, 38, 39, *39*, *40*, 43, 44, 47
  quoted in commonplace books, 19, 22–4, 126, 128, 129–30, 132
  Rubáiyát of Omar Khayyám, 3, 120, 130–2
  Russia's literacy transition, 141, 142, 144, 148
  translations of Eastern poetry, 121–2, 123, 124, 125, 133
Pol, Floris van der, 271
'Popular Law Library' series (Pavlenkov), 5, 168
Popular Physics (Populiarnaia fizika, Ganot), 159
Porteous, James Moir, *God's Treasure-House in Scotland*, 30
Posefsky, Peter C., 160–1
post-Soviet Russia, 5, 172–3
Poulet, Georges, 304
Pound, Ezra, 119
Pownall, Eve, 189
Price, Leah, 11, 26n, 97, 300
Priestley, J. B., 200, 202–3, 204, 214
primers, 164–7, 168, 222, 231, 239, 244, 248
prizes, 292–3, 299–300
Pullan, Matilda, *Maternal Counsels to a Daughter*, 100
Pushkin, Alexander, 140, 143, 150, 169

Quaritch, Bernard, 121
Queensland Bush Book Club, 189, 190–1, 193
Qur'an (Koran), 117, 118, 125, 128

Rackham, Rachel, 104–5
Ramage family, 33
Ramayana, 117, 118, 119

Random House
  of Canada 283, *283*, p11
  live author readings, 282
  Penguin merger, 280
  Reader's Circle newsletters 7, 280, 283, *283*, 286, 288, 289, p9
Rassudovskaia, N., 172
Raty, Hannu, 208
reader response theory, 304
reading aloud
  manuscript magazines, 3, 75, 80, 82, 83, 89
  rural children in Australia and New Zealand, 181, 185–6
  Victorian families, 100
reading groups and societies
  forerunner of the Friends' Hall Literary Society, 85
  see also Society for Purchasing books in Leadhills; Society for Purchasing books in Wanlockhead; Westerkirk Parish library
'Reading tweeps'(Leestweeps), 268
Reading and Writing According to Illustrations (*Chtenie i pis'mopo kartinkam*, Pavlenkov), 166
realism, 144, 145
Red Army readers, 150
Red Cross Record, 191
Reddit, 210, 302, 303, 310
red wall (De rode muur), 262
Regina v. Penguin Books Ltd, 203, 204
religion, books on
  Asian classic literature, 112, 117, 118, 119, 124, 125, 126, 128, 131
  The Bible, 34, 67, 68, 79, 116, 117, 127, 203
  in Leadhills miners' library, 34, 38, *38*, 39, *39*
  Russia's literacy transition, 142
  in school libraries (Scotland), 61, 62, 65, 66, 67, 70, 71

in Wanlockhead miners' library, 36, 37, 38, *38*, *39*, *40*, *43*, 44, 47, *47*
Westerkirk Parish library, *45*
rhetoric, 12
Rhienen, Cees van, 267
Richardson, Samuel, *Pamela*, 38, 46, 47, 203
Richter, Virginia, 111
Ritchie, J. Ewing, 77–8
riyong texts, 220, 221, 222, 223
Robinson, Charlotte, 126, 127
Robinson, Samuel, *Persian Poetry for English Readers*, 124
rode muur, De (red wall), 262
Rodwell, J. M., 125
Roe, Marjorie, 192
Roe, Nicholas, 24
Rogers, G. F., 120
romances, 123, 125, 140–1, 232; *see also* romantic novels
Romanes, George J., 104
romantic novels, 3, 97, 101, 215, 285
Rose, Jonathan, 75
Rossi, Alexander
  Forbidden Books 107, 108, p3
  On the Shores of Bognor Regis, 109–10
Rowlandson, Thomas, *Summer Amusement at Margate, Or a Peep at the Mermaids*, 109
Royal High School library (Edinburgh), 55, 57, 59–60, 62, 66, 67, 68–70
Rubáiyát of Omar Khayyám, 3, 120, 130–2
Rubakin, N. A., 144, 169, 170
Rudd, Kate, 311
Rumi, 128, 130, 132, 133
Rural Reconstruction Movement (Xiangcun jiansheyundong), 6, 238–40, 241, 245–50
Ruskin, John, 96, 101–2, 108–9, 117

Russia
  education (pre-revolutionary period), 138–9, 143–5, 162–3
  literacy transition (pre-revolution), 4, 133, 138–46; *see also* Pavlenkov, Florenty Fedorovich
  lubki, 140, 141, 158
  October Revolution (1917), 138, 157
  post-revolution, 138, 146–53, 157
Russian Word (Russkoe slovo), 139
Rutherford, Isobel, 33

Sabbath school libraries, 55, 56, 62, 65–6, 67, 70, 71
Sadi, 130, 132
  Gulistan (Rose Garden), 121, 125
Saint-Hilaire, Jules Barthélemy, *Le Bouddha et sa Religion*, 117, 118
Salisbury, Jesse, 121
Salmi-Niklander, Kirsti, 76
Samenlezenisleuker (reading together is more fun) Facebook group, 268–9, 274–5
Sanskrit literature, 4, 117, 119, 121, 125, 128, 132
Schepens, Mieke, 261, 263, 267, 269
Schlenker, Barry, 208
school libraries, 2–3
  grammar schools, 2, 55, 57, 58–60, 61, 62, 66, 67, 68–70, 71
  hospital schools, 2, 57, 58, 61–4, 67–8, 70
  parish schools, 2, 55, 57–8, 62, 64, 64–5, 70
  pauper (charity) schools, 2, 58, 61, 64, 67, 70, 71
  rural Australia and New Zealand, 187–8
  Sabbath schools, 55, 56, 62, 65–6, 67, 70, 71
  in Tsarist Russia, 139, 166

358 *General Index*

schools
  commonplace books, 2
  'English' Schools (Scotland), 58
  rural Australia and New Zealand, 5, 180, 181–2, 183
  Scotland, 35, 57–9
  Sunday schools, 88, 163, 181
  Tsarist/imperial Russia, 138–9, 162–3, 165–6
  Xiaozhuang Experimental Normal School, 6, 239–40, 246–8, 249
  see also school libraries
science books
  in China, 226, 242, 247
  miners' libraries, 37, *38*, *39*, 40, 43, 44, 45, 46
  Pavlenkov's literacy project, 5, 158–60, 167–8
Scotland
  education system, 57–9
  grammar school libraries, 2, 55, 57, 58–60, 61, 62, 66, 67, 68–70, 71
  hospital school libraries, 2, 57, 58, 61–4, 67–8, 70
  literary society magazines, 77, 78
  parish school libraries, 2, 55, 57–8, 62, 64, 64–5, 70
  Park Church Literary Society topics, 78
  pauper (charity) school libraries, 2, 58, 61, 64, 67, 70, 71
  Sabbath school libraries, 55, 56, 62, 65–6, 67, 70, 71
  Westerkirk Parish library, 30–1, 44–5, *45*
  see also Society for Purchasing books in Leadhills; Society for Purchasing books in Wanlockhead
Scott, Walter
  commonplace books, 13, 16
  in miners' libraries (Scotland), 41, 51

  Pavlenkov's publication of, 169
  Rob Roy, 41
  Royal High School library books, 68, 69
Scott, W. J., 192
Scrap Book, The (or *A Selection of Interesting and Authentic Anecdotes*), 17–18, 20–1
seaside reading at, 3, 96, 109–11, 112
Settling of Schools Act (Scotland, 1696), 57–8
Seymour, Beatrice Kean, 87
Seymour, William Kean, 87
Shaginian, Marietta, *Mess Mend* series, 151–2
Shanghai
  bookstalls, 221–2, 228, 229–31, *230*
  cholera epidemic, 227
Shelley, Percy Bysshe, 23, 85, 123
  Hellas, 130
Shipp, Horace, 87
Shirras, Alexander, 65
Simon and Schuster book club newsletters 283, *283*, 286, *290*, p8
Sinclair, John, 56
Smiles, Samuel, 133, 214
  Self-Help, 84, 202
Snellman, Leila, 208
Sober Lovelace, The, 141
Socialist Realism, 152
social media
  #shelfie, 215
  as an archive, 312
  authors and book promotion, 8, 281–2, 299–300, 301, 303, 309, 310, 311
  BookTube, 270–1
  online book discussion (Netherlands), 7, 258, 259, 261, 264–75
  The Fault in Our Stars bench, 305, *306*, 308–9, 310, 312
  Tianjin Binhai Library, buzz about, 211

Vlogbrothers, 8, 299–300, 301, 302, 303, 309, 310, 311
Society for Purchasing books in Leadhills, 2, 30, 31, 35, 49
  books, 37–9, *38*, *39*, 48
  membership, 31, 32, 33, 34, 35, 37, 45
  periodicals, 35–6
  pre-society reading community, 34
Society for Purchasing books in Wanlockhead, 2, 30, 31, 33, 37, *38*, *39*, *40*, 49
  asset valuation, 30, 49, *50*
  binding, replacement and book popularity, 30, 45–8, *46*, *47*
  book-choosing meetings, 36–7
  book donations, 30, 35, 39–40, *40*, 42–4, *43*
  books about the Scottish Enlightenment, 2, 30, 48
  booksellers, use of, 30, 40–2, *41*
  Cyclopaedia, 30, 40–1, 42, 48, *50*, 51
  members, 31, 32, 33, 35
  membership, 30, 32, 33, 35, *50*
  periodicals, 35, 36
soldiers, 130–1, 150
Solomon, Abraham, *By the Seaside*, 109
Somerville, Margaret K. B., 63–4
Southey, Robert, 10, 19–20, 123, 128
Soviet Union, 4, 5, 146–53, 168, 169–70
space *see* visual depictions of women readers
Spence, Eleanor, 187
Squire, Alice, *Young Girl Reading in an Attic Bedroom*, 103
St Clair, William, 9, 48
St Martin's Literary Society, 77, 83–4
Stalin, Joseph, 4, 147, 148, 150, 152
Stalinist Russia, 4, 138, 147–53
Statistical Accounts for Scotland, 56, 59, 60, 66
Stein, Gertrude, 131

Steven, William, 61, 64
Stevenson, John, 41
Stirling, James, 32, 35
Stockett, Kathryn, *The Help*, 294
Striphas, Ted, 302, 303
subscription libraries, 8, 20, 132; *see also* bush book clubs; Society for Purchasing books in Leadhills; Society for Purchasing books in Wanlockhead; Westerkirk Parish library
Sunday schools, 88, 163, 181; *see also* Sabbath school libraries
Suzani Samarqandi, 128
symbolism, 144
Sytin, I. D., 139, 143

Tagore, Rabindranath, 133
Taksa, Lucy, 182–3, 186
Talbot, Mary Louisa, 128–9
Tambling, Ernest, 185
Tang Hualong, 242
Tao Xingzhi, 6, 239–40, 241, 244–50
Tatarinov, P., *Wealth Is Useless for a Stupid Son (Fomushka in St Petersburg)*, 141
Taylor, Joan Bessman, 284
Taylor, Susan B., 105
Tennyson, Alfred, 122
  'Akbar's Dream', 4, 131
  Allingham's portrait of, 107
Thacker, Thomas, 82
Thompson, John B., 288
thrillers, 261, 265–6, 267
Thrillzone, 267
Tianjin Binhai Library 211, p7
Tierney, John, 188
Tinsley, Katherine, 183
Toinard, Nicolas, 14
Tolstoy, Leo (Lev), 4, 140, 142, 143, 144, 146, 150, 166
  Anna Kerenina, 142, 266
  Resurrection, 142
Tosh, John, 100

Toulmouche, Auguste
 In the Library (1869), 107–8
 In the Library (1872), 108
Towsey, Mark, 32, 48, 64
Toynbee, Claire, 182
Trotsky, Leon, 147
Trübner, Nicholas, 119
Trübner & Co, 119
Turgenev, Ivan, 143, 144, 271
 Fathers and Children (Turgenev), 159–60
Turner Shaw, Mary, 187
Twitter, 261, 264, 265, 268, 302, 303, 305

United States of America
 Comics Code, 203–4
 see also book club newsletters
USA Today bestseller list, 290, 291
Usenet groups, 258, 259–60, 273
Ushinskii, Konstantin Dmitrievich, 164, 165

Valastro, Buddy, 286
Van der Griendt, Femke, 263, 264–5
Van der Pol, Floris, 271
Van der Vlugt, Simone, 265
van Oostendorp, Marc, 260, 263–4
van Rhienen, Cees, 267
Verheijen, Sander, 267
Vermeer, Suzanne (Paul Goeken), 265
Verney, Georgiana, 212
videoblogging, 8, 270–1, 299–300, 301, 302, 303, 309, 310, 311
Video Spotlight 288, p10
visual depictions of women readers, 3, 96–7, 111–12
 at the beach, 3, 96, 109–11, 112
 discarded books, 102, 107, 108
 household libraries, 96, 103, 105, 106–9
 motherhood and domesticity 98-101, 99, 102, p1
 solitary reading 102-106, 107, p2

Vliegenthart, Sanne, 270–1
Vlogbrothers, 8, 299–300, 301, 302, 303, 309, 310, 311
vlogs, 270–1, 299–300, 301, 302, 303, 309, 310, 311
Vlugt, Simone van der, 265
voyeurism (the erotic appeal of female readers), 104, 108, 110, 111

wanbao quanshu (comprehensive compendia of myriad treasures), 6, 219–27, 231, 232
Wang Yangming, 239
Wanlockhead miners' library see Society for Purchasing books in Wanlockhead
Ward, Edward, *Girl Reclining on a Sofa*, 104
watleesjij.nu, 266, 267, 272
Watson, George, 63
Watson, John Whaley, 128
Webby, Elizabeth, 76
weblogs (Netherlands), 258, 262–5, 267, 268, 269–70, 272, 272, 273, 274
Wegener, 266
Werner, Sarah, 302
Wertham, Fredric, 204
Westerkirk Parish library, 30–1, 44–5, 45
wheeler, James Talboys, *History of India*, 118
Whinfield, E. H., 131, 132
Wilson, Matthew, 34–5
Wilson, Robert, 38
Withrington, Donald J., 57
WLIN see watleesjij.nu
women readers
 book clubs (North America), 282, 284, 285–7, 289
 China, 221–2
 depicted in *Jane Eyre*, 3, 103, 104–5

donors to Wanlockhead, Society for Purchasing Books, 42, *43*
Georgiana Verney's book display, 212
London literary society membership, 77, 78, 80, 83, 87
New Zealand bush book clubs, 190
Russia's literacy transition, 139, 145, 146
of Shakespeare, 22
Wanlockhead and Leadhills reading societies, 33
see also mothers; visual depictions of women readers
Wood, John Warter, 19–20
Woodley, Shailene, 307
Woof, Pamela, 19
Woolf, Virginia, 209, 214
'Middlebrow' article, 199–200
Wordsworth, Dorothy, 35
Wordsworth, William, 'Character of the Happy Warrior', 22–3
Working Men's College (Great Ormond Street), 116, 117
Wright, Judith, 184, 193
Wynne, H., 87

Xiangguo Temple, 229

Xiaozhuang Experimental Normal School, 6, 239–40, 246–8, 249
Xu Teli, 249
Xu Xu, 221–2, 228, 231

Yan Yangchu, 238, 244, 248
Yaohuamen Experimental Primary School, 248
Yasuhide, Fun'ya no, 4, 131
Yohannan, John D., 118, 123
young adult novels
displaying, 198
online discussion (Netherlands), 265, 268, 270
The Fault in Our Stars, 301–313
YouTube, 312
BookTube, 270–1
Vlogbrothers, 8, 299–300, 301, 302, 303, 309, 310, 311
Yu Ziyi, 242, 243, 244

Zeising, Tobias, 263
Zhang Binglin, 241
Zhang Zonglin, 249
Zhou Zuoren, 226
Zimmern, Helen, 124–5
Zonnenberg, Johan, *De schaduwbokser*, 263
Zoshchenko, Mikhail, 151

EU representative:
Easy Access System Europe
Mustamäe tee 50, 10621 Tallinn, Estonia
Gpsr.requests@easproject.com